# MARYLEBONE, GREAT CITY NORTH
## OF OXFORD STREET

'If, Sir, I wished to make such a foreigner clearly understand what I consider as the great defects of our system, I would conduct him through that immense city which lies to the north of Great Russell Street and Oxford Street, a city superior in size and in population to the capitals of many mighty kingdoms; and probably superior in opulence, intelligence, and general respectability, to any city in the world. I would conduct him through that interminable succession of streets and squares, all consisting of well built and well furnished houses. I would make him observe the brilliancy of the shops, and the crowd of well appointed equipages. I would show him that magnificent circle of palaces which surrounds the Regent's Park. I would tell him, that the rental of this district was far greater than that of the whole kingdom of Scotland, at the time of the Union. And then I would tell him, that this was an unrepresented district.'

MACAULAY, speech on the Reform Bill, 2 March 1831

# MARYLEBONE

## *Great City North of Oxford Street*

GORDON MACKENZIE

MACMILLAN

SBN 333 13710 8

*First published 1972 by*
MACMILLAN LONDON LIMITED
*London and Basingstoke*
*Associated companies in New York Toronto*
*Dublin Melbourne Johannesburg and Madras*

*Printed in Great Britain by*
WESTERN PRINTING SERVICES LIMITED
*Bristol*

TO

*John Cowper Powys*

AND

*Joan Frosdick*

# Contents

# List of Illustrations

*Acknowledgements for the plates and maps*

The author and publishers are most grateful to all those who have helped with the illustrations for this book.

Acknowledgement is due to the following:

To the Greater London Council Map and Print Collections for Plates: 5, 6, 10, 11, 12, 13, 14, 16, 17, 18, 21, 23, 24, 26, 27, 28, 29, 31, 32, 33, 37, 38, 39, 46, 47, 51, 79, and maps on pages 39, 149 and 183.

To the Archives Section, Westminster City Libraries, Marylebone Road Branch for Plates: *Endpapers*, 1, 2, 3, 4, 7, 8, 9, 15, 19, 22, 25, 30, 34, 35, 36, 40, 41, 43, 48.

To the Radio Times Hulton Picture Library for Plates: 20, 42, 44, 45, 50.

To Ann Saunders, author of *Regent's Park* published by David & Charles (1969) for the map on page 219 drawn by Bruce Kemp Saunders.

# List of Maps

# Acknowledgements

My first debt of gratitude is to Lord Howard de Walden for his very generous backing of this book, and for his declared faith in it; my second to the Trustees of the Portman Family Settled Estates, who have also generously given it their support. I have, too, to record with gratitude the encouragement I have received from two eminent publishers, Lord Longford and Mr David St John Thomas, both of whom expressed a wish to see this book published.

It has been my good fortune to be able to draw upon the large store of published and unpublished material – including a number of historical monographs – which the St Marylebone Society has issued during the twenty-four years of its very active existence, and to attend many of its lectures. Mr A. J. D. Stonebridge, Honorary Secretary of the Society and former Borough Librarian, whose knowledge of Marylebone's history is probably unrivalled, has helped me with valuable information, and has kindly read the typescript of this book. I am also indebted to Mrs G. M. Ahern, General Editor of the Society's publications and Chairman of its Records section – an outstanding authority on the history of Marylebone and the possessor of a unique library bearing upon the borough's past – for guidance as to source books, and advice about publication. Another leading member, Mrs Norah Nicholls, introduced me to the Society, and has taken a continuing interest in my researches. To Mrs Ann Saunders (Ann Cox-Johnson), formerly Borough Archivist and author of *Regent's Park*, published by David & Charles in 1969, I owe a great deal – not only because she has written the definitive book on the park, but because, in her handlist to the Ashbridge Collection, and her other labours as an archivist, she has enormously facilitated the work of any researcher into the history of Marylebone. I have also to acknowledge a special debt to Mrs Alison Adburgham for information derived from her book, *Shops and Shopping, 1800–1914*, and to Miss Margery Weiner for that obtained from her work, *The French Exiles, 1789–1815*. To Mr

Hugh Phillips, F.S.A., I tender homage for the inspiration and guidance afforded by a unique work, his *Mid-Georgian London*, published in 1964, a topographical and social survey on the grand scale, that must ever be a classic.

Others to whom I am indebted for help of one kind or another are the staffs of the British Museum Reading Room and Students' Manuscript Room, and of the Prints and Drawings Collection at County Hall; Mr K. C. Harrison, Westminster City Librarian, and his Marylebone library staff, and more particularly the Local Collection staff. Mr L. F. Hall and Mr C. M. J. Eldridge of the Howard de Walden Estates Limited, and Mr R. A. S. Brock, Mr P. R. Stansfield and Mr M. J. Coward of the Portman Family Settled Estates, have all at one time or another obliged with their aid. Others I would like to thank are the Dowager Countess of Lucan, Mr Denys Forest, Mr Paul Ignotus, Mr A. J. Kelsall, and Mr Reresby Sitwell. Finally, I must express gratitude to Sir John Summerson, Sir Nikolaus Pevsner, and Mr Howard Colvin, whose works on architectural history have long been my sacred books. To these, I have turned constantly when tracing the development of Marylebone's historic streets and buildings.

Finally, I have as far as possible checked and counterchecked all statements of fact. But in a book of this scale, dealing with a whole district, errors are bound to creep in. In particular, this is so because the scene is constantly changing and putting one's information out of date. I can only hope that my lapses have been minimal.

GORDON MACKENZIE

# Author's Note

Two works must always stand by themselves on the shelf of anyone studying Marylebone's past. One is of course Thomas Smith's time-honoured topography-cum-history, published in 1833, which owed its existence to Marylebone's arrival at the status of a parliamentary borough. The other is Dr F. H. W. Sheppard's modern historical study of the district – *Local Government in St Marylebone, 1688–1835* – a title that hardly does justice to the scope of the work. This book appeared exactly 120 years after Smith, and a mere decade before the borough merged with the City of Westminster. If I refer here to these twin peaks in the annals of Marylebone, it is because I have learnt that even someone attempting a thing much less ambitious than either – and quite different from both – must salute the heights. From these, I constantly took my bearings during this excursion into the circumstances attending Marylebone's rise from a village to the 'great city' so vividly epitomised by Macaulay for the House of Commons of 1831.

I have not thought it necessary to provide this book with notes. There is an ample bibliography, and those scholarly-minded persons who wish to go more deeply into any particular aspect of Macaulay's 'great city north of Oxford Street' – or test any given statement against the views of the authorities they fancy – will of course know where to look for what they want. The rest will no doubt be relieved to see that those persistent, elbow-jogging figures in the text are missing.

I have avoided calling the district of which I write 'St Marylebone'. I apologise to the purists, if this offends them. But nobody uses this version in ordinary speech – and Pepys, and many others after all, called it plain 'Maribone', or even 'Marrowbone'. Thomas Smith, Marylebone's first historian, rather freely rendered Macaulay's phrase for the area north of Oxford Street as 'that great city'. Hence the sub-title of this book.

# 1 . *A Glance at the Past*

MARYLEBONE is both a village and a city. It has at its heart the miniature intimacy of the one, and in its spread and sweep the resources and amenities of the other. Yet, unlike aristocratic – or should it be pluto-aristocratic? – Mayfair, or 'arty' Chelsea, it has no clearly defined social image. It is merely a topographical fact, associated for some with a long, wide thoroughfare; for others with the smallest and most delightful of the Victorian railway termini; for yet others with a waxworks that is a national institution; or perhaps with the Zoo. The very variety of the things it can comprehend – from the Georgian urbanity of the Harley Street area to the fanciful and picturesque villas of St John's Wood, from the B.B.C. to Lord's and the Baker Street of Sherlock Holmes – marks it off as more encyclopaedically all-embracing than any run-of-the-mill borough could be, and explains why, as it offers itself today, it eludes any single social label.

Yet, though it evokes no overriding image in the mind of the man-in-the-street today, as do Mayfair and Chelsea, this has not always been so. For the men and women of the first half of the eighteenth century, it signified a pleasure resort comparable with Ranelagh or Vauxhall, with the excitement intensified by the risk of highway robbery in getting to it. For those of the second half, it won a reputation as London's newest and most fashionable centre of aristocratic wealth, opulent residential development, and artistic activity – a reputation immeasurably heightened in the next century by the creation of Regent's Park, with its splendidly theatrical array of palatial villas and terrace houses conceived on the grand scale, and with a panache which gained it European prestige.

The streets and squares, the essential atmosphere of Marylebone in its booming Regency and Victorian days figure frequently in the works of the great nineteenth-century writers. These were the *mise-en-scène* for many of the events described in the novels of Dickens and Trollope – themselves residents for many years – as well as

those of Thackeray, Disraeli, and a number of others. As for the
list of those who have lived in the district, it contains enough
famous – sometimes notorious – names to fill a fair-sized directory.
Some of these, like those of Dickens himself; Mrs Siddons; Elizabeth Montagu, the blue-stocking; Sir Edwin Landseer; William
Pitt; Constable; the Brownings; Turner; and Lord George Gordon,
of the Gordon Riots, are well enough known as having been
associated with Marylebone. But how many people are aware that
both Dr Johnson and James Boswell lived in the district – though
at different times; that Gladstone, George Eliot, Charles Bradlaugh,
and Herbert Spencer were among its Victorian residents; that
Wagner used to stay there on his visits to England, and feed the
swans on Regent's Park lake; that Cardinals Wiseman and Man-
ning lived at the same house in Baker Street; that 'Ouida' made
the Langham Hotel her home for many years; and that Sir Arthur
Conan Doyle not only planted Sherlock Holmes on the borough,
apparently for perpetuity, but himself practised briefly in Devonshire Place as an ophthalmic surgeon in his pre-Holmes days?

A great many of these celebrated people were associated with
Marylebone at a time when it was the most rapidly developing area
of a London which was itself expanding at a greater speed and more
ambitiously than ever before in its history. It was the period when
the German Prince Pückler-Muskau could write of London, in
1826: 'Now, for the first time, it has the air of a seat of Government,
and not of an immeasurable metropolis of "shopkeepers"', and
when a generation or so later, the French critic and historian,
Taine, could pronounce:

> Paris is mediocre in comparison with these 'crescents', cir-
> cuses, and the endless rows of monumental houses built of mas-
> sive stone, with porticos and carved fronts lining very wide streets.
> There are fifty as wide as the *Rue de la Paix*. There can be no
> question but that Napoleon III demolished Paris and rebuilt it
> because he had lived in London.

Taine might have added that the member of the Bonaparte family
later to become the Emperor Napoleon III had once frequented as
an exile the St John's Wood area of Marylebone, where he had had
the advantage of easy access to the newly-opened Regent's Park. It
seems not unlikely that the famous boulevards of Paris, created
under the Emperor, may have owed something to Nash's transfor-

mation of the old Marylebone Park into a masterpiece of landscaping for the Prince Regent.

These were the great days of what might be called classic Marylebone, when the borough, overflowing with wealth and talent, was developing architecturally and socially at a rate and on a scale which justify the claim that it deserves to be called London's third city. Yet, with all this, Marylebone was once – and in a sense still is – a village. It did not become part of London until well on in the eighteenth century. For hundreds of years, it held a modest place in the minds of Londoners as a pretty little village lying amid fields on the way to Primrose Hill. A village with a parish church, and a manor which had been in earlier times a royal palace and hunting lodge, and a park which had become a pleasure garden – Marylebone Gardens – by the time the eighteenth century came along. Then came the marvellous transformation of the late Georgian and Regency years. And with it a new image was born – that of the most up-and-coming quarter of one of the great capitals of Europe, the scene of the finest and most inventive piece of town-planning that London had known and of its most elegantly-landscaped park, the chosen resort of courtiers and diplomats, and of much of the leading nobility and wealth of the metropolis, the quarter of London which for more than fifty years was that first sought out by all visitors of taste coming to these shores. No wonder that some of the men who lived through these extraordinary developments should have been moved to look upon the area as worthy of the name and standing of a city.

It is perhaps almost impossible in the second half of the twentieth century, when London has grown gigantic and its population more numerous than that of whole nations, to understand the impact which this new and wondrous quarter made upon contemporaries. The splendid wide streets laid out on the grid system, the palaces of Portland Place, the gleaming white and green harmonies of the Nash terraces and the Park, the then novel villadom of St John's Wood, were not only breath-taking in themselves, they represented for the men of those days the latest refinements of their own architecturally urbane age. They were both *dernier cri* and a proof of the prosperity of the nation. And for those who remembered the slower pace of building development in earlier days, they had come at a pace and on a scale which suggested that the country was on the threshold of a new age.

Marylebone's second image, then, was that of London's newest, richest and most fashionable quarter – an area large, opulent, modern and architecturally distinguished; and so filled with people of birth, wealth and talent, and with the artists, craftsmen and tradesmen who ministered to such a community, that Macaulay and others could dub the place a city. Now that Marylebone has become officially part of the City of Westminster, it seems to have missed its chance of achieving formal city status. Yet there seems a case for arguing that Marylebone was in reality the third city thrown up by our metropolis – particularly if the wider dictionary definition is applied. A city, according to one of the definitions given in the 1961 edition of *Webster's New International Dictionary*, is merely 'a place larger than a village or a town'. Marylebone, with a population at its peak in the mid-nineteenth century of over 160,000, certainly filled this bill. Even now, when its resident – as opposed to its daytime business – population has sunk to a mere 70,000 or so, Marylebone still has a claim to citydom, as being unique among the central districts of London for the extraordinary variety of its civic amenities. Neither Chelsea nor Mayfair can compare with it for size or diversity of appeal. Kensington, though greater in size and population, and superior perhaps in the abundance of its museums and stylish stores, cannot really stand in the same class as a quarter which houses at one and the same time the B.B.C., the Zoo, Lord's Cricket Ground, the 'Sherlock Holmes country', Madame Tussaud's and the Harley Street area, and whose park, an incomparable masterpiece, is approached by a thoroughfare of the width and sweep of Portland Place.

# 2. The Manors and the Village

It is a pleasant thought in an age that sees itself as moving towards the full equality of the sexes that Marylebone's first recorded land-owners were both women. Aelfgiva, Abbess of Barking, and Eideva, unidentified, but probably another clerical Establishment lady, held the two manors out of which the borough of Marylebone developed. Domesday Book records that Aelfgiva had the manor of Tyburn – the eastern half of Marylebone – and Eideva the manor of Lileston, the western half. They were, like all great landowners of their day, tenants under the Crown. The manors, about equal in size, covered some 1,500 acres, and together supported no more than 150 people. The present 70,000 or so people living in the area are of course not supported by it; but the enormous increase in numbers aptly illus-trates the effect of urbanisation. The quiet glebes of Norman days have sprouted this monstrous human growth, and where the flocks pastured and the serfs toiled it is now a question of 'permitted den-sities' and the sale of office space at fabulous prices per square foot.

The Tyburn stream – since about 1800 one of London's under-ground rivers – marked the approximate boundary between the two manors. This rivulet with the sinister name flows from sources at Hampstead and Highgate to the Thames at Westminster. Near the point at which it crosses the present Oxford Street, close to Stratford Place, the church of St John the Evangelist was built in the year 1200 to serve the needs of the two manors. The neighbourhood was then deep country, and the little church stood somewhat apart on the fringe of the great Middlesex forest. Maitland, the historian of London, describes it as 'left alone by the side of the Highway'. Depredators, busy then as now – the present St Marylebone Church has to be kept locked because of the activities of vandals – apparently plundered the building so successfully in the latter years of the four-teenth century that it was decided to abandon the exposed site alto-gether. Instead, about 1400 a new church was built half a mile farther up the Tyburn at a point which was to become later the

heart of Tyburn, subsequently Marylebone, village. Here, very close
to the site of the present parish church of St Marylebone – St Mary-
a-le-bourne, or, to be more explicit, St Mary-by-Tyburn – arose the
second, followed in 1741 by the third, of the four parish churches
Marylebone has had in the course of its recorded history.

Here, too, was the manor house, first heard of as early as 1270,
and subsequently expanded into a royal palace and hunting lodge.
And here in the eighteenth century grew to fame the popular
pleasure grounds called Marylebone Gardens, which afterwards for
a brief period even contrived to add to themselves a spa. The long,
winding Marylebone Lane, which follows the course of the Tyburn
river and was the village's first link with the Tyburn Road – now
Oxford Street – terminated near that curious building known in its
day as the Lord Mayor's Banqueting House. This was a relic of the
days when conduits from Marylebone supplied the City of London
with water, and the Lord Mayor made an annual inspection of the
conduit heads, celebrating with a hunt afterwards in the neighbouring royal park and a banquet in what, in spite of its resounding
title, seems to have been little more than a rustic hunting lodge.

Who are the great barons whose names were first associated with
the Marylebone manors? Aubrey de Vere, second Earl of Oxford,
was one. He was the man behind the building of Marylebone's first
church. For the De Veres had acquired the manors of Tyburn and
Lileston very early on in the recorded history of these estates. From
the De Veres, Tyburn passed to the Earls of Warenne and Surrey,
and in the mid-fourteenth century to the Earls of Arundel. The
manor of Lileston had a number of different owners during the
course of the fourteenth and fifteenth centuries, including the
Knights Templars. After their suppression in 1312, it passed to their
rivals, the Knights of St John of Jerusalem. Hence the name St
John's Wood given to a district in the northern part of the manor.
But times were changing, and with them the class of landlord. As
early as the closing years of the fifteenth century, Thomas Hobson,
a commoner of obscure birth, but of some influence as a senior
Exchequer official under Henry VII, had by gradual purchase
acquired three-quarters of the Marylebone manors. The land remained in his family for about half a century until Henry VIII, ever
in search of fresh terrain in which to indulge his ardour for the
chase, decided that the Tyburn estate, only a few miles north of the
built-up area of his capital, would do him nicely. In his customary

way, he offered Thomas Hobson, grandson of the original owner, other properties – in the Isle of Wight and in Southampton – in exchange. Acceptance could not of course be in doubt, and Thomas the second, preferring to remain at large and alive, surrendered a substantial slice of a large area between the Edgware and Tottenham Court Roads, which if it had remained in his family even up to the last century would have made it one of the richest in the country.

Henry's acquisition was dubbed Marylebone Park – the first heard of this name – and was duly stocked with deer, with which it provided sport for him and his successors up to the time of the Civil War. The rest of the Tyburn estate – mostly land south of the present Marylebone Road – was leased out to a variety of owners. The manor itself was retained by the Crown until James I's time, when the freehold of all except the park was sold to a certain Edward Forsett, a safe King James's man and an examining magistrate in the Gunpowder Plot affair. Forsett's daughter and co-heiress was Arabella, wife of one Thomas Austen, and in 1708 her son, Sir John Austen, sold the manor of Tyburn to John Holles, Duke of Newcastle, for £17,500 – a magnate whom Bishop Burnet the historian called 'the richest subject that had been in the Kingdom for some ages'. On his death, Tyburn once again passed to a woman – Newcastle's daughter, Henrietta Cavendish Holles, afterwards Countess of Oxford. The Oxfords, in spite of their ownership of the manor, chose to live outside it, in the then more fashionable area of Dover Street. Lady Oxford, the 'dull but estimable' favourite of that sharp-tongued wit and incomparable letter-writer, Lady Wortley Montagu, maintained the feminine link in the chain of ownership by leaving a daughter as her heiress – Lady Margaret Cavendish Harley, who married the second Duke of Portland. That was in 1734, in the reign of George II. The Portlands held Tyburn – that is to say, the greater part of the eastern half of Marylebone – for some five generations. Then in the 1880s it passed to a sister, Baroness Howard de Walden, of the childless fifth Duke, and about half of it remains in the hands of her descendants today. Meanwhile, the southern part of the manor of Lileston – the western half of Marylebone – had come in the mid-sixteenth century into the hands of a West Country family, the Portmans. Of the northern portion of the manor, the Lisson Grove estate passed to the Milner family, who kept it for some seven generations, until late in the eighteenth century it became the property of John Harcourt and others, Harcourt actually acquiring the Manor House. The St John's Wood estate was Lord Chesterfield's for some years before it was bought in 1732 by Henry Samuel Eyre, a London merchant. It had been in the Chesterfield family for a couple of generations. Both the Portmans and the Eyres have kept their Marylebone estates up to the present day – though by no means in their entirety.

It will be seen from this brief chronicle of the fortunes of its two manors that Marylebone is really the land of the Tyburn. It has a much better title to be called Tyburnia than the district immediately north of Hyde Park, which borders, not the Tyburn river, but the area in which the Tyburn gallows was located. Tyburnia seems to have been a coinage of Thackeray's, but though he included in it the Portman Square neighbourhood, the name has been generally applied to the district west of the Edgware Road. Marylebone in shape is – or, rather, was when it existed as a separate borough – roughly a parallelogram. The base of the figure – the southern frontier – is formed by the northern side of Oxford Street from the Edgware Road on the west to just short of Tottenham Court Road on the east. The western side is formed by the Edgware Road and Maida Vale, and the northern side of the parallelogram by the aptly-named Boundary Road, and by the southern slopes of Primrose Hill. The eastern side of the Marylebone figure runs down the middle of the Broad Walk in Regent's Park, crosses the Euston Road into Cleveland Street – just failing to include the Post Office Tower – and reaches Oxford Street a few score yards short of its junction with New Oxford Street.

Within this perimeter, enclosing some one and a half thousand acres, were the two manors, each with its village – St Marylebone and the much smaller Lileston, the present-day Lisson Grove. Then in the mid-eighteenth century, the swelling metropolis itself, under development by aristocratic landlords, shot out a tentacle northwards and enfolded Marylebone. Within three generations or so, so great were the expansive energies of the first half of the nineteenth century, Marylebone had achieved a population of 160,000 – more than twice today's figure – and had many of the amenities and even the splendours of a city. But the tale of that extraordinary transformation is one that will be told in later chapters. Our concern in this is with the village of Marylebone, which not only gave its name to the later far-spreading conurbation, but has kept something of its topographical identity and flavour right up to the present time. At the heart of the village were of course the manor house and the church – the Old Church, demolished in 1949 because of war damage and decay, but commemorated by a miniature public garden occupying the diminutive site. The site of the manor house is also easily identifiable, though not preserved as such. Pulled down in 1791 after having been a fashionable school for the sons of the nobility for most of the eighteenth century, it was replaced by a range of livery stables, now succeeded by a garage. The front commanded the High Street opposite the church, but a little farther to the north, and the building and grounds occupied the area between the Marylebone Road on the north and the present Beaumont Street on the south.

The appearance of the manor house after Henry VIII had turned it into a palace and hunting lodge is not now known, but in its later stages surviving prints show it as a very extensive range of red brick buildings in the William-and-Mary style with a pedimented garden front, lofty chimneys, and gabled wings. A view published in Victorian times purporting to show the place as it was in the reign of Queen Elizabeth – a many-gabled structure of cosily romanticised aspect – suggests the inventive fancy of that age rather than historic fact. Elizabeth certainly used the manor house as a hunting lodge, and it is known that she entertained the Czar of Muscovy's hunting party in Marylebone Park in 1601. James I was noted for his addiction to hunting, to which he fled whenever he could throw off the cares of state. He must frequently have followed the chase in Marylebone Park, which, as we have seen, he expressly reserved for himself when he sold the manor of Tyburn to Edward Forsett. It is curious to think of Gloriana, and after her 'The Wisest Fool in Christendom', spurring across what is now Regent's Park with their gorgeously colourful courtiers, and being in at the death in the neighbourhood of, say, the Zoo, or one of the big football pitches of today. The contrast between those small groups of figures in the Tudor or Jacobean landscape and the crowds thronging the park today is probably as great as the difference between the wild, lonely, tussocky chase of those days and the formal elegances and picturesque vistas which are the setting for the Nash villas and terraces of modern times.

The first lord of the manor of whom much is really known was Edward Harley, second Earl of Oxford and Mortimer. He acquired the property through his wife, Henrietta, daughter of the extremely wealthy Duke of Newcastle, who brought him a fortune of £500,000. Although they chose not to live within the bounds of the manor, it was they who in 1715, when Harley had not yet succeeded to the title, originated the very ambitious building scheme which brought into being Cavendish Square – at first called Oxford Square – and later that network of fine handsome streets of which Harley Street is the axis. John Prince, commemorated by John Prince's Street, was their surveyor. The task assigned him was to produce a fashionable residential district suitable for an aristocracy beginning at last to take an interest in town houses in the new Palladian style, and of course to provide the Harleys with a fresh and profitable source of income.

If Lady Henrietta was dull – beloved only of that self-sufficiently dynamic character, Lady Mary Wortley Montagu – Harley himself was a personage of considerable interest. His fame as a collector of books and manuscripts, and as a patron of writers and artists, endures. The Harleian MSS are amongst the earliest splendours of the British Museum library. These, during his lifetime, he housed in a building which he had had constructed on the opposite side of the High Street from the manor house. It later became a girls' school, known as Oxford House, and among its pupils was 'Perdita' Robinson, one of the first mistresses of the youthful Prince George, later Prince Regent and King George IV. In a later incarnation the building became Tilbury's furniture repository, and survived into the early 1900s as 35 High Street, Marylebone. After his death, Harley's daughter sold the manuscripts to the nation for £10,000 – more than £100,000 at today's values. The contemporary epithet of 'indolent' applied to the earl seems a strange label for one who collected on the grand scale – medals as well as books and manuscripts – who was, we are told, passionately addicted to building and landscape-gardening, and who surrounded himself with artists and literary men, of whom he was the active patron. Of these, James Gibbs, his architect; John Wootton, the painter of hunting scenes; Rysbrack, the sculptor; and Charles Bridgman, the landscape-gardener, lived upon his estate in Marylebone. His circle also included such names as Sir James Thornhill, Hogarth's father-in-law and the leading Baroque artist of the day; Michael Dahl, the Swedish portrait-painter who was Kneller's only serious rival; and Matthew Prior, poet, diplomatist and secret agent. Pope and Swift

– the latter his frequent guest – were perhaps the greatest names to enjoy his friendship and patronage.

During the three centuries or so preceding the earl's lifetime the religious needs of Marylebone had been served by the little church in the High Street. But, with the creation of Cavendish Square and the fashionable neighbourhood of which it was the nucleus, provision was made not only for a market, but for a church or chapel of ease to suit the convenience of the incoming noblemen and their families. St Peter's, Vere Street, or the Oxford Chapel as it was then called, has, unlike the village church, survived till the present day. Yet architecturally superior as St Peter's is to its rustic predecessor, it was with the village church that many of Marylebone's historic names – some of them, like Bacon, Nelson and Byron, of world renown – are associated.

In its early fifteenth-century form, as well as after its mid-eighteenth-century rebuilding, the Old Parish Chapel, as it came to be known after it had been superseded in 1817 by the present monumental church on the Marylebone Road, seems to have been an extremely modest affair. Marylebone was, after all, no more than a village until well on in the reign of George II. Even then the rebuilding in 1741 was carried out with the strictest attention to economy, and it was not until a couple of generations later that the members of what had then become the wealthiest parish in England and one of the most populous in London woke up to the fact that their tiny church was making them look ridiculous. They sprang into action, and opening their purse strings to the widest extent, produced the present opulent status symbol on its site opposite Regent's Park.

The interior of the little church as it was in the years immediately before the rebuilding in 1741 is shown in one of the plates in Hogarth's *The Rake's Progress*. Peter Quennell has described it as 'a tumbledown edifice then almost in the open country, and because of the remoteness of its situation much favoured for hasty or secret weddings'. It was in this plain little church, in 1606, that the debt-ridden Francis Bacon, aged forty-five, with *The Advancement of Learning* and some of the famous *Essays* behind him and his political rise and fall yet to come, married Alice Barnham, the fourteen-year-old daughter of an alderman dowered with a modest fortune. A contemporary gossip wrote: 'Sir Francis Bacon was married yesterday to his young wench in Maribone Chapel.' The ceremony was celebrated with great pomp, the bridegroom being 'clad from top to toe in purple, and hath made himself and his wife such store of fine raiments of cloth of silver and gold that it draws deep into her portion'. More than a century and a half later a man who, like Bacon, was to make a name first as a writer and then as a politician slipped into the tiny church – its tower was a mere thirty feet high – and married the bride for whom he had already fought two duels. Richard Brinsley Sheridan, whose plays *The Rivals* and *The School for Scandal* have entranced six generations of English playgoers and look like outlasting all but those of Shakespeare, married the singer Elizabeth Linley in Marylebone Church in 1773, and settled in the parish after his marriage. Like the grave but gorgeous Bacon, Sheridan lived far beyond his means, and the Sheridans' house in Orchard Street was always thronged with high society. 'The fair Linley Sheridan', as Fanny Burney called her, gave concerts there, and earned herself the further epithets 'matchless warbler' and 'resistless syren'. Sheridan's oratorical triumphs in the House of Commons were to come later, but it was in his early days in his Marylebone home that he wrote *The Rivals*, and there that he first made his name as a wit and playwright. Perhaps the last marriage of celebrities in the Old Chapel, as it became called after the building of the new parish church, was that of Nelson's Emma with Sir William Hamilton in 1791.

Among the well-known men whose remains lie in the churchyard of the little departed church are James Gibbs, who both as architect and parishioner had been much mixed up in the development of Marylebone and owned six houses there at the time of his death; Rysbrack the sculptor, who lived in the High Street; Allan Ramsay, George II's much favoured portrait-painter and one of Dr Johnson's circle, with a house in Harley Street; and Charles Wesley, brother of the Methodist leader, and author of such famous hymns as 'Jesu, Lover of my Soul', 'Hark the Herald Angels Sing', and 'Love Divine all Loves Excelling'. It is a significant fact that these celebrities, and a number of others less celebrated in whose lives 'Maribone chapel' played some part, were chiefly artists and men of letters. Marylebone in the first decades of its rapid expansion – and indeed for a hundred years and more from the beginning of its population explosion in the mid-eighteenth century – was a magnet drawing to itself great numbers of practitioners of all the arts. In the wake of the numerous noble or wealthy residents attracted to the parish, as it developed into a new quarter of the metropolis, came a multitude of those ready to minister to their needs. Stimulated by reports of its good air, healthy gravel soil, and relatively high situation – compared with Mayfair or Chelsea – and by the growing vogue of the district, those with money to spend and those with skills to exploit flowed in in ever increasing numbers. Portrait-painters, landscapists, engravers, sculptors, architects, and craftsmen of all kinds arrived to inhabit the proliferating rows of streets on the expanding Portland and Portman estates.

During the first phase of the urbanisation of Marylebone, lasting for about a century, the old church, except for its utility-type re-building of 1741 on the same site and scale – went quietly on, grow-ing shabbier and shabbier and less and less suited to the needs of its vast parish. Schemes for its rebuilding in the 1770s, to a design of Sir William Chambers – the leading Establishment architect of the day – never reached the stage of bricks and mortar, in spite of the fact that no fewer than three Acts of Parliament authorising building had been obtained. Finally in 1817 came eclipse with the building of Thomas Hardwick's great classical temple on the Marylebone Road, within a stone's throw of its predecessor, and the last-moment decision that the newcomer should be, not a chapel, but the new parish church. In its later and humbler days the historic little church was converted into a chapel and became known as the Old Parish Chapel. Before its final demolition in 1949, it had won an admirer in Sir John Summerson, who wrote appreciatively of a certain extra-ordinary simplicity and quietude, 'as if here, in rich metropolitan St Marylebone, the village air of Tybourn still turned the vane on the turret. The churchyard was grass-grown and rural till converted into an asphalted playground some years before the war. Headstones leaned this way and that, and the passer-by caught through the railings an improbable, puzzling version of something which seemed to have nothing to do with the twentieth century and little enough with the nineteenth.' So passed the old church, closed for worship as long ago as 1926, and too decayed and damaged after the last war for its dissolution to be arrested in spite of a generous gift from the Pilgrim Trust and the wish of all to preserve it.

Another part of the old village of Marylebone, the burial-ground, survives as a public garden on the south side of Paddington Street. As early as 1731 the population had grown so considerably that the multitudinous dead could no longer be contained within the bounds

of the churchyard. The lord of the manor, Lord Oxford, the creator
of the new Marylebone, was approached and persuaded to provide
a plot of land for the purpose – not far from the church but reas-
suringly remote from the *haut ton* in the Cavendish Square neighbourhood and their fashionable preaching-box, the Oxford Chapel.
The short street linking the burial-ground with Marylebone High
Street was appropriately – or perhaps hopefully – called Paradise
Street, a name now changed to Moxon Street. Thomas Smith, the
historian of Marylebone, writing in 1833, about a century after the
opening of the burial-ground, said that it had been computed that
more than 80,000 people lay buried in this cemetery on the south
side of Paddington Street. He says that the cemetery facing it on
the north side of the street was bought from the Portman family and
opened in 1772. What he does not mention is that many of those
buried in these cemeteries were members of Marylebone's considerable Huguenot community, although the lists of names he
supplies of course point to the fact.

The burial-grounds lay to the west of Marylebone High Street.
On the east side of the High Street and a little farther south was
the main entrance to the celebrated Marylebone Gardens. The Rose
of Normandy public house, demolished only a few years ago, was
built at the point of entry, and the main carriage approach to the
gardens in their later days was through the yard of this inn. These
gardens, so popular in their time, represented what remained of the
grounds of Marylebone Palace, after that palace had once again
declined into a manor house and finally into a school. In 1650,
during the levelling days of the Commonwealth, they had been
detached from the grounds of the Palace and leased out to a
succession of entrepreneurs who had turned them into pleasure
gardens. By 1668, when Pepys visited them, they were sufficiently
developed to win his discerning admiration. They were in their
heyday roughly rectangular in shape, with the northern boundary
running from the High Street end of what is now Beaumont Street
in an easterly direction as far as about half-way between Devonshire
Place and Harley Street, and the southern boundary running from
near the High Street to a point midway between Westmoreland
Street and Wimpole Street and just south of Weymouth Street.
Although the gardens, paradoxically, first became a place of public
entertainment under the stern Commonwealth, it was not until well
on in the first half of the eighteenth century that they began to

achieve fame as pleasure gardens on the pattern of Vauxhall and Ranelagh. At this stage they seem to have been adapted more to the needs of a rising middle class than to the tastes of a pleasure-loving aristocracy. Two bowling greens and their surroundings – one close to the manor house, the other behind The Rose of Normandy, were the nucleus out of which the Gardens developed. Confusingly enough, another tavern, called simply The Rose Tavern, abutted on the first of these greens. This was 'much favoured by persons of the first rank', and provided not only refreshment, but gambling facilities. The line: *Some Dukes at Marylebone bowl time away* refers to this spot. Lady Wortley Montagu has been credited with it, but it is now believed to be Pope's. She may however have quoted it in allusion to the Duke of Buckingham, a constant patron of 'The Rose Tavern' and its bowling green – not the notorious George Villiers, the rake and wit, but John Sheffield, the gaming Duke of Buckingham and Normanby, whose town house became, after re-building, Buckingham Palace. Thomas Pennant, in an account of London published in 1793, wrote of The Rose Tavern that it was 'the place of assemblage of all the infamous sharpers of the time; to whom his Grace always gave a dinner at the conclusion of the season, and his parting toast was, "May as many of us as remain un-hanged next spring, meet here again." '

By 1737, i.e. sixteen years after the Duke of Buckingham's death, the bowling greens had been incorporated in Marylebone Gardens, and the proprietor of the Gardens was charging a shilling a head entrance fee to the public, the price to include refreshments. As the Gardens became more fashionable, the variety of the entertainments provided grew. Balls were given and concerts held, and there were frequent firework displays. A surviving print shows what was known as 'The Orchestra and Grand Walk'. It depicts an avenue of tall, graceful trees, with elegantly colonnaded buildings on either side, a raised open balcony with an orchestra playing, trellised arbours with couples sitting in them, and in the distance an orna-mental alley hung with lights. Here, not far from where the London Clinic stands today, was the heart of the gay pleasure resort, which did not open till the spring and closed down with the coming of autumn.

The music was for a time under the direction of Dr Arne, the English composer and author of *Rule, Britannia*, and Handel's works, as they came out, were often played there. The Reverend

John Fountaine, headmaster of the school which occupied the manor house during most of the eighteenth century, was a close friend of Handel's. Thomas Smith, the historian of Marylebone, tells of an occasion when they were walking in Marylebone Gardens together when the band struck up with a new piece of unknown provenance to Fountaine. Handel asked him for his opinion of it, and got the reply: 'It's not worth listening to – it's very poor stuff.' He was surprised and apologetic when Handel remarked: 'It *is* very poor stuff – I thought so myself when I had finished it.' The composer admitted that he'd worked too hastily on the piece, having very limited time for its production. Fountaine's grandson, who had been at the school in the period just before it closed down in 1791, was the source of this story. He recalled also 'the fine gardens and mulberry trees, and seeing Lunardi or Blanchard, in his balloon high over them'. Lunardi had made the first hydrogen balloon ascent over England in 1784, and Blanchard, the inventor of the parachute – a surprisingly early date for this invention – had crossed the English Channel by balloon the following year, the first aeronaut to do so.

The comparatively small area in which these amusements went on – the size of half-a-dozen football pitches perhaps – contrasts strikingly with the vast spaces and endless acres of Marylebone's second excursion into the realm of the pleasure ground – Regent's Park. It must be remembered that for much of the period of the Gardens' existence, visitors from London had to journey across a wide stretch of open country called Marylebone Fields. This piece of countryside was the haunt of numerous highwaymen and robbers – particularly after dark. Yet the place remained well frequented, and judging by the account of the entrance money taken on a good night in the late 1760s some two to three hundred people must often have been in the Gardens. Parties of patrons from Mayfair would gather at the small alehouse in Wigmore Street and make their way across the hazardous area under the guard of two or three men armed with muskets. A poster advertising the programme in the Gardens for a night in 1765 announces:

Mrs. Vincent's Night: AT MARYLEBONE GARDENS... Vocal and Instrumental Music... There will be a Horse Patrole for the City Road to and from the Gardens, to protect those Friends who intend honouring Mrs. Vincent with their Company.

At the height of their reputation, the Gardens seem to have been equipped with a theatre, a ball-room, and the balcony for the orchestra. The 'Theatre for Burlettas' would be called today the theatre for comic operas. In the summer of 1774, an attempt to hold what the proprietors of the Gardens called a fête champêtre, at the exorbitant cost for those days of five shillings a head entrance money, led to riotous behaviour by some of the public. These people declared that they had been fobbed off with 'nothing more than a few tawdry festoons and extra lights', and reacted by smashing up everything in sight and damaging the stage. But pleasure-garden proprietors in those days – as indeed perhaps always – were a tough breed. Nothing daunted, they returned to the attack with a second fête champêtre, which produced this description:

> The orchestra, boxes, theatre, and every part of the gardens were beautifully illuminated at a vast expense, with lamps of various colours, disposed with great taste and elegance. The grass-plat before M. Torré's building was surrounded with two semi-circular rows of trees, and hedges, prettily contrived, divided, and forming two walks; and between every tree hung a double row of lamps bending downwards; between every break orange and lemon-trees were placed, and the whole was hung with festoons of flowers, and other pastoral emblems. On this place the rural entertainment was held, consisting of singing and dancing... On the left hand of this rural scene was a stile, and a walk which led to a temple sacred to Hymen, and which was transparent, and had a very pretty effect, when viewed at a distance. The gardens were not clear of company at six o'clock next morning.

The M. Torré mentioned here was the highly gifted pyrotechnic artist who directed the firework displays. Admission to the fireworks cost a further shilling – that is, if one viewed them from the open pit of his enclosure. For wealthier patrons, there were better seats at five shillings a head. Dr Johnson, whose enthusiasm for good conversation and the world of letters did not prevent him from enjoying the simpler pleasures of life, caused an uproar at the fireworks one evening. After a long wait in a pit seat to the accompaniment of drizzling rain, while the management, apparently waiting for the empty five-shilling seats to fill up, excused themselves by announcing that the fireworks were damp, he leaped to his feet shouting indignantly: 'It's a mere excuse to save their crackers for a more profitable company!' The Doctor's tremendous bellow started an instant chain reaction among the occupants of the pit seats, and when he suggested that they should threaten to break the lamps a number of young men gleefully started the work of destruction. In his calmer moments, though, Dr Johnson was so perceptive a connoisseur of M. Torré's art that he endowed him with a dubious immortality by bringing him into a critique on the poet Gray. 'Gray', said the Doctor, wielding his literary bludgeon as vigorously no doubt as he had used his cudgel in the pit, 'was the very Torré of poetry; he played his coruscations so speciously that his steel-dust was mistaken by many for a shower of gold.'

Dr Johnson's violent reaction to Torré's procrastinating tactics recalls not only the roughness of the age, but the fact that the management of the Gardens catered for violence. The part known as 'The Bear Garden' contained pits for cock-fighting and dog-fighting, and raised platforms for prize-fighting – both male and female. The female bruisers were probably provided by the celebrated Figg, and James Broughton, the successive lessees of an amphitheatre, known as 'The Boarded House', in Marylebone Fields. Figg, who was the sporting fraternity's hero in his day, would take on any comer at fencing, boxing or quarterstaff, and himself maintained a tough gang of male and female bruisers. A typical contemporary advertisement announced that 'Mrs. Stokes, the City Championess, is ready to meet the Hibernian heroine at Figg's.' Broughton achieved fame but ended his long career as a leading pugilist when he was half-slaughtered by Slack, another mighty bruiser, in a slogging match which ran to ninety-three rounds. Patrons like the Duke of Cumberland, 'Butcher' Cumberland, younger son of George II, whose cruelties after Culloden were as notorious as his London debaucheries, promoted such contests, squandering vast sums on these bloody and barbarous spectacles. There are tales, too, of this hero and the gentlemen of his suite hanging about the shadier parts of the Gardens and indulging their sadistically depraved tastes at the expense of unprotected young women. Another frequenter of the Gardens was the dashing and not unchivalrous Dick Turpin, who is said to have snatched a kiss in the open from the Reverend Dr Fountaine's niece. When she shrieked, half in terror and half in indignation, he is credited with the rejoinder, nicely suited to his image: 'Pray alarm yourself not, Madame. You can now boast that you have been kissed by Dick Turpin!'

While the carriage entrance to the Gardens was through the grounds of The Rose of Normandy in the High Street, there was a back entrance from what were known as 'The French Gardens'. This was in the neighbourhood of the Marylebone Road end of Harley Street – then open country with fields. The French Gardens were the allotments once cultivated by the Huguenot refugees who had fled to London after Louis XIV had revoked the Edict of Nantes in 1685 and made life in France unbearable for Protestants. By the second half of the eighteenth century they had become the resort of what Nollekens the sculptor, and one of Marylebone's best-known residents in his day, called 'cockney florists, their wives and children, and Sunday smoking visitors'. In this area also was the French Chapel, the place of worship of the Huguenot community of Marylebone. Early in 1741 when the crumbling parish church became unsafe for its congregation to use, the Huguenots allowed them to hold services in the French Chapel for a fee of five pounds a year.

In the end, Marylebone Gardens fell victim to the engulfing tide of houses rising all round it. By 1770, Harley Street had been built right up to the edge of the Gardens; Marylebone Fields had disappeared and been replaced by the urban townscape advancing on a broad front from its Cavendish Square–Portman Square base-line; and the rural immunities and amenities of the neighbourhood were fast lapsing. The final blow was struck in 1778. That year the magistrates received so many complaints from neighbouring house-holders about the danger of fire from falling fireworks that the order was given to close the Gardens, and the site was sold to builders. There was, however, a brief Indian summer for this old rival of Ranelagh, a last blaze of glory in the final four years of its existence. In 1773, the City Surveyor, searching for the ancient City Wells famed for their healing virtues in medieval times, found a spring – and next year Marylebone Spa was born. The waters were said to be good for 'indigestion, and for nervous, scorbutic, and other disorders'. An announcement put out by the proprietors ran as follows:

MARYBONE SPAW: Will be open This and Every morning during the Summer, at Marybone Gardens. Admittance ONE SHILLING, for which each person may drink the WATERS, and breakfast on TEA or COFFEE. The Gardens will be open every

Sunday evening for company to walk in. To prevent improper
Company, each person to pay Sixpence at the Door . . .

It seems that the Gardens, though they were closed down in 1778,
had not been disposed of entirely to builders even as late as 1794,
and that there was an attempt that year to open the much reduced
remnant to the public. However, the response was not sufficient to
make the venture a paying one, and the Gardens finally passed out
of existence. A few traces of them survived even to the present century. A writer in 1915 reported that 'trees belonging to the old
garden still remain behind some of the houses in Upper Wimpole
Street. The orchestra of the garden stood upon the site of No. 17
Devonshire Place. A flagstone in the centre of a stable at the back
of No. 28 Weymouth Street is supposed to cover the old well;
another existing sign of the former location of the spring is a
portion of a pump, fixed against the stable wall.'

Old, or village, Marylebone contained two other notable institutions – the Watch House, later the Court House, and the Workhouse and Infirmary. The Watch House originated in the building
which Lord Oxford had put up, at the Oxford Street end of Marylebone Lane, in 1729, to house his manorial court. Four years later,
he made this over to the parish for use as a watch house, or place
of detention for offenders against the law before they were haled
before the justices of the peace. It was to be more than a hundred
years before the London police came into existence, and the maintenance of order was entirely a matter for the local constable and
watchmen. Marylebone was notorious for its disorders at this time.
Riotous outbreaks in Marylebone Gardens, uncivil commotions
among the crowds thronging the pugilistic establishments of Figg
and Broughton, and a superfluity of duellists, highwaymen, and
petty thieves in Marylebone Fields saw to that. The neighbourhood
was so ill famed that Gay made it the subject of telling allusion in
*The Beggar's Opera*. Probably his highwayman hero, Macheath,
was modelled on Dick Turpin, and it is not unlikely that the 'heath'
which forms part of his name referred to the Fields.

Marylebone Watch House contained living accommodation for
the beadle, or parish officer, in the uppermost storey, a watch-
room, a couple of cells for prisoners on the ground floor, and the
court or vestry room on the first floor. In 1803, Lord Oxford's
building was demolished and a new watch house erected on the site.

A third, and larger, building went up in 1825. As the years went by, the watch house began to play the role afterwards assumed by the town hall as the heart and centre of local government. A well-known aquatint by Rowlandson and Pugin shows the building as it was in 1809. It is evening, and the night watchmen in their great-coats are moving off from the large ground-floor room with their lanterns to begin their patrols in the neighbourhood. The Watch House's most celebrated prisoner was James Boswell – apprehended, not as might have been assumed on the night that Dr Johnson caused his disturbance in Marylebone Gardens, but in 1790, six years after his idolised hero's death. His offence was on the face of it a technical one – crying the hour in the streets, which was strictly the prerogative of the watch. Boswell, a heavy drinker who may well have been far from sober that night, said in his defence that he was trying to teach the watchmen a lesson by the emphasis he gave to the actual hour in his crying. For instance, he said, he had cried: 'Past *two* o'clock and all's well,' whereas the watchmen all had the enraging habit of crying: '*Past* two o'clock and all's well!', dropping their voices after the initial 'Past', and so making it impossible to hear which hour it was that had just passed. The Watch House building, in its later form, survived Boswell by 140 years. During the last few years before its demolition in 1935, it was the premises of Bumpus the booksellers.

The Workhouse and Infirmary, an extensive range of buildings with its main façade for much of its existence on Northumberland, later Luxborough, Street, dated back to the middle of the eighteenth century. In its final stage as Luxborough Lodge, an old people's home, it lasted till 1965, after which it was demolished. Lord Oxford's distinguished architect, James Gibbs, one of the few practitioners of English Baroque, was called in to advise on, though he probably did not himself design, these buildings in their original form when they were sited in Paddington Street. In 1775, John White, the Duke of Portland's surveyor, designed a new workhouse, the first to go up on the Northumberland Street site. The old workhouse occupying the north-east corner of the burial-ground on the south side of Paddington Street was turned into the infirmary, in which capacity it survived until its demolition some twenty years later. In 1832, when Thomas Smith was writing his history of Marylebone, there were 1,344 inmates of the workhouse and infirmary, and there were nearly 6,000 people receiving outdoor relief. Mrs M. D. George, in her classic work, *London Life in the XVIIIth Century*, wrote:

While many London workhouses were crowded, ramshackle, insanitary places, perennially ravaged by fever, standards of order and cleanliness, and even sanitation, were being evolved in the richer and better managed parishes, and Marylebone was fortunate in its physician, Dr. Rowley, who was an advocate of the newer methods of treating fevers by bathing, fresh air, and scrupulous cleanliness, instead of what he calls 'the inflammatory practice'. In 1793, Rowley said he had prescribed at the Infirmary for about 400 patients weekly, and he estimated the annual practice there at '14,000 prescriptions'. In 1804, he described the Infirmary as 'an hospital as extensive in seeing numerous patients as any in London, or perhaps in Europe. . . .

A remarkable feature of old Marylebone, until it was filled in in 1764–6, was Marylebone Basin, the reservoir of the York Buildings Waterworks, conduits from which supplied water to the waterworks at Buckingham Street and the Strand. Marylebone, sited as it is on a 'gravel terrace' percolated by the waters of the north London heights, of which the most notable was the Tyburn river, was abundantly supplied with water. Its Basin filled an area north of Cavendish Square stretching from Queen Anne Street to Weymouth Street. On Rocque's map of 1745, this is shown as a long, formal rectangular affair, but it seems to have become in its later years 'a very large, circular and deep pond, fatal to many an inexperienced youth'. Not far from it at that time, too, was a small pond, nearer Oxford Street, called 'The Cockney Ladle'. Chatelain's view of the Basin from the west in 1761 shows several people swimming in it, and a group of fashionable gentlemen and their ladies promenading along the bank. One can imagine that the hygienically-minded Dr Rowley, had he lived in London at this time, would have been none too pleased to see bathing going on in one of the sources of its water supply – though the effect of this no doubt was trifling compared with the consequences of what went into the Thames every day of the year. But the Thames at least is running water, while 'Maribone Bason' was a sheet of still water, probably stinking at times, and as full of bacteria as the rookery of St Giles, away to the south-east, was of human detritus.

# 3. Marylebone Squares

MARYLEBONE in its modern sense as an urban area of London – as opposed to a village on its outskirts – started with Cavendish Square. That was in 1717, and the other large squares of the district – Portman, Manchester, Bryanston, Montagu, and Dorset – followed in the course of the next hundred years. So did Portland Place, which though not a square, was the residential and social equivalent, and at the time of its completion possibly the finest piece of townscape in London. All these squares came into being during the period when the Georgian tradition in architecture prevailed. Though their architectural merits might differ, they all obeyed the same rules of proportion and symmetry, as did the streets which linked them up with one another. In this way, the greater part of what was to become the metropolitan borough of Marylebone was given that urbane and classical character for which it was notable right up to modern times, and which in spite of Victorian intrusions, and now of the latest mammoth housing and office blocks, it still retains in considerable degree.

Cavendish Square struck the note of elegance from the outset. It was begun at a moment in history when England, after the upsets of the Civil Wars and the Revolution of 1688, was at last settling down to a long period of stability, both internal and external. Marlborough's wars were over, and those major political earth tremors, the American War of Independence and the French Revolution, lay many years ahead. Robert Walpole, the apostle of ca' canny, was about to spring into the saddle and keep his firm hands on the reins of government for the next couple of decades. The atmosphere was propitious to a flowering of the arts of peace – and not least for architecture. Palladianism, propelled by Colen Campbell and Lord Burlington, had come to town, and the vogue of the gentleman-connoisseur of 'regular building' was beginning.

Such a connoisseur was Lord Harley, later second Earl of Oxford and Mortimer, lord of the manor of Tyburn. His father-in-law,

John Holles, Duke of Newcastle, had bought the Marylebone estate
in 1708, and on the Duke's death three years later, it had passed to
his daughter, Lady Henrietta Harley. The fact that it was in 1715
that Harley and his wife first conceived the idea of the Cavendish
Square housing estate – for that is what we should call this ambitious project nowadays – is significant. For that was the year
in which Colen Campbell issued the first volume of his *Vitruvius
Britannicus*, that splendidly produced architectural tract for the
times whose elegantly engraved plates recorded the leading classical
buildings in England. Among the many noblemen who subscribed
to the publication of the three immense volumes to which Campbell's work eventually ran were Edward Harley and his father
Robert, the first earl, Queen Anne's chief minister during the last
years of her reign. *Vitruvius Britannicus*, which included some of
its author's own designs, not only furthered the gospel of Palladianism, but gave considerable impetus to the fashion for building
large classical mansions in both town and country. It must certainly
have influenced the Harleys, and contributed to their decision to
exploit their new estate on the northern outskirts of London. Perhaps the determining factor in this was the desire to emulate the
group of Whig landowners who were developing the newly-laid-
out Hanover Square.

Harley was well placed to undertake this piece of early urban
development. He was rich, he had well-off friends ready to take
housing plots, a gifted young architect and a notably shrewd surveyor, and a personal circle of men eminent in the artistic and literary worlds. His passion for building, landscape-gardening, and
the collecting of books and medals, and his distaste for politics and
general society had made him at the early age of twenty-six something of an authority on the urbane life. His total want of business
capacity was provided for in the shape of an uncle, his namesake
Edward Harley, a former Auditor of the Imprest, i.e. an Exchequer
official, who handled the financial side of the Cavendish Square
project. His architect was James Gibbs, the designer of St Mary-le-
Strand, later to be responsible for St Martin-in-the-Fields, the
Cambridge Senate House, and other masterpieces. His well-heeled
friends, prepared to take plots on the estate, consisted of distinguished Tories who had all held posts in his father's administration
under Queen Anne. The most notable of these were Lord Carnar-
von, later Duke of Chandos, a former Paymaster of the Forces and

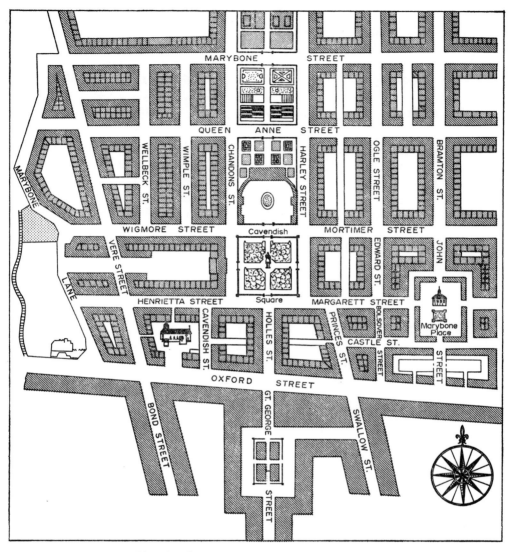

Plan for the Cavendish Square estate 1719,
based on John Prince's plan for Lord Harley

one of the richest men in England; ex-Lord Chancellor Harcourt
and ex-Chancellor of the Exchequer, Lord Bingley.

Fortified by this promise of powerful backing, and stimulated
no doubt by the building activities of their neighbours the Gros-
venors in Mayfair, the Harleys began to lay out Cavendish Square
about 1717. John Prince, their surveyor – commemorated today by
John Prince's Street linking Oxford Street with the south-east
corner of the square – produced an ambitious plan. This provided
not only for a spacious square, but a market, a chapel, and a network of access streets whose western boundary was that ancient
thoroughfare, Marylebone Lane. This narrow, winding country
lane, bordering the Tyburn brook for part of its course, was the
road connecting Marylebone village with London. The Harleys'
new Cavendish Square housing estate was to occupy the fields eastwards of Marylebone Lane as far as the border of the neighbouring
Berners estate at Wells Lane, now Wells Street. The northern
boundary of the estate as drawn by John Prince was along the line
of New Cavendish Street – called on his plan Marylebone Street
– presumably because this was where the new estate would march
with the outskirts of Marylebone village.

Building in Cavendish Square itself started about 1720. But the
'South Sea Bubble' fiasco of that year led to a general shortage of
finance, and building progress on the estate was markedly slow.
Nevertheless, four years later the Oxford Chapel – now St Peter's,
Vere Street – and the Oxford Market had been completed. The market, however was not fully opened until 1731 owing to objections by
Lord Craven, who feared that his Carnaby Market, near by, was
going to feel the draught. It was a country town type building with
an arcaded ground floor and a steep roof with a cupola and a
weather vane. It was sited behind what is now the C & A Modes
store, 200 Oxford Street, and was demolished in 1880. The street
name Market Place and the rebuilt-on square are all that is left to
show where it stood.

St Peter's, Vere Street, called the Oxford Chapel until 1832, has
even now the air of a small Georgian country church. For many
years after it was completed in 1724 – at considerably less than half
the cost of one of the pricier Rolls-Royces of today – it must indeed
have bordered upon open country. It must still have breathed the
air of rusticity, ten years later, when the second Duke of Portland
married his 'lovely little Peggy', celebrated thus in verse by Prior,

St Marylebone as surveyed by John Rocque in 1745
with the boundaries established in 1832 superimposed

and the darling of her father Edward Harley, second Earl of Oxford's circle of artists and writers. Sedately well-mannered outside, the church's interior is all elegance, and it has been called by Sir John Summerson 'a miniature forecast of St Martin-in-the-Fields, exquisitely carried out'. Gibbs, its designer, lived within sight of it, in Henrietta Place. Later Burne-Jones did the altarpiece and some of the windows. In mid-Victorian times, the incumbent there for some years was Frederick Denison Maurice, leader of that group of earnest Christian Socialists of whom the most gifted was Charles Kingsley.

The amenities of the new estate were first enjoyed by the circle of Tory notabilities of whom the Duke of Chandos was the richest by far and easily the most conspicuous – perhaps indeed the wealthiest man in England at the time. This rather colourful adventurer on the grand scale was known as 'The Grand Duke' or 'Princely Chandos' because of the magnificence of his style of life. He had made a vast fortune as Paymaster of the Forces under Marlborough. At his country seat at Canons, Edgware – according to Defoe 'the finest house in England' – he maintained a household of 120 people, with Handel as his private organist and a full choir to back him up. Service in his private chapel was held 'after the manner of the chapel royal', and an orchestra played to him every day at dinner. This monument of conspicuous consumption seems originally to have intended taking the whole of the north side of Cavendish Square for his town mansion. And, indeed, rumour was busy suggesting that his magnificence would be satisfied with nothing less than buying up all the land between the square and Edgware – in order to link his town and country properties in a single immensely long processional way. This was probably pure myth; and the fact is that, having dropped several hundred thousand in the South Sea speculation, he contented himself ultimately with building a couple of unspectacular mansions at the north-east and north-west corners of the square.

Mr Louis Osman, F.R.I.B.A., the distinguished architect responsible for the additions and alterations to the north side of the square in our own day – 1957 – has stated that by 1724 Chandos had already abandoned his idea of building a great palace across the north side of the square. By that time, it seems, his main interest in the area was in its possibilities as the site of a waterworks system for the West End. The 450-ft-long Marylebone Basin, which he had

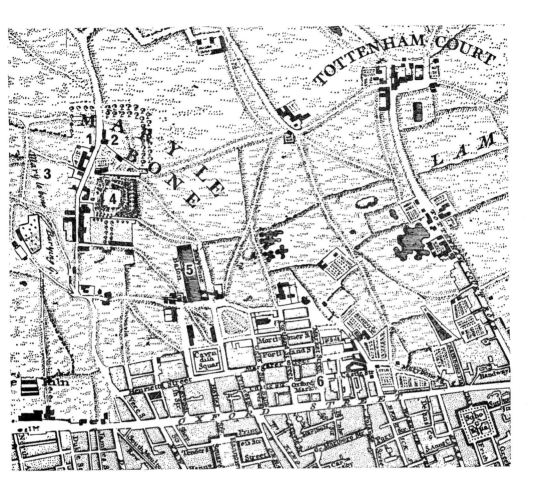

Rocque's map of 1746 with a key to places of interest.

1. St Marylebone Parish Church
2. The School House, formerly the Manor House
3. Burial Ground
4. Marylebone Gardens
5. Marylebone Basin
6. The Oxford Market

originally visualised as the ornamental long water to grace the
northward view from his palace, was to be the basis of the waterworks. Mr Osman thinks that a factor in Chandos's decision not
to build in the centre of the north side of the square was that he
wished to keep it open 'for the conduit that would run southwards
from the basin he was building, which was to act as a reservoir'.
During his work in 1957, Mr Osman found a large and deep culvert
running down 'the centre of the mews on the north side of the
square'. He believes that this was part of Chandos's water-supply
project.

From the outset, Cavendish Square was provided with a central
plot of green turf, railed off, and later this was made the setting
for a statue of the Duke of Cumberland, second son of George II.
The 'Butcher' was shown on his prancing charger in the military
costume of the day. As it was then still the custom to trick out the
effigies of military commanders in the full panoply of togas and
laurel wreaths, this departure caused a lot of indignation, and some
ridicule. A contemporary woodcut, inspired no doubt by a sense of
mockery, gave a back view of the Cumberland statue – vast plunging
buttocks, Hanoverian and equine – filling the foreground, while
sheep grazed around the base of the plinth. The sheep, it seems,
were not a fanciful addition of the artist. They were actually pastured there in the square's earlier days, and must have helped to
maintain the rustic air prevailing during its long unbuilt-up period.

An early resident was Simon, Lord Harcourt, the Tory ex-Lord
Chancellor. He had a mansion built for him on the east side of the
square. But when the house of Lord Bingley, a former Chancellor
of the Exchequer who had died in 1731, came up for sale in 1773,
Harcourt's grandson bought the place. He called his new residence,
on the west side of the square, Harcourt House, and it became a
town house of note, the name surviving to this day, handed down to
a block of flats on the site. This Lord Harcourt, who seems to have
been a man of some mark in spite of being dubbed 'civil and
sheepish' by Horace Walpole, enlarged the house and greatly
improved it. Yet by the time it came into the hands of the Portlands, the Harleys' successors as ground landlords, in 1825, it had
been described as 'a large, gloomy mansion enclosed by a long,
blank wall, rather like a convent than the residence of a man of
Quality'. The high, windowless wall – a print of the day shows it as
reminiscent of the screen wall of the Bank of England – may well

have been for security, since for many of its early years, Cavendish Square stood isolated and lonely on the edge of the notoriously unsafe Marylebone Fields. Thackeray's Gaunt House in *Vanity Fair*, generally thought to be a description of Harcourt House, had 'a vast wall in front, with the rustic columns at the great gate, through which an old porter peers sometimes with a fat and gloomy red face; and over the wall, the garret and bedroom windows, and the chimneys, out of which there seldom comes any smoke now'. All the drab and squalid sadness of early industrial England peeps out for a moment from this vignette of Thackeray's. Like Dickens, he saw the contemporary urban scene through dark-tinted spectacles, and seized upon the gloomy features of an actual mansion to convey moral condemnation of his fictional villain, Lord Steyne.

Harcourt House was renamed Portland House when the fourth Duke of Portland took it over in 1825. The Portlands had been the ground landlords ever since the second duke, 'the handsomest man in England', had in 1734 married the Lady Margaret Cavendish Harley, heiress of the Harleys' Marylebone estate, and so brought the estate into his family. The third Duke of Portland was twice Prime Minister of England. He presided over the coalition ministry of 1783, which followed the collapse of George III's personal rule at the end of the War of American Independence. Twenty-four years later, after his leader, the younger Pitt, had died, he headed the Tory Government which came into power in 1807, and led it until his death in 1809. A steady, reliable person, he seems to have been regarded as one of those likeable, reasonably competent politicians needed from time to time to fill in gaps between really able statesmen.

It was left to the fifth Duke of Portland, central figure of the 'Druce–Portland Case', to attract newspaper publicity on the modern scale, and to be the occasion of a very odd *cause célèbre* seventeen years after his death in 1879. The whole extraordinary affair blew up in 1896, when the widowed daughter-in-law of Thomas Charles Druce, owner of the 'Baker Street Bazaar', who had died in 1864, petitioned the Home Secretary for permission to open his coffin. She alleged that the man known as T. C. Druce had in fact been the fifth Duke of Portland, a very wealthy bachelor noted for his eccentricities. These, the public had learnt, included such expensive whims as the building of an extraordinary network of underground tunnels on his Welbeck estate, the erection of ground-glass screens 80 feet high and 200 feet long on either side of the back garden of Harcourt House – so, with the existing high wall in front, still further shutting himself off from any possibility of being glimpsed by unauthorised persons – and such personal foibles as the sporting of a topper a couple of feet high, tying his trousers at the knee, navvy-fashion, and wearing a long, heavy overcoat in all weathers. Mrs Druce junior's allegation was that the fifth duke had crowned his fantasticalities by creating the personality of T. C. Druce, upholsterer of Baker Street, and by masquerading for years in this borrowed persona. Finally tiring of this tradesmanly role, she deposed, he had liquidated the situation by staging his own death and burial in 1864. If the coffin supposed to contain Druce's body were opened, it would be found to be empty. As far as the world knew, the fifth Duke of Portland had died, a childless bachelor, seventeen years before Mrs Druce came forward with her petition, and his vast fortune had devolved upon other members of his family.

But it now became evident that Mrs Druce's statements, if true, might lead to the duke's ultimately being proved to be her father-in-law. And if that were established, the Druce family might lay claim to some of the Portland millions. At all events the Druces took up the case with the greatest vigour, and although Mrs Druce herself had to retire to a mental home after seven years of intense legal battling, they even went the length of forming a public company, with a capital of £30,000, for the further waging of the struggle. The public, eager to share in what they believed might be the vast profits of this speculation, were quick to subscribe. Finally, in 1907, eleven years after Mrs Druce had first astounded the country with her allegation, the coffin was opened, and found to contain the body of T. C. Druce. With this, the case collapsed, the final scene being the trial that year in Marylebone Police Court of one Herbert Druce, who was found guilty of perjuring himself in the course of his family's frenzied pursuit of this soap-bubble of lucre and lineage. Portland House meanwhile had been demolished in 1903, and replaced by the present block of flats.

Another early resident in Cavendish Square was Princess Amelia, third daughter of George II. She lived for many years in the mansion which Chandos had built at the Harley Street corner of the square, and which he himself occupied for a time. This still survives in part, though much altered. The Cavendish Square frontage is now occupied by Coutts & Co., the old-established bankers, and the site of the Harley Street frontage by various consultants and professional organisations. The Princess, whose engagement to the future Frederick the Great was broken off for dynastic reasons, remained unmarried all her long life. She seems to have been a rather raffish, horsy type, card-playing and snuff-taking; a masculine figure, 'who always drank her morning chocolate in a standing posture'; for ever haunting the stables and discussing the diseases of horses with her grooms with a crude male relish. Contemporary commentators have not been kind to her. The first Lord Holland dismissed her as 'a lively, mischief-making and mischief-meaning woman; has parts without any understanding, and has employed them all her life in doing all the harm she can'. Greville the diarist recalls that 'after the death of George 2nd, somebody asked if the Princess Emily, whose virtue was not thought immaculate, was to have Guards. G.S. [George Selwyn] said: "One every now and then!"' The other house built by the Duke of Chandos at the Chandos Street corner of the square has long since disappeared. Both mansions were designed by Edward Shepherd, who gave his name to Shepherd's Market in Mayfair.

As a piece of townscape, Cavendish Square has now been deprived of its eighteenth-century elegance. The roof-line, first disturbed by Victorian and Edwardian intrusions, has been irretrievably shot to pieces by the insertion of a multi-storey tower block on the south side of the square. This brooding mammoth, housing the British Home Stores, some of the B.B.C.'s innumerable overflow offices, the business premises of various oil companies, and a pub, The Phoenix, looks down across the square at a pair of Palladian façades, the last survivors of its age of grandeur. These comprise four houses, built about 1770 as a speculation, to fill the empty space between the two Chandos mansions. With these, they were originally linked by connecting wings at ground-floor level, thus completing a single architectural composition occupying the whole of the north side of the square.

Today the wings have disappeared. But the two façades, with what Sir John Summerson has called 'their grandiloquent parade of rustics and Corinthian columns', are now linked with one another at first-floor level by a bridge spanning Dean's Mews, the winding cul-de-sac to which they form the entrance. The bridge is the backdrop for Epstein's 'Madonna and Child', which has been suspended from it – a brilliantly imaginative stroke which gives the tensely conceived work the height and commanding position of a cathedral altarpiece. Behind the easterly of the two façades is Heythrop College, founded in Louvain as far back as 1614 for the education of English Jesuit students, but now part of the Faculty of Theology of the University of London. The college, transferred to England from the Continent following the French Revolution, was moved to Cavendish Square in 1970 after nearly half a century near the Oxfordshire village of Heythrop. It is the successor in its distinguished London premises of the children's school attached to the Convent of the Holy Child Jesus, a latterday order of Catholic nuns established in England in 1846 by Cornelia Peacock, of Philadelphia, and in Cavendish Square in 1851. The westerly building, after a long period of dingy dereliction, has been renovated and its stonework cleaned. It is now occupied by a commercial firm.

Lady Mary Wortley Montagu, that witty letter-writer and friend of the leading wits of her day, Pope's intimate and afterwards the target of his venom, moved to Cavendish Square as early as 1731. Her close friendship with Henrietta Harley, Countess of Oxford, may have accounted for the move. At this time, she was already in her early forties, and her never very happy marriage was more or less on the rocks. In a few years' time she would leave England, in fruitless pursuit of her passion for a young Italian, Francesco Algarotti, twenty-three years her junior and markedly ambidextrous in his amatory tastes. Though she did not know it at the time, her principal rival for his attentions was her own intimate friend Lord Hervey, whose memoirs of George II's court are shot through with malice hardly inferior to Pope's at his most scarifying, and who did not hesitate to ridicule her to Algarotti. She might well have suspected this attraction, for she had long before made her classic remark – that there were three sexes: men, women, and Herveys. Lady Mary left England, and Cavendish Square, in 1739, and for the rest of her life – apart from its last few months – lived abroad. But her husband, the cold-hearted, handsome Mr Wortley she had eloped with thirty years before, and whose self-centred indifference to her had finally drained away her wifely feelings, lived on in the square – probably retiring to a smaller house as it became clear that she was not going to return to England.

Two only of the most notable men and women who have lived in the square are commemorated by a blue G.L.C. plaque. This is not due to indifference on the part of London's rulers, but to the fact that the G.L.C.'s policy is, it seems, to slap on one of these medallions only where the original house of the celebrity survives. It is in general disregardful of new buildings occupying sites where the famous have lived. This not only helps to preserve a properly reverential attitude on the part of sightseers – who can touch the very bricks which encased the great man or woman – but probably prevents London façades from becoming one immense polka-dot surface of blue medallions. It is also an added indication to the knowledgeable of the architectural period of a house.

Cavendish Square's two plaques commemorate Asquith and Quintin Hogg – not our present talented and irascible politician, but his grandfather, the founder of the Regent Street Polytechnic, and the philanthropist from whom he clearly derives his moral fervour. Hogg lived on the east side of the square, Asquith on the west. One is apt to forget that Asquith became the Earl of Oxford and Asquith. His fame rests with the name he had as a commoner, not with his title of nobility. Similarly, Edward Harley, the creator of Cavendish Square, is remembered, if at all, by the fact that he gave his name to a famous street, and not as Earl of Oxford and Mortimer. After all, English genealogy is bursting at the seams with earls of Oxford – the De Vere family alone having produced twenty of them. No. 20 Cavendish Square became Asquith's home in 1894, the year he married Margot Tennant, and he did not sell it until 1919, though of course he moved to Downing Street during the period of his long premiership of nearly nine years. The house is now the premises of the Cowdray Club.

Henry Mayhew, in his classic work, *London Labour and the London Poor*, published midway through the nineteenth century, has shown Cavendish Square as seen through the eyes of a crossing-sweeper. He describes 'Billy' as the 'man who for many years has swept the long crossing that cuts off one corner of Cavendish-square, making a short-cut from Old Cavendish-street to the Duke of Portland's mansion'. Billy, he says, told him that in the good old times he had made 'hats full of money', and 'the very first day I was at work, I took ten shillings. I never asked nobody; I only bowed my head and put my hand to my hat, and they knowed what I meant.' He had seen Queen Caroline, wife of George IV, pass through the square after her trial: 'They took the horses out of her carriage and pulled her along. She kept a-chucking money out of the carriage, and I went and scrambled for it, and I got five-and-twenty shillin.' At this time, the Queen, who was staying at Lady Anne Hamilton's house in Portman Street, had the sympathy of most of the public in her refusal to renounce her title at the King's behest. The ladies and gentlemen of Marylebone sent her a loyal address. They mustered in Welbeck Street in 135 carriages, and then drove to the house she later took in Hammersmith to assure her of their loyalty.

Billy also told Mayhew that 'all the time the Duke of Portland was alive, he used to allow me 7s. 6d. a week'. This would have been the fourth duke, of whom history has nothing to say – not even Thomas Smith's history of Marylebone. Billy recalled that 'one of the best friends I had was Prince E... [probably Prince Paul Esterhazy], as lived there in Chandos-street, the bottom house yonder. I had five sovereigns give me the day he was married to his beautiful wife.... Then there was the Earl of Gainsborough. He lived in Chandos-street, and was a particular nice man and very religious. He always give me a shilling and a tract.' Billy the crossing-sweeper's memories also extended to Portman Square in the early years of the nineteenth century. The indefatigable Mayhew elicited his impressions of the scene when Castlereagh's house was attacked at the time of the Peterloo 'massacre'. Castlereagh was peculiarly identified in the public mind with the harshly repressive measures of Lord Liverpool's Tory administration – directed against the populace, and against any kind of reform. It was the period when Shelley wrote his blistering lines in *The Mask of Anarchy*:

> I met Murder in the way –
> He had a mask like Castlereagh,

and when Cobbett's *Political Register* thundered weekly against the tyrannies of a reactionary establishment. Billy could remember 'the mob at the time of the Lord Castlereagh riots. They went to Portman-square and broke all the windows in the house.'

Portman Square was the nucleus of the Portman estate, just as Cavendish Square was the nucleus of the Portland – now the Howard de Walden – estate. It was not laid out though until some forty years later. That is to say, the work began about 1761, by which time the earlier square was thoroughly developed, and its access streets ready to link up with a major housing project on the neighbouring Portman estate. The occasion for such a project was provided by the succession to the property that year of Henry William Portman, of Orchard Portman and Bryanston. He gave immediate instructions for a square and streets to be laid out. And so there came into being slowly over the next twenty years that five-acre rectangle of fine houses destined for a century and a half to be one of the most fashionable residential areas of London.

The rate of development was largely dependent upon the speculative builders to whom the construction was let out. They certainly took their time, and it was not until 1768 that the first houses – on the south side – began to be occupied. Most, if not all, of the houses on the south, east and west sides were built by the brothers Adams – Abraham and Samuel – not to be confused with the celebrated Adam brothers, who were also involved in the development of the square.

Building on the north side does not seem to have started until 1773, when Robert Adam began his celebrated Home House, now the Courtauld Institute. The Countess of Home, widow of the eighth earl, was a great heiress from Jamaica, and she spared no expense in providing herself with a splendid palazzo. Famous for its superb first-floor music room, and its unusually long frontage, it offered an immediate challenge to another leading hostess of the day, Elizabeth Montagu. This lady, also a widow with vaulting social ambitions, and a noted blue-stocking to boot, promptly secured a lease on a large site at the south-west corner of Gloucester Place. Building diagonally across the site, and using 'Athenian' Stuart as her architect, she produced in the course of five years an even vaster and more imposing mansion than Home House. This piece of magnificence, separated merely by the width of the road from her rival's domain, was inaugurated with a breakfast for seven hundred people. Mrs Montagu then dubbed the poor Countess of Home 'The Queen of Hell', and proceeded to take the mickey out of her by throwing parties even more sumptuous than hers, and by constantly monopolising public attention with every kind of ingenious gimmick. There was, for instance, her 'Feather Room':

The 'Feather Room' was an idea which seems to have sprung from her own fertile brain.... Large canvas-mounted frames were hung round the room, and upon them were feathers collected from all her friends, no matter whether peacock plumes, pheasant tails, or even cock's feathers....

There was, too, the faultless elegance of her architecture:

> Horace Walpole, who went to sneer, was surprised into praise.
> 'Instead of vagaries, it is a noble edifice. When I came home I
> recollected that, tho' I had thought it so magnificent a house,
> there was not a morsel of gilding. It is grand, not tawdry, not
> larded and embroidered and pomponned with shreds and
> remnants.'

Her generosity was on the grand scale: 'Every May Day, any
sweep who chose to present himself at Portman Square between one
and five in the afternoon was regaled with roast beef and pudding
on the lawn.' The targets of this particular gesture were the
wretched little imps who were actually sent up the chimneys – and
not their masters – and Thomas Smith, the historian of Marylebone,
suggests that the publicity her action received may have contributed
to subsequent legislation preventing this practice.

And if all this were not enough, the wretched Countess of Home
could reflect on the fact that the magnificent rival who had chosen
to build on her doorstep enjoyed an income of £10,000 a year, had
been visited in her great mansion by the King and Queen, was the
author of an *Essay on Shakespeare* publicly refuting Voltaire, was
hailed as a leading wit of the day, and had been called by her friend
Dr Samuel Johnson 'a very extraordinary woman'.

Fanny Burney, the novelist and diarist, once described Mrs
Montagu as 'brilliant in diamonds, solid in judgment, critical in
talk'; at another time, she remarked rather ambiguously 'as a member of society she is magnificently useful'. Physically, she seems to
have been a rather thin, sharp-faced woman, and 'Peter Pindar',
the satirical versifier, lampooned her as 'Old Uganda', declaring
that she had 'more beard than female grace'. He was writing of her
when she was over sixty, but accounts of her at earlier stages of her
career suggest that his hint that she lacked some of the feminine
graces was not unfair. If she fell short in physical attractions, she
was certainly a commanding personality, and she appears in her
own way to have impressed herself upon her leading contemporaries, over many years, almost as unforgettably as did Dr
Johnson in his. Indeed, the Great Cham himself could not afford
to ignore her celebrated salon. For the 'Madame du Deffand of
London' insisted on good conversation rather than card-playing,
and her blue-stocking circle included his beloved Mrs Thrale,

Hannah More, Hester Chapone, and Fanny Burney. Fanny, as a youthful diarist, had as early as 1777 sketched the reactions of Dr Johnson and Mrs Thrale to a dinner invitation from Mrs Montagu:

> Chocolate being then brought, we adjourned to the drawing-room. And here, Dr Johnson being taken from the books, entered freely and most cleverly into conversation; though it is remarkable he never speaks at all but when spoken to; nor does he ever *start*, though he so admirably *supports* any subject. The whole party was engaged to dine at Mrs Montagu's. Dr Johnson said he had received the most flattering note he had ever read or that any body else had ever read by way of invitation. 'Well, so have I too,' cried Mrs Thrale; 'so if a note from Mrs Montagu is to be boasted of, I beg mine may not be forgot.' '*Your* note,' cried Dr Johnson, 'can bear no comparison with *mine; I* am *at the head of the Philosophers,* she says.' 'And I', cried Mrs Thrale, 'have all the Muses in my train!' 'A fair battle,' said my father. 'Come, compliment for compliment, and see who will hold out longest.'

Of the leading architects of the latter half of the eighteenth century both Robert Adam and 'Athenian' Stuart made contributions – and outstanding ones at that – to the building of Portman Square James Wyatt, then at the outset of his immense and varied architectural output and known only for his Oxford Street Pantheon, was also involved. He designed Nos. 11–15 on the north side, now, like so much else in the original square, demolished. Wyatt was himself living in Marylebone, which was his home for the rest of his life. He built himself a delightful small house near Portland Place, and his workshops were close to the Queen's Head and Artichoke, a public house in Marylebone Park.

The houses designed by Wyatt in Portman Square, begun in 1773, were not completed till 1784. This may well have been due to the spate of commissions for public buildings and country houses he was then getting. The square rapidly became extremely fashionable, and by the time Dickens and Thackeray began to write was one of the smartest addresses in London. Thackeray, the coiner of the term 'Tyburnia' to describe the square and the area westward of it to beyond the Edgware Road, was especially interested in the neighbourhood. It provided the locale for the snobbish upper-class families which were the target of his satire and the staple provender

of his novels. He also had a personal interest in Portman Square
because a cousin of his, a wealthy Miss Thackeray, lived there. Of
her he wrote in 1853 – the year *The Newcomes*, with its marriage
market theme, began to appear –

> I went to a concert at the house of a cousiness of mine who has a
> fine mansion in Portman Square, and £6,000 a year to bestow
> upon any one who marries her; there were as many sneaks about
> her as in the very politest circles, and people were as eager to get
> to her party as to a Duchess's.

One of those who inhabited the square in its Victorian heyday
was George William, fourth Baron Lyttelton, Gladstone's brother-
in-law, a friend of Macaulay, and a fine classical scholar. This
Liberal politician and ardent educational reformer is one of the two
contenders for the original of Disraeli's Coningsby, the other
being Lord Strangford, who lived in Harley Street. Lord Lyttelton
had the curious experience of being given notice by the whole of
his domestic staff when he told them he intended to leave Portman
Square for Grosvenor Place. From the housekeeper and butler
downwards, they protested that they could not think of going to
such an outlandish neighbourhood. This may sound strange to
modern ears, when Grosvenor Place lies near the heart of one of
the most fashionable urban areas of London. But it must be remembered that in early Victorian days Belgravia was only just coming
into existence. It took several decades before it was finally built up.
Victoria Station itself was not built until 1860, and was merely an
assemblage of wooden shanties for the next half-century, until the
present structure went up in 1908. Belgravia, with its houses arising
on reclaimed marsh land, must have looked a dreary waste for many
years. To the eyes of retainers used to the elegant urbanities of
Marylebone – the great city north of Oxford Street, of Macaulay's
remark in 1831 – it probably seemed like the end of the earth.
    The social distinction attached to a Portman Square address dur-
ing the nineteenth century is reflected in the novels of Trollope as
well as in those of Thackeray. The town house of the Earl of Brentford in *Phineas Finn* was to be found there, as was that of the
blue-blooded De Courcys in *The Small House at Allington*. Trollope,
who himself lived in Montagu Square only a few minutes' walk
away from Portman Square, must often have seen upper-class
Englishmen of the De Courcy type frequenting it:

The De Courcys had never been plain. There was too much hauteur, too much pride . . . too much nobility in their gait, to allow of their being considered plain; but they were not a race nurtured by Venus or Apollo . . . tall and thin, with high cheek-bones, high foreheads, and large dignified cold eyes.

Such indeed was the charisma attaching to localities like Portman Square that all those of any social pretensions living in neighbouring streets would include the name of the square in the addresses on their visiting cards or headed notepaper. Typical of this was George Richmond, the much sought-after portrait-painter of the mid-Victorian era. He lived in York Street, half a mile or so away from Portman Square, but his address was nevertheless 'York Street, Portman Square' – a signal to potential patrons that he lived in the right neighbourhood, and that a portrait by him would mean no more than a short drive in one's carriage to the pleasant studio of a socially acceptable artist. Similarly when Tennyson, on 27 September 1855, read the newly-written *Maud* to a select audience consisting of D. G. Rossetti, the Brownings, and Miss Arabella Barrett – Mrs Browning's sister – that literary event took place at '13, Dorset Street, Portman Square'. This was probably the Brownings' address during a brief absence from Italy. But the point is immaterial. The significant fact is that for the poet, as for the painter, the *point de repère*, socially speaking, was Portman Square.

Portman Square indeed seems to have acted as a magnet for institutions as well as individuals. It could of course have been pure coincidence that the barracks of the 2nd Life Guards were situated in King Street – now Blandford Street – a few minutes' walk from Portman Square. But in an age when a colonel of the Grenadier Guards could use his influence with the Duke of York to prevent his battalion being present at Waterloo because he wanted to remain in a desirable post in Bavaria, one may well wonder if the social life of the officers was not the determining factor in the siting of the barracks. These ceased to be used as such in 1833, when they were superseded by the Regent's Park barracks. But the buildings, covering nearly two acres, were utilised for what became the King Street Bazaar. Here 'the Nobility and Gentry of the Neighbourhood' resorted in large numbers, and horses and carriages, saddlery and harness changed hands. Here there was 'stabling for nearly 400 Horses, a capacious Riding School, Standing for 500 carriages, a

Ladies' Bazaar for the Sale of Miscellaneous Articles, the entrance
for which is in Baker Street; a Suite of Rooms for the Sale of Furniture; and a splendid Saloon for the reception and display of
Works of Art.' Later, all these horsy splendours faded away together, presumably with the miscellaneous articles and the objets
d'art, and all that remained was the furniture – in the shape of
Druce's repository. This survived, on the opposite side of Baker
Street, until modern times but finally disappeared in 1971.

Within five years of the appearance of the first houses in Portman
Square in 1768, another great building project was afoot, this time
on the Portland estate. Half a century had elapsed since the Harleys
launched their Cavendish Square scheme, and during this interval
the Marylebone Road had come into existence. The famous 'New
Road', as it was called, was London's first by-pass. It had been cut
in 1756 through the fields from Paddington to Islington, enabling
sheep and cattle from the north to be brought to market at Smithfield without the need to drive them through Oxford Street and
other fashionable central streets of the metropolis. The coming of
the new thoroughfare provided a fresh means of access to the Portland and Portman estates, and gave a further fillip to their
development. By the early 1770s, development on the Portland
estate had filled up most of the area between Oxford Street in the
south and the Marylebone Road in the north. As Thomas Malton
said, writing of this period in his *A Picturesque Tour through the
Cities of London and Westminster:* '. . . houses rose like exhalations
in the parish of Mary-le-bone.'

There was however an area north-east of Cavendish Square to
which this was an exception. Here on the present site of the
Langham Hotel, Lord Foley, a cousin of Edward Harley, had
obtained a lease and built a large mansion in 1758. This imposing
building, costing £30,000, was – as Dr F. H. W. Sheppard in his
*Local Government in St. Marylebone, 1688-1835* was the first to
point out – sited right across the axis of a north–south road provided
for in the original estate plan of the Harleys. For reasons apparently
unknown, he was allowed to get away with this gross infringement
of the ground landlords' rights. Indeed, the Foley family later
extracted from the Portlands an undertaking, legalised by a private
Act of Parliament, that they would leave the ground north of Foley
House unbuilt upon for ever. The provision was that 'a large street
or opening' was to be left between the frontage of the mansion and

Marylebone Park, so that the view from the house should remain unobstructed in perpetuity. On this basis, plans were in existence for the building of a large square to be called Queen Anne's Square. Carrington Bowles's map of 1766 shows that, had this been realised, it would have occupied much of the site of Portland Place.

By 1773 the housing boom had reached such proportions, and the pressure to live in fashionable Marylebone was so great, that a move was made to exploit this promising area in a big way. With finance provided by the extremely rich and vastly eccentric John Elwes, already a considerable property-owner in Marylebone, the Adam brothers were roped in, and produced an ambitious scheme to make Foley House the southern terminal of a 'street of palaces'. The agreement of the Foley family was obtained by an undertaking that the street – or, strictly speaking, the close, for it was to have gates at its northern entrance – would be 125 feet wide. This was the width of the Foley House frontage, and in this way the view from the mansion was to be kept unobstructed. So Portland Place, which Nash was to call 'the finest street in London', came into existence – its width and spaciousness determined by the whim of a private leaseholder who had died years earlier!

The wealth flowing into England from India and America on the successful termination of the Seven Years War in 1763 had led to the Marylebone housing boom. Similarly, it was the outbreak of the War of American Independence in 1775, and its unfavourable course for England, which put an end to the boom for a number of years, and took much of the steam out of Robert Adam's palatial plans for Portland Place. It seems that he lost interest when he realised that he was not going to be able to bring off an even greater architectural feat than his Adelphi buildings of a few years earlier. With the abandonment of the original scheme for a series of detached private palaces, he handed over the project to James Adam, who produced something much less ambitious, but still a great deal more spacious than the ordinary run of town houses. His units, reminiscent of the Bath terraces, were long blocks occupying the whole length between intersecting streets, and foreshadowing the splendid terraces with which Nash was to surround Regent's Park. These pilastered and pedimented compositions in which a number of large houses sheltered behind what appeared to be the façade of a single monumental building were James Adam's way of producing the requisite grandeur on a reduced budget. With their shallow fronts, recessed windows, and delicate ornamentation – Adamesque friezes, plaques and roundels – they provided a not unworthy setting for what was soon admitted to be the finest street in all London.

It is difficult today, when Portland Place has been reduced to an architectural hotchpotch, and transformed into a huge thoroughfare for modern fast-moving traffic, to visualise what it looked like in the first few decades of its existence. It was in the beginning essentially an aristocratic enclave, with its back turned on London and its face towards the quiet fields leading to Marylebone Park. The only access to what must have had the air of being a large country seat on the fringe of the metropolis was through its gates giving on the green hinterland of the Marylebone Road. It had the privacy and the exclusive views of parkland which Nash – influenced doubtless in part by this pilot experiment in urban rusticity – was to achieve thirty years later for his Regent's Park villas and terrace houses.

One of the earliest illustrations of Portland Place is Thomas Malton's attractive aquatint of 1800. It gives a view looking northwards to the fields. The shut-off nature of the place is well conveyed, and the striking contrast with the roar and bustle of today enhanced by the presence of a performing bear in the foreground of the picture. A drawing of 1816, done by the architect J. B. Papworth, himself a Marylebone resident, shows further building development, somehow subtly foreshadowing the aura of Victorianism so soon to arrive. But the atmosphere of a close was long maintained and we are told that: 'It was a common thing on summer evenings to see the inhabitants in evening dress strolling up and down the pavements.'

One of the earlier residents in Portland Place was James Holroyd, first Earl of Sheffield, the close friend of Gibbon the historian, who also made his home in Marylebone – in Bentinck Street – for a number of years. Sheffield outlived his friend by nearly thirty years, and edited his memoirs, which appeared in 1795, the year after Gibbon's death. He was a man of action, and a vigorous Whig politician who won his peerage for the part he played in bringing about the legislative union of England and Ireland in 1801. During the Gordon Riots he had been in the House of Commons on the day when the mob tried to invade it. He is said to have seized Lord George Gordon by the throat and threatened to run his sword through him the moment the first of the mob entered the building. Fortunately for Lord George, the mob was diverted in another direction which offered the chance of more loot, and violent action against him became unnecessary.

Even fifty years after Portland Place had come into existence, it was still very much a preserve of the aristocracy. Thomas Smith, the historian of Marylebone, writing in 1833, recorded a list of residents which included the Earls of Mansfield, Sheffield and Stirling, Viscount Boyne, Lord Walsingham, and the dowager Duchess of Richmond. The Sheffield family which had so befriended Gibbon lived there for several generations. Yet, by the middle of the century, it seems that Portland Place had ceased to be favoured by the nobility, many of whom had presumably gone off to the newly-built Belgravia. The American, Slidell Mackenzie, in his *American in London*, published in 1848, wrote:

> Portland Place is still wider and more vast than Regent Street. It is of more ancient construction. The houses are of unpainted brick, and are all private dwellings. No omnibus is permitted to pollute with its presence these precincts, *though now guiltless of nobility* and abandoned to the abode of aspiring merchants and bankers. Compared with Regent Street, it had a certain air of staid respectability, not a little augmented by the occasional display of funeral hatchments, on which family arms were emblazoned, with angels, hour-glasses and various mournful emblems of the tomb to announce that death had been busy within.

It is clear from this that the solid Victorian mercantile element, satirised by Dickens with such gusto, had infiltrated the street in force during the sixteen years which had elapsed since the Great Reform Bill. Nevertheless, it is noteworthy that buses were not allowed to use it, and that a Portland Place address still connoted very considerable social status. The proof of this was evident in the number of embassies to be found there. Talleyrand when French Ambassador resided there, and it had been the home at different times of the Spanish, Polish and Turkish Embassies, the Swedish Legation and the Italian Consulate. The Swedish Embassy is there, as is the private residence of the Turkish Ambassador. The Chinese and Polish Embassies are still there.

In the now remote year 1896, when Lord Salisbury, that bearded father-figure, was Her Majesty's Principal Secretary of State, the

Embassy of Imperial China was the scene of untoward doings. The storm-centre was the revolutionary, Sun Yat-sen, the begetter of republican China. In exile in London, he had been nobbled by the Embassy staff and locked up in a room at 49 Portland Place. But he succeeded in smuggling out an appeal for help to the surgeon, Sir Edward Cantlie, his former tutor. Cantlie approached the British Foreign Office, who intervened and secured his release, thus paving the way for the ultimate birth of the Republic. Since it took Sun Yat-sen ten unsuccessful risings to achieve this object, one must believe that the F.O. had released a man of destiny and, whether intentionally or not, made history. One may also reflect, a little ruefully, that in letting out Sun Yat-sen, the Foreign Office started the chain reaction which led to the present Maoist régime in China, which cares as little for any sort of British intervention as for Sun's old pigtail.

One of the most colourful figures of modern times to choose Portland Place for his London residence was the late Edgar Wallace. To a generation to whom James Bond is beginning no doubt to seem 'old hat', it is perhaps necessary to explain who Wallace was. They should know that the author of *The Four Just Men* and *The Ringer* loomed equally large – as provider-in-chief of thrillers for their fathers – in an age when the public was not limited to a diet based on the scabrous exploits of spies and secret agents. In 1928, when he decided that only the sweep and splendour of Portland Place were large enough to contain his magnificence, this wholesaler in the production of crime literature was earning, from his nearly one hundred and seventy-odd novels and plays, about £50,000 a year. A nameless orphan brought up by a Billingsgate fish porter, he had risen in thirty years from newsboy to the world's best seller. He loved showmanship, and adored self-display, no matter how brash it might seem to the world at large. He was determined that the symbol of his success – the silhouette of the heavy face with the long, projecting cigarette-holder – should be universally known. From his perch in near-by Clarence Gate Gardens, that canyon of mansion flats leading to Regent's Park, he transferred himself to 31 Portland Place. There, encased in a sound-proof glass cabinet, he dictated, we are assured, at the rate of three to four thousand words an hour to a secretary in another room – linked to him presumably by dictaphone. Another secretary and numerous servants were kept busy ministering to the incessant needs of his fourfold *persona* as novelist, dramatist, patron of the turf, and man-about-town. It was characteristic perhaps of his restless dynamism that he left Portland Place in 1929 as suddenly as he had arrived there the year before – for a new setting in the Carlton Hotel.

Langham Place, which is a kind of appendix to Portland Place created by Nash as part of his Regent Street scheme, was the home during 1836 of Daniel O'Connell. The great champion of Catholic Emancipation, then in his sixty-second year, was exercising his extraordinary oratorical powers on immense audiences in many parts of England. He was M.P. for Kilkenny in the United Kingdom parliament, and had become so popular – because of his powerful support of the reform movement here – that he was boasting he would be offered a post in Lord Melbourne's Whig Cabinet.

At this point in time, his path crossed that of the young Disraeli, avid for publicity and pushing his fortunes with the Peelite Tories. 'Dizzy' had no personal dislike of O'Connell, who had in fact bidden him to dinner and tried to help him in his attempt to get a seat in Parliament. But he was not going to lose an opportunity of demonstrating his capacity for invective before his Tory masters. He denounced O'Connell in a speech as an incendiary, and accused the Whigs of 'grasping his bloody hand'. He got a reply, blistering even for those days, from one who was a tried pastmaster in the art of personal abuse. O'Connell stigmatised Disraeli as 'an abominable, foul and atrocious miscreant', and added:

> He possesses just the qualities of the impenitent thief that died upon the cross, whose name I verily believe must have been Disraeli. For aught I know the present Disraeli is descended from him, and with the impression that he is I now forgive the heir at law of the blasphemous thief that died upon the cross.

This was duel-provoking language, and Disraeli immediately issued a challenge. O'Connell, who had once killed his antagonist in an affair and vowed never to fight again, ignored the challenge. His son, Morgan O'Connell, had only recently fought a duel on his father's behalf, and likewise avoided a meeting. The final outcome – a sign of the changing times – was that Disraeli was arrested by the Marylebone police and bound over to keep the peace.

Of the three great mansions which have stood near the south end of Portland Place, Chandos House is the only survivor. Foley House and Langham House, the other two, were built successively upon the site now occupied by the Langham Hotel. Lord Foley's mansion was demolished at the time Nash was planning his Regent Street scheme, and a house of Nash's designing built for Sir James Langham, a Northamptonshire baronet. This pleasant stuccoed building, which had a sweeping Ionic colonnade running the length of its south front, formed a continuation of the west side of Portland Place. So, unlike its predecessor, it had no frontal view up Portland Place to the park. The reason for this was not far to seek. Nash had bought the land from Lord Foley, probably intending that his new Regent Street should run on in a straight line from the southern end of Portland Place. His agreement with Sir James Langham had provided that he should be the architect, and also no doubt that the house should be sited so as to leave room for Regent Street to be on the same axis as Portland Place.

All seemed to be going well when it was discovered that the line of march of the new street was going to involve Nash in insuperable difficulties with the owners of houses in Cavendish Square, whose back views would have been affected. He therefore prepared to swing the street eastwards along a line which would have brought the backs of the houses in Regent Street close to the front windows of Langham House. Sir James was furious – not only at this, but because his newly-designed mansion was showing signs of tumbling down. But there was little he could do. Nash held the whip hand. He owned the land. Langham was forced to buy enough of it to protect his view, and Upper Regent Street was deflected still farther eastwards. His house – he had called in another architect to put things right structurally – stood until 1864, when it was demolished to make room for the Langham Hotel.

Chandos House, built as far back as 1769–70, stands at the junction of Chandos Street and Queen Anne Street. Safely aloof there from the path of the Nash building hurricane, it has survived in good condition to show what Robert Adam could do at the height of his powers. Today, the site appears a rather cramped one, but it must be recalled that originally the house was free-standing, and that there was an uninterrupted view from the east front over the gardens of Foley House at the southern end of Portland Place. The west front also looked out over a garden towards that of Major-General Robert Clerk, for whom Adam had built a house with a frontage on Mansfield Street, in large grounds. The mansion was

built for the third Duke of Buckingham and Chandos – the last of
the line of that 'Princely Chandos' who had domiciled himself
round the corner in Cavendish Square a generation earlier. The
Chandos Street façade, even now when jostled by later buildings of
no particular merit, has an air of notable dignity and distinction.
But, for all its fine proportions, admirable portico, and proud display of ornamental iron-work, it is surely a little austere, a little less
inventive than Robert Adam at his most ingenious? For some tastes
the stable front on Duchess Street may make the greater appeal as
more completely in the Adam idiom.

In the Duke's time, stabling for twelve horses, and space for
four coach houses, lay behind this façade. With its monumental
front of receding planes in shallow relief, its coupled pilasters,
its pair of couchant sphinxes, and its sensitively-placed iron anthemion balustrades, it must have been an impressive curtain-
raiser to the prancing horses and the splendid equipages garnished
with ducal arms which jingled and rattled back and forth during
the London season. Chandos House remained in the Duke's family
for well over a century, but there was a variety of tenants over
the years. By 1817, Prince Paul Esterhazy, Austrian Ambassador
at the Court of St James's for nearly thirty years and one of the
most lushly apparelled men of that age of dandies, was in residence. In his time, Chandos House was the scene of entertainment on the most lavish scale. His extravagance was such that
he finally ruined himself, but not before he had impressed himself upon London society as a man who, in spite of his taste for
oriental splendour, was a warm and lovable personality, 'benevolent,
friendly, and courteous to everyone'. His appearance at the coronation of Queen Victoria was of such glittering sartorial magnificence
that a contemporary versifier was moved to record that

> 'Twould have made you crazy to see Esterhazy
> All jewels from jasey to di'mond boots.

After Esterhazy went in 1842, four further Austrian Ambassadors
in turn succeeded him there. In the present century, the most
notable owner has been Viscount Kemsley, the newspaper magnate,
who in 1927 bought most of a 999-year lease for £40,000. The place
remained in the Berry family until 1963, when it was sold to a
property company. Since 1964 it has been sub-leased to the Royal
Society of Medicine. The present owners seem to be keeping it in

excellent condition. The smooth ashlars of the Chandos Street front have been cleaned, and the area railings with their lamp standards and torch extinguishers are gleaming in black picked out with gold. Inside a four-year programme of redecoration to Robert Adam's original requirements has been recently completed.

Chandos House is within a stone's throw of a church which has suffered scenic extinction. As is well known, Nash, the designer of All Souls Church, Langham Place, was satirised in a contemporary print which showed him spitted on the spire of his church. Were he alive today, one can imagine that he, good-humoured as he was, might have his own candidates for pictorial lampooning, i.e. the architects of the Langham Hotel, Broadcasting House, Broadcasting House Extension (a scenic offence), and the St George's Hotel. These outsized structures, whatever their individual merits or de-merits, are collectively an example of the grossest bad manners in architecture. By their height and positioning, they have deprived All Souls of every iota of significance as a piece of townscape. The Langham Hotel, when it came in 1864, diminished the church's relevance to the Regent Street scene, and the other giants com-pleted the business of destroying its key role in Nash's great triumphal way from Carlton House to Regent's Park.

All Souls Church, admitted by modern critics to be a work of great ingenuity and distinction, was completed in 1824. Nash's dust-up with Sir James Langham, whose house lay on the other side of Langham Place, was now some years behind him. But there were other dogs ready to bark at anything done by the man who was the King's favoured architect – 'Prinny' having come to the throne since the earlier fracas. One of these yelpers announced in Parlia-ment that he would 'give a trifle to have this church pulled down'. Apart from political motives and natural jealousy, it was the unfami-liar sight of a spire rising from a classical building which stuck in the gizzards of the critics. Even Thomas Smith, anxious to do all honour he could, in his history of Marylebone, to one of the borough's architectural show-pieces, remarked sourly: 'Its novelty surprises, but does not produce delight.'

Nevertheless, at the time he made this comment – 1833 – All Souls had already become one of the most fashionable places of worship in London. The list of those who had thought it worth-while to pay for seating accommodation of suitable grandeur there included the Duke of Portland, Lord Dufferin, Lord Duncannon,

Lord Bridport, Lord Strangford, and other magnates. It is to be doubted if the quality of the architecture had much to do with their decision to patronise the church, but they certainly knew a place of social distinction when they saw it. The noble residents of Portland Place and the Harley Street area – at a cost of rather under £20,000, of which the Church Commissioners had contributed nearly £13,000 – had been provided with an elegant place of worship almost on their doorsteps.

The altar-piece in their new, spacious building – it could accommodate nearly 1,800 people – was the gift of George IV himself. It was the work of Richard Westall, R.A., a friend of Sir Thomas Lawrence (who must have painted the portraits of all the leading nobility in London). Against the festoons of a great crimson curtain hanging behind the altar, Westall had given them his 'Christ Crowned with Thorns'. No matter that the irrepressible Paul Sandby – who had probably bestowed drawing lessons upon the daughters of some of them – had dismissed Westall as 'very gaudy in his colouring, and has a face like a monkey'. Most of them cared not a jot either for his colouring or his face; enough that he was a fashionable painter patronised by the King, an intimate of that renowned and courtly prince of painters, the P.R.A., Sir Thomas Lawrence.

All Souls was refurnished in 1876 by Sir Arthur Bloomfield, son of a distinguished Bishop of London, a restorer of many cathedrals and churches, and himself a Marylebone resident. The talented and witty Goodhart-Rendel made some improvements in 1928, and it fell to him to restore the fabric after the blasting and burning of the second world war, when as the close neighbour of the B.B.C., All Souls was in the front line of the German blitz. The church was rededicated in 1951.

Manchester Square, the second large square to be built on the Portman estate, went up between 1776 and 1788. Unlike most London Squares, it has built-up corners, the streets of access entering it elsewhere than at the corner angles. This, together with its somewhat smaller area than Cavendish and Portman Squares, gives it a snug and rather sheltered look. Most of the north side is occupied by Hertford House – the Wallace Collection – a very large red brick mansion, approached by way of forecourt and a prominent portico, with balustraded roof. This once great town house, transformed into a jewel-case containing the pictures, porcelain, furniture and armour squirrelled away by the opulent Hertford family over a century, has an air of quiet and secluded leisure rare in contemporary London. The many superb clocks in cases of Boulle or other fine craftsmanship ticking away in its vast and splendid rooms still tell of a time that rolled on no faster than the lumbering family coach.

Hertford House had a predecessor in Manchester House, built by the fourth Duke of Manchester in 1776, when the square was in process of being created. Time carried him away in 1788 – the year of the square's completion – and the mansion became the residence of the Spanish Ambassador. Hence Spanish Place, where the now demolished Spanish Chapel went up in the 1790s, and then St James's, Spanish Place, its present successor, sited in George Street. This robustly conceived Gothic Revival R.C. church was decorated by J. F. Bentley, architect of Westminster Cathedral, with the kind of loving skill and taste which our own times saw miraculously revived in Sir Ninian Comper.

Manchester Square is not only physically dominated by Hertford House, but seems to have had little history apart from that of the house and its owners. That brilliant hostess, Lady Blessington, lived there briefly in the last days of the Regency – but that was before her marriage and the days of her fame. William Beckford, author of *Vathek*, an oriental novelette as fantastic as his monster neo-Gothic palace of Fonthill, had a house in the square, but his life there seems to have gone unrecorded. It is true that that proconsular personage, Lord Milner, lived on the west side of the square, but his lustre was gained in Egypt and Africa, and he cannot really be considered as involved with the locality. The Hertfords, on the other hand, were so involved, and for several generations. Their magnificence, their superb art collection, and their association with Royalty in the shape of the Prince Regent gave them colour, and by the time of the third Marquess of Hertford – prototype of Thackeray's Marquess of Steyne in *Vanity Fair* – they had taken further root in the district with the building of St. Dunstan's Villa in Regent's Park.

Much has been written about the third marquess, and a great deal said, and his notoriety as one of the most libertine of the Regency rakes is always stressed. His wealth, and that of his half-Italian wife, daughter of the Marchesa Fagnani by some gentleman unknown – but suspected to be either the Duke of Queensberry or Horace Walpole's witty friend George Selwyn – was fabulous. Maria, or Mie-Mie, Fagnani – 'never before did a lady have so many fathers' – inherited vast possessions from both her putative fathers, who vied with one another in claiming paternity. Several London houses, and a villa at Richmond, came her way on their demise, together with the fattest of monetary legacies from both papas. The Prince Regent was the intimate friend of the third marquess, as he had been of his father, the second marquess.

It was with the father's second wife, Lady Hertford, that 'Prinny' had one of his later liaisons. In 1811, he abandoned Mrs Fitzherbert, to whom he'd been secretly married for twenty-six years, and surrendered to the dominating Isabella Hertford, whom Sir Shane Leslie has dubbed his empress rather than his mistress. The corpulent middle-aged prince – he was a rather worse-for-the-wear forty-nine – was for ever in Manchester Square visiting his almost equally balloon-shaped lady. A contemporary print of the usual savage kind satirised the heavyweight pair under the caption: *Manchester Square Cattle Show*, and Tom Moore, with his turn for *vers de société*, let fly with the following 'from the diary of a politician':

> Through M–nch–str Square took a canter just now –
> Met the *old yellow chariot*, and made a low bow.
> This I did, of course, thinking 'twas loyal and civil
> But got such a look, oh, 'twas black as the devil!
> How unlucky! – *incog.* he was travelling about,
> And I, like a noodle, must go find him out!
>
> *Mem.* When next by the old yellow chariot I ride
> To remember there *is* nothing princely inside.

Work on Montagu and Bryanston Squares was started about the time the Prince Regent began his affair with Lady Hertford. Marylebone was becoming more and more fashionable, and development was pushing steadily northwards from Oxford Street. It was felt that the district, situated on higher ground than Mayfair or Westminster and bordering for the whole length of its northern edge on open country stretching away to the heights of Hampstead and Highgate, was a good healthy place to be in. Mrs Montagu, an inhabitant of Portman Square for the last couple of decades of the eighteenth century, declared that she had never felt so well anywhere as there, and christened the square 'the Montpelier of

England'. The building of Montagu and Bryanston Squares coincided with the launching of Nash's great Regent's Park scheme. The knowledge that this was afoot must have greatly encouraged David Porter, the 'eminent builder' and ex-chimney sweeper, who was mainly responsible for the construction of these two elongated rectangles of high-class housing. Although he appears to have begun building as early as 1810, he is unlikely to have known until a year or more later that the success of his venture was going to be guaranteed by the choice of Marylebone for the most splendid development scheme London has ever seen – the Regent's Park.

The architect employed for the layout of the new squares was James Thompson Parkinson, who was also responsible for some of the neighbouring streets. Parkinson, a young and relatively inexperienced man, was the son of a solicitor who was adviser to the Portman and other big London estates. Smith, in his history of Marylebone (1833), probably reflects the general opinion in his own day when he writes that the two squares 'are said to be the best examples of well constructed town residences'. Certainly they became very fashionable. By the early 1840s, when they had been in existence for a generation, they came in for some caustic criticism from a contributor to the encyclopaedic work *London*, edited by Charles Knight. He wrote:

> *Montagu Square* and *Bryanston Square* are twin deformities, the former of which is placed immediately in the rear of Montagu House. A range of balconies runs along the front of the houses in Bryanston Square, but the inmates seem to entertain dismal apprehensions of the thievish propensities of their neighbours, for between every two balconies is introduced a terrible chevaux-de-frise. The mansions in Montagu Square are constructed after the most approved Brighton fashion, each with its little bulging protuberance to admit of a peep into the neighbours' parlour. These two oblongs, though dignified with the name of squares, belong rather to the anomalous 'places' which economical builders contrive to carve out of the corners of mews-houses, behind squares, and dispose with a profit to those who wish to live near the great.

Bryanston Square, which is the wider of the two and has architecture of greater pretensions – the elevations are Parkinson's – is on the axis of the Marble Arch to the south, and of St Mary's, Wyndham Place to the north. But the intended vista is interrupted for much of the year by the mass of foliage on the trees in the square garden. The west side of the square has been almost entirely reconstructed as a single block of flats whose lines observe most of the old classical proportions and conventions. In spite of this attempt to preserve harmony, the result is displeasing and unconvincing. Montagu Square has kept many of its older houses, and its central garden is more secluded than its counterpart in Bryanston Square. The latter's great plane trees are strikingly lofty and graceful – even for the squares of a city whose planes are among its outstanding graces. Perhaps the most socially celebrated inhabitants of Bryanston Square were the Blessingtons, who went there after their marriage in 1818 – not long before they helped launch the splendid Count d'Orsay upon his career as leader of fashion on both sides of the Channel.

At No. 39 Montagu Square lived Anthony Trollope, and quite a number of the leading characters in his novels had links with Marylebone. Mr Slope, in *Barchester Towers*, had his church in Baker Street; the town house of the 'wicked Marquis' of Brotherton, in *Is he Popenjoy?*, was in Cavendish Square. Incidentally, is this a case of Trollope joining Thackeray and Disraeli in taking the third Marquess of Hertford as the model for his aristocratic villain, and likewise locating him in Cavendish Square? In *Orley Farm*, Thomas Furnival, the barrister who appeared for Lady Mason in both trials, lived in Harley Street. *Phineas Finn*'s Earl of Brentford had a mansion in Portman Square. Trollope must have met the models for some at least of the characters in his innumerable novels in upper middle class society in Marylebone. Among these perhaps was Frith, of 'Derby Day' fame, who has pointed the contrast between Trollope's books and the man himself – for us today the bearded old codger with gleaming glasses shown in the most frequently reproduced photograph. Frith, who knew him well, wrote: 'The books, full of gentleness, grace, refinement; the writer of them, bluff, loud, stormy and contentious; neither a brilliant talker nor a good speaker; but a kinder-hearted man and a truer friend never lived.'

St Mary's, Wyndham Place – better known perhaps as St Mary's Bryanston Square – a church begun by Smirke in the same year, 1823, that he started the building of the British Museum, has been in service since 1824, The building, architecturally speaking, was clearly intended as an eye-filler closing the vista from Oxford Street

through Bryanston Square to Wyndham Place. It has a handsome
portico, but suffers from a high, weedy tower which takes all the
punch out of its designer's conception. The church cost some
£20,000 – about the same as All Souls, Langham Place. The first
incumbent, Thomas Frognall Dibdin, nephew of Dibdin the song-
writer, was a noted bibliographer who had been librarian to Earl
Spencer at Althorp. By the time he began his ministrations to the
select citizens of Bryanston Square, he had produced *Bibliomania*,
*The Bibliographical Decameron*, and other works, all apparently
sought after avidly by the connoisseurs of the day. Had he lived
today, a title like the second one would have brought him a spate of
offers from those leading publishers who dabble in fashionable
pornography.

Dorset Square, the last of Marylebone's major squares to be built,
was probably started about 1814 – three years after Lord's Cricket
Ground had been moved from the site – and building was still in
progress in 1822. It marked yet another stage in the steady northward advance of the developing Portman estate. The supervising
architect was J. T. Parkinson, moving on from the laying out of
Montagu and Bryanston Squares. In Dorset Square, he produced
something less ambitious than these, but nevertheless, unlike them,
a true square, with its attendant advantages of appearance and
layout. The houses, though obeying the classical canons of the time
and wearing the traditional garb of brown stock brick, were distinctly more modest in their pretensions. Nor has Dorset Square
ever been as fashionable as its two predecessors, whose very propin-
quity to modish Portman Square in its brilliant Victorian heyday
made them seem extensions of it.

Whose are the resounding names that should have made this
pleasant, civilised square a familiar part of London's history? It
is difficult to say. A blue G.L.C. plaque tells us that George
Grossmith the elder lived on the west side. But it would be too
much to assume that this gifted actor and entertainer, who was not
even born until a generation after the square had come into being,
was the first or only person of note to live in Dorset Square. Nor is
it likely that the G.L.C. are refraining from further commemorative gestures because the original houses which sheltered other noted
people have been demolished. Here, if anywhere, we have a place
which still retains most of its pristine buildings. And one, and one
only, is identified as having had links, not with celebrated people,

but with two historic though utterly different organisations – the Bertram Mills circus and the S.O.E., the Special Operations Executive of the second world war. Here, at No. 1 Dorset Square, on the corner with Melcombe Street, a second plaque indicates that the Bertram Mills headquarters, which suspended its activities in 1940, was replaced, at this dignified house with the Trafalgar balcony, by a branch of the S.O.E. whose secret agents were parachuted into France to help the Resistance movement against the Germans. The tale of the perilous missions undertaken by one of these men, and of his sickening treatment in a Nazi concentration camp, has been told by Bruce Marshall, in *The White Rabbit* – a document calculated to make the ordinary inhabitant of Dorset Square thankful that he can sit quietly at home.

Dorset Square, then, though existing now in an age which has produced some pretty unpleasant years, points to an era which, architecturally at least, was civilised. Together with the neighbouring Gloucester Place, it strikes an almost unbroken late Georgian note in architecture – the note which still distinguishes much of Marylebone and gives it its classic quality. A little to the north of the square the basically Georgian architecture of the older parts of Marylebone gives way in one direction to the Regency of the Park, and in another to the basic, though now much diluted, early nineteenth century and Victorian villadom of St John's Wood.

# 4. Oxford Street Frontier

'A DEEP hollow road, full of sloughs; with here and there a ragged house, the lurking place of cut-throats, insomuch that I never was taken that way by night, in my hackney coach, to a worthy uncle's, who gave me lodgings at his house in George Street, but I went in dread the whole way.'

This description of Oxford Street in the early eighteenth century provides a piquant contrast with the great urban thoroughfare of today, when the principal hazards are overcrowded pavements and a street choked with motor traffic. Now, when Oxford Street is separated from the country to the north by ten miles of built-up streets – instead of looking out over the fields towards the village of Marylebone – it is hard indeed to think of it as the Tyburn Road, as it was then called. This was the miry track leading to Tyburn Tree, the gallows set up outside London at the northern approaches to Hyde Park. Tyburn, a name which has become synonymous with the place of execution, was a hamlet on the Roman road linking Hampshire with Suffolk. In medieval times, when London had expanded, this road became the main route between the capital and the south-west. Tyburn the hamlet merged in the fifteenth century into the village of Marylebone. And Marylebone Fields, the area between it and London, became the notorious haunt of highwaymen and thieves of all sorts. Thus an atmosphere of violence, whether with the state's blessing or without it, pervaded the early history of the road which was destined to develop into one of the great shopping streets of the world.

It was Thomas Pennant, whose *History of London* appeared in 1790, who as a boy suffered such terrors on those journeys to his uncle's after dark, even though made in the shelter of a coach. By the time his book appeared, he was an elderly man, and the Tyburn Road of his younger days had been transformed into fashionable Oxford Street, one of the most elegant shopping thoroughfares in Europe, and a street renowned for the brilliance of its lighting.

Much of this extraordinary sea-change had taken place in the couple of decades before 1790. As late on in the century as the mid-1750s people were able to gather blackberries on the north, or Marylebone side of the street. It was by this time well built up with houses, but the locality appears still to have retained much of its rural character.

During the early and middle years of the eighteenth century the street, westward of what is today Oxford Circus, was a country road sloping down to a dip where a fifteen-foot-wide bridge carried it over the Tyburn brook. Stratford Place now stands just north of the point where this wooden bridge – simple enough perhaps to be called a culvert – used to be. It was known as Banqueting House Bridge because a country house used by the Lord Mayor of London for hunting banquets stood until 1737 in the field now occupied by Stratford Place. Between the bridge and the Edgware Road the road rose steadily again from the level of the miniature valley formed by the Tyburn brook.

Eastward of the Oxford Circus of today, building had started at the Tottenham Court Road end as far back as 1718. Thomas Rathbone, probably a relation of Dr John Rathbone, the first doctor to live and practise in urban Marylebone, began building there on the Berners estate about that time, and gave his name to Rathbone Place. A Marylebone gardener, Thomas Huddle, carried on the good work when, some twenty years later, he undertook to build up the whole 220-yard Oxford Street frontage of the Berners estate. Between 1746 and 1763, Berners, Newman, Nassau, Eastcastle and Mortimer streets were laid out, and by 1773 the Berners estate had been provided with some 230 houses, and the Middlesex Hospital with its present site. Farther west along Oxford Street, just behind the main street frontage, stood the Oxford Market, its high turret visible over the roof tops. Near by, still in the fields up to the middle of the century, were the Boarded House, the haunt of pugilists and prizefighters, and the Adam and Eve tavern.

Oxford Street was for many years controlled by a turnpike trust which was responsible for the whole route between St Giles's Pound – which stood at the Tottenham Court Road intersection – and the village of Kilburn. There were toll gates both at the Tottenham Court Road end and at the Edgware Road junction. This western gate was known as the Tyburn turnpike, and was for a time sited at the intersection of the Bayswater and Edgware Roads on the precise spot where the notorious Tyburn Tree, the triangular gallows on which a dozen people could be hanged at the same time, had stood from 1571 until 1759. Before 1571, gallows at Tyburn had been erected as and when needed. After 1759, there was a reversion to the earlier practice.

Famous victims of these instruments of barbaric inhumanity in earlier times were Roger, Earl of Mortimer, the overthrower of King Edward II, 'taken off' in 1330 when Tyburn was merely a barren heath; Perkin Warbeck, pretender to Henry VII's throne, whose jocular jingle of a name has been dutifully remembered by generations of school-children who would certainly have forgotten him had he been called John Smith; Elizabeth Barton, the so-called 'Holy Maid of Kent', a pallid nun who got swept into the path of that royal juggernaut, Henry VIII, and promptly ground into the earth for preaching against his divorce of Catherine of Aragon; and Robert Southwell, the extraordinarily gifted Jesuit priest and poet, who survived thirteen torture sessions, to die half-strangled and wholly disembowelled for some other splendid dynastic reason.

These Tyburn scapegoats of remoter times were the precursors of an enormous host of human beings who dangled year in and year out – for almost any conceivable offence, from murder to pocketing a piece of bread – from the branches of the 'Deadly Never-Green', as the Tree was dubbed. An old print shows Queen Henrietta Maria, the year after she married Charles I, kneeling under the Tree in prayer for the souls of the Catholic martyrs who had perished there. This incident produced an official complaint against the Queen's French retainers, Catholic zealots who were thought to have pushed the seventeen-year-old Henrietta into making this gesture. Since the arrival of the Jesuits in England in 1580, there had been a series of plots against the Protestant monarchy, culminating in the Gunpowder Plot. This had provoked a reaction of corresponding intensity, and Jesuit leaders like Southwell, and Campion before him, had followed the path to Tyburn.

Yet these, after all, like the Mortimers and Warbecks before them, had knowingly flung their lives into the scales, staking them on great issues. But vast numbers of those done to death at Tyburn were poverty-stricken unfortunates who had transgressed some minor article of the law. These were made a rare show for a populace whose brutal gusto for the spectacle of human suffering and indignity led then to treat these scenes like a Cup Tie match, or the finals at Wimbledon. Hogarth's 'Idle Apprentice', a typical case

of the petty offender whirled away to insensate extinction, was
strung up before the gaping throng for picking pockets:

Tom (Idle) goes to his death escorted by cavalry and foot-
soldiers, and accompanied in the cart by his own coffin and a
proselytising Methodist preacher. On a waggon, Mother Douglas – obviously a keen amateur of public solemnities – is raising
her eyes and lifting a glass of gin. The hangman smokes his pipe
as he lounges above the scaffold, along the gallows cross-bar.

It was not the pity of such scenes as this which in 1783 caused the
removal of the Tyburn gallows from its prominent pitch in Marylebone. The wealthy and aristocratic residents of the richest parish in
the kingdom had not yet developed that kind of sensibility. What
the inhabitants of the great mansions and fashionable squares of the
future Tyburnia objected to was the influx of the rabble into the
select neighbourhood they had created. Frequent executions meant
frequent incursions by the mob, and that they would not endure. In
the last twenty years or so before the Marylebone local authorities
finally got rid of the gallows, they took over a piece of land at the
corner of the Edgware Road and what is now Bryanston Street, and
requested that the executions should be held there. When in 1783
the place of execution was transferred from Tyburn to Newgate,
considerable relief must have been felt in Portman Square, whose
elegant mansions had arisen within little more than a stone's throw
of the gallows ground and its concomitant concourse of sweaty
nightcaps. After all, by that year those fashionables, Mrs Montagu
and the Countess of Home, were installed in their palaces on the
north side of the square. And they needed quiet enjoyment of the
locality for their routs and balls, for the carriages to roll up
unmolested and the chairmen to set down their powdered and
pomaded charges unruffled and exquisite.

The age of refinement had set in in Oxford Street. With the
coming of wealth and aristocracy had come artists and craftsmen,
shops and coffee-houses. Wyatt's Pantheon, the new 'winter Ranelagh', that urbane puff-ball mimicking Saint Sophia – the site is
now occupied by Marks & Spencer's Pantheon store on the south
side of Oxford Street – had added a note of elegance and sophistica-
tion to the whole neighbourhood. Horace Walpole – early on the
scene, naturally – had visited it with the French Ambassador, and
duly written off to Sir Horace Mann (that unwearying human

letterbox): 'Imagine Balbec in all its glory!' Gibbon, from the quiet luxury of his Marylebone home a couple of streets away, had become a subscriber to its masquerades. These, and its theatre, together with the daring and splendour of its smart architectural pastiche, had raised the tone of the street to a pitch which astonished foreign visitors to London.

To the remarkable development of the later 1770s, and the 1780s, the youthful Wyatt's tour de force was a mere prelude. Walpole, scrutinising the urban scene of 1776 with his usual intense interest, remarked:

> They have been building ever since [i.e., ever since his father got lost in the new squares of London thirty years earlier] and one would think had imported two or three capitals. London could put Florence into its fob-pocket . . . As its present progress is chiefly north, and Southwark marches south, the metropolis promises to be as broad as long. Rows of houses shoot out every way like a polypus; and so great is the rage of building everywhere, that, if I stay here (Strawberry Hill) a fortnight, without going to town, I look about to see if no new house is built since I went last.

In the van of this mania for development was the Oxford Street area, coming into flower at the high noon of the era of Georgian architectural perfection. Under the inspired leadership of the Adam brothers, and the influence of such masters as Chambers, Holland and Wyatt, London was becoming one of the centres of European elegance. The movement in the arts which was to culminate in the extreme refinement of the Regency was well launched. Sophisticated cabinet-makers like Chippendale and Sheraton, potters like Wedgwood, designers and sculptors like Flaxman and Nollekens, the Adam brothers in interior decoration, Reynolds, Gainsborough and Romney in portrait painting, and a host of gifted craftsmen in textiles, jewellery, and glass, were providing London with furnishings of a quality and finish which have never been surpassed, and which still command the highest prices in the art market.

Oxford Street, at the entrance to this newest fashionable residential quarter of the metropolis, attracted shops where such choice furnishings could be displayed to the most profitable advantage. These shops themselves were of a distinction and elegance which evoked the astonished admiration of foreign visitors. Sophie von la

Roche, Germany's first woman novelist, who spent much time in England in the 1770s and 1780s, wrote of Oxford Street with almost bated breath.

This street alone contained as many lamps as the whole of Paris, so that the scene, with shops open till ten p.m., and brightly lit, cheated the Prince of Monaco into believing all this brilliancy in his honour . . . The lamps, which often consist of two, three, and sometimes four branches, are enclosed in crystal globes, and being attached to iron supporters, are placed at a small distance from each other. They are lighted at sunset, both in winter and summer, as well as when the moon shines as not.

Again, writing to her children, she strikes a lyrical note.

We strolled up and down lovely Oxford Street this evening, for some goods look more attractive by artificial light. Just imagine, dear children, a street taking half an hour to cover from end to end, with double rows of brightly shining lamps, in the middle of which stands an equally long row of beautifully lacquered coaches, and on either side of those there is room for two coaches to pass one another; and the pavement inlaid with flag-stones, can stand six people deep and allows one to gaze at the splendidly-lit shop fronts in comfort.

Sophie speaks also of a shop in which children's, and even dolls', shoes could be bought. This recalls the fact that a specialist in children's shoes, Daniel Neal – whose store was long established in Portman Square, but has now removed to Oxford Street – started business on the Portman estate as early as 1837. In Sophie's time, however, it was not the shoe shops, but the furriers who had begun to entrench themselves in Oxford Street. Nicholay's Fur and Feather Manufactory – later furriers to Queen Victoria and the reigning families of Austria, Belgium, Prussia, Russia and Spain – appeared there as early as 1780. A hundred years or so later, they were taken over by Debenham and Freebody, whose fabulous fur department originated in Nicholay's. Another early arrival was Sneider's, established in 1785, and in the first rank of the fur business for many years.

But, splendid as were the Oxford Street shops of Sophie's day, it was not until England had recovered from the Napoleonic wars that the great stores which are still famous today arose. Among the earliest was Peter Robinson's. In 1833, Peter Robinson, son of a Yorkshire haberdasher, opened a linen draper's shop at 103 Oxford Street. By this time, linen drapers, boot and shoe makers, and hosiers and glovers in the street were each numbered by the score. Competition was formidable. But Peter Robinson's has endured, and today presides over an Oxford Circus with which it is almost coeval.

Not far away in Wigmore Street, in the year Peter Robinson's opened, was Clark and Debenham's small shop, a draper's which had been in existence since 1778. William Debenham, a Suffolk farmer's son, had bought a partnership in what was then Flint & Clark's as far back as 1813. At first, no doubt, this establishment depended largely upon the patronage of the neighbouring grandees in Cavendish Square. Hence the name Cavendish House given to the shop, which was later to become famous as Debenham & Freebody's. William Debenham himself is supposed to have taken his name from the little town of Debenham in Suffolk. Debenham's as a great store has always stood somewhat apart – not only geographically, but in *ambiance* – from the ruck of its peers in Oxford Street. Rebuilt in 1907 and swathed in a sort of architectural tea-gown of Doulton's white Carrara tiles, it breathes an infinitely leisurely atmosphere, as of Edwardian great ladies going about their lawful and opulent occasions on some golden afternoon outside time. Debenham's celebrated for its lace – and its ladies' lavatories. As a souvenir booklet issued by the firm reminded its patrons, the rebuilt Debenham's included 'a luxuriously appointed suite of Dressing and Retiring Rooms'. A later and less inhibited writer noted that 'mahogany seating completed the sanitary fitments which bore the name of "The Cavendish"'.

James Marshall's shop, the bud from which that very fashionable bloom Marshall & Snelgrove's flowered, opened in Vere Street in the profitable year 1837 – the year of Queen Victoria's accession. Marshall was partnered only by a Mr Wilson until Snelgrove, a Somerset boy, came along in 1848, was taken into partnership, and contributed his highly distinctive name to the firm's title. Early on in its ascent of the modish ladder, Marshall & Snelgrove's sprouted a branch in Scarborough – possibly because Marshall came from Yorkshire. Open only during the season at what was one of the smartest combined seaside resorts and spas, the firm reinforced its grip upon the nobility and aristocracy, achieving what was practically a corner in the blue-blooded clientèle of the day. For years after the establishment had obtained an Oxford Street frontage and assumed its present-day appearance, the original Vere Street entrance preserved an atmosphere of exclusiveness such as only the English know how to foster.

If Marshall and Snelgrove's – rather than Swan & Edgar's, as some allege – was the launching pad for that runaway rocket of 1864, the elopement of Lady Florence Cecilia Paget and the Marquess of Hastings, is this not a further proof of the aristocracy's natural affinity for this store? Henry Chaplin, the rightful fiancé, left abandoned amidst a gauzy mass of bridal fripperies near the sacred Vere Street entrance whilst the lovely lady shot like a dose of salts through the mazes of M & S, to emerge panting into the arms of the villainous Hastings, posted artfully by the Henrietta Street bolt-hole! What more could a store need than its selection by these two as the only possible stage for their elopement?

John Lewis, another young man from Somerset, had graduated as buyer of silks and woollens for Peter Robinson's when in 1864 – what an eventful year it was – he hived off into a minuscule shop at the corner of Oxford Street and Holles Street. Like Debenham's, his establishment was within easy reach of the carriage folk in Caven-dish Square round the corner. Indeed, the carriage folk were all around him, for Holles Street was still an extremely exclusive resi-dential offshoot of the square itself. It cultivated its memories of Byron, born there the year before the outbreak of the French Revo-lution, and was not unmindful of the fact that the reigning ruler of France, the Emperor Napoleon III, had lived there in exile with his mother, Queen Hortense, a mere generation back. Notwith-standing the proximity of all this top brass of the fashionable world, poor Lewis is said to have taken 'less than 20s.' on his opening day.

But worse was to come. At a later stage, his very success in attracting sales in this wealthy district led him to seek the expansion of his store by acquiring leases over neighbouring residential premises as they became available. He seems to have ignored the fact that the terms of these leases precluded his using the houses so acquired for business purposes. Litigation with the ground landlord, Lord Howard de Walden, ensued, and the unyielding Lewis be-came so embittered at what he regarded as persecution of an enter-prising businessman that he had a large sign erected at the corner of Oxford Street pointing to 'Lord Howard de Walden's Monument of Iniquity' – presumably his house in Cavendish Square. In spite of a compromise offer which involved changing the outside of the shop to look like a private house, he hung grimly on. Finally, he even allowed himself to be sent to prison for disregarding a court order to reinstate the properties. Still maintaining his splendid life style, he drove off to Brixton Prison in his own carriage. Lewis in fact was one of those robust Victorian characters, larger than life and vigorous to a fault, which our own conforming, though permissive, age conspicuously lacks. He lived to be over ninety, surviving until 1928.

Dan Harries Evans, of Llanelly, bought No. 320 Oxford Street in 1879. Like William Debenham and James Marshall before him, he had no doubt been attracted in general by the wealth and smartness of Marylebone as a district, and in particular by the sales potential of the Cavendish Square residential complex. At all events, the premises he selected had their other frontage on Old Cavendish Street. Here, helped by his wife, who did the dressmaking, and her brother and sister, he built up a retail trade which made lace its speciality. It was in 1902 that Mr Bourne and his brother-in-law, Mr Hollingsworth, small drapers from Westbourne Grove, decided that Oxford Street was a good bet – even at its less fashionable end, east of Oxford Circus. Today, with a whole island site at their disposal, and doing a general trade, they are one of the larger independent stores of London, and have a solid prestige of their own.

But when they came to Oxford Street in the early days of King Edward VII's reign, they were felt by some at least of the staffs of the earlier-established institutions to be a blot upon the high-toned landscape. An employee of Peter Robinson's, reminiscing about the dear departed days of splendid serfdom enjoyed by a small élite of purveyors to the nobility, sadly recalled that:

> Oxford Street was a superior shopping street until Bourne and Hollingsworth brought the general trade and then Selfridges. We were family drapers . . . the carriages would drive up and the duchesses would step out. Customers would discuss Sunday's sermon with you, give all their family news, and say their married daughter would be in during the afternoon.

The name Gillow in connection with cabinet-making goes as far back as the last decade of the seventeenth century, originating in

1. View of the north side of Cavendish Square, *circa* 1800, by Thomas Malton. The corner houses, similar in design, were built for the first Duke of Chandos. He lived for some years in the one at the north-western corner, which also had a long frontage on Harley Street. This was later the home of Princess Amelia, a daughter of George II. The two imposing Palladian buildings in the centre of the north side were built in the early 1770s and still survive. In our own time a bridge has been constructed between them, and this is the backdrop for Epstein's great bronze *Madonna and Child*.

2. A view, probably about 1830, of Montagu (later Portman) House, by Thomas Hosmer Shepherd. Montagu House was designed for Elizabeth Montagu, the celebrated bluestocking and society hostess, by James (Athenian) Stuart, and completed in 1782. It was destroyed by enemy action during the Second World War, and the Portman Hotel now occupies the site.

3. A view of Marylebone Gardens by a Continental artist, undated, but probably during the latter part of their existence. The gardens, which lay to the east of the northern section of Marylebone High Street, became fashionable during the mid-eighteenth century, though perhaps less so than Vauxhall Gardens. The view illustrated here is the 'Orchestra Grand Walk', and the members of the orchestra can be seen in their bandstand on the right of the picture. The row of buildings on the left includes the theatre, known as 'The Theatre for Burlettas', that is, the comic opera house. The gardens were also the scene of firework displays, and contained enclosures for prize-fighting, cock-fighting, and dog-fighting.

4. Edward, Lord Harley, second Earl of Oxford and Mortimer (1689–1741). He was the founder of urban Marylebone, and gave his name to Harley Street.

5. Mrs Elizabeth Montagu (1720–1800). In her mansion at the corner of Gloucester Place and Portman Square she vied with the Countess of Home in neighbouring Home House, now the Courtauld Institute, in the splendour of her entertainments.

6. John Elwes, rich miser, and colourful eighteenth-century eccentric. He provided some of the finance for the construction of Portland Place.

7. John St John Long, known as 'The King of Quacks', set up in Harley Street in 1828. He attracted a vast feminine clientele, but fell into disrepute, and died following the deaths of two of his patients.

8. An engraving of the School House in Marylebone, formerly the Manor House, show-ing it as it was in the late eighteenth century. The view is of the west side of the building, seen from the High Street. A garage now stands on the site, at the corner of Beaumont Street.

*The upper part of High St. Marybone. near the Turnpike*

9. This pen-and-ink sketch of *c.* 1777 attributed to Nathaniel Smith but perhaps by S. H. Grimm, is of Marylebone High Street, looking southwards from near the turnpike gate of the New Road (Marylebone Road). To the left can be seen the school house gables with the clock turret.

10. The equestrian statue of the Duke of Cumberland—
'Butcher Cumberland', victor of Culloden—which stood
in the Cavendish Square garden for the best part of a
hundred years until its demolition in the mid-nineteenth century.

11. A view of the west side of Cavendish Square in 1808. Harcourt House, with its high
screen wall, is seen in the background. The mansion was renamed Portland House when,
in the 1820s, it was taken over by the fourth Duke of Portland. It was demolished in
1904. Thackeray may have used the house as his model for Gaunt House in *Vanity Fair*.

12. This view of Marylebone Parish Church in 1750 is from the east side of the High Street. The building is the small, reconstructed church of 1741. Richard Brinsley Sheridan, the playwright, was married in this church in 1773, and Nelson's Emma married Sir William Hamilton there in 1791. This building was superseded by the present imposing church in the Marylebone Road in 1817, but was not finally demolished until 1949.

13. A view of Portland Place in 1809, looking southwards to Foley House, now the site of the Langham Hotel. At this time Portland Place was an aristocratic enclave with its back turned on London and its face towards the quiet fields leading to Marylebone Park.

14. The north side of Portman Square in 1813. Home House, designed by Robert Adam for the Countess of Home, is the last house but one on the north side before the group of poplars is reached. Now the Courtauld Institute, it is the only complete building surviving from the original square.

15. The Oxford Market, completed in 1724 but not fully opened until 1731, was part of what was in effect the Cavendish Square aristocratic housing estate. It was demolished in 1880 and the street name Market Place, just east of Oxford Circus, is all that is left to show where it stood.

Lancaster. Robert Gillow of this long-established family of joiners and cabinet-makers, with his son Richard as partner, opened a branch of his firm in Oxford Street around 1760. For some time, all their furniture was made in Lancaster and sent to London by sea. The name Waring seems a good deal less well known – Browning's tag – 'What's become of Waring?' – would appear to apply. Waring & Gillow's as such does not really materialise until 1906 when their present swashbuckling great building was completed. Sir Nikolaus Pevsner, in his *Buildings of England*, relaxes his scholarly restraint sufficiently to label it 'riotous Hampton Court Baroque'. He speaks of 'ships' prows with cornucopias' at the corners. This odd feature must have provoked many a question from children riding on bus tops with their dads and mums. It is certainly playful in an exuberantly Edwardian way suggestive of the massive 'advance and recess' of the patrician paunches and bosoms of the period.

The Gillows supplied furniture and fittings to the nobility, who in the 1780s and 1790s were moving into the district in large numbers, giving it that enormous injection of wealth which acted like a lodestone on the retail trade of London, and helped to make Oxford Street the first shopping street in Europe. A note survives showing that the Gillows were helping in 1784 to fit out the second Lord Hardwicke's house at 18 New Cavendish Street. There is mention of 'very large white satin window curtains with pink satin ribbon binding and pink silk broad fringes with white buttons', showing that as far back as this they had already extended their business from cabinet-making to other furnishings.

The two most remarkable shopping institutions in Oxford Street are, curiously enough, the most recently established – Selfridge's in 1909 and Marks & Spencer's in 1930. Both are the creations of men of empirical genius, able to discern from farther off than most the requirements of a new age. Gordon Selfridge brought to the world of English emporia the first whiff of those transatlantic breezes which have blown so hard ever since. He blew away the 'props' of the small, rigid, custom-bound Edwardian shopping scene and substituted scenery, décor, concepts of a large loose-fitting variety more in harmony with the land of the Grand Canyon and the Empire State Building. He also brought with him a sense of urgency, hustle, and the frontiersman's need to see his vision realised in the shortest possible time.

From the laying of the foundation stone in 1908, a mere twelve months went by to the completion of his massive store – not, it is true, on the vast scale of today – that was to come later – but on one quite large enough to rivet the attention of the shopper in 1909. Nowadays, when Selfridge's has been part of the London scene for two generations, it is almost impossible to imagine the impact of this New World leviathan, that seemed to have sprung up almost overnight out of nothing, upon an arising mass public invited for the first time to 'come in out of the cold' and taste the sweets of consumer spending in an atmosphere tailored precisely to their needs.

Hitherto, with few exceptions, the big London stores had catered exclusively for an élite of birth and wealth. In the world of journalism. Alfred Harmsworth with those money-spinning novelties the *Daily Mail* and the *Daily Mirror* had shown where the customers of the future lay. Selfridge, like Northcliffe, opened his arms to the Little Man and the Little Woman. And, with a personal capital of £300,000 and an expertise gained in Marshall Field's store in Chicago, he flung at them everything he had in his armoury. Many weeks before the great shop – or community centre as he called it himself – opened, he already had 1,200 employees on his pay-roll, most of his star buyers drawing salaries well above the London rates. An extremely ambitious press advertising campaign heralded an inauguration to the sound of trumpets, and an avid public was treated to window-dressing and interior displays such as were undreamt of in their experience.

'Selfridge Green' the colour chosen to symbolise the store, blossomed everywhere – in carpeting, wrapping paper and string, delivery vans and bill-heads, and in the flag flying over the main entrance. Connoisseurs might raise their eyebrows at the fancy dress in which Daniel Burnham, the Chicago architect, had tricked out the giant columns of the main façade, but the public were entranced with the scale and exuberance of the whole thing, and with the invitation to walk round the 130 departments and use the writing, reading and rest rooms, the post office, information bureau, restaurants, and roof garden, and finally to walk off with their gift souvenirs of purse calendars and shopping notebooks.

Soon an Ice-Cream Soda Fountain and a Bargain Basement – the first in London – were added to the attractions, and a perfumery and cosmetics counter was planted – with what was then daring

effrontery – just inside the main entrance to lure the feminine custo-
mer with its wafted odours. The slogan was coined: 'Why not
spend the day at Selfridge's?' So was born – in London at least – the
modern concept of the store as a recreational centre where goods
changed hands, a microcosm of pleasure, colour, and thronging
people to draw you and your money out of their wonted haunts.

Gordon Selfridge saw the great store of his day as in some sense
a community centre where sales took place; Simon Marks very early
on grasped that the store in his must emphasise staff welfare and
training as the prime element in the sale of goods of unmistakable
style and quality to a mass public. Both men, it is instructive to note,
came from backgrounds where it was understood that enlightened
self-interest presupposes a lively interest in benefiting all the selves
in the community.

Gordon Selfridge had emerged from a small co-operative farming
community in the Middle West; Simon Marks from a section of
the Jewish Diaspora, with its tradition of communal responsibility
and the intimate interplay between wealth and charity. Both understood the needs of a great retail business because their origins pre-
disposed them to understand the needs of society. They were natural
sociologists with a shrewd business sense. Lord Sieff, in an interview
with Kenneth Harris, has made it clear that Marks and he were per-
petually driven on by a curious compound of moral and mercantile
perfectionism which they seem to have found inseparable the one
from the other.

The firm founded in Leeds in 1884 by Michael Marks sprang
from the idea of the penny bazaar. Michael Marks had arrived in
England in the early 1880s as a Jewish refugee from what was then
Russian Poland. He had settled in Leeds, starting as a travelling
bagman walking from village to village in the Yorkshire dales, and
by the time he took Spencer into partnership in 1894 had established
a chain of penny bazaars. Spencer, a stolid-looking Yorkshireman
with a walrus moustache, died at fifty-three in 1905; Marks at only
forty-four in 1907. By this time there were more than sixty branches
distributed throughout the country, and the pace of expansion was
gathering momentum. By this time, too, Simon Marks, Michael's
only son, was a shareholder in the firm. At nineteen, he was too
young and inexperienced to have any say in the direction of the
business, but from 1916 onwards, when he was twenty-eight, he
took the helm as chairman.

Thus the man who was later to become Lord Marks of Brough-ton, aided by his brother-in-law, Israel Sieff – they had married one another's sisters – began that extraordinary adventure which was to make the name of Marks & Spencer's perhaps the most famous today in all British retailing, and a magnet of European, if not world, dimensions. Early on in their business lives the two young men were brought under the crucial influence of that master mover of men and moulder of events, Chaim Weizmann. Lord Sieff, the survivor of this enlightened partnership, has told how Weizmann educated them in 'the scientific, technological, empirical attitude to life'. And in particular how he impressed upon them, half a century ago, the important future awaiting man-made fibres.

But they were still learning, and it was to America that Simon Marks went in 1924 for the forward-looking ideas on store manage-ment which were to be the key element in the venturesome philo-sophy that turned technological advance to so sure an account. He came back with the vision of a new Marks & Spencer's patterned partly on Woolworth's, but embodying a 5s. ceiling on sales, goods of fine quality, lavishly improved premises, and a policy of staff welfare and trust in employees probably unprecedented in Britain in a firm of comparable size.

M&S, which had advanced upon London from the Midlands as early as 1903 – making its first penetration at Brixton – took up a commanding position in Oxford Street in 1930. This, the Marble Arch Store as it is called – now being expanded into what will be the biggest store of the whole chain – represented the firm's arrival at the frontier of Macaulay's 'great city north of Oxford Street'. The next year they entrenched themselves still further in Maryle-bone with the transfer to Baker Street of their head office. Michael House, with its giant-pilastered façades and heavily enriched attic stories, somewhat in the style popularised by Selfridge's, was a feature of Baker Street for the better part of a generation. It still exists, but is now in other hands. In 1958, the head office was trans-ferred to a very large modern building on the opposite side of the street. Here, four great blocks of curtain-walled office space sit upon an extensive podium. Three of these belong to the new Michael House. This large building occupies, among others, the site of Druce the furniture people's former premises, which themselves arose on the site of the old Horse Bazaar, formerly the barracks of the 2nd Life Guards.

On the north side of Oxford Street, almost opposite the site of Marks & Spencer's present day Pantheon premises, there stood for a number of years a building known as the Queen's Bazaar. Thomas Smith, writing in 1833, described it as comprising 'a Ladies' Bazaar for the Sale of Miscellaneous Articles, and galleries for the reception and display of works of art'. The art side of the establishment, with its dioramic views and its 200-ft. 'Physiorama' gallery, reflected the early nineteenth century's taste for optical illusions and *trompe-l'oeil* of a kind which later culminated in the technically sophisticated illusionism of the cinema. Establishments of this kind had been introduced into England by Daguerre and Bouton, and the most celebrated of them was the Diorama in Regent's Park.

The site of the Queen's Bazaar was later occupied by the Princess's Theatre, which had its main entrance on Oxford Street, and stretched back as far as Eastcastle Street. This theatre in its turn was taken down and rebuilt in 1880, and finally demolished in 1931, when a block of shops and offices called Princess House was put up on the site. The Oxford Street ground-floor frontage, enlarged, is occupied by a big Woolworth's. The Princess's Theatre gained celebrity between 1849 and 1859 because of Charles Kean's Shakespearian revivals there. It was here under him that Ellen Terry started her career as a child actress in 1856 and Sir Henry Irving his London career in 1859. Later under the management of Wilson Barrett, it became for a time the home of melodrama. Next door to the theatre at one time were Princess's Concert Rooms, where Frampton's Salle de Danse, a much patronised night haunt of the 1850s, attracted the kind of clientèle of which Michael Sadleir has written so hauntingly in *Fanny by Gaslight*.

A little farther east along Oxford Street, the small Berners estate had a frontage extending from Wells Street to Rathbone Place, and stretched as far north as the Middlesex Hospital and Ridinghouse Street. Its centre of gravity was Berners Street, famed in earlier days as the home of many leading painters, sculptors and architects, and in later times for the Berners Hotel and Sanderson's wallpaper establishment. The estate came into the possession of the Berners family as far back as 1654. In medieval times, it had been part of the possessions of the leper hospital of St Giles, founded by Matilda, wife of Henry I, in 1101. It was still part of the lands of a religious foundation, the hospital of Burton St Lazar, at the Dissolution of the Monasteries, and so suffered the customary fate of being grabbed by Henry VIII and disposed of to one of his favourites.

The Berners Hotel has arisen on the site of the banking house of Stracey, Fauntleroy and Graham, and of the town house of Henry Fauntleroy. The unfortunate Fauntleroy – unlike 'Little Lord Fauntleroy' the velveteen-clad hero of the Victorian novel, the only other Fauntleroy to come to the public's attention – had an unhappy ending. He was publicly executed in front of Newgate Gaol in 1824 for forging his partners' signatures on banking documents, and selling off the company's assets. The Bank of England is said to have suffered to the tune of some £300,000 as a result of his operations. Some of today's fallen pillars of tycoonery might well have been deterred from their interlocking company promotions or their fabulous-interest-paying finance houses had they faced the prospect of as drastic a penalty. Today, the Western world treats its swindlers less barbarously, reserving its savagery – in the shape of flame-throwers and saturation bombing – for distant victims in developing countries.

The Berners Hotel, one gathers, used to be a place where real English ladies, up from the country on a shopping spree, poised themselves before plunging into the flood of Oxford Street bargain sales. Today, like most other hostelries, it is in the main channel of the many through which the mighty Mississippi of foreign tourism roars and thunders as it breaks over the capital on its way to Stratford-on-Avon and other beckoning Meccas in the west and north.

Berners Street also contains Sanderson's – the home of heavenly wallpapers and exotic fabrics and furnishings – another of the shopping institutions of the Oxford Street area. Sanderson's building, opened in 1960 – the centenary year of the firm's foundation – is the most striking piece of architectural modernism that the big stores of the Oxford Street area have to show. Arthur Sanderson, the begetter of the firm, and his three sons who over the years acquired 999-year leases on no fewer than nine contiguous houses in Berners Street, would have opened their eyes pretty wide to see this glass curtain-walled giant of a building which has sat its backside down on the long strip of first-class selling space they eased out of the Berners estate. Arthur Sanderson would have noted that his grandson, Ivan, had taken a hint from those Yankees – whose civil war messed them up so badly in the year after he opened his business – and had offered his customers drive-in facilities for their cars in the basement.

A mere step from car to lift, and then they can choose – if they live long enough – from among 6,000 fabrics and 2,500 wallpapers. In case they are bored by the old-fashioned floor-by-floor division of the traditional big store, they can savour the novelties of a glass-walled spiral in which alternating one-storey and two-storey 'display areas', like 'raindrop roundels looped together', swing themselves around and above a central courtyard. Here a gleaming boulder of basalt presides over an array of weeping beeches, spouting water, star-scattered pebbles, evergreens, and terrazzo flooring, to make one big eyeful of a Japanese garden, or some such outdoor house-and-garden bibelot. For those who like the traditional, and prefer their feet to the lift, there is an early send-off to the ascent of the spiral in the shape of a stained glass mural by John Piper hovering near ground-floor level.

The biggest thing that ever happened to the Berners estate is the Middlesex Hospital. At the time its 999-year lease was granted in 1754 by the Mr Berners of the day, the family had had the estate for exactly a hundred years. The site was described as 'a good place for snipe-shooting'. It was in fact on the extreme edge of the built-up area in a marshy, pond-besprinkled part lying to the west of the road linking the district of St Giles's with the manor of Tottenham Court – the rustic forerunner of the Tottenham Court Road of today. There was a curious coincidence in the new hospital's arising on the site of the old leper hospital of St Giles. The Middlesex Hospital had in fact been in existence for nine years, under the name of the Middlesex Infirmary, when the new site was acquired in 1754. Housed in two small dwellings in Windmill Street, belonging to a Mr Goodge, it had been a very small affair. But, like the name of the unknown Goodge – now for ever blazoned to the public in the shape of a street and an Underground Station – it was destined to bulk very large in modern times.

By the time of the major modern reconstruction of 1935, it covered many acres of ground, and it now includes a host of departments and institutes, not forgetting the rather alarmingly named Institute of Nuclear Medicine. During its long career, the Middlesex – apart from ministering to the needs of the general public of these islands – has served such diverse elements as the people of the original gin-sodden rookeries of St. Giles's and Soho, the unhappy émigrés from France who flocked to the area during the French Revolution, the victims of a number of wars from the Napoleonic to the Second World War, and latterly patients from a growing number of foreign countries. Cancer and the coronary diseases, and other plagues of the affluent society, are now the prime enemies it has to fight; in 1754, it was smallpox, four out of every five people in the district being marked by it.

The Middlesex has an unrivalled prestige as one of the most superbly equipped of the great London teaching hospitals, and has been the target of a shower of princely bequests, including £250,000 from the diamond king Henry Isaacs Barnato – which went to its cancer wing – and far more than that sum from Sir Edward Meyerstein, the stockbroker. His largesse, expressed in a variety of gifts, covered not only the rebuilding of the east wing, but the provision of a students' residence, and a sports ground at Chislehurst. The names of the wards and departments of the hospital set forth on the wall of the main entrance commemorate a fantastic farrago of benefactors – possible only to categorise in broadest outline as composed of great doctors, duty-driven members of the Royal family, enlightened ground landlords, philanthropic peers, merchant bankers of vision, and tycoons of industry and commerce of all the kinds that come.

What does emerge above all from this roll of names is the soaring generosity and public spirit of the Jewish element in the community. The quartet of murals by Cayley Robinson, a follower of Puvis de Chavannes, is a proper frame for this index of benefactors. Much more than the customary exercise in the day-before-yesterday's clichés, the paintings have a sensitivity and life that can only arise when the artist is properly damning the patron and pleasing himself. The fourth panel is an excellent instance of this. The wounded soldiers of the first World War, in their blue slops and red ties, are not the grotesque zombies to which the figures of so many a mural artist have accustomed us, but at one and the same instant touchingly alive, and as remote in their period feeling from our 1970s as Cavalier or Roundhead.

Almost within the shadow of the Middlesex, but a bit nearer to Oxford Street, stands the church of All Saints, Margaret Street. It is hardly an eyecatcher today, except for its high-riding broach spire, since the varicoloured and patterned brickwork which was its architect Butterfield's sign-manual has lost the brilliance which won Ruskin's admiring approval. It springs from a comparatively little plot of Marylebone's earth, and its Gothic Revival designer has most ingeniously tucked a whole relatively tiny complex of ecclesiastical buildings centring on the church into this restricted Tom Tiddler's ground. For the general public in modern times, All Saints has signified Romish ritual, and music – fine choir-singing especially – and little else. But for the Cambridge Camden Society and its dedicated architect, who dreamed of a model church and brought it slowly to birth over the years 1849-59, it symbolised a way of life in which true Gothic building pointed the way to heaven. It was the spirit of Pugin and his crocketed and pinnacled Houses of Parliament marching on in banded brickwork and dazzling mosaic. Today, with its choir-singing no more than a memory, it is pinning its faith to the creation of an Institute of Christian Studies.

The eminent Dr Pusey, of Tractarian fame, laid the foundation stone of this fantastically costly church. £70,000 may be a mere trifle for a public building today, but in early Victorian times it was more than somewhat, and the splendour of its furnishings reflected that fact. Sir Nikolaus Pevsner has called it 'the most remarkable and the most important church' in Marylebone. Architecturally speaking this may be so, but with all its dedicated purism, its costly panoply of marbles, carving, mosaics, stained glass, and gilding; its glittering reredos, heraldic chapels, and lights gleaming before dim shrines, it somehow fails to make anything like the impact it should. Perhaps the scale is too small, the setting too cramped and smudged with the grime of neighbouring Victorian commercialism for it to seem, architecturally speaking, much more than an obscure appendage to the rag trade world which has sprung up all around it.

Oxford Street, although it has never made much of a splash as a residential street, still contains what was for many generations one of the great private palaces of London. Aldborough House, better known as Derby House, went up soon after the Pantheon in that miraculous decade for fine buildings the 1770s. The Hon. Edward Stratford, later to succeed his father in the Irish earldom of Aldborough, built both the mansion and much of Stratford Place with its other large houses in the years 1773–5. The spot he chose was about halfway along the north side of the fashionable western section of Oxford Street. Here, in the Conduit Mead, the field where the Lord Mayor's Banqueting House had stood, his surveyor, Richard Edwin, designed for him a palazzo so Adamesque in its interiors that for years it was credited to Robert Adam. The present familiar Palladian façade is in essence the house of those days, but enlarged and with the wings heightened in the present century. The owners now are the Oriental Club, who have modernised the premises and turned them into a place of great comfort and convenience.

Edward Stratford, by that time Earl of Aldborough, completed Stratford Place – 'a handsome pile of buildings in the form of a battledore' – in the late 1780s after he had recouped himself financially by a second marriage with an heiress. He also moved into the house next door and let the mansion itself. The earl, who had a more than eighteenth century taste for building on the grand scale, was frequently very hard put to it for funds. A Fellow of the Royal Society, the label 'the Irish Stanhope' suggests that his bent was a scientific one. He was certainly rather eccentric, went to prison towards the end of his life for contempt of the House of Lords – he was convicted of libelling the Lord Chancellor – and is said to have made fifty-one wills. Aldborough House passed out of the Aldborough family early in the nineteenth century, and then through a number of hands, until in the present century it was acquired by that very active politician and patron of the Turf, the late Lord Derby, with whose name it is still generally associated.

Lord Derby found the place, big as it was, not large enough for the grand scale of his entertainment, and extended the mansion eastwards, absorbing the whole of the old stables area in the process. The political breakfasts at Derby House were a celebrated feature of his régime. During the last war, the house became the temporary refuge of Christie's the auctioneers. But the best known owner of post-war times was Walter Hutchinson, the publisher, who turned the place into the National Gallery of British Sports and Pastimes. Here for some years, until his death, he exhibited hundreds of sporting pictures out of his vast collection of over 3,000 paintings and coloured prints. With his disappearance from the scene, the gallery closed down, and Londoners were no longer able to step into the quietude of this backwater off Oxford Street and enjoy the art of Constable, Stubbs, Morland, Landseer, Munnings, and many other masters, collected together within the walls of a mansion still redolent of patrician grandeur.

Two of the smaller estates of Marylebone at the time the Earl of Aldborough was developing Stratford Place were the Edwardes estate and the Hinde estate. These two tiny enclaves, of valuable, or potentially valuable, urban property formed – together with the Stratford estate itself – a buffer between the southern portions of those giants, the Portland and Portman estates. And the word "buffer" is peculiarly appropriate as far as the Stratford property is concerned, since the Earl of Aldborough by planting his exclusive, aristocratic close in the position he did, frustrated a plan to link the Portland and Portman estates by extending Henrietta Street – now called Henrietta Place for this reason – westwards.

By dumping Stratford Place down right astride the path of this early piece of town development, he effectively prevented the creation of an unbroken east–west thoroughfare parallel to Wigmore Street, i.e. a direct route from the south-west corner of Cavendish Square to Portman Street. Thomas Smith, the historian of Marylebone, says that the intention had been to make this a really handsome street. Large, uniform houses on the model of Harley Street were clearly envisaged. But the speculative builders, on whom the ground landlords relied to supply houses they had provided for in their layouts, would not play ball. They declined the risk of building and trying to sell large houses to modish people in a street which had no direct access to Cavendish Square – the centre of fashion for the whole neighbourhood.

The consequences of their attitude were felt mainly on the Edwardes estate, which lay, in a largely undeveloped state, to the west of Stratford Place. Here building over an area between James Street and Stratford Place was particularly badly affected, resulting in the creation of a slum district of narrow courts and mean alleys which has persisted to this day. Barrett Street and Gee's Court and the depressed purlieus behind C&A Modes' big store remain as evidence of the blight which fell upon the neighbourhood. The shabby streets and buildings are still with us, but happily not the foetid, overcrowded rookeries of Thomas Smith's day and earlier. These stretched as far west as Orchard Street, occupying the whole of the present site of Selfridge's.

The Franco-American traveller, Simond, who lodged in Orchard Street in 1810, described the collection of filthy courts and passages, inhabited by Irish labourers. They filled every cellar and garret, and their riotous behaviour made the nights hideous. He wrote: 'The noise was such (on Saturday nights) that it was impossible to sleep, but nothing could be done as no watchman would risk his life among them'. This sleazy quarter was bounded on the north-east by the southern reaches of winding Marylebone Lane. The houses in this part of the lane had been built along the banks of the Tyburn brook, a small and narrow stream which as urbanisation proceeded declined into an insanitary drain. As a result, about the end of the eighteenth century, it was covered in, and the course of the stream and its tributaries became a series of passages and footways between the former riverside dwellings. This was a further slum-creating factor, additional to the artificial impediment to good town-planning caused by the construction of Stratford Place astride the path of east-west development.

On the tiny Hinde estate, lying immediately to the north of the Edwardes estate, and bounded on the east by Marylebone Lane and on the west by Spanish Place, exactly the opposite had happened. Much about the time Stratford Place was going up, Jacob Hinde, who had come into his estate through his marriage with Anne, daughter of Thomas Thayer, agreed to the local authorities' proposal that the Portland estate should be linked with the Portman by way of a street running across his land. In this way, Hinde Street, joining up Bentinck Street, on Portland land, with Manchester Square and Berkeley Street, on Portman ground, came into being. There was no obstacle in this case to the course of east–west development. Gibbon the historian, whose address was 7 Bentinck Street, Manchester Square, was thus in a position to have himself conveyed direct to Manchester Square should the Duke of Manchester bid him to some rout or party. Manchester Square, the nearest haunt of nobility, was of course a required part of his address as a gentleman of coat armour.

In 1787 – the year Gibbon finished the last three volumes of *The Decline and Fall* – a chapel went up at the west end of Oxford Street, in what is now Bryanston Street. The Quebec Chapel seems to have been built, a trifle belatedly, to commemorate the Battle of Quebec, which had been fought nearly thirty years before. It appears to have retained its military connection – for Thomas Smith, writing in 1833, reported that the 2nd Regiment of Life Guards used to attend Sunday service there when their barracks were situated in King Street – now Blandford Street, the site of the barracks now being covered in part by Marks & Spencer's head office. Also, when permission was sought in 1911 to demolish the chapel, it was alleged that it had originally been the riding school of the Portman Barracks. This was a Foot Guards barracks which occupied the ground on which Granville Place was later built – some time about 1860 – and which had an entrance in Portman Street.

The Quebec Chapel was done away with in 1912, and Sir Walter Tapper, an exponent of Sir Gilbert Scott's particular brand of four-teenth century Gothic Revivalism, raised on the site the Church of the Annunciation, a rather refined evocation of the medieval past. Out of the same stable as St Cyprian's, Clarence Gate Gardens, its small red bricks, towering buttresses, and clean lines, show a masterful hand fashioning the inner vision with the strictest artistic precision. Inside, the vision is no less unfaltering and the rule of taste nowhere broken. Up there in the vaulted heights, the clerestory windows look down upon an impeccable array – golden rood on arched golden rood loft, carved and traceried screen, altar with massive reredos displaying its painted triptych, soaring organ pipes in their enriched case, brilliantly coloured representations of the Stations of the Cross with figures in high relief adorning the nave walls, etc, etc.

High Anglo-Catholicism is so high here apparently that Roman Catholics readily mistake the place for papal ground, and there are notices in the porch directing them to the nearest R.C. churches. A late sacristan, a lady commended in a gold-lettered inscription for her care of the church, is neatly commemorated by a pair of wrought-iron gates set across the entrance arches of the nave. These, kept locked between services, act as a kind of dumb sacristan – alas, deterring the inquiring visitor as well as thieves and vandals.

The Oxford Street area, like the principal shopping centres of other great capitals, has a hinterland which at different times has been noted as a haunt of highly commercialised prostitution. This seems to have been largely located in that eastern part of Maryle-bone lying between Great Portland Street on the west, and Cleveland Street on the east, and bounded by Oxford Street itself on the south, and the Euston Road on the north. The Victorian age in particular contrived to make of this a sordid district of mean streets and shady businesses that seemed an appropriate backdrop to the dubious fleshly pleasures which it hawked. Even in the eighteenth century, for much of which it was bordered by the fields of the open countryside, street names such as Night Pit Lane,

Wrestling Lane, or Hartshorn's Rents, proclaimed its sleazy character. The Prussian traveller, J. W. von Archenholz, in his book *A
Picture of England*, which appeared in 1789, noted that it had been
estimated that there were some 50,000 prostitutes in London. Of
these, he said, 13,000 lived in the parish of Marylebone, 'the largest
and most populous of any in England'.

There were, he noted, different classes of tart: 'The lowest sort
live under the direction of an old bawd who furnishes them with
cloaths. Others live in houses of their own, or in furnished lodgings.
The uncertainty of the payment makes the proprietors of those
houses demand double the ordinary rent. Without such lodgers,
there would be thousands of empty houses in the west end of the
town.' Of the 13,000 ladies of pleasure who had flocked to the pickings of wealthy Marylebone – or been corralled there by their male
'protectors' – no less than 1,700 occupied entire houses to themselves. This élite of harlotry, the massed *poules de luxe* of a quarter
which was attracting most of the moneyed aristocracy of London,
appears to have lived quite extraordinarily free from any interfer-
ence from the authorities. Von Archenholz noted that:

> These last live decently and without being disturbed. They are
> mistresses in their own house, and if any of the magistrates should
> think of troubling them, they might shew him the door; for pay-
> ing the same taxes with other householders, they are entitled to
> the same privileges. Their houses are neatly and sometimes mag-
> nificently furnished, they have waiting maids, house maids, livery
> servants, and some of them even keep a carriage. Many of them
> have annuities, which they have obtained from their seducers,
> or which they have coaxed out of their lovers in the moment of
> intoxication . . . The testimony of these nymphs, even of the
> lowest among them, is received in courts, and this gives them in
> general a certain pride, and principles, which it is difficult to
> reconcile with their course of life.

It is known that these princesses of the *demi-monde* lived somewhat farther west than the common-or-garden battalions commanded by the 'old bawds'. Certainly the pretensions of the more
celebrated among them were of no mean order. Kitty Fisher's, for
instance, was a name of glittering notoriety in the early years of
King George III's reign. This provokingly beautiful, vivacious and
witty woman, noted for her intelligence and spirit, died at twenty-

six – 'a victim to cosmetics' – after having been absolute mistress of the world of pleasure for seven or eight years. Reynolds painted her many times, and even celebrated her in verse (found among his papers) and an army of young fashionables hung upon her skirts. By the time Von Archenholz's book appeared, she had been dead more than twenty years, but not her memory, for clearly there were still stories told about her.

The priestess knew her value, and she exacted an hundred guineas for every night spent in her arms. The late Duke of York, brother of the present King, made one offering at her shrine. When he left her in the morning, he gave her a bank note for fifty pounds, which was all he had about him. This present offended Miss Fisher, who ordered her servants, before he was out of hearing, to tell him when he called again that she was not at home; to shew the contempt she had for his present, she ate the note on her bread and butter to breakfast.

Michael Sadleir, in his novel *Forlorn Sunset*, has painted an unforgettable picture of the dreary squalor of north-eastern Marylebone in mid-Victorian times, and of the trade in young women which went on. Like all his books, this novel is based on the closest study of the area at the period selected – the 1860s and 1870s – and is almost the prose equivalent of the documentary film. There is even a street map of the district, so concerned is the author to show that his fictional characters are based upon real persons who once lived, and suffered, and died upon this particular plot of earth. In the chapter 'Girl to Let', Lottie Heape, the illegitimate child of a jobbing plumber and a Farnham barmaid, treads the predestined path of waifs of her background imported into the area – rapid transfer, under threat of violence from her 'protector', from one man with money to burn to another. From a start as a small-time music-hall turn – the hall being a convenient place for pick-ups – she is transferred by her exploiter to the post of mistress of a rich Jewish business man. When he is murdered one night returning home on foot after dark, she is thrown back on to the market, and drifts from one mischance to another till her own violent death in a back street affray. Michael Sadleir sets the scene of her pitiful career thus:

. . . slanting south-eastward from the Metropolitan Railway Station at the top of Portland Road [now Great Portland Street] to where Rathbone Place debouched into Oxford Street was an

area favoured by harlots of every grade. The north-westerly section of this area, centring on what had been Norton Street but by
now (in the pathetic belief that a change of name meant a change
of heart) re-christened Bolsover Street, was a low-class flesh-
market of a rowdy and scandalous kind. It was not dangerous in
the sense that Granby Street [near Waterloo Bridge] and its
alleys were dangerous. Late at night its bullies and thieves might
well molest unwary strangers, but it was too accessible from every
side to function by daylight as a robbers' lair. It was, however, a
public nuisance, and flaunted its trade in shameless squalor. Every
house in Bolsover, Carburton, Clipstone, and the two Charlton
Streets, as well as in Cirencester Place and the Upper part of
Great Titchfield Street, was a brothel, a rooming house, a common lodging-house, or a tavern with access to the upper floors.

What were the Marylebone local authorities doing to clean up this
nauseous part of their borough? Sadleir's researches seem to have
led to the conclusion that they were largely powerless in the face of
these activities. They were unable, it appears, at this period at any
rate, to raise sufficient funds to clear the worst sites and rebuild and
re-house the inhabitants of the district. Nor could they even manage
the smaller expenditure involved in large-scale prosecution of the
owners of disorderly houses. Sadleir suggests that the vested
interests of wealthy men in certain parts of the borough proved one
of the most potent brakes on any action. In *Forlorn Sunset* he was
writing of a period before the full impact of those two formidable
social reformers, Baroness Burdett-Coutts and Miss Octavia Hill, had
made itself felt.

Sadleir's topographical precision makes it clear that the dens of
the lowest-class prostitution were in this north-western section of
Marylebone's eastern purlieus. He points the contrast with the
southern part of the area:

> Very different was the south-east section of this district of
> *chambres ouvertes*. Berners Street, Newman Street, and Rath-
> bone Place ranked almost with the purlieus of St James's for
> elegance and decorum. Of actual bagnios there were very few,
> and these were costly and luxurious. For the most part the ladies
> lived in well-appointed rooms and entertained a small and recog-
> nised clientèle, or were under the direct protection of a single
> individual of influence and wealth.

It seems likely that the reason for the comparative decorum of this south-eastern section was the fact that the seraglios were there superimposed upon a residential district which had been one of some standing. In the late eighteenth and early nineteenth centuries, the Berners Street area had been the centre of Marylebone's artistic quarter – the Chelsea of the borough. In the mid-Victorian days described in *Forlorn Sunset*, it doubtless treasured memories of the time when Constable, Opie, Benjamin West, Sir William Chambers, Fuseli, Barry, Stothard, Bacon, and scores of other leading names in the arts, had given a special distinction to the place – which anyhow lay too close to the then ultra-smart shopping quarter of Oxford Street for the sleazier type of bagnio to be able to flourish.

'Bagnio, a warehouse where women of the town are to be found in complete parcels.' In 1772, the Frenchman Grosley offered this rather quaint definition of the now obsolete word first used to describe a public bath-house, and then by extension a coffee-house, and finally a brothel. In his *A Tour to London*, published that year, he informed his readers that women of the town were 'more numerous than at Paris, and have more liberty and effrontery than at Rome itself'. Grosley seemed much impressed with the order and regularity of the whole business, the fixed prices, and the way the tarts appeared to give the magistrates very little trouble – in this last respect confirming the impression gained by Von Archenholz, seventeen years later:

About nightfall they range themselves in file in the foot-paths of all the great streets, in companies of five or six, most of them drest very genteely. The low taverns serve them as a retreat to receive their gallants in; in those houses there is always a room set apart for this purpose. Whole rows of them accost passengers in broad daylight; and above all foreigners. This business is so far from being considered unlawful that the list of those who are in any way eminent is publicly cried about the streets. This list, which is very numerous, points out their places of abode, and gives the most circumstantial and exact detail of their features, their stature, and their several qualifications for which they are remarkable. A new one is published every year and sold under the piazza of Covent Garden with the title of the *New Atlantis*.

Hogarth, who used parts of Marylebone as background in scenes

from *The Rake's Progress*, has brilliantly evoked an orgiastic
evening in a bagnio. The place depicted has been identified as the
Rose Tavern, Drury Lane, but could no doubt have been paralleled
in most of its features by some similar den near the Boarded House,
or certain of Marylebone's taverns. The room is filled with young
tarts, the Rake lounges half-sozzled on a chair in the foreground.
Sharing his seat, a pouting minx has one hand inside his partly-open
shirt, while the other picks his pocket. There is only one other male
client, and him a blowsy dame has encircled in a firm half-nelson.
A porter near the door is bringing in a huge silver platter and a
candle. In the foreground, a fleshy young piece – technically known
as the 'posture-woman' – is undressing. Her role, according to the
painter Jean André Rouquet, Hogarth's contemporary and the ex-
pounder of his works in France, was to whirl herself around naked,
striking poses of the crudest indecency. Finally she would collapse
flat on her back on the platter. And the candle? He would leave his
readers to guess where that went, as she lay spread-eagled like a
larded chicken – '*et l'ivresse et l'esprit de débauche feront trouver
plaisant un jeu, qui de sang-froid ne le paroit guères.*'

# 5. Harley Street and Around

HARLEY, the family name of that Earl of Oxford who created Cavendish Square and its neighbourhood, and in so doing annexed the village of Marylebone to London, was given to the principal street linking the two. Harley Street, begun about 1729, was a long time a-growing. Like Cavendish Square, it hung fire through many decades, taking more than a century before it was completely built up. Nearly a quarter of a century elapsed from its beginning until the arrival of the first residents in 1752. As late as the opening years of George III's reign, it remained for the most part merely an architect's layout. 'Harley Fields', as they called it then, was 'a dreary and monotonous waste between Cavendish Square and Marylebone Village'. But from the 1770s onwards the rate of development quickened enormously, as did the fashionability of the street. The making of the Marylebone Road in 1756 – the famous 'New Road' – London's first by-pass, cutting through the fields from Paddington to Islington – had given fresh impetus to the development of Harley Street. So had the disappearance, a couple of decades later, of Marylebone Gardens. These abutted on the line of the street, interfering with its back garden and mews space. With their removal, the full length of the street much as we know it today came into being – a wide, dignified thoroughfare, ruler-straight, from whose Cavendish Square end looking northwards, one has that enchanting distant green glimpse of Regent's Park closing the vista.

Harley Street became the main axis of that grid of streets occupying the area between Baker Street, on the west, and Portland Place on the east; and between the 'New Road', on the north, and Oxford Street on the south. The rectangularity of their layout, and the classical restraint of their houses, indicated – and still indicates where houses have not been replaced by Victorian and later additions – very clearly the age in which they came into existence. The Harley Street house, built of brown London stock brick, and conceived on a large scale, displayed a flat façade to its well-bred

counterpart across the street, and its lines emphasised the horizontal
and the symmetrical – in so far as quiet urbanity would allow any
emphasis at all. The wrought-iron balconies at first floor level delicately drew attention to the tall sash windows of the reception
rooms looking out on them, and to the smaller windows of the
two floors above. Below the balconies – or in some cases the single
balcony running across the whole front – a rather solid double
frontdoor with fanlight over, set in a bland expanse of stuccoed
walling, was flanked by large, discreet windows. Wrought-iron
railings guarded the deep, narrow basement area and marched up
the short flight of steps leading to the front door. This architectural
garb set the pattern for the whole neighbourhood, though in most
of the other streets between Baker Street and Portland Place the
scale was smaller and the turn-out a good deal more modest.

Harley Street's perhaps over-careful attention to architectural and
social good manners accounted for what has seemed to some critics
a rather ponderous general effect – particularly when combined
with the over-all air of size and solidity. Famous men have not been
wanting who found the houses dull and dreary. Disraeli was particularly contemptuous, caustically dismissing 'our Gloucester
Places, and Baker Street, and Harley Streets, and Wimpole Streets
and all those flat, dull, spiritless streets, resembling each other like
a large family of plain children, with Portland Place and Portman
Square for their respectable parents', and complaining that 'you
must read the names of the squares before you venture to knock at
the door'. Dickens in *Little Dorrit* gives Mr Merdle, the swindling
financier, a residence in Harley Street, and in describing a dinner
party there takes a brilliantly fanciful side-swipe at the street and its
inhabitants:

> Like unexceptionable Society, the opposing rows of houses in
> Harley Street were very grim with one another. Indeed, the man-
> sions and their inhabitants were so much alike in that respect that
> the people were often to be found drawn up on opposite sides of
> dinner tables, in the shade of their own loftiness, staring at the
> other side of the way with the dulness of the houses.

It is probably significant that the houses which Disraeli and
Dickens found so dull and distressing to the spirit, are more likely
to be commended today for their Georgian good manners. Victorian
romanticism, even if it now shows some signs of reviving, is anti-

pathetic to the spirit of the age. The Gothic Revival fantasies which 'Dizzy' and 'Boz' admired have had a lot more mud slung at them than has ever adhered to Harley Street. Mr Merdle's dinner party which Dickens described with such verve and irony contained, besides 'Bar' and 'Bishop' and 'Horse Guards', and other such professional grandees, 'a famous Physician, who knew everybody, and whom everybody knew'.

At this time – *Little Dorrit* was first published in 1857-8 – there were fewer than twenty doctors in Harley Street, and the great invasion which was to make the street a synonym for doctordom lay ahead in the last decades of the nineteenth century. Those who first came to inhabit what was to be a very fashionable locality from the reign of George III onwards were drawn in part from the aristocracy and the well-born and well-to-do elements in society; in part from leading figures in the government and the armed services; and in part from persons of distinction in the spheres of scholarship, the arts and sciences, and diplomacy. For a single street, the range was extremely wide, and, in this, characteristic of Marylebone at this period of its extraordinarily vigorous expansion. In the Harley Street of those days the aristocracy and the meritocracy seem to have lived side by side, and to a certain extent off one another – the nobility providing the entertainment and the money, and their distinguished neighbours the professional glitter and the artistic services.

A key figure in Harley Street's earlier fashionable days was Allan Ramsay, the portrait-painter, and one of that band of gifted Scots – including Robert Adam, Lord Mansfield and David Hume – who astonished London with their brilliant gifts. Ramsay's home at No. 67 (now No. 45) was for many years a centre of the best society, in all the senses of that term. This remarkable man, whose name is less well known to the general public than it deserves, not only rivalled Reynolds and Gainsborough as a portraitist, but excelled as a conversationalist, counting men as different as Dr Johnson and Horace Walpole as his friends, and Rousseau and Voltaire as his correspondents. As a popular practitioner of his art, and principal portrait painter to George III, he made a fortune out of his brush, but left it to the more ambitious Sir Joshua to hold the limelight, while he spent much time in travel. At his Harley Street home he converted a set of coachmen's rooms and a hayloft into a studio, rebuilding these in the form of a long gallery. It is said that when he was engaged on his first portrait of Queen Charlotte, he had all the

Crown Jewels, and the Regalia as well, sent to him in Harley Street. He then demanded a guard for their safekeeping, and had sentinels posted in the front and rear of his house. His gift for painting women was outstanding, and his success with George III such that royal commissions were showered upon him. One of these was to paint ninety pairs of whole-length portraits of the King and Queen. For these, we are told, he received two hundred guineas a pair, the actual work being done by his apprentice Philip Reinagle, at a cost to him of fifty guineas a pair.

This highly profitable series of royal likenesses was destined for hanging in government offices. Though he was extremely well off and very hospitable, Ramsay's personal tastes seem to have been far from luxurious. Boswell, who used to visit him with Johnson, described him as 'a man who would not give away half a crown, but would get up in the middle of the night, and ride to serve you ten miles in heavy rain'. Anne Porter, a friend of his daughter Amelia, said his home was 'agreeable but not elegant', and everything was always upside down. What she valued there was the opportunity of meeting 'very clever people', and the 'vivacity and information' in Ramsay's talk.

Ramsay's house is now one of two occupied by Queen's College, the first college in London for the higher education of women. With its projecting, colonnaded porch, this institution is immediately distinguishable in a street whose houses are so well drilled at keeping their ranks. Propelled by a group which included Tennyson, Charles Kingsley, Frederick Denison Maurice, and other earnest Victorian intellectuals, the Governesses' Benevolent Institution, founded in 1845 'to raise the tone of female education', was whisked off on a tide of enthusiasm and transformed into Queen's College for Women in 1848. It started, under Queen Victoria's patronage, with a couple of hundred students, and was preluded by a clarion call from the Poet Laureate:

> Girls,
> Knowledge is now no more a fountain seal'd;
> Drink deep, until the habits of the slave,
> The sins of emptiness, gossip, and spite
> And slander die. Better not be at all
> Than not be noble.

Tennyson then introduces a young lady called Melissa – presumably his conception of a Queen's College student – depicting a kind of Alma-Tadema figure which might have come from his own 'rose-bud garden of girls';

> A rosy blonde, and in a college gown
> That clad her like an April daffodilly.

Since his day, Queen's College students – rosy blondes or not – have numbered some notable names among them, including Gertrude Bell, Octavia Hill, Elizabeth Garrett Anderson, and Katherine Mansfield.

Harley Street, long before it ever attracted the doctors, seems to have been a magnet for leading members of the armed forces. Wellington himself, as Sir Arthur Wellesley, lived at No. 11, setting off from his house there to conduct the Peninsular War campaign. Admiral Hood, later Lord Bridport, lived at No. 7 (now 16), and Admiral Lord Keith at No. 45 (now 89). Lady Keith was Dr Johnson's little favourite, Esther Thrale, the 'Queeney' with whom he delighted in romping when she was a small girl. Lady Nelson, who survived her doom-led admiral by a quarter of a century, lived for many years afterwards in Harley Street, and died in her house there. During part of their married life, the Nelsons were guests in Cavendish Square, only a few minutes' walk away from the Harley Street house. Lady Rodney, widow of another admiral of the classical period of British naval renown, also chose Harley Street to live in after her husband's death. At No. 71 (now 37) lived the Earl of Mulgrave, military adviser to William Pitt both in and out of office – as it were the 'Prof. Lindemann' of his day – and one of those in the corridors of power who first recognised the outstanding talents of Wellington, and pushed his promotion.

No. 73 Harley Street has the distinction of having housed first Sir Charles Lyell, the geologist who revolutionised our ideas on the age of the earth, and then Mr Gladstone. Today, when we hear so much of 'student power', and of the violent scenes it can lead to when politicians are harried and shouted down by youth en masse, it is salutary to remember that the hairy-handed mob of Victorian days did not hesitate to break the G.O.M.'s windows when they surged down Harley Street in 1878 to demonstrate against his opposition to Disraeli's pro-Turkish policy, and his fiery campaign against Turkey's 'Bulgarian atrocities'. Public feeling ran very high in favour of 'Dizzy', then Prime Minister, recently ennobled as Earl of Beaconsfield and idolised by Queen Victoria, whom he had just made Empress of India and was courting with nicely-calculated gallantries.

More than eighty years before Gladstone's day, one of Harley Street's most distinguished social figures had taken up residence at a house close to the one which was to be his. Count Simon Woronzow, the Russian Ambassador, who went to live there in 1792, eventually made England his home, and married his daughter off to the 11th Earl of Pembroke. He entertained a very wide circle of acquaintances, ranging from the Prince Regent and the future King Louis-Philippe to the humbler citizens of Marylebone. He gave in a princely way to a variety of charitable institutions, and on his death left £500 to the poor of Marylebone. Woronzow Road, St John's Wood, commemorates the man who during his lifetime gave away – so Thomas Smith records – more than £4,700 a year in charity – a vast sum in those days, also the Woronzow Almshouses.

Stafford Northcote, first Earl of Iddesleigh, at one time Gladstone's private secretary, lived at No. 86, only a few doors away from the great man's own house. Disraeli, too, had one of his young men, Lord Strangford, poet and politician and one of the two contenders for the post of model for the hero of *Coningsby*, living at No. 68 (now 43). Strangford is said to have fought the last recorded duel in England – in 1852.

The decade which saw the profound peace of mid-Victorian England shattered by the Crimean War and the Indian Mutiny brought to Harley Street that charismatic figure, Florence Nightingale. Entrusted in 1853 with the charge of the Hospital for Invalid Gentlewomen, then languishing at 8 Chandos Street, she sprang into immediate action. The hospital was promptly transferred to No. 1 Upper Harley Street (now No. 90), where amid the fashionable and the successful – and the handful of pioneering doctors who had dared to come so far west of what was then their traditional territory in the City – it was bound to attract the maximum of attention. By October the following year, 1854, she had made such a name for herself and her hospital that she was able, in her characteristic lightning way, to be off for the Crimea with a party of thirty-eight nurses, within a week of proposing this daring and then unheard-of experiment. Not, however, before she had done some execution upon the 'Sairey Gamps' of her day. 'I have changed one housemaid', she wrote in a quarterly report of this period, 'on account of

her love of dirt and inexperience, and one nurse, on account of her
love of opium and intimidation.' A plaque commemorates her
presence in Harley Street, but the Florence Nightingale Hospital in
Lisson Grove is her real monument. This mid-Victorian-looking
building, standing unshielded by any forecourt from the relentless
roar of modern motor traffic along Lisson Grove, actually went up
in its present form in 1909. It provides for women patients a reason-
ably-priced alternative to treatment in a State hospital or a private
nursing home.

Perhaps the best-known building in the Harley Street area today
is one of its twentieth-century additions – The London Clinic. This
very solid pile has a long frontage on the Marylebone Road, and its
main entrance in Devonshire Place. But it has a courtyard approach
and entrance from Harley Street, and is thus at least partially in the
status-conferring thoroughfare. With its stepped-back upper storeys,
prominent pantiled roof and curiously Italianate air, it seems to
assert its difference from a mere State-supported hospital. It is of
course a hospital, but a luxurious private establishment with a
seemingly magnetic attraction for the more opulent type of Oriental
patient – particularly from the Arab world. King Hussein of Jor-
dan and the Sheikh of Kuwait have frequently patronised this
Shangri-la of the nursing world, and the late Emile Bustani, the
Lebanese politician, businessman and entrepreneur who became so
well known to the British press in the late 1950s and early 1960s,
enjoyed retiring there and entertaining his friends from his bedside.
Like so many Arabs, he seemed to regard a cure in an English hospital as a highly pleasurable experience, quite apart from any divi-
dends in restored good health which it might yield. Perhaps an
element in the attraction for the Arab is the presence of so many
pretty young nurses, with its suggestion to the un-Westernised mind
of a new hareem to hand whenever wanted. The oil kings, Paul Getty
and Nubar Gulbenkian, have both in their time sampled the cosset-
ing of The London Clinic, and the many celebrities it has attracted
over the years since its foundation in 1932 include the Duke of
Windsor, Charlie Chaplin, Elizabeth Taylor, and Gilbert Harding.
Emile Savundra took refuge there between the sheets before the
repercussions of his financial juggleries finally caught up with
him.

By the time the London Clinic came into existence, a generation
ago, the doctors were in full possession of Harley Street and the

immediately surrounding area. They had been there in force for
fifty years. The most famous name among the first great inrush of
medicos in the last quarter of the nineteenth century was that of
Morell Mackenzie. He is vaguely remembered nowadays as the
throat specialist who got a knighthood for attending the German
Crown Prince, husband of Victoria, the English Princess Royal, and
whose reputation and career came to grief when the Prince died
soon after of cancer of the larynx. Actually, it was Mackenzie's
book on the affair, published in June 1888, which upset medical
opinion both in Germany and England, and which earned him the
formidable displeasure of Kaiser Wilhelm, the Prince's son and
successor as German Emperor. The All-Highest was perhaps provoked by the knowledge that Mackenzie suspected a syphilitic complication as having contributed to the outcome. Sir Morell is of more
interest nowadays as having been responsible for what was perhaps
the first suggestion of a causal connection between smoking and
lung cancer. He sounded a warning through the *Strand Magazine*
in 1892, the year of his own death.

His consulting rooms were at 19 Harley Street; those of another
celebrated Harley Street Scot, Sir James Mackenzie, the heart
specialist, were at No. 133. This son of a Highland farmer belonged
to the next generation of doctors, and did not reach Harley Street
until 1907, when he was fifty-four. He survived until 1925, and lived
to come to some very interesting conclusions about the strain put
upon the hearts of young soldiers in the First World War. He was
able to show that a large proportion of so-called valvular heart
disease and heart arrhythmia patients were not cardiacally diseased
at all, and in fact perfectly capable of normal physical effort, without ill effects. He attended Lord Northcliffe in his last illness, and
is said to have been threatened with a revolver by that pain-
demented megalomaniac.

Both Sir Morell and Sir James Mackenzie attained a measure of
celebrity – which is more than can be said for Dr William Rowley.
Yet surely the first member of the medical profession to practise in
Harley Street deserves remembrance. Rowley, an army surgeon
from 1760 to 1765, settled down to general practice thereafter at No.
66 (now 47) Harley Street. Describing himself as a 'man-midwife',
he built up a very profitable connection, and made a comfortable
fortune. He was bitterly opposed to vaccination, and claimed to
have discovered a cure for cancer. He was the same Dr Rowley who

in the 1790s was medical superintendent of the Marylebone work-house and infirmary, and was notable for his advocacy of modern methods of hygiene (see p. 36). Another of the early medical arrivals in the street, John St John Long, who set up there in 1828 at No. 41 (now 84), was perhaps the first of the fashionable doctors to make his name in Harley Street. That he came ultimately to be known as 'The King of Quacks' in no way lessens the social significance of this artist turned therapist. So magnetic was the power of the man, and the fame of his 'cures', that he became a kind of Pied Piper of the medical world, drawing lady patients after him to such an extent that, at the height of his career, he had Harley Street jammed daily with the carriages of his rich female devotees.

With the use of lotions and inhalants, he struck a new, and seemingly bewitching, note in the medicine of the day, and his luck held long enough for London to buzz with his successes. Doubtless the laying on of hands involved in his methods, coming as it did from a man of his good looks and peculiar charisma, titillated the ladies, ministering to the unappeased sensuality of tired business-men's wives and stimulating the erotic fantasies of well-heeled debutantes. The yards of mysterious pink tubing to which he plugged in whole bevies for their inhaling sessions probably produced a kind of collective hysteria which reinforced the effect of the private massage sessions that followed. And then he had a local habitation and a name in a street which had been outstandingly fashionable for more than a generation. His female clientèle could make an outing of the thing – just as they did of their visits to some favoured and modish preacher at his smart church. Instead of summoning this doctor to their homes like a superior servant bidden attend the mistress – as had been their mothers' way – they them-selves were forced by the fashion he had so deftly created to make a pleasurable pilgrimage to the temple of Aesculapius. And the gossip it provoked and fed! This was an added and potent incentive to rich and bored females in an age which neglected their minds and forbade them any career but that of housewife or harlot.

John St John Long – what a splendid incantatory name for this medical high priest! – rode the waves of his current of popularity for some years. Then, suddenly, he struck a couple of concealed rocks in the shape of two fatalities, one after the other. Two young women died under his ministrations. He was taken to court in each case and charged with manslaughter. Found guilty in the first case, he escaped with the astonishingly mild penalty – he was making more than £10,000 a year – of a £250 fine. He was acquitted in the second case, but now his career was wrecked, and his life soon after ended. He died of tuberculosis at no more than thirty-six – a cometlike creature who shot across the skies of London society with crackling brilliance, and was probably forgotten as promptly as the entertainments of the year before last. Yet, he was socially significant – he pioneered the road which was to lead to the 'bedside baronets', and bring the leading members of the medical profession into the highest social circles on a footing of equality.

Two of these socially distinguished medicos, Sir Frederick Treves and Lord Dawson of Penn, had their consulting rooms in Wimpole Street, Sir Frederick at No. 6, and Lord Dawson at No. 32. Treves, the older man of the two by eleven years, was born in 1853. A surgeon of great skill and inventive resource, he made his name socially speaking as far back as 1902 when he successfully operated on King Edward VII for appendicitis. In so doing, he unwittingly launched the cult of appendectomy as a fashionable nostrum. Dawson, who survived Treves by some twenty years, dying in 1945, was physician-in-ordinary to three generations of British monarchs, beginning with Edward VII, and reached the exceptional elevation of a viscountcy. His extraordinary abilities and his personal distinction fitted him admirably for the role of senior statesman of the medical world.

It is usual to draw attention to the now almost universally known fact that Elizabeth Barrett lived in Wimpole Street, and eloped from her father's house there with Robert Browning. *The Barretts of Wimpole Street*, with its phenomenally long run in the early 1930s, was responsible for perpetuating this piece of information. It is less well known that the Barretts lived for a while at 74 Gloucester Place before they moved to Wimpole Street, and that ten years after their marriage in 1846, the Brownings returned briefly to Marylebone, staying with a cousin of Elizabeth's in Devonshire Place.

Among the earlier residents in the street was Edmund Burke, who arrived in 1757 at the age of twenty-eight and stayed for three years. At this time he was merely a rising writer, and the start of his spell-binding oratorical career in the House of Commons lay some years ahead. Chance led him to the Harley Street area of Marylebone, the most up-and-coming quarter of London, and one in which he was within easy walking distance of a number of men of distinction. Burke's health was poor at this time, and on arriving in London, he went to live in the Wimpole Street house of his physician, Dr Nugent, married his daughter, and settled down in his household. Nugent frequented literary society, and was one of the first members of The Club – founded in fact in 1764, a little later than this period – where Dr Johnson did verbal battle with all comers in company with Reynolds, Garrick, Goldsmith and Fox, and other leading men of the day. Mrs Montagu, the society leader and bluestocking – whose palazzo in Portman Square was not to go up for another twenty years, but whose friends included some Marylebone intellectuals – met and approved of him. Marylebone in fact turned out to be the best possible springboard for the splendidly gifted head of eloquence and fount of political thought called Edmund Burke.

At No. 1 Wimpole Street, but with its main frontage on Henrietta Place, is the too too solid building of the Royal Society of Medicine – Roman monumentality marred by machine-age motifs. This was completed for the Society in 1912 when it moved from Hanover Square, drawn inevitably into the Harley Street area, one presumes, by the magnetic attraction of its massed medical forces. The Royal Society of Medicine, formed in 1805 by secession from the Medical Society of London (whose premises are in neighbouring Chandos Street), flourished so mightily that after a mere hundred years or so of existence, it was able to absorb seventeen other more specialised medical societies. It has been described as 'the premier medical society of the English-speaking world', and is renowned for its encyclopaedic library.

Henry Hallam, the historian, who lived at No. 67 Wimpole Street, would certainly have approved of the Society's motto: *Non est vivere sed valere vita*. For if 'life is not living, but being healthy', the collapse and death of his son, Arthur Henry, in 1833 at the age of twenty-two was a classical instance of the force of the dictum. Tennyson, whose life was intertwined with the victim's, was moved to write *In Memoriam*, the Victorian public received the most moving and characteristic of the age's threnodies, and poor Wimpole Street was dismissed, in a line dripping with the Gothic gloom of the period, as 'the long, unlovely street'. Hallam senior seems to have been a rather overpowering character. He had a fantastic speed of utterance, could drop the most appalling bricks in company, and was deftly pinned down for posterity by Sydney

Smith with the remark: 'And there was Hallam with his mouth full of cabbage and contradiction.'

Whether Wimpole Street is – or was in Tennyson's time – unlovely is surely a matter of personal taste or predilection? Certainly, Tennyson showed himself as high Victorian in his tastes as Dickens and Disraeli when he condemned the look of this typical street of the Harley Street grid. The classical regularity of the area was too much in the style of their fathers, too near to these Victorians in time, to be acceptable to them. But Wimpole Street, whether unlovely or not, is certainly not a long street. Strictly speaking, it runs, today at least, only from Henrietta Place to Weymouth Street. From thence northwards it becomes Upper Wimpole Street, and its final slightly wider continuation to the Marylebone Road is called Devonshire Place. Wimpole was the Cambridgeshire seat of the Harleys, and since all the earlier streets on their Marylebone estate were given names commemorating that family and its connections, a Wimpole Street was predictable in the first rush of christenings after the naming of Oxford (later Cavendish) Square. It seems probable that Wimpole Street was begun about the same time as Harley Street, i.e. about 1729, and that like that street it grew slowly. Rocque's map of the Marylebone district in 1745 shows both Harley and Wimpole Streets as having got no farther northwards from their starting-points in Cavendish Square and Henrietta Place than Marylebone Street – the New Cavendish Street of today. All the building in both streets seems to be on their western sides only. Probably the proximity of the Marylebone Basin reservoir – until its filling in in the mid-1760s – delayed the development of the eastern side of Harley Street. But it is not clear why Wimpole Street, too, apparently remained unbuilt on on the corresponding side.

Today, Wimpole Street retains much less of its eighteenth century character than does Harley Street. Victorian and later additions occupy the whole of the southern part of the street. Indeed, so prolific is it in cosily late Victorian or Edwardian versions of Renaissance architecture, as well as in specimens of what Sir Nikolaus Pevsner has identified as the French Loire style – eleborately carved façades in rose-pink terracotta – that Messrs. Dickens, Disraeli and Tennyson, had they lived to deliver their judgments later, might have taken a rather more indulgent view of this part of the area at least.

Welbeck Street, the third of the three main north–south thoroughfares of the Harley Street complex, is much shorter than the other two, and much more diluted with such non-medical elements as hotels, architects' offices, professional associations' headquarters, and business premises generally. In earlier days, it too was a fashionable residential street. It was named after Welbeck Abbey, the Nottinghamshire seat of the Dukes of Portland, and its most famous – if not infamous – resident was Lord George Gordon, that aristocratic weirdie whose anti-Popish demonstrations, the Gordon Riots, cost London £180,000 worth of property destroyed and several hundreds of lives. This high fantastical, preserved for posterity in literary form by Dickens in *Barnaby Rudge*, ended his life in Newgate prison at the age of forty-two, thirteen years after the riots – not for turning London bloodily upside down, but for libelling Marie Antoinette two years before the French Revolution. By this time, he had adopted the Jewish faith, as Israel Abraham George Gordon, and retreated behind a vast beard. As 'Peter Pindar', in a contemporary squib, wrote of him:

> Here, a prime favourite of a sainted band,
> Hell in his heart and torches in his hand,
> Lord George by mobs huzza'd, and, what is odd,
> *Burning* poor Papists for the *love* of God.

Lord George directed the riots from his Welbeck Street house. Among the more celebrated of his Marylebone neighbours who seem to have been endangered by his activities was Charles Wesley, the hymn-writer brother of John Wesley, the Methodist leader. Wesley, nothing if not topical in his output, promptly produced a hymn: 'Upon notice sent one that his house was marked', and followed up with some stirring verses, of which one stanza ran:

> 'Havock!' the infernal leader cries;
> 'Havock!' the associate host replies;
> The rabble shouts, the torrent pours,
> The city sinks, the flame devours!

Though no damage seems in fact to have been done to Charles Wesley's house in the riots, his close friend Lord Mansfield, who used often to walk over from Bloomsbury, suffered badly. That leading member of the band of successful Scots entrenched in the English establishment, whose pronouncements as Lord Chief Justice had shown him to be tolerant of Roman Catholics, was attacked in his Bloomsbury Square home, and he and his wife got away by the back door only a few moments before the house was set ablaze. But the place was destroyed, and his entire library and papers lost. Kenwood, his much more famous home – his country residence as it was then – only escaped, it is said, because the landlord of 'The Spaniards' had the presence of mind to ply the rioters with so much liquor that they could stagger no farther. Mansfield was seventy-five at the time of this attack, and he and Lady Mansfield then made Kenwood their permanent home. It still survives, this Hampstead mansion designed by Robert Adam – another of the Scottish top people of that day – and its superbly conceived and decorated library, spacious rooms, and landscaped park are enjoyed each year by thousands of visitors.

Another colourful eighteenth-century eccentric who chose Welbeck Street for his town house was John Elwes, the rich miser and Marylebone property owner, who provided some of the finance for the construction of Portland Place and Portman Square. His does not seem to have been the more usual case of the self-made man turned skinflint as a result of his struggle for wealth. Already, before he inherited a cool £250,000 from an uncle, he was described as having his 'chief residence' at his own seat of Marcham, Berkshire. He appears to have been very far from the kind of broken-down, creeping, Scrooge-like miser with whom Dickens has familiarised us. Passionately fond of horsemanship, and 'one of the finest riders in Europe', a product of the 'Riding Academy at Geneva', he would sit up whole nights gambling for thousands of pounds with 'the most fashionable and profligate of the time'. Then, he would walk out as day was breaking – not to go home to bed, but to Smithfield Market to inspect the cattle being driven in from a farm of his in Essex, and to stand in the grey light of some cold or wet dawn haggling with a carcase butcher over a shilling this way or that. He would then walk home, even in the foulest weather, rather than pay for a coach. His obsession with dodging expenditure of any kind (other than on games of chance, presumably) would lead him, we are told, into sitting for hours in wet clothes to avoid lighting a fire, and at one time he went about for a fortnight in a wig which he had picked up from a ditch while riding through a country lane. The frontispiece to a contemporary biography is entitled: 'Mr Elwes robbing a bird's nest to recruit

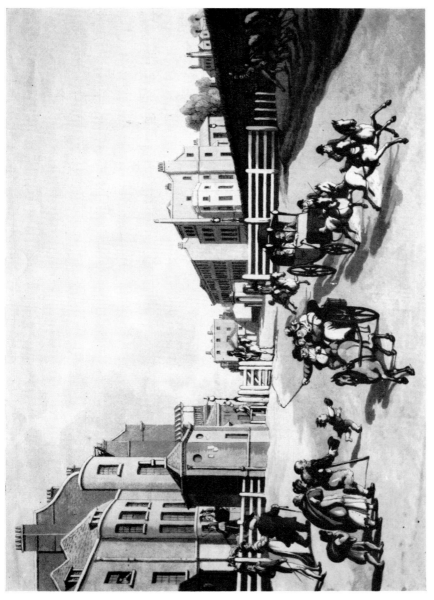

16. A Rowlandson print looking eastwards down Oxford Street from its junction with the Edgware and Bayswater Roads, near where Marble Arch now stands. On the left is the Tyburn toll-house—occupying the spot where 'Tyburn Tree', the old gallows, had stood until 1759—and on the right the wall of Hyde Park and the roofs of the houses in Park Lane.

17. An unusual sidelong view of curving Sussex Place, a Regent's Park terrace completed in 1822. It was recently entirely reconstructed behind the original façade and now houses the London Graduate School of Business Studies.

18. This Ackermann print of Oxford Street in 1813 shows the then monumental entrance to Stratford Place in the right foreground. Stratford House, at the end of Stratford Place, was built in the 1770s, that miraculous decade for fine buildings. Edward Stratford, later Lord Aldborough, built both the mansion and Stratford Place, with its other large houses. Among more recent owners of Stratford House was the seventeenth Earl of Derby, politician and ambassador to France, who enlarged the mansion and rechristened it Derby House. Today the owners are the Oriental Club, who have modernised the premises and turned them into a place of great comfort without sacrificing elegance.

19. Thomas Hardwick (1752–1829), the architect of St Marylebone Parish Church, and the man who rebuilt St Paul's, Covent Garden, after it was burnt down in 1795. He lived in Berners Street.

20. Count Alfred d'Orsay (1801–1852), artist and supreme dandy of his age, settled in England, and with the Countess of Blessington maintained a fashionable and literary salon.

21. Thomas Hood (1799–1845), poet, journalist, and humorist, lived for some years in St John's Wood. He is best known now for such socially-conscious poems as 'The Song of the Shirt' and 'The Bridge of Sighs'.

22. Sir Lawrence Alma-Tadema, O.M. (1836–1912) was a popular painter. His house in St John's Wood, still standing, was a stately pleasure-dome.

23. 'The Progress of Steam' is an artist's fantasy of 1831, but a steam carriage did in fact make its appearance in 1828 travelling through Regent's Park at five-and-a-half miles an hour.

24. Middlesex Hospital was founded as an infirmary in 1745, and is here shown when rebuilt as a hospital in 1755. The Middlesex, still in Mortimer Street, was remodelled in the nineteenth century and reconstructed in 1935.

25. Sir Edwin Landseer (1802–73), perhaps the most popular painter of the Victorian era, lived in St John's Wood all his adult life. His paintings of animals combined with his charm endeared him to an enormous public.

26. William Powell Frith (1819–1909), painter of *Derby Day*, was among the many artists who settled in St John's Wood. He survived to a great age and was seen about St John's Wood long after his great painting contemporaries were mere memories.

27. Herbert Spencer (1820–1913), the evolutionary philosopher, settled in St John's Wood in 1889.

28. George Eliot (1819–80) lived in Marylebone for many years—latterly in the Lisson Grove area, on the Regent's Canal North Bank. She wrote *Romola* and other classics during this period.

29. Holford House, Regent's Park, situated near the Zoo, was designed about 1832 for James Holford by Decimus Burton, the most celebrated of Nash's team of architectural executants. It rivalled the Marquess of Hertford's neighbouring *palazzo* for size and magnificence and was destroyed by bombing during the Second World War.

30. Mrs Siddons's house at the north end of Baker Street, showing the big windows of her drawing room with their famous view towards the Clarence Gate entrance to Regent's Park. Chalfont Court, a block of flats, now occupies the site.

31. Hanover Terrace, Regent's Park, completed in 1823, was designed by John Nash himself. Among its famous residents have been Charles Dickens and, in modern times, Alfred Noyes, Edmund Gosse, and H. G. Wells.

32. Foley House, completed in 1758, occupied the site of the Langham Hotel and was built by the second Lord Foley, a cousin of Edward Harley, Earl of Oxford and Mortimer. His family subsequently obtained an undertaking from the ground landlord which secured them an uninterrupted view northwards towards Marylebone Park, and so left the ground free for the ultimate creation of Portland Place. Foley House was demolished *circa* 1813, and its successor, Nash's Langham House, in 1864.

his fire'. He refused to educate his two sons, on the ground that 'putting things into people's heads takes money out of their pockets'.

This dashing moneygrubber, who was clearly as tough as they come, is said to have been extremely gentle, courteous, and engaging in manner. One wonders what happened when he decided to patronise Marylebone Gardens, that fashionable resort a few fields away from his house. Did he get in on the strength of his charm alone? Or were his bawbees kept intact by his slipping through some hole in the hedge unobserved?

The Harley Street area, in its medical context, stretches as far north as Park Crescent – heavily damaged during the war and now rebuilt. It includes also the east–west streets, Queen Anne Street, New Cavendish Street (formerly Marylebone Street), Weymouth Street, and Devonshire Street. Perhaps the most famous name in medical annals that the area has known is Lord Lister's. No. 12 Park Crescent was his London headquarters from 1877 to 1908. The image of this pioneer of the antiseptic has been somewhat tarnished by time, and by the onslaughts of Almroth Wright and George Bernard Shaw. Shaw, after castigating him for his wholesale use of the carbolic spray, which 'poisoned the microbes, the patient, and the surgeon simultaneously', remarked that Lister was not publicly discredited, as that would have shattered the faith of the public in his profession. Instead, his methods – except the aseptic cleanliness – were silently scrapped, and 'he himself enshrined in the medical Valhalla, symbolised by his statue in Portland Place.' In the present era of the antibiotic, with its new and puzzling problems of unpredictable side-effects and resistant strains of organisms, Lister's work seems to belong to some far-off palaeolithic period in clinical medicine.

# 6. The Regent's Park Area

NASH, it is known, originally intended to build fifty-six villas in Regent's Park. The Chancellor of the Exchequer of the day – the year was 1811 – quickly cut him down to twenty-six. The final figure of villas actually built was eight. But Nash also ringed the park with ten great stuccoed terraces, seven smaller terraces or places, a handsome crescent, a square, a barracks, a church, and a couple of residential estates whose unit was the cottage orné, and various other important architectural amenities. On top of this, he provided a serpentine lake and a canal. He did not, however, produce the elegant palazzo, or Petit Trianon, with which his master the Prince Regent intended to present himself, as the cynosure of all this architectural display gracing the grandest of garden cities. The Regent had become King by 1820, and the building of Buckingham Palace had superseded the idea of a pleasure dome in the park. The long water across which his Trianon was to face Cumberland Terrace was also never to materialise. What had been achieved, and it was more than twenty-five years before it was opened to the public, was the most beautiful park in London – not the palatial city-in-a-park of which the Regent had dreamed and for which Nash had planned.

The Regent's vision of a rural retreat for himself and a circle of congenial courtiers remained unrealised. Lack of funds, his changed interests on coming to the throne, and his death while the scheme was still in course of development, ensured that of the major features of his ideal city only the terraces and a handful of villas came into being. Had things worked out otherwise, and the First Gentleman in Europe succeeded in creating for himself a villegiatura of such urbane splendour, there were those who doubted whether either the taste of the architecture or the tone of the tenants would be such as to do the metropolis any credit. Such people clearly feared that a whole hatch of Brighton Pavilions was being gestated, and that 'Prinny' would encourage an equally garish rout of courtiers to inhabit them. As a correspondent of Leigh Hunt's put it: 'Depend upon it, if the Regent carries out his plans, we shall see a stucco town arise on the skirts of his palace – rows of pavilions *in petto*, with vistas of little pale gingerbread domes, erected by royal place-men, half-pay swashbucklers, and superannuated sirens.'

This prophecy was not of course realised, and the Regent never did more than drive in the park named after him, or visit friends who had villas there, like the Marquess of Hertford – the 'Caliph of Regent's Park' – or perhaps, strictly incognito, Mrs Fitzherbert, the wife whom he had secretly and illegally married when a young man of twenty-three, and whom he never quite got out of his system.

The park then, as it has come down to us, has as well as the fine terraces on the Outer Circle for which it is renowned, an amount of unencumbered space never intended by Nash or by his patron. We are beneficiaries of the fifty odd villas that were never built. The cult of the picturesque, under which each villa was to be so sited as to appear to its inhabitants to be alone in its private park, belonged to an aristocratic age which was already dying when Regent's Park was opened to the public in the second year of Queen Victoria's reign. With most of the villas out of the way, it was possible to pursue a policy of making the park a place of recreation for the mass of citizens newly enfranchised under the Great Reform Bill of 1832.

The area on which the landscape gardeners and planners went to work was the site of the old Marylebone Park, that hunting chase which Henry VIII had made, and which the Crown had kept possession of ever since. The Duke of Portland's lease over the handful of farms into which the park had been transformed since the days of the Commonwealth had expired in 1811. The moment was ripe for men of vision and enterprise to act. Nash and the Prince Regent were two such men. But it was John Fordyce, Surveyor-General of H.M.'s Land Revenue, an able Scot, who fired the fuse which set the whole thing going. One of the pioneers of town-planning in Britain, the features he adumbrated in four reports issued between 1797 and 1809 were largely retained by Nash when he was made architect to the project. Fordyce was dead, however, within two months of his last report, and it was left to the genius of Nash to overcome all obstacles to the realisation of London's finest piece of town-planning.

The site had great natural advantages. It lay, to use Nash's words,

at 'this Apex of the Metropolis', that is to say, at the farthest point
northward to which western London had then pushed. It was, thus,
on one of the major lines of development – a piece of practically
untouched countryside lying alongside urban and urbane Marylebone, itself a rapidly expanding quarter of notable opulence. Geographically speaking, it was on a slightly elevated, well-watered
ridge at the foot of Primrose Hill and the Hampstead heights. Here
three farms lay scattered over an area of some five hundred acres. A
few farm buildings, some cottages and workshops and a couple of
taverns – the 'Jew's Harp' and the 'Queen's Head and Artichoke' –
diversified the rural scene.

Nash set to work with vigour to transform this picture of nature
unadorned. But the task was formidable, and even after the first ten
years much remained to be done. The principal hazards were financial, and most of these had to be overcome by Nash acting alone.
The country was still at war with Napoleon when he started, and
the aftermath of that great struggle was felt till at least 1820. The
park and its amenities hung very much in the balance until that
time. In those early years, 'men of rank and fortune' who, on the
announcement of the scheme, had rushed in large numbers to apply
for villa sites in the park, failed to proceed any further. As Nash
put it, 'the disposition to building suddenly became paralysed'.
Great difficulties, technical and financial, were encountered in
getting the Regent's Canal constructed. Embezzlement by one of its
promoters offered an additional complication. Park Crescent, the
first part of the building programme to be undertaken, was left high
and dry for three years when its builder went bankrupt. Nash was
attacked in Parliament for failure to achieve progress with the park.
His castigator, Thomas Creevey, an amusing diarist, but a neg-
ligible politician, denounced the canal scheme as a mere job,
intended to benefit Nash and his assistants at the expense of the
Crown. 'Peter Pindar', the bludgeon-wielding satirist of the day
joined the chorus of hostile architectural critics with:

> Master Nash, Master Nash,
> You merit the lash
> For debauching the taste of our Heir to the throne.

But once the lean years were past, and the palaces and pleasances
of a new and splendid park began to take shape between 1820 and
1830, Londoners awoke to the fact that the churned-up piece of

waste land they had learned to live with at Marylebone for the past decade had been transformed into a dream of elegance and beauty. The architect James Elmes, whose book *Metropolitan Improvements* was the classical manifesto of the time on Nash's achievement in beautifying London, described Regent's Park in 1827 as a 'scene of ever-varying delight'. Thomas Hosmer Shepherd, the young artist who illustrated this work, may have lacked something in accomplishment, but he certainly covered the waterfront in the thoroughness with which he recorded the new look which Nash had given London. His restrained, orderly representations of the buildings of the period have been so frequently reproduced in modern books on the Regency era that we have come to see Nash's work – as it originally was – through his eyes.

And it was certainly worth looking at – particularly the park. By 1827, when *Metropolitan Improvements* began to appear in parts, most of the stylish villas – 'rural mansions for wealthy men', as Elmes defined them – and the palatial terraces as well, had been completed. Under the baton of Nash, grand conductor of all and himself executant of some of the works, a band of architects which included Decimus Burton, James Thomson, and John Joseph Scoles had produced, as a backdrop to the green vistas of the park, an array of palaces in gleaming white stucco of a kind, and on a scale, never before seen in England. Park Crescent, completed in 1821, had been followed the same year by Cornwall Terrace. The year 1822 had seen the completion of York Terrace, the approach via York Gate to the grandiose and newly-built church of St Marylebone; of Hanover Terrace with its fine view across the lake; and of curving Sussex Place with its Oriental cupolas hinting that Brighton Pavilion fantasies were still much to the royal taste. Clarence Terrace, a serene and shapely piece of work by Decimus Burton, had come in 1823. Clarence Gate, by which Baker Street debouches on the park, had been added to close the gap between this range of buildings and Cornwall Terrace.

1823 had also seen the completion of Park Square East, with its Diorama, or early version of the picture palace. In 1824 had come Park Square West; and Ulster Terrace, smaller in scale than most of the terraces, its trim bows suggestive of the typical Regency house as we visualise it today. Largest of all the ranges of building, Cumberland Terrace, Nash's own masterpiece – that series of palaces linked by triumphal arches which was to have had the honour of facing the Regent's own pavilion (his *guinguette*, or hedge-tavern, as it had been sarcastically dubbed) – had been finished by 1826. So had neighbouring Chester Terrace, vast too, but distinctly less grand, with the triumphal arches at the extremities. Then, small-scale Cambridge Terrace, also of 1826; and finally Gloucester Gate in 1827, where the scale of a Nash design for the cornice of this row of terrace houses facing the park was so altered by the executant architect, J. J. Scoles, as to spoil the façade in the eyes of connoisseurs. (Nash, characteristically enough, didn't mind.) 1827 also marked the completion, but not the opening – that had to wait until 1829 – of the most spectacular building of the whole lot, the giant Colosseum. With a dome rather larger than St Paul's and a massive Doric portico, it was built to house a panoramic view of London as one sees it from the top of that cathedral. Its huge silhouette, rising where Cambridge Gate now is, was a landmark for miles around.

Thus, some fifteen years after the start of the great enterprise, Nash had something to show for his mighty and laborious work – something which not only impressed his countrymen, but won him European admiration. Visitors from the Continent began to come to London expressly to see his 'metropolitan improvements'. And some among these found Regent's Park the feature that impressed them most. As early as 1822, Chateaubriand, then French Ambassador to the Court of St James, noted that great changes had taken place since he had last been in London as a French émigré at the time of the Revolution. 'Wide streets', he wrote, 'lined with palaces have been cut, bridges built, walks planted with trees: Regent's Park, near Portland Place, occupies the space of the old meadows filled with herds of cows.' In 1826, Prince Pückler-Muskau, the German traveller and horticultural connoisseur, observed that London was 'extremely improved in the direction of Regent Street, Portland Place, and the Regent's Park'. Though rather critical of what he conceived to be Nash's variety of architectural styles, he had nothing but admiration for the park:

Faultless, on the other hand, is the landscape-gardening part of the park, which also originates with Mr Nash, especially in the disposition of the water. Art has here completely solved the difficult problem of concealing her operations under an appearance of unrestrained nature. You imagine you see a broad river flowing on through luxuriant banks and going off in the distance in several arms; while, in fact, you are looking upon a small piece of standing, though clear, water, created by art and labour. So beautiful a landscape as this, and surrounded by an inclosure of magnificent houses a league in circuit is certainly a design worthy of one of the capitals of the world; and when the young trees are grown into majestic giants, will scarcely find a rival.

An American visitor, Slidell Mackenzie, writing in the 1840s, was so fascinated by Regent's Park that, in his book *American in London*, he included a detailed description of its leading architectural features. Not content with this, he presented the park itself as a kind of dreamlike Watteau landscape, inhabited by figures who might have graced the *Départ pour Cythère*. Viewing the scene from near Sussex Place ('a curious group of buildings in the Chinese taste'), he writes:

From this point the grounds of the park are to be seen with all their beauty. They present a great variety of agreeable objects, groves, gardens, sheets of water, the indentations of whose shores imitate the graceful caprice of nature, interspersed with villas, lodges, airy bridges, and the view being closed in the distance by the nave and towers of St Catherine's, the dome of the Coliseum and the colonnades of the adjoining terraces. The inhabitants of these mansions enjoy, in the heart of a great city, the sight of whatever is pleasing in the prospect of the most highly ornamented scenes of rural life – for even sheep and cattle are not wanting to complete the picture of pleasant rusticity.

The marked contrast with New York was in this American visitor's mind; for in painting an idyllic picture of what this favoured quarter of London had to offer, he compared it with 'the dust, tumult, and deafening clatter of Broadway' besetting the mansions of New York city magnates. Recalling the human scene in Regent's Park, he continues:

While many rolled over the smooth avenues in luxurious equipages, others of either sex ambled on beautiful and highly-mettled horses, followed by neatly-dressed and equally well-mounted grooms; while others, with an air of not inferior enjoyment, rambled on foot over the gravelled walks of the enclosures, or, seated on rustic benches at the sunny side of a grove, or by the margin of the water, pored over the pages of some attractive author . . . The laugh and lively prattle of children, too, gave to the scene its most pleasing character of animation. Some were ferried over the water in pretty wherries, while others, hanging over the railings of the airy bridges which spanned the stream, seemed delighted to divide their luncheon with the majestic swans which sailed proudly below, and which for a moment forgot their stateliness and dignity in their eager efforts to catch the descending morsels.

If there is a touch of Tennyson at his most namby-pamby in this last description, it is nonetheless a genuine tribute to the splendid amenities with which Nash had endowed this northern quarter of the capital.

One of the first of the Regency rakes to enjoy these amenities was Francis Charles Seymour-Conway, third Marquess of Hertford, whose ostentatious magnificence had surprised even the Czar when as Lord Yarmouth, he had been appointed Envoy Extraordinary to the Court of Russia. This millionaire man of pleasure, some of whose activities have been noted in an earlier chapter, got Decimus Burton to design him a villa in the park. Here, in a spot not far from what is now the western border of the Zoo, he installed himself as early as 1825, and here he carried on some of that fantastically luxurious entertaining which, together with his wit and dissipation, earned him the nickname 'The Caliph of Regent's Park', and doubtless decided Thackeray and Disraeli to use him as a model for their aristocratic libertines. The diarist Greville called him 'a sharp, cunning, luxurious, avaricious man of the world' who supported himself by gaming until his marriage put him into the possession of an enormous fortune. Thereafter, he was 'puffed up with vulgar pride'.

Since he helped to build up the 'Wallace Collection', in his Manchester Square house, and assisted the Regent in forming one of the finest of the royal collections of pictures, his activities were clearly not all 'counter-productive'. At his Regent's Park villa – called St Dunstan's after the church of St Dunstan's-in-the-West, whose clock with life-size striking figures he had bought and installed there when the church was rebuilt in 1831 – he is reputed to have kept a seraglio. In this Italianate mansion – with its sweeping, horizontal roof-lines, broad eaves, and portico based on the Athenian Tower of the Winds – he also housed a remarkable collection of bronzes, marbles, and furniture, together with an extensive library of Italian books, a windfall possibly from his marriage with the heiress Maria Fagnani. A noted feature of the building was the splendid reception room which it was his habit to use for breakfast parties. Very lofty and sumptuously furnished, it had a roof in the shape of 'a large tent-like canopy with a spiral finish of copper' -- an early foreshadowing no doubt of the hyperbolic paraboloid roof of today, as well as a graceful bow in the direction of 'Prinny's' oriental dream architecture.

A much later occupant of St Dunstan's Villa was the first Lord Aldenham, the merchant banker, scholar and bibliophile. He was succeeded there by his son, the Hon. Vicary Gibbs, editor in collaboration with his uncle, J. E. Cockayne, of *The Complete Peerage*. It was fitting perhaps that one of the begetters of this vast, scholarly work in many volumes – a verbal tapestry presenting the British peerage in depth and *in extenso* – should have been as splendidly housed as some of those he chronicled. Another merchant banker, Otto Kahn, of the house of Kahn, Loeb, had the villa from 1914 to 1917, in which year he surrendered the lease so that the place could be used as a training centre for blind and disabled soldiers and sailors. St Dunstan's Institute for the Blind, as this was called, moved in 1920 to St John's Lodge, another of Nash's fine villas. The final occupant of note was the first Lord Rothermere, who had the place from 1934 to 1936 and who in 1935 returned the celebrated striking clock to the façade of the church of St Dunstan-in-the-West. In 1937 the villa was demolished and Winfield House built for the Countess Haugwitz-Reventlow – the Woolworth heiress, Barbara Hutton. With the break-up of her third marriage – to the film star Cary Grant – she handed over the remainder of the Crown lease to the United States Government, which in turn was granted a new 99-year lease. Since 1954, Winfield House has been the private residence of the U.S. Ambassador. Just as in the Marquess of Hertford's day St Dunstan's Villa housed a renowned collection of objects of *virtu*, so today during Mr Annenberg's residence, Winfield House is the home of his private art collection, one of the finest in the world, whose masterpieces were exhibited at the Tate Gallery in 1969.

St John's Lodge – now St John's Hall – to which St Dunstan's Institute for the Blind betook itself in 1921, and where it remained for seven years, has perhaps the most splendid position in the whole park. On rising ground close to the Inner Circle, it looks out and down across a great sweep of parkland to the Zoo and Primrose Hill. It was designed by a little-known Northumberland architect, John Raffield, of Seaton Delaval, for Charles Augustus Tulk, M.P., an intimate of Coleridge and a friend of the Brownings, who combined radicalism in politics with Swedenborgianism and Theosophist beliefs. Raffield, whose design was exhibited at the Royal Academy in 1918, is said to have worked under the Adam brothers, and their influence is evident in the house he produced. Though it was Regency enough in feeling to satisfy Nash, its flat, pilastered façade, small pediment, and anthemion ornaments recalled Portland Place or the Adelphi. A boldly projecting, pyloned portico, provided with the fashionable stubby Doric columns and a couchant lion on top, struck a more contemporary note. Sir Charles Berry's mid-19th century alterations to what was no more than a medium-sized villa have done away with most of this. The visitor today is confronted by a greatly enlarged, strikingly palatial building, with another storey added to the centre block, and extensive wings.

Tulk had the place for ten years. The next owner of note was the Marquess of Wellesley, Wellington's elder brother. Governor-General of India, Foreign Secretary in Spencer Perceval's government of 1809-12, and finally Lord-Lieutenant of Ireland, he was a busy man, and St John's Lodge provided only an occasional residence for him during the years 1829-33. The owners of the villa for nearly half a century beginning from 1842 were the Goldsmid family. Sir Isaac Lyon Goldsmid, Baron de Goldsmid de Palmeira in the peerage of Portugal and the first Anglo-Jewish baronet, came of a family of bankers which had used its money greatly to the advantage of Britain, the country of its adoption. One of the founders of the London docks, Goldsmid was also a prison reformer, philanthropist and educationist, as well as an ardent advocate of the removal of Jewish disabilities. President of the Royal Society, F.R.G.S., Fellow of the Linnaean Society, London University and University College Hospital owed their foundation largely to him. A man so well endowed with abilities and sensibility, so variously gifted and cultivated, was well able to appreciate the splendid site in Regent's Park. He entrusted the enlargement and transformation of Tulk's original building to Sir Charles Barry in 1847, with the delightful results which survive in the main in the place as we see it today. The interior decoration he gave to Ambrose Poynter,

architect and artist – father of the better known Sir Edward, later
President of the Royal Academy. Poynter provided the long ball-
room and other rooms with murals of high quality in the late Italian
Renaissance style.

Sir Francis Goldsmid, son of Sir Isaac, followed his father as
tenant of St John's Lodge. The first Jewish barrister and the first
Q.C., he was one of the promoters of the Reform Synagogue. St
John's Lodge remained in the hands of the Goldsmid family until
1887. A couple of years later it was acquired by the third Marquess
of Bute. Here indeed was another extraordinary man – even more
many-sided than Isaac Goldsmid, and a figure to set the imagination
alight. The kind of larger-than-life-size figure, gifted but enigmatic,
around which John Buchan romances used to centre, he was in
fact probably the model for the hero of Disraeli's novel *Lothair*, the
tale of the immensely rich young nobleman whom adroit priestly
influence almost succeeds in steering into the church of Rome.
Though the incidents of the novel of 1870 bore no relation to most of
the facts of Bute's life, the stir made by the actual affair in 1868, in a
still militantly Protestant Britain, had been memorable. The public
apostasy of a nobleman of such great possessions and promise as the
heir to the Marquessate of Bute presented one of those imbroglios
involving the English aristocracy which peculiarly appealed to Disraeli's romantic imagination. Hence, *Lothair*, considered by some to
be his best novel.

Bute's was a character in which a desire to do public service and
to be active in the world warred with an intensely devotional cast
of mind. In his not very long life – he died at fifty-three in 1900 – he
played such worldly roles as Mayor of Cardiff (there was family
property there) and Rector of St Andrew's University – holding
both offices twice – and he was behind the restoration of many
ancient religious buildings. But he was at heart a scholar and a
mystic. A linguist, with a special interest in Hebrew, Arabic and
Coptic, he travelled widely, and his versatile mind led him up many
bypaths of knowledge. He had a specialist knowledge of heraldry
and was one of the leading authorities of his day on religious ritual.
In later life he devoted himself to the study of psychic phenomena,
and became Vice-President of the Society for Psychical Research.

St John's Lodge he turned into the spiritual hub of his withdrawn mystical life. Here he had a domed circular chapel constructed which housed a great crystal ball. The central rooms of the

villa he redecorated with heraldic emblems and astrological symbols. His gardens became open-air extensions of his chapel, a series of terraces and arboured retreats, sanctuaries for his own solitary walks. Here, a tall, cowled and bearded presence, he would pace endlessly in those ultimate years, meditating on psychic and theological mysteries, lost in strange, perhaps eerie, realms of the mind. His chapel has now gone, demolished in 1959, but his gardens remain. They are part of the park, and open to the public. But they are still secluded behind great trees, and few people visit them. Beautiful as they are, they are a little *triste* – as though the seeker still sought and found not.

Bute's heart, when he died, was buried in Jerusalem, on the Mount of Olives. That was his wish. His widow kept St John's Lodge until 1916. Then came the wartime hospital for disabled officers, and in 1921, St Dunstan's Institute for the Blind. For six years, St Dunstan's enjoyed this splendid position in the park, and then in 1927 it moved out. But Sir Ian Fraser, later Lord Fraser of Lonsdale, the war-blinded moving spirit of St Dunstan's, has a house in the grounds. Bedford College's history department now occupies St John's Lodge – now called St John's Hall – succeeding the University of London's Institute of Archaeology in that pleasant spot.

Feminine learning has almost a stranglehold on the park, for Bedford College is also entrenched at the next Nash Villa along the Inner Circle, known as 'The Holme'; in extensive buildings on the South Villa site, also on the Inner Circle; and in Park Square East, on the old site of the Diorama. 'The Holme', one of the earliest villas in the park, was designed by Decimus Burton for his father, James Burton, the builder. Its garden façade overlooks the lake, and the view of the villa seen across the lake from the Outer Circle has often been reproduced from an old print of Regent's Park. James Burton was one of the most remarkable builders even London has known. Not only was he Nash's great stand-by in the building of Regent's Park and Regent Street, but he built much of Bloomsbury, including Russell Square, and parts of the Eyre estate in St John's Wood. Outside London, he built extensively in Tunbridge Wells and St Leonards-on-Sea. It has been estimated that this energetic and venturesome man was responsible for the erection of some £2,000,000 worth of housing. Besides so many houses, he produced ten children, Decimus the architect being the best-known member of the family, with James Burton the younger, a noted Egyptologist, as the runner-up in the celebrity stakes.

On the site now occupied by the big red brick buildings of Bedford College's main halls, appeared in 1827 the third of the large stuccoed villas on the Inner Circle – South Villa. This seems, judging from T. H. Shepherd's view, to have been an imposing looking place with a fine pedimented Ionic portico supported on an arcaded loggia, and with bow windows both on ground and first floors on the side facing the lake. The most interesting, though not the first, tenant of South Villa, George Bishop, a wine merchant with a taste for astronomy, had the place from 1834 till his death in 1861. He built an observatory in what is now Queen Mary's Gardens and pursued his hobby so successfully that he became President of the Royal Astronomical Society. After his death, this observatory was removed to Twickenham. Bedford College, named after its original premises in Bedford Square, acquired a lease of South Villa in 1908. Over the years it grew too large for the villa, which was demolished and replaced by the present extensive academic buildings. All that now remains of South Villa is the pretty octagonal gate lodge near York Bridge. The land on which the villa and its collegiate successor were built was once occupied by Marylebone Park Farm, the largest of the three farms into which the area was split up before the formation of Regent's Park.

Curiously enough, another of the park's original villas, Holford House, was the property for many years of a leading wine merchant. This splendid Regency gentleman's rural residence, sited between the Marquess of Hertford's villa and the Zoo, no longer exists. It was totally destroyed by enemy action during the Second World War. When it was designed, about 1832, for James Holford, general merchant and wine importer established in Lisbon and London, it rivalled the Marquess of Hertford's villa – St Dunstan's – for size and magnificence. Decimus Burton once again, as so often in the park, was called in to do the designing. He produced a building of real panache, whose chief features were a vast pedimented portico, a balustrade with roof urns, and semicircular bays at either end of the façade. In this opulent retreat, Sir James Holford, as he became, held solitary state amidst a retinue of servants until his death in 1855. For the next couple of generations the villa was the home of the Regent's Park Baptist College. When the college moved out in 1927, the place was turned into flats.

Ten years before he provided Holford with his eye-catching villa, Decimus Burton at the age of twenty-two, had been entrusted by Nash with the designing of his second work in the park – Grove House. He already had to his credit 'The Holme', built for his father. Charges by the Crown Commissioners, administrators of this royal park, that this first product of Burton's, done at the age of eighteen, was ugly, and 'deformed' the park, he survived with ease. Indeed, he went on at remarkable speed to produce the Colosseum and such other early achievements as the Hyde Park Corner Screen and the Wellington Arch on Constitution Hill. These famous monuments were thrown off within a few years in the middle 1820s.

But in 1822, when George Bellas Greenough, the geographer and geologist, commissioned him to design a villa on a site between the newly-opened Regent's Canal and St John's Wood Chapel, his architectural wings were really still being fledged. Yet the house which he produced, the sole villa in Regent's Park to survive almost unaltered to today, proved to be an essay in the Greek Revival style of the most complete assurance. It has been called a classic of Regency villa architecture, and it is certainly a building whose stylishness makes an instantaneous impression. The dominant theme was a circular one – circular entrance hall, central pillared rotunda, and drawing room with semicircular portico. Leading off the rotunda, at one end, are rooms originally designed to be a dining room and a billiard room, and at the other a couple of libraries. The two libraries probably reflected the fact that Greenough was a scientist of distinction in two fields. A President of the Geological Society, and a founder member of the Geographical Society, over which he also presided, his major contribution to knowledge was the mapping of British India. He was too – rather naturally perhaps with the Zoo almost on his doorstep – an early member of the Zoological Society.

The Marquess of Linlithgow, one-time Viceroy of India, was the last private resident at Grove House. This was between 1947 and 1952, when the Midland Bank indulged its chairman in this very pleasant way by taking a lease of the villa for him. Of the five tenants who, after Greenough's death in 1855, had preceded Lord Linlithgow, his immediate predecessor, Sigismund Goetze, was by far the most interesting personality. A keen patron of the arts, and himself a fashionable portrait, landscape and historical painter, he was probably more intimately a part of his elegant home than any of those who came before him. Goetze, a man of considerable wealth, acquired a lease of Grove House in 1909, when he was forty-three. Early on in his connection with the place, he converted the stables into a big top-lit studio. He specialised in large-scale murals, and the outstanding example of his work in this field are the frescoes with which he decorated the first floor of the Foreign Office – free of charge. Symbolic of the origin, development and expansion of the British Empire, they are today perhaps no more than nostalgic reminders of an age when the British people seemed to collect colonies and engender dominions almost in their sleep. Had the British Museum accepted a similar free offer he made to decorate the dome of the Reading Room with allegorical figures, Goetze might be better remembered than he is as a decorative artist. Sad that this ingenious attempt to win lasting notice should have failed.

His own splendid drawing room at Grove House, with its views in the direction of the canal and the park, he set aglow with seventeen panels depicting scenes from Ovid's *Metamorphoses*. These, regrettably, were painted over at the time the present tenants, the Nuffield Foundation, moved in in 1954, and all that now remain are his decorations in the entrance hall. Here the Signs of the Zodiac are diversified by the Four Seasons and the Days of the Week, striking a note of Renaissance classicism that somehow typifies the man. Goetze died in 1939, and his wife Constance in 1947, but not before they had proved themselves generous benefactors to the part of London they had made their home. The large, gilded wrought-iron gates at the entrances to Queen Mary's Gardens are their gift, as are the two fountains in the gardens. They also presented the statue of St George and the Dragon which stands at the crossroads in front of St John's Wood Church.

Hanover Lodge is the only survivor of three well-known residences in this south-western part of the park, the other two being Albany Cottage and Sussex Villa. It has been the home of many notabilities, of whom the most famous were Joseph Bonaparte and Admiral Lord Beatty. Famous as the name Beatty was in the First World War and after, his fame as a man and a sailor was equalled, if not surpassed, by that of an earlier naval man, Thomas, 10th Earl of Dundonald, better known as Lord Cochrane, who owned Hanover Lodge in the 1830s and 1840s. In the years immediately after Nelson's death, Cochrane won the name of the most daring and resourceful junior officer in the navy. His successes against the French fleets, gained by brilliant audacity and extreme tactical ingenuity, caused Napoleon to nickname him *Le Loup des Mers*. But if he was a wolf, he was a lone one, and he had the awkward habit of snarling at his elders, or rather of outspokenly criticising senior naval officers. This drawback, plus his conviction and imprisonment in 1814 for being involved in an attempt to rig the Stock Exchange by spreading a rumour that Napoleon had fallen from power, led to the interruption of his British naval career for fourteen years.

At the time of his disgrace, this extraordinary man was also Radical M.P. for Westminster, and he was expelled from Parliament and struck off the navy list. His sentence had included a heavy fine and being condemned to stand in the pillory – the last such sentence in England – and he is said to have been saved from this humiliation only because Sir Francis Burdett, his fellow member and one of the most popular men in the country, had threatened to stand there with him if the sentence were carried out. Cochrane spent the years 1818-28 in the service of the Chilean, Brazilian, Peruvian and Greek navies, all of which he reorganised and commanded. As each of these countries was fighting for its independence, he also took part in their liberation struggles, earning admiration, honours and monetary rewards. The 10th Earl of Dundonald, as he had become on his father's death, made his come-back in England in 1832. In that year, he received a 'free pardon', and was gazetted a rear-admiral. Later he was given back his K.C.B., and made C-in-C of the North American station. Before he was finally buried in Westminster Abbey on his death in 1860, a repentant and grateful country had at last recognised that this strange maverick was one of its great men – not only an outstanding naval commander, but a passionate reformer, and an inventor of high ability. His early advocacy of the employment of steam power in warships, and his celebrated 'secret warplan', involving the use of sulphur in a way foreshadowing the use of gas in the First World War (it was rejected by the authorities of the day as too inhuman a weapon!) had marked him out as a mind of the rarest foresight. He lives on in the novels of Captain Marryat, who served under him as a midshipman, and has perpetuated the memory of this giant of the roughest and toughest days of the British Navy.

Neighbours of Dundonald's at Hanover Lodge during the 1830s and 1840s were Lord Hertford across the way at St Dunstan's Villa, and Francis Grant, the fashionable portrait painter, afterwards Sir

Francis Grant, P.R.A., who lived at Sussex Villa, a few hundred yards away on the same side of the Outer Circle. This rising Scottish painter, as he was during Dundonald's tenancy of Hanover Lodge, was to become one of the most successful artists of his time. Sussex Villa, designed by Nash himself, became Grant's home in 1840 – the year he painted his picture of the young Queen Victoria attended by Lord Melbourne and other leading noblemen, a *succès fou* which turned him into a celebrity. Grant at the outset of his career had the friendship and patronage of Sir Walter Scott, and at Sussex Villa was only a few doors away from Scott's elder daughter, Sophia. She had married Lockhart in 1820, and they had settled in London, at 24 Sussex Place, in 1825 when her husband became editor of the *Quarterly Review*.

Grant was one of those immensely viable types, destined from the word go to brilliant social success of a kind that brought outstanding monetary rewards to the fashionable portrait painter in the Victorian heyday of the art. Handsome, courtly, well-connected by marriage, passionately fond of fox-hunting, he was just the man to tickle the fancy of a wealthy aristocracy by presenting them with mirror images of flattering grandeur. At first he concentrated on the production of single portraits, but soon he began to specialise in hunting scenes in which his noble clients could be seen and recognised at their favourite sport. *The Melton Hunt*, commissioned by the Duke of Wellington himself, sent Grant's stock rocketing up, as did his popular image of the young Queen Victoria. He settled at Melton Mowbray, devoted himself to perpetuating the likenesses of noble riders to hounds, and died there, his Mecca, at the age of seventy-five.

Sussex Lodge as it came to be called, was the home in more modern times of William Hall-Walker, later Lord Wavertree, a noted patron of the Turf, who bred Minoru, the horse which won the Derby for King Edward VII. In the 1920s, Lady Wavertree made her two fine grass courts available for tennis exhibitions. In these, such stars as Borotra, Suzanne Lenglen, Tilden, Patterson, and Betty Nuthall – golden names of a now remote past – created each summer 'an attractive but tiny sort of tennis Ascot'. The proceeds went to an invalid children's orphanage. Sussex Lodge finally bowed itself out in 1957, when it was demolished to make way for the new building of the Royal College of Obstetricians and Gynaecologists.

Albany Cottage, the third of the notable villas on the south-western perimeter of the park, was a fine example of that Regency
whimsicality, the *cottage orné*. Its site today is occupied by the large
neo-Georgian mansion housing the Islamic Cultural Centre, a building which was the creation of Lady Ribblesdale, another rich
American woman who, like Barbara Hutton, has left her mark on
the park. Albany Cottage was an elegant architectural confection
put up for the dandy and diarist, Thomas Raikes. This tall, bulky
Old Etonian, the friend of Beau Brummell, adored dress and the
life of pleasure. A clubman to the finger-tips, he was by profession
a city merchant, as his father had been before him. He would spend
his mornings at his counting house in the City, and then drift up
to the West End later in the day, to lounge at the Carlton Club, of
which he was a founder member, or sit in the big bay window at
White's where he did his betting.

This daily journey earned him the nickname of Apollo, 'because
he rose in the east and set in the west'. A crony of the Prince
Regent, he is described in the hey-day of his dandyism as dressed
in 'a surtout closed to the extent of three buttons, plaid trousers, and
black cravat'. The surtout was a kind of frock coat. Raikes's
appearance was taken off by the artist Robert Dighton in a carica-
ture entitled 'The Prince of Rakes'. Captain Gronow, in his vividly
written reminiscences, tells a tale of how Raikes drew upon himself
a witticism of Count D'Orsay:

> Tom Raikes . . . having one day written an anonymous letter to
> D'Orsay, containing some piece of impertinence or another, had
> closed it with a wafer, and stamped it with something resembling
> the top of a thimble. The Count soon discovered who was the
> writer, and in a room full of company thus addressed him: 'Ha!
> ha! my good Raikes, the next time you write an anonymous
> letter, you must not seal it with your nose!'

Raikes' tenancy of Albany Cottage was during the late 1820s and
the early 1830s, when he was in his fifties. The family's links
with royalty – his brother and sister also lived in the park, at
this time a mark of royal favour – seem to have started with his
mother, who was lady-in-waiting to Princess Amelia, an aunt of
George III. This tough old female lived in Cavendish Square, and
reference has been made to her tastes and reputation in an earlier
chapter.

The City connection at Albany Cottage persisted, for the next tenant of any real note was William Meyerstein – noted perhaps more for the son he produced than for the skill that enabled him to make a fortune in London, the city of his adoption. The Meyersteins were a Jewish family from Hanover, and William's son, Edward, was knighted for his enormous benefactions to philanthropic causes. The tale of his outstanding contributions to the Middlesex Hospital has been touched on in Chapter 4.

All the buildings so far described were exercises in the classical taste of the day – variants on the Greek temple theme, garbed in the white stucco which has come to seem Nash's hall-mark. But there were two exceptions to this. Both were built in the mid-1820s, and both were in the Gothic Revival style. They were of course intrusions upon the unity of Nash's over-all scheme, and as such distasteful to him. The more important was a group of buildings just north of Cumberland Terrace. This was St Katharine's Hospital, a home for poor clergy and their widows, and consisted of a church, two ranges of living quarters and, on the opposite side of the Outer Circle, a Master's House. The Hospital and its inmates had been chased out of their original home near the Tower of London – where they and their predecessors had dozed quietly since the year 1147 – as a result of industrial development. This was in 1825, when their land was needed for the making of St Katharine's Dock. They were granted a site in the park, and Ambrose Poynter, a pupil of Nash's disliked by his master, (as we have seen, he later decorated St John's Lodge) was given the job of designing the new hospice.

An up-and-coming young man, with a sense of the new horizons in architecture, he produced buildings in the Tudor style, judging this no doubt both *dernier cri* and particularly suitable for an ancient institution of the type. That he was not mistaken was soon demonstrated by the comments of his fellow architect, James Elmes, whose *Metropolitan Improvements* was published soon after the buildings went up. Elmes noted approvingly that the Master's House looked like 'the habitation of the Prior to some mitred abbey' and the stables like the abbey's tithe barn. It all seemed delightfully monastic, he thought. This it must be remembered was the heyday of the *Waverley Novels*, and Scott's *The Monastery* and *The Abbot* had recently contributed their quota to a romantic yearning for the Gothic past.

The first occupant of this piece of latter-day Tudor was another intimate of the royals of the day. Not 'Prinny's' friend this time, but the Duke of York's private secretary and aide-de-camp, Colonel, later Lieutenant-General, Sir Herbert Taylor. Taylor's post as Master of this institution was probably a sinecure, and the Master's House a grace-and-favour residence in a fashionable part of London. An able man of the world, a linguist, and no doubt a diplomat, he had the ticklish job given him of buying back the Duke of York's letters to his discarded mistress, Mary Anne Clark. This was after the notorious affair of her sale of commissions in the army, in which she used the duke's name to make large sums of money. Taylor got the letters at an enormous price, and an agreement that the witty, impudent, totally impenitent Mary Anne would abandon Gloucester Place, Marylebone, for the Continent, and keep her mouth shut about the royal family – and particularly about the man she called 'that big baby', the Duke of York. A flying bomb destroyed the Master's House in 1944, and the site has been cleared and become part of the park. The church, now the Danish Church in London, has recently been renovated, as have the other hospital buildings.

Abbey Lodge, the other Gothic Revival building once to be seen in the park, went up about 1826. It was built facing Park Road on a site next to Hanover Gate now occupied by the big block of flats which has inherited the name. Nothing is known of its early history, apparently – not even the architect's name. Thomas Smith, the historian of Marylebone, writing in 1833, doesn't mention it or show it on his map. The first indication of an occupant of whom anything is known is in 1842, when Charles Norris, artist and author, was the tenant. He had the place for about a year. And about all that can be said of him at this date is that he was celebrated for his strong resemblance to Napoleon at a time when memories of the 'Corsican Ogre' were still very much a part of the furniture of men's minds, and that he left a collection of architectural drawings. He was succeeded by Baldomero Espartero, Duque de Vitoria, a Spanish general who came from that famed locality, La Mancha. Espartero spent five years quietly at Abbey Lodge following his fall from power in 1841. He had been Regent of Spain for a couple of years, and was to be Head of State again for another couple in the mid-1850s. He was not the only eminent exile to seek refuge in the fashionable Marylebone district, the Bonapartes and many famous

Frenchmen had been there before him, and the Hungarian national leader, Kossuth, was to come after him.

The family with whose name Abbey Lodge is most closely associated are the de Bunsens. This Anglo-Prussian partnership – Elizabeth, daughter of Samuel Gurney the Quaker banker, and her husband, Baron Ernest de Bunsen, son of a former Prussian Minister in London, had the villa for more than half a century, from 1851 to 1903. One of their sons, Sir Maurice de Bunsen, was a well-known British diplomat, and was accredited to Vienna as ambassador at the time of the outbreak of the First World War. Their daughter married Baron Deichmann, a member of the German upper crust and a friend of Bismarck, who settled in England as a young man and devoted himself to a life of hunting and coaching. Baroness Deichmann spent her childhood at Abbey Lodge, and after her husband's death lived at the family home again from 1911 to 1924. During the eight years intervening between the ending of her parents' tenancy of Abbey Lodge and her return, it was occupied by Emil Fuchs, an Austrian painter and sculptor who was a friend of King Edward VII. Abbey Lodge was demolished in 1928 after being unoccupied for four years.

Enough has perhaps now been said to make it clear that the villas in Regent's Park have never at any time been solely an aristocratic preserve. In fact about a third of the tenants whose names have been mentioned were business men of one kind or another. This is not to deny that throughout the park's existence, residents have tended to be either influential or wealthy, or both. Indeed, for the first ten years or so after its completion, it was not open to the public at all. It was in fact treated as a great private estate, shut off from the outer world by its railings and gates. Even after the public were allowed in in 1838 there were still parts of it strictly private, a state of affairs which lasted until well on into the present century.

A. D. Webster, in *The Regent's Park and Primrose Hill*, published in 1911, speaks of 'the Enclosure or the Private Grounds'. This was the whole area between the lake and the Outer Circle, from York Bridge in the east to Hanover Gate in the west, which was 'reserved for the use of keyholders'. Clearly the intention was to keep the grass and the lakeside walks as a sort of front garden for the tenants of the big terrace houses facing the south side of the lake. The large villas on the north of the lake – South Villa, The Holme and St John's Lodge, all of course had their own extensive grounds, each with its lakeside view. A further sign of the long reign of privacy in the park was the comparatively late arrival of the bridges over the lake. Clarence Bridge, now so much used by the mass public of today, was not made until 1884, and the Boat House Bridge and the long bridge near St John's Hall, till the years 1904–6.

Secure in their privacy as the residents of the park may have liked to feel themselves, by the latter part of the nineteenth century their immediate neighbourhood had attracted to itself three of the great public spectacles of the age – the Colosseum, the Diorama, and Madame Tussaud's. The first was on the Outer Circle, the second in Park Square, and the third – from 1884 onwards – just behind York Terrace. Against the comparatively low roofline of Regency London, the Colosseum, with its enormous dome rising to a height of 112 feet, just could not be overlooked. It went up in Nash's time, and managed to keep going through many vicissitudes for about fifty years. It was a sort of White City or Wembley Exhibition of the first half of the nineteenth century, specialising in 'spectaculars' – from the original breath-taking panorama of London as seen from the top of St Paul's Cathedral – painted by a single man on nearly an acre of canvas and viewed from galleries high up in the dome of the building – to a variety of marine caverns, grottoes, glens, mountain ranges, and a cyclorama.

One of the earliest lifts seen in England was used to take visitors up to the viewing galleries. A visitor of 1838 was clearly completely taken by surprise when unwittingly introduced to this latest marvel of science:

> There is a curious contrivance in this building. The first time that I visited the Colosseum I was not aware of it. I went with a friend. We entered the building. 'Step into this room', said he. A door opened, and we entered a beautiful little bijou of a place. Upon a table in the centre were several books and magazines. I took up one. A bell rang. I was getting amused with the magazine. Again a bell rang. The door opened. 'You can step out here, if you please,' said a man, not the one who had let us in. We stepped out, and my astonishment was great at finding that I had ascended to the top of the building, room and all. The room is purposely contrived to ascend and descend, to save visitors the fatigue of travelling up the all-but-interminable staircase.

Edmund Yates, the Victorian journalist and novelist, whose

father, the actor-manager Frederick Henry Yates, was joint owner of the Colosseum at one stage in its fortunes, has described the Cyclorama – a circular panorama which surrounded the spectator:

> To the Coliseum, some years before its final fall, was added the Cyclorama – an extraordinarily realistic representation of the earthquake of Lisbon. The manner in which the earth heaved and was rent, the buildings toppled over, and the sea rose, was most cleverly contrived, and had a most terrifying effect upon the spectators; frightful rumblings, proceeding apparently from under your feet, increased the horror, which was anything but diminished by accompanying musical performances on that awful instrument, the apollonicon. Never was better value in fright given for money.

The Diorama, housed in a building in the centre of Park Square East, was opened in 1823, and survived for twenty-five years. It consisted of a revolving auditorium, and two picture rooms, each of which came into view in turn. It was a French invention, and was brought to England by Bouton and Daguerre. It was capable of producing effects of great realistic power. The two Frenchmen used it to show landscapes in France and Germany conceived in the highly romantic genre of the period:

> The views represented have the appearance of reality, not only from the effect of the paintings, highly wrought, but from the effect produced by the various degrees of light brought to bear upon them. Thus, in a cathedral some time since exhibited, you gazed upon the interior of an edifice in broad and opening day. Gradually the light faded away, and finally and almost imperceptibly, object after object became indistinct and darkness reigned. Then the candelabra were lighted in the edifice, a procession of monks was seen to cross the distant isle (sic) of the cathedral and finally the whole building became crowded with figures not there previously. There is no effect that cannot be produced in this admirable establishment. Sunrise and sunset; dawn and twilight; moonlight; the obscuration of the sun by a passing cloud; and the shadows of leaves and trees cast upon the ground when the sun again bursts forth, are all faithfully delineated, and without anything like theatrical effect.

The effects produced by the displays in the Colosseum and the

Diorama depended of course upon a whole array of factors – light, height, movement, sound effects, and above all *trompe l'oeil* painting. But the third of the popular forms of entertainment which found itself a site in Marylebone, Madame Tussaud's, relied solely for its appeal on waxwork figures counterfeiting celebrities. Its founder, a Swiss woman who had learnt her art in Paris, had stumbled by chance upon the fascination of the macabre. This had happened when she had been compelled during the French Revolution to attend guillotinings and make masks of the severed heads. Emigrating to England in 1802, she brought her collection of the famous and infamous with her, and after trying a variety of places finally settled in 1835 in Baker Street at the popular Horse Bazaar. Here, among such diversions as the Glaciarium, or indoor ice rink, set amid what appeared to be the mountains of Baker Street, Madame Tussaud's started on its career of developing into a national institution.

The game of strolling round these galleries inhabited by life-size figures of the famed or the notorious dressed in their habits as they lived, and frequently set in their natural habitats, made an instant appeal to the great British public. Their bottomless snobbery and unappeasable love of make-believe were fed by these jaunts among the gilded and the ghastly. They could admire, jeer, or shiver as the mood took them. The Tussaud family soon saw that, great as the pull of their William the Conquerors or Henry VIIIs might be, topicality was the bait with which to catch the rising middle class. They seized their first chance with the great opera singer, Malibran, whose superb vitality and youthful allure had taken the English musical audiences of 1836 by the throat. When she collapsed and died suddenly during the Birmingham Musical Festival of that year, at the age of twenty-eight, they rushed out an effigy of her that drew the public in in vast droves. From that moment they seem never to have looked back. By 1884 they had grown too big and too ambitious for their premises in Baker Street, and that year they moved to the present much larger site in the Marylebone Road. Neither the devastating fire of 1925 nor the German block-buster in 1940 did more than prove their powers of reincarnation.

*Punch* and other journals have frequently recorded the impact of Madame Tussaud's upon the cockney mind in the Victorian era. But one of the lesser known tales about the place concerns that dandy and aristocrat, the Count D'Orsay. The Count's splendid extravagance had resulted in his being dunned for debt from one end of the metropolis to the other. As a result, he dared not show his nose in public, at some periods of his life, without danger of arrest by the watchful tipstaffs. D'Orsay, though best known in his character of fashionable trend-setter and society leader, was of course an artist. He numbered Landseer among his friends. One day, so the story runs, when he was undergoing a period of self-imposed house arrest and had become very tired of his own premises, he asked Landseer, whose house he had managed to reach, muffled in his cloak, if he could not suggest some outside diversion. He got the reply that the only possible public entertainment available at mid-day was Madame Tussaud's. D'Orsay had never seen the place, and was only too keen to go. They succeeded in making a 'soft landing' at the Baker Street establishment, and started to go the round of the galleries. But soon they noticed that two extremely watchful-looking men seemed to be following them everywhere. D'Orsay feared that he had failed to shake off the law, and was going to be arrested. One of the men came up, bowed, and asked if he were addressing the Comte D'Orsay. When told yes, he lowered his voice confidentially and said: 'Madame Tussaud, the old lady you saw as you came in, asks if you would do her the honour to let her model you in wax?' 'In wax,' came the relieved shout in reply, 'in marble, bronze, iron, my good fellow! Tell her, with my love, she may model me in anything!'

If the Regent's Park residents were well supplied with places of entertainment within their immediate neighbourhood, their spiritual needs were equally well looked after. St. Marylebone, the parish church, was situated just south of York Terrace; Trinity Church (now Holy Trinity), to the east of Park Square; and St John's Wood Chapel (now St John's Wood Church), not far from Hanover Gate. And now the twentieth century has brought with it St Cyprian's, Clarence Gate, a minor masterpiece. Thomas Hard-wick's St Marylebone, which was completed a couple of years after Waterloo, is a rather grand affair. It represents a belated attempt by a very wealthy parish, after havering for nearly half a century, to replace their patched-up ancient village church by something that would proclaim their solid splendour. It probably cost nearer seventy than sixty thousand pounds – perhaps the best part of a million at today's values – and had a seating capacity of between three and four thousand people. Nash, at work on the building of

Regent's Park at the time of its construction, seized on the opportunity for a piece of scenic bravura, and aligned the York Gate entrance on the church. Hence the short avenue known as York Gate,
whose altogether delightful sweep of buildings links park and church.

Benjamin West, the P.R.A. of the day and a parishioner himself,
contributed an 'Annunciation' and a 'Holy Family' from his own
brush. For the former, a vast transparency to span the organ arch,
measuring seventeen feet by eight, he horrified the vestrymen by
charging £800; the latter, an altar-piece, was, he indicated, a free
gift. A significant oddity in the design of the church was the two
wings flanking the chancel diagonally. Here the Duke of Portland –
ground landlord of so much of Marylebone – and other grandees,
had their family pews, a couple of rooms to each wing, equipped
with fireplaces, and no doubt other mod. cons. Originally, too, the
note of lordly comfort – indeed of pleasurable diversion – was continued in the nave, where two galleries, one above the other, sustained the theatrical impression produced by the peers' private
boxes perched on either side of the altar. To add to the atmosphere
of exclusive grandeur, Charles Wesley, son of the great hymn-writer
and private organist to the Prince Regent, was retained to provide
suitable music for the fashionable congregation. Order throughout
the great building was maintained by three beadles, one at the main
entrance – no doubt to keep out the straggling poor – and one in
each gallery. Ten pew-openers marshalled the ranks of local society
into their strictly graded, hired, and paid-for slots.

Since those remote days of the Regency, much has been changed
in the church. The upper galleries have gone from the nave, an apse
has been added at the chancel end, and the organ has been moved
from its central position. The anomalies and theatricalities of the
Prince Regent's era have given way to a traditional style of furnishing. But St Marylebone remains a conspicuously opulent-
looking temple of religion; the gilded caryatids ringing its high
tower – a landmark of the area – remind one that this was the place
of worship once of the richest parish in England.

In contrast with the pomp and circumstance of Hardwick's great
church – still triumphantly self-assertive at the end of its unspoiled
vista – Holy Trinity, Albany Street, now no longer a church but the
headquarters of the Society for Promoting Christian Knowledge,
seems monstrously null. Its site, farmland when the church was consecrated in 1828, has been elbowed out of its scenic existence by the

surrounding buildings. The White House, nine storeys high, and Euston Centre – which might be ninety, it towers so high over the church – have dwarfed it into the appearance of some vestige from Lilliput. Strangely enough, the battering of the weather and the hazards of time, plus the fumes of the traffic-choked Marylebone Road on its doorstep, have done little damage to the fine profiles which Soane gave the outsides of his masterly buildings. But surface texture and colour have long ago lost their 'bite' and impact, and faded into that dun dinginess with which London slowly abolishes its architecture. A curious feature of the façade is the open-air pulpit, built to commemorate a popular preacher. Into the carcase of this rather under-privileged work of Soane's, it is amusing to recall that Allen Lane and his 'Penguin Books' fitted themselves for a while in the 1930s – in the crypt. Trinity Church was supplied at less than a third of the cost of St Marylebone, and would now appear to have been 'remaindered'.

The third of the quartet of Marylebone churches serving the needs of the Regent's Park area is St. John's Wood Church. As this is now also the parish church of St John's Wood, it will be dealt with in the next chapter. At the time it was completed in 1814, it was merely a chapel of ease to St Marylebone Church. The fourth of the Regent's Park churches, St Cyprian's, Clarence Gate Gardens, standing just south of Park Road, by the Francis Holland School, is a Gothic Revival masterpiece of the early twentieth century. An unpretentious red brick exterior, with buttresses and traceried windows, hardly prepares one for the exhilarating quality of the interior. There are no pews, and the great sweep of the empty, light-filled nave, with its fine proportions and its tall, delicately vigorous piers, is a breathtaking prelude to the serene splendour of the very large openwork rood screen. Ninian Comper was the architect of this church, and the designer of all its decorative features – fittings, screens, and glass – and of the striking font-cover, a gilded tabernacle rising to its slender apex.

The fabric of the building was completed in 1903, but much time and the slow accumulation of funds were required for the addition of the various features – the rood screen not being finished until 1924, and the canopy over the high altar until as late as 1948. 'Refined medievalism' is the epithet applied to St Cyprian's by the Rev. Basil Clarke, in his book on London churches. At the consecration, he says, the floor was strewn with flowers and rushes, and the

church is unrivalled as 'an expression of the best of Anglican
Catholicism in the reign of Edward VII'. The driving force behind
the creation of St Cyprian's, the Rev. Charles Gutch, seemingly both
a religious and a social and philanthropic force in the neighbourhood in the latter half of the nineteenth century, did not live to see
the church built. He succeeded only in getting a temporary structure put up. His lack of success in achieving a proper church was
due, we are told, to the ground landlord's dislike of high church-
manship. Lord Portman refused to grant him a site for a permanent
church. His heir took a more liberal view, and St Cyprian's eventually appeared, posthumous but splendid – and on the site of
Gutch's own house.

Charles Gutch was the focus of a variety of movements for
helping the poor, the sick, and the underprivileged. His church-
manship might be high, but he understood instinctively what it was
like to be down in the kennel. Grinding poverty amid surroundings
of sickening squalor prevailed in large parts of Lisson Grove, a few
minutes' walk away from his doorstep in Ivor Place. These slums
had been building up for at least fifty years when he arrived on the
scene in the mid-nineteenth century, and by the time he died in
1896, they constituted a well-established blot upon the borough of
Marylebone. It would probably be unjust to saddle the Great Central Railway – later the L.N.E.R. – with the whole responsibility for
the further social decline suffered by Lisson Grove and the southern
part of St John's Wood during the first half of the twentieth century. But it is difficult not to see it as the major factor in that
process. Lisson Grove's slums had originated in the beginning of the
nineteenth century, when poor Irish labour was brought into the district for the building of the Grand Union and Regent's Canals. But,
in making their Marylebone Station terminus, the Great Central
Railway were not content with cutting a swathe through sordid
tenements and crumbling cottages; they also swept away a large
part of the district's most flourishing residential area, lying between
Lisson Grove itself and Park Road.

Here, on either side of the Regent's Canal, had grown up streets
of pleasant villas, with gardens running down to the water's edge.
Neighbouring this to the south was Alpha Road, the main east–west
axis of what might well have been dubbed 'the Park Village on the
other side of the Park' i.e., the opposite side of the park from Park
Village East and Park Village West. And finally to the south of

what we should now call this attractive housing estate were two squares – Blandford Square and Harewood Square. This well-to-do neighbourhood where most of the more favoured social strata were concentrated was demolished practically in its entirety in the years immediately preceding the opening of Marylebone Station in 1899. The whole locality had a strong literary, artistic and cosmopolitan flavour, being the home at different periods of – to name only a sample – George Eliot; Benjamin Robert Haydon; Mary Lamb, sister of Charles; Samuel Palmer; C. R. Leslie, R.A., Constable's biographer; Charles Rossi, the sculptor responsible for the giant caryatids on the tower of St Marylebone Church; Ugo Foscolo, the Italian poet; Kossuth, the Hungarian revolutionary; the tightrope walker, Blondin; and, for a very brief period, the great Sarah Bernhardt.

Marylebone Station was the last of London's great termini to be built. It came a little too late to make any showing in the modern transport race. 'Last, loneliest, loveliest', Kipling's epithets for Auckland, New Zealand, in his *Song of the Cities*, can, odd as it may sound, be construed, without too much twisting, as applying to this terminus. It came after all the others; it is the smallest and least frequented; if not exactly lovely, its Victorian gentleman's Jacobean country house appearance, breathing an unwonted atmosphere of repose and leisure, is more subtly beguiling than any architectural perfection could be. And then, most potent of all, it has about it the beauty of the doomed. It was the last terminus to come, and it looks like being the first to go.

It is in fact, after a mere seventy years' existence, threatened with redundancy. A modernised Paddington, we are told, will readily look after most of its functions, and the remainder will be dealt with by other methods of transport, now conveniently available. There is a built-in irony in this destiny. For Sir Edward William Watkin, Bart., M.P., one of the great forces behind transport in Britain in the latter part of the nineteenth century, and a early champion of railway unification and the Channel Tunnel scheme, had the fiercest struggle of his life in wringing the new terminus out of the many conflicting interests involved. And above all in silencing the cricketing interests at Lord's, who saw their sacred turf in danger of being abbreviated by a railway cutting. Even this, he achieved by the exercise of financial gamesmanship – and recourse to a tunnel instead of an all-too-visible cutting.

A Manchester man, and an early associate of Cobden and Bright in the Free Trade struggle, Watkin viewed Marylebone as merely the link between his railway interests in the Midlands and lines to the south coast and the Channel Tunnel, which he hoped might ultimately connect the English and French railway systems. After campaigning up and down the country, and in and out of Parliament, and pulling the many strings that were at his disposal as a major railway administrator and financier, he succeeded in 1894 in getting the project moving – only to succumb to a disastrous stroke. He was out of the battle, and it was left to Lord Wharncliffe, his successor as chairman of the Great Central Railway, to bring the scheme to completion and inaugurate the new terminus.

So short of funds were the Great Central Railway by the time it came to the building of the terminus that they were apparently unable to afford the services of an architect, and the architectural design was left to a member of the Engineer's staff. The result was the nostalgic little building we know, with its whiff of provincial England far away and long ago. But when the first train puffed out of the station in March 1899, to the plaudits of that group of top-hatted, frock-coated grandees invited for the occasion, it passed through a residential area of Marylebone which had literally been wiped off the face of the map. Harewood Square had entirely disappeared. Blandford Square, where George Eliot had lived in the early 1860s, had been virtually bisected. The whole of the pleasant Regent's Canal-side and Alpha Road suburbs had vanished, yielding place to goods yards, wharves, coal depots, and – a few years later – a power station. Scores of streets and hundreds of houses had been done away with, and a number of ancient and well-beloved land-marks removed. In short, industrialism had, in one sudden stroke, taken over an entire residential quarter of London. The symbol of the transformation was the Grove Road power station chimney, an imaginatively conceived piece of 'infernal' architecture by the late Sir Charles Reilly, whose dark implacable silhouette now towers over the industrial jungle below.

This is the debit side of the picture. The credit side, such as it is – apart from the convenience and commercial advantage of a new terminus in this part of the metropolis – lies chiefly in the destruction of some of the slums of Lisson Grove. Some 4,500 inhabitants of these areas had to up sticks and move elsewhere. About half of these were resettled in other existing accommodation, and the rest housed in six five-storey apartment blocks built by the Great Central Railway. Wharncliffe Gardens, as they were called, went up in St John's Wood Road, on the site of Sir Edwin Landseer's house and garden.

Another large structure diversifying the Marylebone scene was the Hotel Great Central, built at the same time as the terminus, and linked to it by a graceful canopy spanning the station yard. This 700-roomed Jacobean-style, red-brick monster, tricked out in the terracotta dressings of the time, and topped by a clock tower, is perhaps an expression of the enormous optimism behind the whole venture. It was sumptuously furnished, and was launched with suitable splendour and publicity. One wonders how often in its comparatively short life as a hotel it was filled to capacity. It was taken over by government in both world wars, and since then has been used as the headquarters in turn of the L.N.E.R. – which absorbed the Great Central Railway – the British Transport Commission, and the British Railways Board. This building too will become redundant when B.R.'s offices are moved to St Pancras Station.

It will be seen then that, although Sir Edward Watkin wrought mightily and turned a whole quarter of London upside down, his works are not likely to endure. In the Second World War, his vast goods depot on the Alpha Road site was bombed out of existence, and the Westminster City Council have acquired it for municipal housing. If both his terminus and his hotel disappear in the near future, as is only too likely, we may see the land occupied by these buildings and the extensive station approaches reverting to residential use, with big blocks of flats and perhaps a hotel or two to meet the rocketing needs of tourism in the metropolis. Thus, in the course of a couple of generations – a mere moment of time in the history of cities – Watkin's calculated venture may have bowed itself out.

Another calculated risk of this period of Marylebone's history proved itself a miscalculation within a very few years. In the flush of enthusiasm aroused by the arrival of the new terminus and its eye-filling hotel, it was decided to rebuild the Portman Market, in nearby Church Street, on an ambitious scale. At a cost of £35,000 – a considerable sum in 1900 – an entirely new structure was put up, with nine large avenues of shops converging on a central domed hall. This was the modernised successor of the extensive market buildings which already existed on the site. It was located so as to take advantage of a goods yard brought to Lisson Grove by the new railway. Shoppers of today, who only know Church Street Market as a small street market, with the business done on stalls by the kerbside, may be surprised to learn that the market we see in the 1970s is the puny successor of the huge, covered Portman Market, which flourished for over seventy years from its foundation in 1830. It occupied a space of some three acres on the north side of the street, and dealt in meat, vegetables, fruit and hay on a large scale. Thomas Smith (1833) estimated that the cost of building the market had been originally about £60,000, and he thought that it was already – only three years after its foundation – in a fair way to rivalling Covent Garden. And this because, unlike other London markets of the day, everything in it was under cover – stabling, storehouses, abattoirs, and livestock pens.

The modernisation of 1900, an attempt to take advantage of the new rail links with the district, failed to inject fresh life into the market, and by 1906 the buildings were up for sale by auction. It was reported in the press at the time that the company owning the market had never been able to let more than about half the shop accommodation available, and that expenses in general had been very high. Possibly bad management was an element in the situation. It has been suggested that permission to costers to put up their stalls just outside the market building led to undercutting and a considerable loss of business. At all events, this attempt to ride the crest of the Watkin wave of enterprise foundered.

Before the coming of the railway, Church Street had been linked directly with Regent's Park by means of Alpha Road. This fine, broad straight thoroughfare continued the line of Church Street east of Lisson Grove, and debouched on Park Road opposite Kent Terrace. Thus the underprivileged northern quarter of Lisson Grove was easily accessible to the carriage folk of the park area. They probably drew some of their domestic staff from the pool of labour so conveniently near by, and they could reach the Old Marylebone Theatre, in Church Street, after the shortest of drives along a straight route. The fact is that the arrival of the railway, with its multiplicity of tracks, tunnels, cuttings, goods yards, coal depots, wharves, and other industrial trimmings, scattered over an area of seventy acres, set an angel with a flaming sword between poor Lisson Grove and the paradise of Regent's Park from which it had been detached! The physical obstacle created was formidable,

33. The shut-off nature of Portland Place is well conveyed in Thomas Malton's attractive aquatint of 1800. In the background can be seen the railings dividing the northern end of Portland Place from the fields bordering the Marylebone Road and the Park. This splendid quarter of London was designed by James Adam, younger brother of the more famous Robert. Among celebrated residents have been such diverse personalities as Talleyrand and Edgar Wallace.

34. George Shillibeer started the first public bus service in London in 1829. Three horses, driven abreast, carried a load of twenty-two passengers, all inside, from the Yorkshire Stingo public house, near the Edgware Road end of the New Road (Marylebone Road), to the Bank and back again. The fare was a shilling and included the use of a newspaper.

35. Volunteers on parade in Dorset Fields during the Napoleonic Wars. The houses whose backs are visible in the distance are on the north side of the Marylebone Road. The parade is taking place on ground used for the building of Dorset Square in 1814. The Volunteers are being presented with their colours.

36. Henry Fuseli (1741–1825), the Swiss-born painter who became Professor of Painting at the Royal Academy, and later Keeper, after a drawing by Sir Thomas Lawrence.

37. An unusually informal sketch of Sarah Siddons (1755–1831), the great actress at about the age of fifty. It is probably by George Henry Harlow, a pupil of Sir Thomas Lawrence.

38. Sydney Smith (1771–1845), wit, journalist, and cleric. Mrs Siddons 'developed convulsions' and had to be led away from the table, speechless with laughter, at their first meeting.

39. This photograph of Elizabeth Barrett Browning (1806–61), the poet, was probably taken when she lived in her father's house in Wimpole Street.

40. 'The Yorkshire Stingo', the well-known public house which stood in the Marylebone Road until the late 1960s, is the background here to a Regency print. For a period in the 1830s and 1840s, plays were staged there in the Royal Apollo Saloon, a concert hall-cum-theatre at the rear of the main building.

41. St John's Wood Chapel, now St John's Wood Church, after a drawing by Thomas Hosmer Shepherd. It was designed by Thomas Hardwick and completed in 1814, and was for many years a chapel of ease to St Marylebone Parish Church.

42. J. M. W. Turner (1775–1851) by Daniel Maclise, the history painter, who sketched famous contemporaries for *Fraser's Magazine* during 1830–8.

43. The sculptor Joseph Nollekens (1737–1823) made a vast fortune out of his portrait busts. He lived in Mortimer Street, Marylebone.

44. Emma, Lady Hamilton (1765–1815), Nelson's mistress, was married to Sir William Hamilton, the diplomat, antiquary, and authority on volcanoes, in Marylebone.

45. François René, Vicomte de Chateaubriand (1768–1848) took refuge in England during the French Revolution and lived there for some years between 1793 and 1800, making his home in Marylebone.

46. George Dance's vivid sketch of James Boswell (1740–95) with its thrusting inquisitive nose, rather obsessive fixed stare, and dew-lapped chin, exactly hits off the biographer of Dr Johnson.

47. This sketch of Benjamin Robert Haydon (1786–1846), history painter, man of letters, and gifted diarist, conveys something of the fiery quality of this tragic near-genius.

48. George Romney (1734–1802), portrait painter on the grand scale, lived for many years in a house on the south side of Cavendish Square. His many portraits of Nelson's Emma Hamilton helped to gain her celebrity.

49. Edward Gibbon (1737–94) whose stately, sardonic periods have enriched English literature as greatly as his vast erudition illuminated history, lived at 7 Bentinck Street, Marylebone, from 1773 to 1783.

50. Lord George Gordon (1751–93), anti-Catholic agitator associated with the Gordon Riots, lived in Welbeck Street. Dickens gave him added notoriety by portraying him in *Barnaby Rudge*.

51. The Eyre Arms is here shown in 1820. It stood at the corner of the Finchley Road and Grove End Road and was demolished in 1928 to make room for Eyre Court, a big block of flats. In its heyday its large, well-laid-out grounds, theatre and ballroom attracted great crowds of visitors.

and though a new road was built across the railway over the Ross-more bridge, south of the old Alpha Road, it had an industrial and not a residential character, and proclaimed only too clearly that Lisson Grove had been flung into outer darkness.

Lisson Grove is a pleasant name, suggestive of rustling leaves, for a place which in the eighteenth century had still been a village. Lisson village had its grove, its green, and its pond in those days. As we have seen in Chapter 1, Lileston, or Lisson, was the westerly one of the two manors comprising the territory which later became the borough of Marylebone. The manor house of Lisson village stood on the site now occupied by the headquarters of St Dunstan's – the home for service war blinded – at the western end of the Maryle-bone Road. Lisson Green – the village green – on to which the manor house looked, took up most of the area between Lisson Grove and the Edgware Road. Although even as early as 1745 the map shows a group of buildings at the south-west corner of the green, where the pond also stood, London did not begin to take the village into its lengthening grip until the beginning of the nine-teenth century, when an increasing number of painters and writers started to settle in and near the village. Meanwhile workmen from the purlieus of Paddington Green, on the other side of the Edgware Road, flowed in to populate an area of temporary hutments on the northern fringe of the green.

By the time Marylebone became a parliamentary borough in 1832, Church Street – or New Church Street as it was then called – was already in the heart of the slum area of Lisson Grove. It had how-ever one feature of distinction – a theatre, founded the same year. The Old Marylebone Theatre, or the Royal West London Theatre – to select only two of its better known names during the 110 odd years of its existence – was sited on the south side of the street, oppo-site the Portman Market. The history of this long-lived old home of the British drama has been chronicled by Mr Malcolm Morley for the St Marylebone Society, with love, skill, and a wealth of detail. After a variety of later-life incarnations, as a cinema, a stadium, etc. – it is said to have had the deepest stage in London – the audi-torium and the stage were heavily damaged by a German bomb in 1941. The Marylebone Borough Council bought the freehold in 1959, and have used the site for housing and a public library follow-ing the theatre's final destruction by fire in 1962.

Charles Dickens, with his compulsive addiction to the theatre and

private theatricals, must often have visited the Old Marylebone
Theatre – particularly during the eleven years he himself lived in
the borough. Nearly all the famous novels of his early and middle
years were written at No. 1 Devonshire Terrace, at the park end of
Marylebone High Street. But it was not until 1866, when he had
left Marylebone, that his editorship of the magazine *All the Year
Round* involved him in a row with Joseph Cave, then lessee of the
theatre. The magazine's theatre critic, it seems, in an article entitled
*Mr Whelks at the Play*, had adopted a style of chilling condescension
towards a double bill put on at the Old Marylebone – *The Water
Cress Girl* and *The Black Doctor*. Cave, enraged by this superior
attitude, and either believing or affecting to believe that Dickens
had written the article himself, rushed to distribute a hand-bill
alleging that the great man had been in a state of vinous non-com-
prehension when he attended the play. Mr Dickens was sarcastically
invited to come and run the theatre himself if he thought he knew
such a lot about the drama. As it turned out, it was one of Dickens'
staff who was responsible for the review. The charge of inebriation
probably came rather near the knuckle, for Dickens had begun to
drink under the strain of ill health and the other excessive stresses
of his last years. He threatened a libel action unless the statement
were withdrawn. It appears that it wasn't, but that he took none.
He was only four years away from his death, and perhaps felt that
he had enough on his hands without inviting further publicity of a
kind that might have dragged his clandestine affair with Ellen Ter-
nan into the limelight.

The Yorkshire Stingo, a celebrated pub which stood just east of
the Lisson Grove manor house and had its main frontage on the
Marylebone Road, was the liveliest spot in the neighbourhood for
much of the eighteenth and nineteenth centuries. This ancient hostelry, which only ceased to exist a few years back, was heard of as
long ago as 1684, i.e. when Charles II was still reigning. Its proprietor opened a large bowling green and tea-gardens in the 1760s,
and from about 1790 on held a May Day fair, whose sports and
jollities eventually attracted such huge and often unruly crowds
that the local residents took fright and ultimately got the fair sup-
pressed. For a period in the 1830s and 1840s, a concert-hall-cum-
small-theatre, known as the Royal Apollo Saloon, was built out into
the tea-garden. Some of the plays staged here were based on
Dickens novels. The Yorkshire Stingo itself figured in a drama put

on at the Old Marylebone Theatre in 1844. This was called *Jack of Paddington; or The Omnibus Conductor, the Informer and the Felon*. It dealt with the hazards of using the first London bus service which from 1829 on ran from the Bank to Paddington, via the New (Marylebone) Road, with a stop at the Yorkshire Stingo.

With this piece the Old Marylebone billed another play, a melodrama with a strong local interest, entitled *The Shore Devil; or the Lone House at Mary-le-bone*. Those were the days when many houses in Marylebone still stood in the midst of large gardens, and when some backed on to fields and the open countryside. After dark, the atmosphere in these places – particularly where there were small households – must have been sufficiently creepy at times. Only candlelight was available then to the nervous householder, or the flickering primitive gas jets, with that 'night-must-fall' feeling coming on, which novelists of the day like Wilkie Collins or Mrs Oliphant could describe with such potent effect.

# 7. St. John's Wood

As an early forerunner of the garden city, St John's Wood was the
direct offspring of Regent's Park. The launching of Nash's great
scheme had immediate consequences in this untouched rural area
to the west of the park. Here for the best part of a century the Eyre
family of City merchants and port wine importers had owned some
500 acres of farm land. What turned out at this late stage of their
ownership to be a tremendous financial windfall had been acquired
quite by chance in 1732. In October of that year, Henry Samuel
Eyre, a well-to-do, well-connected – his mother was a Lucy of
Charlecote Park – middle-aged merchant of New Broad Street,
Bishopsgate, was visited by Lord Chesterfield's confidential man of
business. The future author of the celebrated letters to his son was
in need, it seemed, of £20,000, and to get it was ready to sell his St
John's Wood estate. Wit, diplomat, and cultivator of the graces, he
had not long before succeeded to his father's earldom, and it may
be needed money to live in the style to which he soon hoped to be
accustomed. At all events, the business was done, and Eyre became
owner of the forty-five fields which were to yield his great-nephew
so golden a harvest in the reigns of George IV, William IV and Victoria – he lived till 1851 – and other generations of Eyres thereafter.

His great-nephew, a second Henry Samuel, a colonel in the
Guards at the time he came into the estate in 1823, seems to have
been well advised. The opportunity which Nash had so conveniently made for him was not left to slip by unexploited. But he
inherited from his mother, and it seems likely that it was she who
actually started the policy of developing the estate. At all events the
great James Burton himself, and other speculative builders, moved
in and took up the sites offered by the Eyre estate. It is significant
that the building unit chosen was the villa. Pairs of semi-detached
villas, set in their own large gardens, were used for the first time in
the building history of this country. Thus from the outset it was
clear that St John's Wood was to be a modest reflection of Regent's

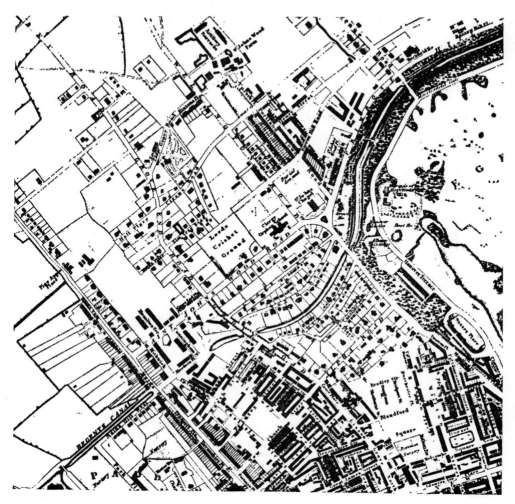

St John's Wood from Greenwood's Survey of 1827

Park – a rustic housing estate for the middle classes, an elegant suburban retreat for those who wished to babble of green fields.

The development of the Eyre estate came at a peculiarly opportune time to attract the right type of resident. It was not only that many people of moderate means who could not afford a house, let alone a villa, in fashionable Regent's Park, wished to get as near to the area as they could; it was also that many London dwellers were heartily tired of the urban scene. They had lived with the classical eighteenth-century architecture of their fathers and grandfathers longer than they cared to remember. The beginning of the industrial era, with its introduction of Londoners to the industrial slum, reinforced their desire to escape into a different atmosphere, 'away from it all'. The cult of the romantic, a yearning for the Gothic past and for a leap out of the stark present into the supposedly 'merrie England' of long ago, had them by the throat. Disraeli expressed one aspect of their feelings when he denounced the streets and squares of Marylebone as tame, insipid, and uniform. These solid, middle-class citizens, tied by their business or professional interests to a life in London, wanted a new milieu. Escape from the 'broiler-house' existence of endless, ruler-straight rows of terrace houses built two generations or more ago and beginning to decay, held out a strong allure. Exciting, up-to-the-last-moment housing in the latest modish novelty, the villa, beckoned from the borders of the Regent's dream park, that city-in-a-park described ecstatically by James Elmes, the architectural critic, as 'a scene of ever-varying delight'.

The deciding factor, however, was probably the Eyre estate's proximity to London. In an age of horse transport, it was an enormous advantage for the citizen's rustic box to be within easy carriage drive of his place of business in the capital. St John's Wood fulfilled this requirement, being little more than three miles from the City. That was the practical attraction for the business or professional man. But there was another class of potential resident for whom the Eyre estate held out an immediate appeal – the artist. An outlook on green fields, with country quietude and fresh air was a big element, no doubt, in bringing all types of resident, but for the artist it offered special advantages. He needed somewhere out of the rush of urban existence – what poor Haydon called 'the continued rush of fashion which never left me any rest' – to gestate his works and bring them to completion. He needed, too an uninterrupted north light for his studio – not easily obtainable in a built-up area – and, if a landscape painter, he probably required the inspiration of the rural scene.

As we have seen in earlier chapters, Marylebone in the late eighteenth and early nineteenth centuries was one vast hive of painters, sculptors, architects, and other artists and craftsmen. They had moved in from the 1760s onwards, seeking the good air and good light of what was then a relatively unbuilt-up quarter of London, and following in the wake of the rush of rich aristocracy and well-off professional men into the area – ready-made patrons for their works. The Berners estate, with Berners Street as its hub, was the headquarters of this Chelsea of earlier days, and here such men as Constable, Nollekens, Sir William Chambers, Fuseli, Opie, Richard Wilson, Benjamin West, and Sir David Wilkie, to name only a few of the more famous, had their houses and their coteries. A little farther west in the parish, as it then was, lived J. M. W. Turner, Romney, and Allan Ramsay. Many of these outstanding artists were dead by the time St John's Wood was well and truly launched. But other names of note, intimately associated with the Victorian era, were coming up.

One such, the very quintessence of Victorianism to our way of thinking today, was Edwin Landseer's. His was the resounding name which inaugurated the reign of the artists in St. John's Wood. He went there as a young man in 1824, and stayed there all his life till his death in 1873. He had been brought up in Marylebone, where his father, John Landseer, had his home in Queen Anne Street East, now Foley Street. As a boy, he had rambled all over the open countryside between St John's Wood and Hampstead, learning the topography and sketching the views. He was an ideal person to savour the delights of the new neighbourhood — sensitive and knowledgeable, yet both sociable and a lover of field sports, and able through his immense popularity with high society and royalty to bring the most favourable publicity to bear upon the district of his choice. Landseer was the symbol of St John's Wood as a centre for artists and artistic living in its opening and middle phases, just as Alma-Tadema was a symbol of that side of the place in its later and closing phases.

St John's Wood had been developing for well over a decade before Landseer's arrival. Some of this early building seems to have taken place in the St John's Wood Road and Regent's Canal areas, with St John's Wood Chapel, and Lord's Cricket Ground and Tavern as the main centres of public resort. The construction of the Regent's Canal was itself one of the main factors in the early development of the St John's Wood district, for the Eyre estate made the sale of its land to the canal company dependent upon the building of first-class houses along the banks. Since the canal was begun in 1814, it is clear that the villas on North Bank and South Bank, as they were called – which were demolished when the Great Central Railway lines into Marylebone Station were constructed – were among the earliest parts of St John's Wood to be developed. By 1820, however, Peter Potter's plan showed that development had also taken place on the two other estates included in the district – the Harrow School estate on the west and the Portland estate on the east. The former was a long, narrow strip running from just south of St John's Wood Road northwards to Kilburn, with its frontage on the Edgware Road. Its major property, Hamilton Terrace – the finest street in the district – had not yet been developed, but there had been some building along the Edgware Road. The other was an isolated outlying part of the main Portland estate situated between Primrose Hill and St John's Wood High Street. Both these properties were much smaller than the Eyre estate. The Harrow School estate was an area of high-quality housing, but Portland Town, as it was called, developed into a poor neighbourhood, and was largely pulled down and rebuilt around the turn of the century.

If one selects the year 1824, the year of Landseer's arrival, as a good date to take stock of the early development of St John's Wood, it becomes clear that most of the housing progress had been in the south and east of the district. By that date, St John's Wood Road, in which he had settled, was already largely built up with villas, each having its own garden. North of that road, Elm Tree Road, Circus Road, Hall Place, and Grove End Road each had a considerable sprinkling of villas set amid gardens – all in the best Regent's Park-at-one-remove tradition. On the east side of 'the New North Road' – the Finchley Road – the government had acquired a part of St John's Wood Farm for a military riding school as early as 1822, and this they were to build in 1825, the year after Landseer's arrival. It became in 1880, and has remained, the Artillery Barracks – the training school of the Royal Horse Artillery. After the Second World War, it was the home of the King's Troop of the R.H.A., whose special function it is to take part in the great ceremonies of State.

The barracks have been rebuilt to suit today's needs. South of St John's Wood Road, the Regent's Canal–Alpha Road housing estate was already dotted with villas and their long strips of garden. Eastwards, Portland Town Road — as St John's Wood High Street was called then – and its immediate neighbourhood showed line upon line of terrace houses, the only villas on this estate being in the Avenue Road area.

Judging by the commemorative tablets in St John's Wood Chapel, among the earliest residents of the district must have been a colony of retired officers and officials of the East India Company, and their wives and families. This element preceded the artists. At the time the chapel – as it was called until early on in the present century – was completed in 1814, Marylebone was still expanding at a tremendous rate. New churches were needed to accommodate the spate of residents pouring into the district, and there was an urgent need for a new cemetery. The site eventually selected for the cemetery was just beyond the south-west boundary of the park. Here six acres of agricultural land were bought from the ground landlords, Mr Eyre and the Duke of Portland, at a price of £600 an acre, and on this a chapel was built and provision made for a burial-ground. In this spot, then deep countryside, a century and a half earlier, so the tale runs, the bodies of thousands of Londoners killed by the Great Plague had been buried in mass graves. The vestrymen of Marylebone, it seems, had in 1814 hit by chance upon a locality worthy of commemoration by Sir Thomas Browne himself, who actually lived through the time of that appalling pestilence. As the coiner of the phrase 'dormitories of the dead', the author of *Urn Burial*, had he been alive, would no doubt have commented appropriately in his splendid and stately prose upon the decision to reopen this particular dormitory after little more than a tenth of a millennium had passed.

Thomas Hardwick, then already at work on St Marylebone Church, was asked to design the new chapel. Hardwick was the father of the better known Philip Hardwick, the designer of the celebrated arched entrance to the old Euston Station. A very experienced architect of sixty-two, living in Berners Street, he once had Turner the painter in his office at a time when that whimsical genius had not realised where his talents lay. Hardwick produced a handsome little brick building, with an Ionic portico and a stylish bell turret. He gave it an attractive interior, lit by fine big windows. Thomas Smith noted approvingly that the inside of the chapel had 'a very novel and pleasing appearance, the pillars and pews being painted white, and having mahogany mouldings on the tops'. White is still the predominating theme in the decoration, and with the gold which has been added since the post-war redecoration, gives the whole church an atmosphere of serene and luminous tranquillity that is peculiarly its own. If St Paul's, Covent Garden, is 'the handsomest barn in England', then St John's Wood Chapel, created by the man who some twenty years before had been given the job of rebuilding Inigo Jones's classic church almost as it stood, from the master's designs, may have caught something of the original genius. Hardwick's miniature 'barn' is clearly one of a long line of descendants from the 'barn' prototype.

The chapel was originally intended to be a chapel of ease for St Marylebone Church, i.e. both an overflow chapel and a more convenient place of worship for people living on the north-western outskirts of the parish. Among those who found it 'easier' to go to St John's Wood Chapel was that *grande dame* of the stage, Mrs Siddons. This was in her later days, when she had given up acting, and retired to a fine house at the top of Baker Street, overlooking the park. From this mansion, with its large bow window facing Clarence Gate, she could bowl along Park Road in her carriage, taking her surviving daughter, Cecilia, to Sunday service at 'the new chapel'. The road too was new over which these fashionable ladies were driven. It had not existed until the cemetery and chapel came into being, and a route was needed to reach them from Marylebone.

From her pew in the 'Mid Aisle East', the stately and apparently rather forbidding Mrs Siddons was doubtless in a good position to see and be seen, and to overawe the simpler members of the congregation. But the chapel was also patronised in these early days by a large number of Anglo-Indians – as British officers and officials who had lived long in India were termed in an age less race-conscious than we are today. Some of these had made reputations in the service of the East India Company, and were almost certainly formidable characters themselves. They had settled, on retirement, in the rural outskirts of Marylebone, and St John's Wood Church contains many monuments to their memory. Among them the oddest was certainly one John Farquhar, who from his great wealth gained in India deserves to be called a nabob, though his manner of life was on the whole very far from nabob-like.

Like John Elwes before him (see Chapter 5), he was that strange phenomenon the miser-millionaire. During the earlier years of St John's Wood Chapel, John Farquhar had a house in Park Road, where he lived alone with one old woman, his servant. The place was a mass of books and papers, everything scattered about, and covered in dust and dirt. Farquhar himself presented so poverty-stricken an appearance that he was several times offered charity by people who had mistaken him for a down-and-out of gentlemanly origins. Yet this Aberdeenshire Scot, who had gone to India in the mid-eighteenth century as a boy cadet in the East India Company's Bombay Army, had returned from that country with a fortune of half a million pounds, which was to treble itself before his death. Lamed during his military service as the result of a wound, he had left the service, gone into business in Bengal, become an expert in the manufacture of gunpowder, and finally sole contractor for explosives to the Government of Bengal. So rich was he that by the year 1822 he was able to spend £330,000 in buying that vast white elephant, Fonthill Abbey, from William Beckford. He seems to have lived there only occasionally, and when the tower collapsed in 1825, he prudently converted the rest of the building into a woollen factory. Some years earlier, when Nash had had to face the nasty problem of the bankruptcy of the speculative builder engaged in building Park Crescent, Farquhar had stepped in and agreed to guarantee the money needed to finish the construction.

Also like Elwes, Farquhar seems to have been a man of the most courteous manners, and to have restricted his skinflint attitude to the matter of his own comfort. He is said to have given large sums away in acts of charity. But he died without making a will, and his vast estate was divided up amongst seven nephews and nieces, who all put in an appearance for his funeral at St John's Wood Chapel. Marylebone was clearly prodigal of human oddities in the late eighteenth and early nineteenth centuries. Elwes and Farquhar were certainly very curious eccentrics – but Richard Brothers, the 'Nephew of God', and Joanna Southcott, the 'Woman cloathed with the Sun' (the poet and humorist Hood called her 'that cackling hen-prophetess') – were far out on the lunatic fringe. Both these religious fanatics, fabricators of cults and self-deifiers though they were – ended up by being buried in St John's Wood Chapel cemetery – in Joanna's case through a trick involving the use of a false name.

In its last phase before achieving the status of a church, St John's Wood became a chapel of ease to Christ Church, Cosway Street. That was in the year 1899. Cosway Street, named after the dandified little miniaturist whom the Prince Regent delighted to patronise, visiting him at his house in Stratford Place, links the Lisson Grove district with the Marylebone Road. Here in the early 1820s, Philip Hardwick delivered himself of a church which Sir John Summerson has labelled – architecturally speaking, of course – 'soulless'. The interior, before its post-war redecoration, was said to be gloomy, and the exterior as it now presents itself is dingy and depressing. Lisson Grove, ever since Marylebone Station and its extensive yards and depots steam-rollered their way into the place at the turn of the century, has been the Cinderella of Marylebone districts. Even before that it had its slums. But in 1899 when Christ Church in a lordly way took over St John's Wood Chapel as a chapel of ease, Lisson Grove, ecclesiastically speaking at least, must have been a remarkably flourishing place. The incumbent, the Reverend Oswald Pryer Wardell-Yerburgh – the very name carries with it the odour of prosperity – seems to have presided over what was practically a clerical army corps, and a congregation large enough to fill a small cathedral. 'He had', say John Oliver and Peter Bradshaw, in their book *St John's Wood Chapel, 1814–1964*, 'four Curates, twenty-two sidesmen, nine servers, a choir of 20 men and 30 boys'. There were at that time a thousand people in his church at Evensong, 1,400 pupils in the Sunday Schools, and more than 3,000 callers a year at the Church House. He topped all this off by having his own 'Superintendent of the Hymn Boards'. Now, seventy years later, the scene has completely changed. St John's Wood Chapel has been a flourishing parish church since 1952 and scheduled as an historic building since 1954. Christ Church, in spite of internal redecoration and the efforts made to save it, has the outward appearance of having gone down in the world.

Within a few minutes' walk of St John's Wood Church is that other ancient institution, Lord's Cricket Ground. It is fairly general knowledge that Thomas Lord's original ground was in what is now known as Dorset Square. But it is far less commonly known that the St John's Wood Road ground represents the third pitch he had in Marylebone. Lord, that 'sharp lad from the north' – a Yorkshireman born in Thirsk in 1757 — first appears on the cricketing scene as a groundsman at the White Conduit Cricket Club in Islington.

Here at the age of thirty he was deputed by some of its noble patrons to find them a better ground. He succeeded in getting a lease – or perhaps an agricultural tenancy – of the piece of ground on the northern outskirts of Marylebone, later known as Dorset Square. Thus was born the Marylebone Cricket Club, and the potent initials, M.C.C. So far, so good. More than twenty years roll by, and the ground landlord, Mr Portman, declined to renew the lease except at a much higher rent. Mr Portman, who was clearly no cricketing enthusiast, saw that a much better thing could be made of the ground by granting building leases and developing it as a square. Thomas Lord departed in 1811, taking his turf with him, to a site about half a mile farther north. This he had had the foresight to acquire as early as 1808. But hardly had he got there, and the club recovered from the adverse effects of the move, than a fresh devil, in the shape of the Regent's Canal Company, presented itself and demanded Mr Lord's new ground for the building of the canal. So, still hitting the northward trail – and again taking the sacred turf with him – he once more executed a half-mile trek, and reached his final haven in St John's Wood Road. This, the present Lord's, he opened in 1814.

Lord received much help and encouragement from one of the great sporting characters of the time – George Osbaldeston, known as 'Squire' Osbaldeston. Steeplechase rider, renowned master of fox-hounds, dedicated cricketer and cricketing enthusiast, he fought a celebrated duel with Lord George Bentinck, son of the fourth Duke of Portland and friend of Disraeli. The venue, rather appropriately perhaps in view of their lawless intentions, was Wormwood Scrubs, and the two performers in the splendid drama seem to have gone through the life-saving antics sometimes resorted to. Bentinck, it is said, fired first, missed, and bawled out: 'Now, Squire, it's two to one in your favour!' 'Why, then the bet's off,' yelled Osbaldeston, and fired into the air. Reconciliation, however, seems to have been delayed for several years – perhaps because neither of the honourable gentlemen was able to display any justificatory wound. That was in 1831, when the 'Squire' had reached the ripe age of forty-four. The same year he matriculated in that peculiar sport of the Corinthian age, the equestrian 'spectacular'. He won a thousand-guinea bet that he would not ride 200 miles in ten consecutive hours by completing the course in 8 hours, 42 minutes. Since he changed his horse at the end of every four miles, he must have used fifty horses in this mad marathon – and come away with a pretty sore seat. Osbaldeston – surely Sir Walter Scott's hard-riding Sir Hildebrand Osbaldistone in *Rob Roy* must have been taken from him, perhaps unconsciously since the name is hardly changed – was a thick-set man of great muscular strength. Cricket absorbed him so wholly in his later years that he settled down at 2 Grove Road, St John's Wood, within walking distance of Lord's. There he died at seventy-nine, in 1866.

Thomas Lord himself also settled down on the spot. His house at the north-east corner of the ground overlooked the pitch. There he stayed until a couple of years before his death in 1832. His last two years had been spent in retirement in the Hampshire village of West Meon. Meanwhile, another institution had grown up nearby – Lord's Tavern, the famous pub used by patrons of the game. 'Squire' Osbaldeston must have been a familiar frequenter of this place, as he certainly was of the Eyre Arms, another of the early places of assembly in the district deserving mention. This resort, which was far more than a mere pub, seems – as its full name, 'The Eyre Arms and Assembly Rooms' indicates – to have been something much more like the great assembly rooms found in the eighteenth century in cities such as Bath and Cheltenham. It could hold 1,500 people at the height of its career, in the building designed by John White junior, district surveyor of Marylebone, in 1820. No doubt it had existed as a small tavern for some time before this. After the transformation, it developed from a local pub to a place of resort for Londoners in general. Excellently sited on the Finchley Road, at the Grove End Road corner, its large, well-laid-out gardens, theatre and ball-room attracted crowds of visitors. Balloonists made an early airfield of it, taking off on their glorious technicolour ascents into the clouds. Firework displays and all sorts of celebrations were held there, including the rehearsal for the 'Eglinton Tournament' – medieval fun and games for the nobility and their ladies, in which the future Emperor Napoleon III laid about him heartily in the company of an English marquess and a brace of earls.

By 1836, when the Eyre Arms had become a noted resort for Londoners, Landseer was a rising celebrity, and easily the best known person in St John's Wood. He had been there twelve years, and his original country cottage had been replaced by a house, 'small, but rather aristocratic and dignified in aspect'. No. 1 St John's Wood

Road was, for the home of a popular – indeed for many years the most popular – Victorian painter, distinctly austere and, internally at least, rather bourgeois in atmosphere. Alma-Tadema, whose sybaritic temple of art went up in Grove End Road half a century later, would not have been seen dead in it. The great painter of dogs, stags, lions and other sporting beasts lived in fact in a rather larger dog-kennel or den. A cosy, comfortable artist-cum-sportsman's bachelor retreat, it may have been aristocratic and dignified, but rather, one senses, as the large bloodhound in his famous *Dignity and Impudence* is – in the simplest and nicest possible way. His studio – the studio was usually the show-piece with the artist-aesthetes of St. John's Wood at its zenith – was dark, gloomy, and totally void of decoration. Even the stove in this main work-room, near which 'Lass', his favourite collie, used to lie curled in a chair, shed a ponderous gloom.

Landseer never married, but was looked after by his sister, Jessie. Born, artistically speaking, to the purple – that is to say, father, brothers, friends, all artists – he had been trained with the minutest care for the career of an animal painter. Pitched practically puling among the Royal Academy pundits of his father's day – he had first exhibited at the Academy at the age of thirteen – he was trained from the word go by men of the calibre of Fuseli and Haydon. The mark of the beast – in the opposite to the general sense of that term – was on him from the outset. Fuseli would shout: 'Where is my little dog boy!' when he was still a small, curly-headed child, and Haydon would lecture him on the artist's need to know animals intimately, by dissecting their bodies. He was made to draw, paint, etch at home; to study intensely first domestic, then wild, animals. At the menagerie at Exeter Change, Strand – where the Strand Palace Hotel now stands – he was first introduced to lions. Lions thereafter became a regular part of his life – and as we know, he left their effigies (weighing seven tons each) in Trafalgar Square.

So much for the technician. But artists of the universal popularity of a Landseer are also great men of the world, diplomatists of the brush, courtiers of the canvas. Ordinary men writ very large, their tastes must be bang on centre. Above all, they must entertain, in the fullest sense of the word. Landseer not only painted animals, he hunted them and shot them. He could be trusted not only to visit Abbotsford, stay with Scott and paint him and his dogs, but to meet

his sporting friends and go deer-stalking with them. Victoria and
her Albert could invite him to teach them how to etch, and then
commission pictures like *The Drive, Shooting Deer on the Pass*, safe
in the knowledge that he would enchant them equally as artist and
as sportsman when discussing the finished product. He was too, it
seems, a gifted mimic and a delightful anecdotist. No wonder then
that his house in St John's Wood was for many years a Mecca for
the society of the day, a place thronged with visitors. One of these
was that witty and worldly parson, Sydney Smith. Perhaps he didn't
really retort, when laughingly invited by Landseer to sit for his
portrait: 'Is thy servant a dog, that he should do this thing?' It
doesn't matter. The significant thing surely is the legendary quality
of both the painter and the wit.

Most of the desirable things came Landseer's way – immense
popularity, a knighthood in the days when artists rarely got
honours, the friendship of the powerful from royalty downwards,
money enough to live very comfortably. He not only hit the fancy
of the Victorian aristocracy and upper middle class with his broad
treatment of sporting themes and the chase after game – *Monarch
of the Glen* stuff – but appealed to an enormously wider public with
his prolific output of 'faithful doggie' pictures. *The Old Shepherd's
Chief Mourner*, typical of his exercises on the theme that the dog
is man's best friend (with the implication that it is often a better
friend than most men) touched a chord that was – perhaps still is –
very near to the heart of the British public. Perhaps the strain of
melancholy that lay behind this suggestion, and which overcame
him in the end, accounted for his never marrying? This great
popular enchanter had a streak of morbidity in him, hated showing
his work to anybody in the unfinished state – at one stage in his
later life, visitors were only allowed to look at work in progress in
a mirror – and by the time he was sixty had fallen into a state of
severe mental depression. He recovered only to refuse the Presidency
of the Royal Academy. A railway accident in which he was involved
a year or two later completed his mental downfall. On his death in
1873, a press article drew a picture of his state of mind suggestive of
the passing of Edgar Allan Poe rather than that of the genial artist
who moved so easily in society, delighting the good couple at Bal-
moral equally with his friends at St John's Wood. 'Beset by a vision
of his own funeral, he lay silent and tolerating no interruption, his
vital forces sinking under his too easy and long indulgence in

images of terror and mystery.' A far cry, this, from *Dignity and Impudence.*

Landseer, by settling in St John's Wood, had made it fashionable for artists to colonise the place. C. R. Leslie, genre and portrait painter, had migrated to St John's Wood the year after Landseer went there. He settled first in St John's Place, and then at nearby Pine Apple Place, both in Maida Vale. Better known now for his friendship with Constable, and his biography of him, than for his own work as illustrator and portrait painter – once highly rated – Leslie had been born in Marylebone, of American parents. He had returned with them to America at the age of five, and after their deaths been sent back to England at seventeen to study art. With the exception of the year 1833–4, when he went to America to take up the post of Professor of Drawing at the U.S. Military Academy, but almost immediately relinquished it, he spent the rest of his life in England. He was Landseer's friend as well as Constable's, and in 1824 when he was thirty and Landseer only twenty-two, they visited Scotland together and stayed with Sir Walter Scott at Abbotsford. After Leslie's death in 1859, his son G. D. Leslie, also a painter, whose stated aim was 'to paint scenes from the sunny side of English domestic life', used to assist Landseer by painting details of still life on to his canvases. He would also play billiards with the ailing master during his periods of depression, or whisk him off to a theatre.

A contemporary of G. D. Leslie's who lived in St John's Wood was that romantically-fated Frenchman, James Tissot, who first had a home in Springfield Road and then took the house in Grove End Road which Alma-Tadema afterwards made his own. 'Tissot', says Montgomery Eyre, 'was esteemed far and wide as a painter *par excellence* of the charms of the ladies.' This remark has a period charm of its own, and one can almost hear the click of the billiard balls and smell the cigar smoke as the words fall from some heavily-moustached male of two generations ago. Tissot indeed had an eye for feminine beauty in general, but the focus was so frequently on one individual face that a Dante and Beatrice legend came to attach itself to him. He arrived in London after the Franco-Prussian War of 1870 – or rather fled under suspicion of having been a member of the Paris Revolutionary Commune. He was in his mid-thirties, had studied at the École des Beaux Arts under Ingres, had had his picture *The Meeting of Faust and Marguerite* bought by the

Luxembourg, and produced a series of studies, *La Femme à Paris*, foreshadowing his abiding interest in contemporary woman, her clothes and her social preoccupations. There was something of the stylish photographer's gift about his productions, and he certainly cut a caper or two in St John's Wood, where his Gallic *empressement* made its mark in feminine circles. His house in Grove End Road, he adorned with a double colonnaded approach in a style which may have helped to prompt the Pompeian fantasies of his successor, Alma-Tadema. This period pergola survives, in a rather defused condition, to the present day, when the whole pipe-dream of a place has subsided into flats.

Tissot seems to have suffered some soul-cataclysm in the early 1880s, when he popped off to Paris, and then made for Palestine, where he spent a number of years collecting material for illustrations to the Bible. In a roundabout way this escapade appears to have been connected with his mysterious Beatrice, whom he is said to have married just before her death. Himself, he rented an abbey in France and died there just after the turn of the century at the age of about sixty-six. Not, however, before he had collected over a million francs from the firm of Lemercier for his Bible pictures. Like some other fated figures before him, it was in his heart rather than in his pocket that he suffered.

St John's Wood was the home for many years of W. P. Frith, one of the wealthiest artists of the Victorian age. At 114 Clifton Hill, he was some way off the fashionable Grove End Road and the artistic and literary cliques clustering about the St John's Wood Road area. But the man responsible for such best-selling articles as *Derby Day* and *The Railway Station*, and whom Queen Victoria commissioned to paint the wedding ceremony of the Prince of Wales – Edward VII – for £3,000, an astronomical sum in 1863, was well able to look after himself. In fact so well did he do so, that, born in 1819, he survived until 1909, 'a pleasant-faced, alert old gentleman', says Montgomery Eyre, writing in 1913, who was 'always busy in the mornings with his paints and brushes and in the afternoon was ready for a stroll and a chat'. The pleasant old gentleman, besides giving a lot of pleasure to a lot of people in his time, had done some quite first-rate business with the picture trade. *The Railway Station* – Paddington, of course, instantly recognisable as substantially the Paddington Station of today – was commissioned by Flatow, the dealer, for £4,500, plus the copyright and a preliminary sketch. The canny Frith, however, still had a further card up his sleeve – the right, which he had reserved from the first, to exhibit the picture at the Royal Academy. For this he got another £750 from Flatow. The only time Frith put a foot wrong – significantly, not with the dealers, but with his public – was when in 1870 he gave them a work entitled *The First Cigarette*. They were outraged to see that it represented a young lady of the first fashion smoking in public. She is seated at a table in what appears to be a park café, and the waiter is giving her a light (no doubt an added impropriety). For the painter whom the Queen had delighted to patronise, the father of daughters of his own, an R.A. and a pillar of the Establishment, blatantly to publicise such decadence was no doubt the moral equivalent today of turning the camera on a pop group cannabis session – if indeed today has any moral equivalent.

Like other shrewd Victorian artists with a large public, Frith understood the value of introducing portraits of well-known men and women into his large-scale renderings of topical scenes. In this way, he incorporated into these life-sized mirrors of the Victorian world a 'spot-the-celebrities' element of a type sometimes found nowadays in the press. In 1883, for instance, he exhibited at the Royal Academy a large picture entitled *Private View at the Royal Academy, 1881*. With this he really went to town in a big way, crowding on to the canvas likenesses of Gladstone, Browning, Huxley, Tenniel, Du Maurier, Irving, Sala, Ellen Terry, Lily Langtry, Trollope, Oscar Wilde, and himself. In his autobiography, he admits that he was out to pepper the picture with notabilities – 'persons eminent in various walks of life', he calls them, but quickly adds that the *raison d'être* of the work was to satirise the aesthetes. Taking his cue no doubt from Gilbert and Sullivan's *Patience*, he introduced into the picture a 'family of pure aesthetes absorbed in affected study of the pictures', and 'a well-known apostle of the beautiful, with a herd of eager worshippers surrounding him' – the ineffable Oscar himself, of course.

By 1883, however, Frith had no need to look as far afield as Wilde, then domiciled in Chelsea, to find an apostle of the beautiful. In Alma-Tadema, St John's Wood possessed a high priest of the cult of 'that Lady Beauty', whose flying hair and fluttering hem were so passionately celebrated by D. G. Rossetti in both the verbal and the graphic image. Rossetti and Wilde are of course great names, and it is not suggested that the talented Dutchman who contributed his quota to assuaging the *fin de siècle* longing for pipe-dreams of the classic past was of their company. His scenes of languid luxury where marble terraces look out on sun-dappled seas, and the eternally youthful, propped on beds of amaranth and moly, seem to suggest that lotus-eating is the only life, were, it appears, the sincere reflection of his own temperament. That they were also profitable was extremely convenient for him, for he clearly needed the money for the transformation of his home environment into a temple of the arts. First at Townshend House and then in Grove End Road, he created for himself a kind of hedonist's carapace-for-living that could only have flourished in that particular era. So compulsive were his dreams, and so prestigious his art in its day, that he was first knighted and then in 1902 made an original member of the newly-instituted Order of Merit – in company with Lords Kitchener and Roberts, Florence Nightingale, George Meredith, and other towering figures. In an age before the 'telly' elevated pop singers and reduced royalty and the rest of us to a single level, he was visited in his studio by King Edward VII.

It is strange to think that, in spite of the trumpetings of his prophets, not a wrack of all this remains. He died in 1912, but when in 1961 the public library of his own borough, Marylebone, was offered two of his major works, *The Roses of Heliogabalus* and *The Finding of Moses*, as a free gift – with the sole proviso that they should hang on its walls – the offer was declined on the grounds that there was no space. Escapist art of the lushly luxurious kind in which he dealt is not even a smoke puff on the distant horizon into which the speed-wake melts. *Whispering Noon, Rose of All the Roses, Dolce Farniente, A Roman Emperor, The Shrine of Venus, The Parting Kiss, He Loves Me, He Loves Me Not, Wandering Longings, The Year's at the Spring, Pleading* – they all plead in vain for any public interest in the 1970s. Yet the man himself and his career remain a fascinating spectacle.

Laurens, later Lawrence, Alma-Tadema was born in Holland in 1836, studied art in Antwerp, and specialised in the painting of historical subjects. Attracted by the prospects for this kind of thing in flourishing mid-Victorian London, he visited St John's Wood about 1866, and attended a fancy dress ball given by Gambart, the Belgian art dealer, at his own house in Avenue Road. Alma-Tadema and his wife were still in the house when it was partially destroyed by an explosion of gas – a curious foreshadowing of the fate of his own first house in England which was also partially destroyed in the Regent's Canal barge explosion of 1874. This affair, probably the greatest explosion in London up to the time of the First World War, had an effect almost as devastating as one of the big block-busters of the Second World War.

Alma-Tadema, by now married for the second time, had settled in 1871 at Townshend House, near the Macclesfield Bridge over the Regent's Canal. With his taste for the creation of a markedly artistic environment, he had transformed the place into a kind of aesthete's nest, a famous feature of which was the long, narrow panel-paintings in the hall, all framed in white, and all contributed and painted by artist friends. In the early morning of 2 October 1874, five barges loaded with cargoes consisting partly of explosives – five tons of gunpowder, says one account – were being towed along the canal when one of them blew up just as it was passing under the Macclesfield Bridge, annihilating the crew of three in an instant. So great was the force of the explosion that not only was the iron-framed bridge wrecked, but the lodge-keeper's house at the park gate was destroyed, and the banks of the canal stripped of vegetation and devastated for a considerable distance. The blast blew in windows over a wide area, and the mighty rumble of the disaster was heard all over London and beyond. Townshend House, close to the bridge, was filled with dust and rubble, and the windows came in on the terrified Alma-Tadema children – a couple of little girls – who, with their governess and the servants, were alone in the house at the time. Alma-Tadema's own bedroom was heavily damaged, and he probably owed his life to his prior engagement elsewhere. Among the odder consequences of this formidable explosion was the fact that the blast damaged Joanna Southcott's tomb in St John's Wood Chapel churchyard, and that the authorities thought it necessary to post troops around the Zoo for fear that damage there might result in the escape of dangerous wild animals. (None in fact did escape.) For months afterwards, fragments of the blown-up barge and scatters of hazel-nuts – part of another cargo – were found in the neighbourhood.

Alma-Tadema made this setback the occasion for moving off to Grove End Road, where he bought the house which Tissot had occupied till his departure for Paris and the Holy Land. He retained the celebrated colonnade, and used part of the old house as the nucleus of his new and highly idiosyncratic dwelling. Like Lord

Leighton, his distinguished senior and rival in the art of concocting classical charades in paint, he produced a house which was part museum and part jewel-case. Once past the front door – figured wood with an elaborately worked bronze surround, and the word *Salve* over the lintel – you were in for all the more eclectic delights. The hall, the staircase, the studio, the atrium, flowing now up, now down, led you on past apse and balcony to a whirling assault on the senses by ceramics, marbles, stained glass, painted wood, brass, and aluminium. Windows of Mexican onyx, rose-garlanded friezes, Pompeian ceilings, Persian tiles, Roman fountains, highly-polished woods, a grand piano of oak inlaid with ivory, mother-of-pearl, and tortoise-shell – all working together to produce that hard gem-like flame in the mind so warmly recommended by Mr Walter Pater – made it the most talked-of house in London.

Time has been unkind to Alma-Tadema's house, which he sought to transform into a reflection of the world of his classical fantasies. Houses such as his become faintly ridiculous in the English climate. They belong of right to the southern sun and the wine-dark sea. Their social justification past, they retreat behind house agents' boards, and expose to the public gaze merely their cracking walls, or some dome or column weathered like streaky bacon. The little, bearded, koala-bearlike painter who so impressed our grand-parents has gone with all his rout. 'The St John's Wood Clique', that band of Academicians and near Academicians who caught some of Alma-Tadema's reflected glory, and frolicked so greatly to their own delight in 'The Wood' of the 1870s and 1880s are even less remembered than he. Nobody can now tell you what kind of people Stacy Marks, Philip Hermogenes Calderon, W. F. Yeames, Frederick Walker, G. A. Storey, or D. A. Wynfield were, or what sort of pictures they painted. Even such names as George du Maurier and Val Prinsep have become pretty hazy memories. Only their houses, where they survive, can tell us a little about them.

One of the oddest of the artists' houses of 'The Wood' – not belonging to a member of the 'Clique', but nevertheless the home of a sculptor, John Adams-Acton, is still to be seen in Langford Place, off Loudoun Road. In scale it is to an ordinary St John's Wood villa as a dwarf or gnome might be to a human being. Its high, narrow gables, squeezed together, resemble a couple of witches' hats, and below them protrudes a weirdly-shaped bow window with a bulbous glass upper portion rising to a peak like a

Norman soldier's helmet. The façade of this basically German folk-tale cottage has a whole repertoire of medieval features in miniature at first-floor level, as though the architect had suddenly been seized with a dream of the Tudor past, and decided to have a toy long gallery with all the trimmings, down to bricks in a herring-bone pattern beneath his range of windows. At the other end of the façade, clearly living in another age and mood, he has plumped for a minuscule French window opening on to a balcony. That this weird bag of Gothic whimsies – now bisected into two dwellings – was once called 'Sunnyside' adds just the right grotesque note.

One wonders whether it was Adams-Acton himself – he died in 1910 at a fairly ripe old age – who was responsible for the design of this fey little place. He is said to have been an extremely prolific sculptor, and to have 'peppered India with statues of generals and administrators' – undesirable perhaps, but not necessarily a sign of madness. It is not hard to believe that 'the house has an uncanny atmosphere, particularly the room behind the Gothic window, which may have been used by Mrs Adams-Acton for her seances.' A final touch of the ultra-odd is provided by the information that Sarah Bernhardt, looking for accommodation for herself and pet tiger in St John's Wood, tried unsuccessfully to rent the place.

The 'St John's Wood Clique' who made such a splash in their day in the 'Grove of the Evangelist' – as Bulwer Lytton facetiously dubbed 'The Wood' – were, of course, just a drop in the ocean of artists who have made the place their home in the course of its more than a century-and-a-half's existence as a London district. Some have been well enough known in their time, but in the perspective of five or six generations they do not count for much. That is, as individual names they have little to say to us now, although their choice – in their hundreds – of St John's Wood as their place of residence was the reason why, before Chelsea was ever heard of as an artists' neighbourhood, 'The Wood' became synonymous with artistic and indeed literary London. It was only after 'The Wood' had been flourishing for fifty years and more that, early in the second half of the nineteenth century, Chelsea began to come into prominence as a fashionable artists' quarter. Whistler, surely, one must hold greatly responsible for that – the supreme artist-dandy, his outsize aureole of publicity spotlighted Chelsea and started a Thames-side migration.

Summerson, in his *Georgian London*, calls St John's Wood

'London's most humane suburb'. He was thinking of its unique,
gardened villas, as opposed to the stucco terraces of other early-
nineteenth-century suburbs. But the humane quality of the place
expressed itself also in human life there, and in the way in which it
has been a magnet for political exiles. Prince Louis Napoleon
(Napoleon III), Wagner, Kossuth, Foscolo – to quote only the bigger names – all lived in, or frequented, the 'Grove of the Evangelist' in their time. Foscolo, the Italian poet and patriot and near
genius, dashing, but irritable and pathetic, was the first to come.
Disappointed in his hope that Napoleon would liberate Italy from
the Austrians, he had fled to England in 1816 after service in the
French armies. He arrived in St John's Wood about 1822, after
several moves, and settled in the Alpha Road neighbourhood. Like
so many artists and literary men of the time, he was constantly in
debt and under threat of imprisonment. Digamma Cottage, his elegant bungalow beside the Regent's Canal, represented the apogee of
fashionable comfort achieved by the fiery little red-haired exile.
Entirely built, furnished, and sustained on credit, it housed him for
the short two or three years that he and his friends were able to
stave off his creditors. His reputation as poet and patriot had preceded his arrival in England, and he was given the entrée
immediately to influential circles of the Whig nobility. But his displays of temperament made him personally unwelcome to many,
and his inability to organise his life counterbalanced the effect of his
generous and powerful personality. Macready the actor, and Haydon with his very similar temperament, were among the number of
noted artists and writers of the day who were friendly with him.
Digamma Cottage, with its statuary, fine carpets and furnishings,
became a haunt of literary circles. Here Foscolo, with a domestic staff
of three attractive young women, wrote and entertained, and provided hospitality for other Italian exiles, including Panizzi, later to
be the most eminent of the British Museum's nineteenth-century
librarians. Here, too, he employed a succession of secretaries to
translate for him, one of whom, Cyrus Redding, was later a well-
known journalist. Staff troubles – an ex-secretary seduced one of his
'Three Graces' – led to a duel on Primrose Hill in which the dis-
dainful Italian stood rigidly to attention to receive his antagonist's
shot. When it had missed, he fired his own pistol into the air, and
stalked off the field.

An interesting impression of the neighbourhood at this period, and of the local shopkeepers' idea of Foscolo emerges from an article in a periodical called *The New Monthly Magazine*. The writer records that, strolling near Regent's Park, he lost himself in a wilderness of cottages and villas, amongst which he came on Foscolo's bungalow:

There was a brass plate on the door, with the inscription *Digamma Cottage*... While the **F** placed above it, though comprehensible to the learned, serves only to announce to the common eye, through its resemblance to one of the characters of our alphabet, the name of the celebrated owner. This information I obtained from a butcher's boy, who was passing and who assured me that the 'F' stood for Foscolo, the great Italian poet, and that the Digamma was the Latin for 'Die Game'; which proved, what all the world said, that he was a true patriot into the bargain.

Foscolo died in 1827 at the comparatively early age of forty-nine. In 1871, after the success of the Risorgimento and the setting up of the modern Italian State, his remains were removed to the church of Santa Croce, Florence, and buried beside those of such leading Italians as Michelangelo, Galileo, Machiavelli and Alfieri. Four years after Foscolo's death, two other eminent exiles arrived in London – ex-Queen Hortense of Holland and her son, Prince Louis Napoleon, later, the Emperor Napoleon III. Queen Hortense settled in Holles Street, Cavendish Square, and after her death in the year of Queen Victoria's accession, Prince Louis, who had failed in his first attempt to establish himself as the ruler of France, returned to London. This was his first return. After his next return, following his abortive second attempt on the throne of France and five years' imprisonment in the fortress of Ham, he frequented St John's Wood, and more particularly a house in Circus Road. He was often there in 1847, visiting the beautiful Miss Elizabeth Haryett, or Howard, a protégée of Lady Blessington. Her home, Rockingham House, was at the corner of Circus Road and Elm Tree Road – or rather perhaps the home of a major in the 2nd Life Guards whose mistress she was, and whom she abandoned for the Prince. This fashionable courtesan, the daughter of a bootmaker, who had run away from home, gone on the stage, and then run through a succession of rather raffish male protectors of aristocratic background, had achieved a position on the fringes of society by a combination of

superb good looks and outstanding intelligence. Influential admirers
such as the Duke of Beaufort not only took her up, but made her
very large gifts in money. Prince Louis on becoming her reigning
protector benefited by her wealth at a time when he was glad
enough to be financed. Indeed, she is known not only to have supported him, but advanced him large sums of money.

His coup d'état and emergence as the Emperor Napoleon III
must have unduly raised her hopes for herself as his *maitresse en
titre*. When he married Eugénie de Montijo, a Spanish countess, in
1853, the ambitious Miss Howard was, to put it mildly, more than
a little upset. It took the threat of banishment to America, the title
of Comtesse de Beauregard and the estate which went with it, plus
the payment of between £300,000 and £400,000, to keep her away
from Paris and embarrassing appearances at court. She was advised
to travel, did so, and married a young Englishman named Trelawny
whom she met in Florence. They were divorced after eleven years,
in 1865, and she died the same year. But not before she had
reappeared in Paris during the seasons of 1864 and 1865 'driving a
superb pair of bays and manoeuvring in such fashion as to meet
their majesties' equipage as often as possible and stare at them.'

Napoleon III was in the honeymoon years at the outset of his
imperial venture when in 1855 Wagner, living abroad because he
had become embroiled in revolutionary activities in 1849, paid the
first of his visits to London. He stayed, as he did on subsequent
trips, with his friend Ferdinand Praeger at 22 Portland Terrace –
now Wellington Road – St John's Wood. The house was demolished in 1905, so that it is impossible to pay Wagner the tribute of
a blue commemorative plaque, as has been recently done for Berlioz
in Queen Anne Street. Much of the scoring of *The Valkyries* was
done in Praeger's house, and Wagner became a familiar figure in
St John's Wood High Street. The two were also frequently to be
seen in Regent's Park. Montgomery Eyre's tale that they spent their
time there feeding French rolls to the swans and ducks at the Hanover Gate end of the lake is entirely credible. One need not even
wonder whether when 'one swan in particular attracted the great
composer's attention', it really caused him to shout: 'There is a
swan fit to draw the chariot of Lohengrin!' Nothing would be
more in character. After all, it seems certain that he regarded the
whole of animal creation as merely a property bestiary from which
he could select specimens for his Teutonic mythology. In *The*

*Valkyries*, which he was working on at the time, a couple of property rams used to be brought into service to draw Fricka's chariot. In *The Twilight of the Gods*, a swan is actually shot, and in *Siegfried* a bear appears. Had Wagner troubled to walk a few hundred yards beyond Regent's Park lake to the Zoo, who knows if the chimpanzees or a gorilla might not have made their way into *The Ring*?

In 1849, when Wagner had temporarily bowed himself off the German scene, Louis Kossuth, the Hungarian revolutionary leader, fled to Turkey. A couple of years later he came to England, and for most of the rest of the 1850s he remained here. Attracted like Louis Napoleon before him, and Wagner after him, to St John's Wood, he settled at 21 Alpha Road.

Perhaps the earliest of the colony of writers and journalists to take an interest in St John's Wood was Cyrus Redding. As far back as 1808, i.e. six years before the building of St John's Wood Chapel, he is found writing to his friend Matthew Tearle on the merits of the place as a rustic retreat: 'Beautiful fields – green lanes, clear air – the very place for lovers of quiet and the lovers of Nature – why don't you build a villa in the heart of St John's Wood?' Redding was a very well known journalist in his day, and his writings have furnished a lot of information about literary and other circles in the first half of the nineteenth century. Thomas Hood, poet, humorist and journalist, was among the first of the better known literary figures to be associated with the neighbourhood. He was already broken in health when he arrived in 1842, and he survived only three years in the green surroundings he found so refreshing. Settling first in lodgings at 17 Elm Tree Road, and then in a house in the Finchley Road – he called it Devonshire Lodge and described it as 'just beyond the Eyre Arms, three doors short of the turnpike' – he produced, among much else pumped out to keep the family going, *The Song of the Shirt* and *The Bridge of Sighs*. A couple of farewell performances, these, with which he is almost solely identified in the public mind of a century-and-a-quarter later. Like Dickens and others of his friends, he was sickened by the black misery of nineteenth century industrial slums – even to proving that the prostitute and the sweated seamstress could wring music out of a man half dead himself. There is no denying of course that this was the kind of thing – as he probably knew – that his guilt-ridden public wanted. Manifestos like these, whatever their motivation, made their mark in the public consciousness and contributed their tittle to the slow erosion of the crasser exploitations.

Hood's humorous verse, which kept him afloat during his stressful career – cut short at forty-five – has dated. But some of his private humour, as expressed in his letters, remains alive and delightful. He was not only an impenitent punster, but bubbling over with the perpetual natural effervescence of a Lear or a Lewis Carroll. A letter from Elm Tree Road to a little girl tells her: 'I promised you a letter, and here it is. I was sure to remember it, for you are as hard to forget as you are soft to roll down a hill with. What fun it was! only so prickly I thought I had a porcupine in one pocket and a hedgehog in the other. The next time, before we kiss the earth, we will have its face well shaved.' That was in 1842. Later that year he had a visit in Elm Tree Road from Dickens, then established at 1 Devonshire Terrace, where urban Marylebone debouched on Regent's Park. With him came his 'pair of petticoats', Mrs Dickens and her sister, his beloved Georgina Hogarth. Maclise, the painter, who also accompanied him, had recently sketched the three of them in profile standing together – a dashing, beardless, youthful Dickens and two slim young women. It was an accolade of youth – and blooming, successful youth – for the ailing Hood. Dickens was to come again, bringing Longfellow with him. Hood was popular with his fellow literary men, and when he collapsed under the strain of producing his one-man periodical, *Hood's Own*, Dickens, Browning, Landor, and others rallied round him and got out a whole number on his behalf.

One of his writer neighbours, and a good friend, was Douglas Jerrold, who lived in Circus Road. Humorist, playwright, wit, and the backbone of *Punch* for many years, he had leapt into distinction at an early age when working as a compositor for the *Sunday Monitor*. He had been to see *Der Freischütz*, Weber's opera, with its catchy German folk tunes and ghostly terrors in the romantic Faustian style, written a critique on it on the inspiration of the moment, and dropped it into his employer's letter-box. Next morning he had had his own copy handed to him to set up, with an editorial note to the anonymous correspondent asking for more of the same kind of thing. Before long, he was dramatic critic of the paper and launched on a career of intensive play-writing. Like Maclise, Jerrold belonged to the circle of Dickens's close friends, and he is one of the group, including Carlyle, shown in that artist's sketch of 1844 as listening raptly to a first reading of *The Chimes* by a be-haloed Dickens. He had a very handsome face, with the fine eyes and something of the clear-cut perfection of feature of the matinée idol, and a great mane of hair in the Henry Irving style. With these tremendous advantages, however, he combined a tiny and curiously truncated body.

An early inhabitant of St John's Wood of a rather later vintage than the Hoods and the Jerroldses was the great T. H. Huxley, biologist and father of modern agnosticism – and grandfather of Julian and Aldous. He arrived there in 1850, and spent forty years – almost all the rest of his life – there. The first out of at least five different houses he lived in in the district was 41 North Bank – his brother George's home – one of the pleasant canal-side villas, south of St John's Wood Road, which were swept away when the extensive approaches to Marylebone Station were built. Douglas Jerrold was still alive when Huxley came to the neighbourhood, but the two greatest personalities in the world of writing and writers to be associated with 'The Wood' – George Eliot and Herbert Spencer – had not yet settled there. Huxley, a young man of twenty-five with a medical training, was just back from a four-year cruise as assistant surgeon aboard *H.M.S. Rattlesnake*, which had been surveying the waters between the Great Barrier Reef and the Australian coast. He had seized the opportunity with that sense of the crucial moment which seems to be a built-in component of the really distinguished mind. His papers on the marine animals he fished up in those then remote waters hooked the Royal and Linnaean Societies so firmly that he was made an F.R.S. at twenty-six. He was on the up-and-up when he arrived in the neighbourhood, and he became a celebrated man before many years had passed.

After a number of moves, Huxley built himself a house in Marlborough Place, and it is this site, No. 4 – now a cottage hospital – which bears the blue plaque commemorating him. Here he spread himself. As his son and biographer, Leonard, wrote, it was 'built for comfort, not beauty', and designed 'to give each member of the family room to get away by himself or herself if so disposed'. The Huxleys were a hospitable family, and their many friends had an open invitation to drop in at their Sunday evening parties. High tea – and no doubt much high thought when George Eliot, G. H. Lewes, and Herbert Spencer were of the party – was dispensed at 6.30. Music frequently followed, since the Huxley daughters sang, and most Victorian families were accustomed to provide their own entertainment. Poetry recitals – another popular form of indoor sport in those days, at which the highest score could only be obtained by collaring Tennyson for the job – were not allowed to infiltrate No. 4 Marlborough Place. No doubt, they would have interfered with the splendid verbal drives of T. H. himself, the all-over-the-court agility and tremendous smashes of G. H. Lewes, or the sly-curling shots of Herbert Spencer lobbed from his favourite arm-chair. However, the Huxleys had on one occasion apparently sufficiently relaxed their guard for Sir Henry Irving, then recently launched in his actor-managership at the Lyceum Theatre, to break into recitation of *The Dream of Eugene Aram* 'with great effect'.

Marlborough Place is on the central plateau of St John's Wood, which slopes fairly steeply away to Maida Vale on the west, and more gradually to the Finchley Road on the east. It was certainly a very pleasant spot when the Huxleys moved there about a hundred years ago. So too was North Bank, close to the Regent's Canal, where a few years earlier George Eliot and G. H. Lewes had settled themselves at No. 21 – 'The Priory'. This was a lower-lying part of 'The Wood', but attractively situated, with its gardens running down to the green slopes of the pre-industrial canal. The Alpha Road estate, of which it was the northern section, was pleasantly close to Regent's Park, and had easy access to it by way of Kent Passage.

In that ardently non-permissive age, the George Eliot–G. H. Lewes ménage was of course regarded as scandalous in the extreme. A clandestine mistress, or a string of them, was perfectly acceptable. But an open union between an undivorced married man and a highly respectable woman was an affront to the conformist herd. As a visiting American intellectual, Charles Eliot Norton, wrote in 1869: 'She is not received in general society.' He added that the women who visited her were either 'émancipée' or had 'no social position'. The situation was embarrassing, but judging by the hosts of famous persons who made their way to 'The Priory', she hardly suffered from social isolation; in fact the moral quarantine to which she was subjected probably only served to insulate her from boring society nonentities.

She may or may not have had a face like a horse. To some her disproportionately large features were a stumbling-block coming between them and their ideal of the complete Victorian authoress.

Charles Eliot Norton clearly disliked her. Her talk, he found lacking in brilliance, her manner too intense, and he accused her of 'bringing her face too close to yours', and 'speaking in low, eager tones'. Norton was determined to like nothing about her. Even her house, dismissed as 'a little, square two-storey dwelling standing in a half-garden', was frowned upon for being 'within one of those high brick walls of which one grows so impatient in England'. To another American visitor, John Fiske, who visited 'The Priory' in 1873, she was 'simple, frank, cordial and matronly', yet could state an argument as cogently as any man. He records that Herbert Spencer – who had been her friend for twenty years at the time, and had first introduced her to Lewes –thought her 'the greatest woman that has ever lived on the earth'. Lewes himself seems to have been a very odd person – odd in dress, odd in manner, and capable of arousing the strongest dislikes. Massively hairy even for a society which cultivated much facial hair, he had a Gallic *empressement* which made Norton condemn him as failing in social tact and taste, although reluctantly admitting that he was 'very vivacious, very entertaining'. Mrs Gaskell, the novelist, thought him repulsively familiar, Frederick Locker-Lampson, elegant versifier, spread the rumour that 'he was literary among men of science and scientific among literary men.'

He was certainly a man of extraordinary versatility in an era when the sacred cow, specialisation, had not yet been heard of. Basically a man of letters and a journalist, he had all the scientific disciplines at his finger-tips (some hinted that they got no farther than there). He had founded and edited *The Fortnightly Review*, so advanced in its liberalism, and written a life of Goethe that became a classic. But these were merely the peaks in an extraordinary range of interests. A contemporary wrote of him that he 'began life as a journalist, a critic, a novelist, a dramatist, a biographer, and an essayist; he closed it as a mathematician, a physicist, a chemist, a biologist, a psychologist, and the author of a system of abstract general philosophy.' He was in fact the kind of man who in our day would be replaced by a dozen faceless specialists all judging life in terms of one restricted discipline.

Montgomery Eyre gives this picture of life at 'The Priory':

George Eliot's plan of life at North Bank was to devote the morning, usually from 9 a.m. to one o'clock, rarely longer, to writing; to spend the afternoon driving or walking in Regent's Park with Lewes, she with a certain weird sibylline air, he not unlike some unkempt Polish refugee of vivacious manners, swinging their arms as they hurried along at a pace as rapid and eager as their talk. The evenings were usually spent at home, reading or playing. Occasionally they would visit a theatre in the evening, and sometimes in the afternoon attend a concert or an art exhibition, or visit the Zoological Gardens.

If George Eliot impinged on the consciousness of the local shop-keepers solely as the large-faced lady who paid weekly visits to the post office-cum-grocer's shop in Church Street, off the Edgware Road, Herbert Spencer was equally well known as the oddly dressed old gentleman who lived, with the two sisters who were his house-keepers, at 64 Avenue Road. Here is the account of the début of this establishment, as described by one of them:

At last, on the 23rd of September 1889, at twenty minutes to five in the afternoon, he drove rapidly to the door in his carriage – a shabby little victoria – and, stepping quickly out, slowly ascended the steps, leaving the innumerable rugs, cloaks, etc., he had brought with him to follow. He shook hands cordially, and then entering the dining-room, sank in silence into an arm-chair. The silence lasted several seconds, after which he informed us that he had been feeling his pulse! Luckily it had been beating regularly, and conversation, to use the hackneyed phrase, 'became general'.

Spencer, a man of sixty-nine, was not only a valetudinarian, but a crotchety old bachelor in his habits. His life was organised down to the minutest detail – his own methods of bed-making had to be strictly adhered to – and he had a system of his own for indicating whether he was incommunicado or not. The sisters learned to understand that the ostentatious wearing of ear-pads was tanta-mount to a declaration that he required absolute silence and solitude. He, on the other hand, learned that their cooking was not to be despised, and that he might safely abandon his original intention of lunching each day at the Athenaeum in favour of a succulent repast in his own home. He had intended to be a bed-and-breakfast man. A succession of dreary lodgings had bred in him a distrust of the cooking landlady. As an evolutionary philosopher – indeed, *the* evolutionary philosopher of the Victorian age – he was to learn that graduation from a landlady to a brace of housekeepers was, in the sphere of alimentation, like his definition of evolution 'a change from an indefinite, incoherent homogeneity, to a definite, coherent heterogeneity'.

St. John's Wood has been written of by novelists as the semi-rural retreat where men of rank or wealth kept their mistresses in the not-so-distant past. Victorian and Edwardian writers have tended to sentimentalise about the place, stressing the idyllic seclusion, rhapsodising about 'Phryne at her ivied lattice-window', or informing us that 'the thrush and blackbird (and some say even the nightingale) still carol from lawn and bushes', and handing out similar codswallop – as the present down-to-earth generation would label it. This is no more than to say that there has always been a hint of Shangri-la about 'The Wood' – from the days when the original crop of villas was visualised as an elegant extension of 'Prinny's' paradisal park. In the 'Grove of the Evangelist' the rakish and the rural were always dashingly intertwined, and the *monde* and the *demi-monde* encouraged to mingle in a perpetual *fête galante* in the ample gardens of the Eyre Arms, or some other appropriate spot.

This splendid image, so assiduously built up by our forefathers – and now so firmly erased – was reflected in the large number of variations on the villa theme, and the extreme oddity of some of them. There were of course two basic types, both deriving from Nash's *cottage orné*. In one of these, a rectangular white-stuccoed box was soberly capped by an attractive, shallow-pitched slate roof. Everything about the façade was symmetrical, from the half-visible windows in the basement to those with shutters on the first and second floors. If the porch had a hood, it was ogee-shaped; if there was a balcony, it was one of those with elegantly curved roofs, and you had the feeling everywhere that suburban comfort was still the creature of the classical disciplines. The other type, straining in the opposite direction, reflected nineteenth century romanticism. Its prototype was the Elizabethan mansion and, less frequently, the medieval castle. It was all cosy irregularity – high narrow gables, dripstone mouldings over mullioned windows, oriels, weird little dormers, projecting porches; or sprouting towers, turrets and miniature battlements.

Both these basic types of dwelling, the classical-reminiscent and the Gothic Revival, though varying considerably in size, avoided undue height. Not so some of the mid- and late-Victorian villas. Built of a whitish brick that soon turned grey, they sprouted up, monstrous in size and bulk and vaguely Italianate in style. Such buildings – Carlton Hill still contains some good specimens – were the precursors of the *fin de siècle* period in 'The Wood', when every kind of architectural 'weirdie' was acceptable. If Loudon Road – until recent development totally altered the scene – was the principal show-case of the gabled and mullioned villa, the classically-restrained box type was seen in most abundance in such parts as Hamilton Terrace and Acacia Road. Walled gardens were a *sine qua non* for all residences of any pretensions. No 'Woodman' with proper patrician longings could be without one. Hence the reference in the preface to Montgomery Eyre to 'a thousand and one gardens, a thousand and one miniature groves of almond and lilac half-hidden behind ivied walls'. 'Here in St. John's Wood', it is added, 'a brave last stand is being made against the Philistines.' That was 1913. Today the Philistines, in the shape of 'the modern tenement house', i.e. the block of flats, are well within the gates, and most of the villas are already gone.

# 8. *Artists and Writers*

URBAN Marylebone, as we have seen, was the creation of the eighteenth century. Its first literary and artistic circles were formed of men whose minds had been moulded on the same principles as governed the building of its streets. Regularity, proportion, symmetry, balance, sobriety – these in general were the watchwords guiding writers like Johnson, Boswell, Gibbon, or artists like Romney, Joseph Nollekens, Sir William Chambers – to give only the outstanding names associated with, or having some connection with, Marylebone. With the nineteenth century and the Romantic reaction, the big names include Dickens, Trollope, and the Brownings in the field of letters, and Constable, Turner, Wilkie, among painters. These were great names indeed – perhaps the greatest ever associated with the district – but it was not they but their eighteenth century predecessors who made Marylebone the pre-eminent literary and artistic quarter of the metropolis for the best part of a hundred years.

The seed of Marylebone's urban development, sown in the 1720s with the building of the Cavendish Square neighbourhood, began to flower with real vigour in the later 1760s. The Seven Years' War, with the great colonial acquisitions it brought this country in India and America, had resulted in unprecedented prosperity. This highly profitable war had ended in 1763. The influx of wealth following it, and the rapidly expanding population of London, had given a great fillip to the development of the Harley-Portland estate, so conveniently situated north of Oxford Street. It was the beginning of the period about which such observant travellers as Von Archenholz could write: 'It is computed that forty-two thousand houses have been built in London between the years 1762 and 1779 . . . The sagacious North thought proper to lay a tax on brick; but . . . the rage for building only increased . . . There has been, within the space of twenty years, truly a migration from the east end of London to the west.' As Caleb Whitefoord, maker of couplets from lines lifted from adjacent newspaper columns, wrote:

Removed to Marylebone for the benefit of the air –
The City and Liberties of Westminster.

Although the sagacious Dr Samuel Johnson did not himself move to Marylebone in the 1760s, he had in fact lived there earlier, and had close friends living there. It had too been the scene of an important turning-point in his career as a scholar and writer. Johnson had arrived in London in 1737, a country schoolmaster from Staffordshire accompanied by his pupil, David Garrick – the master to seek his fortune from his pen and the future actor to study for the bar. Soon after this, Johnson brought his wife to town, and they took lodgings at 'Mrs Crow's, 6 Castle Street, near Cavendish Square'. Castle Street, like Cavendish Square itself, was still on the edge of the open countryside – the notorious Marylebone Fields where highwaymen and thieves abounded – and Marylebone proper was still a village. Marylebone Gardens, the northern Ranelagh, lay to the east of the village, and its firework displays and other amenities proved an attraction which Johnson, loving life in all its aspects, could not resist. This period in his career antedated his meeting with Boswell by nearly thirty years – Boswell was still unborn when Johnson came to London – and its details escaped the idolatrous magnifying glass of the supreme biographer. It was the time when the Great Cham of literature was still obscure, pensionless, and without his honorary doctorate – a time when his movements and his every word were not registered with the faithfulness of a tape-recording by the all-pervasive Scot who played pilot-fish to his whale.

Johnson worked, in this opening phase of his long climb to fame, as a journalist. *The Gentleman's Magazine*, a monthly founded by the printer Edward Cave, a cobbler's son, a few years earlier, was the first 'magazine' in England to be called such. It was, as the word implied, a store – a storehouse of articles reprinted from the journals and newspapers – in fact, the first *Reader's Digest*. Johnson helped transform this collection of reprints into a forum for original articles, biographies, and parliamentary reports – mostly written up by him from a few sketchy hints – and book reviews. Five years of this – by which time he had become the dominant force in the enterprise – and he was sufficiently known to be drawn in 1742 into the outstanding scholarly venture of the decade. This was the cataloguing of the splendid library of Edward Harley, second Earl of Oxford – Marylebone's ground landlord – who had died the previous year. Thomas Osborne, a bookseller, had bought this, i.e. Harley's books, for £13,000. (His manuscripts would have to wait until 1754 before they were bought for the nation.) This was a ridiculously low price for a fabulous library of some 40,000 volumes, many sumptuously bound, on a great variety of subjects. Osborne himself described it as 'a more valuable collection than perhaps was ever in the hands of any bookseller', and immediately sought the help of scholars in cataloguing and disposing of it. Johnson attended a meeting in the library building in Marylebone High Street, along with Martin Folkes, President of the Royal Society, and other *literati*, and he and William Oldys, who had been Lord Oxford's literary secretary, were retained for the job of publicising and cataloguing the collection. Later, they edited what came to be known as the *Harleian Miscellany* – reprints of selected rare pamphlets from the library.

This enterprise not only enormously increased the extent of Johnson's reading and his general knowledge, but it helped to make his reputation as a scholar and a writer. By the time Marylebone started to become a fashionable neighbourhood in the late 1760s, he had climbed to the heights. With a government pension of £300 a year – more than £3,000 a year nowadays – membership of 'The Club', that exclusive group of leading men of letters and the arts which included Burke, Reynolds, Goldsmith, Garrick and Fox, an unrivalled reputation as a wit and a polemicist, an assured position in society, and Boswell as his unpaid publicity agent, he frequently found himself back in Marylebone visiting friends who lived there. Allan Ramsay, the most distinguished of these, lived, as we have seen earlier, in Harley Street. Both Johnson and Boswell were welcome in the house of this gifted portrait painter, writer, and conversationalist. A formidable talker, he stimulated Johnson, who told Boswell: 'I love Ramsay. You will not find a man in whose conversation there is more instruction, more information, and more elegance, than in Ramsay's.' Johnson's extraordinary dominance, even among the outstanding men of his circle, is shown in the anecdote told of a party given by Ramsay at his Harley Street house for Sir Joshua Reynolds. Johnson was late in arriving, and they began to discuss him in his absence. Boswell stung Robertson the

historian into objecting when he announced that he worshipped
Johnson. Johnson, said Robertson – remembering perhaps that he
himself was a leading member of the Church of Scotland – was certainly a man of many outstanding gifts, but not a proper object of
worship. Anyhow, he was unfortunately a narrow-minded person in
many respects, and could not, for instance, bear the slightest
criticism of the Anglican Church. As he was finishing his sentence,
Johnson came into the room, and all, in Boswell's words, became
'as quiet as a school on the entrance of the headmaster'. What was
the secret of this remarkable power? Perhaps, underlying the
immense moral conviction, stinging force of invective and discon-
certing presence, the Doctor's tremendous physical strength was
sensed by all who came near him. They felt themselves to be within
the field of force of some strange potency which, disturbingly,
might manifest itself in any sphere, moral, intellectual, or physical.

'A Tom-Tit twittering on an Eagle's back' – a contemporary's
jeer at Boswell's relations with Johnson, seems a conclusion a good
deal less obvious two centuries later. Nowadays, in our post-
Freudian world we do not easily accord eagle status to even the
most venerated figures of their time – and a great deal more is now
known about James Boswell. The finding of the Boswell Papers,
and their editing and publication by a team of Yale University
scholars, have enormously added to our knowledge of this prodi-
gious biographer. If we know a whole lot more about his erotic pur-
suits, and his love of haunting the great, we are also much better
posted on the extraordinary industry, enterprise, and skill which
made him one of the outstanding journalists of his age. An
eighteenth century Malcolm Muggeridge and David Frost rolled
into one, his two greatest scoops were his interviews with Voltaire
and Rousseau, and his political achievement the bringing of Paoli,
the Corsican leader, to London. Among his many affairs – many
admittedly squalid – he included a period of delicious flirtation in
his early days with Belle de Zuylen, known as *Zélide*, the young
Dutch woman writer and *esprit fort* who was scandalising Nether-
lands society in the 1760s. But characteristically he shied off even
the idea of marriage with a beauty so cool and forthright, so contemptuous of the Establishment in all its aspects.

Paoli settled in Marylebone in 1769, in a house near the south end
of the Edgware Road. But Boswell, though often visiting friends
there, did not become a resident till 1790. There, however, he spent

Marylebone from Greenwood's Survey of 1827

the last five years of his life at his house at 122 Great Portland Street – three minutes' walk away from where Broadcasting House stands today, and whose microphones, had he lived in this age, he would certainly have been invited to use. By this time, the decent Scots body Margaret Montgomerie, the wife whom he'd finally settled down with, was dead, and one of his daughters was keeping house for him. Deprived of the moral and intellectual stimulus so long provided by Johnson, he had given way to his penchant for heavy drinking. It was to this period of his life that his detention in Marylebone watch-house (see Chapter 2) belonged. But though he had become a sozzler, he had by no means lost his capacity for pawky repartee. He is his own reporter, as usual, for the story that 'Lord Mountstuart said it was observed I was like Charles Fox. "I have been told so," said I. "You're much uglier," said James Stuart, with his dry drollery. I turned to him full as sly and as droll: "Does your wife think so?"' This rejoinder from so successful a womaniser as Boswell had been must have caused at least a momentary qualm. Boswell had joined Lord Mountstuart, son and heir of the Earl of Bute, as his travelling companion when they met in Italy on the Grand Tour as young men. James Stuart was Mountstuart's younger brother.

Had Boswell settled in Great Portland Street a decade earlier, he would have had as his neighbour, a few streets away, a writer whose reputation has remained as unfading as his own. James Boswell cared for Edward Gibbon as little as did Samuel Johnson; and Gibbon heartily disliked the pair of them. The fact that all three were members of *The Club* made matters no easier for them. The Doctor and his devoted publicist could not avoid the sight of the historian holding court among his admirers. Jowled, corpulent, suave, ironical, tapping his snuff-box as he rounded off some elegant period, the stylish splendour of his clothes and the Gallic *finesse* of his manner irritated the pontificating Johnson and his bumptious impresario as acutely as the detached scepticism of his works. Gibbon, for his part, dismissed Johnson as a bigot and a crabbed persecutor of all who failed to share his view; Boswell, as a journalist and not a scholar, hardly came into his purview.

Gibbon's house in Marylebone, in which he lived from 1773 to 1783, was at 7 Bentinck Street, 'the best house in the world', as he called it. He was thirty-five years old when he moved into this comfortable London mansion, and had been working for several years on his masterpiece. *The Decline and Fall of the Roman Empire* was to occupy him for another sixteen years, and to become 'an old and agreeable companion'. His father had recently died, and he himself, a bachelor, was now well enough off financially to employ a staff consisting of a housekeeper, a butler, a cook, and four maids. He also had a parrot, and a Pom called Bath, 'the delight of my life, pretty, impertinent, fantastical'. The rooms of this pleasant retreat were hung with a pale blue flock wall-paper with a gold border, and the decorations were by Adam. The book-cases in the library were white picked out with gold. The place filled him with the pride of ownership, and by August 1773 he was writing to his friend, J. B. Holroyd, inviting him to 'make Bentinck Street your inn. I fear I shall be gone; but Mrs Ford (his housekeeper) and the Parrot will be proud to receive you.' Phoebe Ford was Dr Johnson's cousin – no doubt her presence in Gibbon's household in this capacity was an acute irritant to the irascible Doctor.

In the year he left England to spend the rest of his life in Lausanne, Gibbon's portrait was painted by Romney, then at the height of his powers. Romney's fine house in Cavendish Square was only a few minutes' walk away from Gibbon's snug and elegant retreat in Bentinck Street. They knew one another socially through Hayley, the poet and writer, an acquaintance of Gibbon's who was Romney's most intimate friend. This was the period when 'the man in Cavendish Square' – as Reynolds called him so disdainfully – was devoting himself to innumerable portraits of Emma Hart, later Nelson's Lady Hamilton. Emma, then living in the Edgware Road as the mistress of the Hon. Charles Greville, had Romney so absolutely in her net that time stood still for him while he posed her for one subject after another till he had practically exhausted mythology. As *Cassandra, Euphrosyne, Diana, Ariadne, Iphigenia, Calypso, A Bacchante, A Pythian Priestess, Circe, Sensibility, Contemplation, Lady Macbeth,* and *Joan of Arc,* not to mention a bagful of other roles, she, 'The Divine Lady', utterly absorbed the whole being of his sensitive, vulnerable, withdrawn artist who had challenged and was beating Sir Joshua at the game of fashionable portrait-painting. Her progress through Romney's life was a triumph, just as it was to be later through that of that other genius, Nelson. Nevertheless, it was conducted discreetly enough to avoid trouble with Greville, her protector.

It has been estimated that Romney produced some 2,000 pictures, sketches, and drawings during the twenty-three years or so of his residence in Cavendish Square. This phenomenal rate of production was the result of very long hours of work at a quite extraordinary speed – in fact a speed quite clearly detrimental to the quality of his output. He was an obsessional worker, who cheerfully put in thirteen hours a day, which might include five or six sittings, and he made no exception of Sundays. His regular output was once more interrupted in 1791, when the 'Divine Lady' turned up again, after an absence of five years in Naples as the mistress of Sir William Hamilton, the British Ambassador. Sir William was famed for his interest in antiquities and volcanoes. When Emma had installed herself with him in 1786, a correspondent wrote that Sir William 'has lately got a piece of modernity which will fatigue and exhaust him more than all the volcanoes and antiquities in the Kingdom of Naples'. Notwithstanding this prediction, they had come home to get married, and Sir William allowed her to resume her sittings for the painter whose portraits had given her such immense publicity. It was, seemingly, halcyon days again for the shy painter, so lonely in his fame, and so apparently undemanding of the woman he adored. Not only did she sit to him, but she used No. 32 Cavendish Square as a stage for the display of herself to an admiring aristocracy. 'She performed in my house last week', wrote Romney with unmixed admiration, 'singing and acting before some of the nobility with most astonishing powers. She is the talk of the whole town, and really surpasses everything in both singing and acting that ever appeared. Gallini offered her two thousand pounds a year, and two benefits, if she would engage with him, on which Sir William said pleasantly that he had engaged her for life.'

Romney's house was on the south side of Cavendish Square. His studio was in his garden, which ran down in the direction of Oxford Street. From this vantage-point he could get an excellent view of that pitiful procession of meat carts which until 1783 passed so regularly along Oxford Street on its way from the Old Bailey carrying condemned prisoners to the Tyburn gallows. At the time Romney arrived in the square, the south side was still only partially built up, and the Tyburn processions could be seen by a number of the residents. One of these was the Earl of Harcourt, who had been George III's governor when he was Prince of Wales, and whose large mansion on the west side of the square – later Portland House – was defended by a very high wall. Next door to Harcourt's mansion, going southwards, was the town house of the Barrington family, of which Dr Shute Barrington was then the owner. A connoisseur of the arts, as Bishop of Salisbury, he was responsible for the fine lay-out surrounding the Cathedral, and for architectural improvements in Durham and elsewhere. It was this house which became Mr Asquith's in 1894, and is now the Cowdray Club.

Royalty, in the shape of Princess Amelia, an aunt of King George III, was housed at the Harley Street corner of the square when Romney settled there in 1775. This rather tough old character died in 1786. For years she had held a small court of her own there, at which Horace Walpole – her 'Prime Minister' – held the floor, 'dining with her thrice a week and regaling her with all the gossip of the day'. At the opposite, the north-east, corner of the square was the house of the Earl of Gainsborough, a pious nobleman accustomed to handing out tracts at the slightest provocation. The equestrian statue of the Duke of Cumberland, on his massive prancing charger – set up in the middle of the square, free of charge, by a Lieutenant-General Strode 'in gratitude for private kindness and in honour of public virtue' – must have been a perpetual reminder to Princess Amelia of the private habit of her remarkably unvirtuous and chronically impecunious brother, William Augustus, Duke of Cumberland, in coming round and trying to touch her for a few hundred pounds. Perhaps her gesture in having his statue re-gilded in 1783 was an attempt to appease his ghost with yet more gold!

A portrait bust of the Duke, as of other members of the royal family, was done by Joseph Nollekens, the most fashionable maker of these likenesses of his day. The sculptor's house and studio were in Mortimer Street, in the heart of that Berners Street quarter of Marylebone which was beginning to attract so many artists when he settled there in 1771. Sir William Chambers, the architect, was already living in Berners Street then, and Richard Wilson, the landscape artist, in Charlotte Street; also living in the quarter were Benjamin West, P.R.A.; John Bacon, the sculptor; Ozias Humphry, R.A., a close friend of Romney's; John Opie, R.A.; Henry Fuseli, R.A.; the architects, Joseph Bonomi and William Porden; Flaxman the sculptor; and James Barry, R.A.; John Varley and Peter de Wint, the water-colourists; Thomas Hardwick, the architect; John Constable himself, and many other celebrated artists were to settle there in his lifetime.

Nollekens, a tiny, bow-legged man with a large head and a beak of a nose, was at once a fine artist, a hard-headed business man, and a quite monstrous miser. He realised from very early on in his career that the making of busts was for a popular sculptor a means of coining money – particularly when the subjects were so celebrated that numerous replicas were called for. Nollekens charged 120 guineas a bust, and for such famous pieces as the heads of Pitt and Fox, he was able to sell a hundred casts of each. Such replicas went at six guineas each. For statues, of course, he received much more – £4,000 for the statue of Pitt, and correspondingly big sums for the other notabilities. Just as John Bacon was the best sculptor of his day for funerary monuments, and Thomas Banks the best for historical pieces, so Nollekens was unchallenged king of the *bustos*, as the eighteenth century – taking the artistic lead in all things from Rome – so long continued to call them. Smith, the historian of Marylebone, says that he died worth nearly £300,000. Whether his fortune reached this enormous sum for those times, or was merely £200,000, as stated by J. T. Smith, his pupil and biographer, it was amassed not only by great industry and the strictest attention to all possible devices for profit-making, but by the most fantastic parsimony. He started by faking antiques in Rome during his ten years' training there, and went on to smuggling (using the interiors of his casts as receptacles). By the time he returned to England in 1770, he was already worth £20,000, and 'the shrewdness which he had shown in selling damaged Venuses and Emperors in Rome he now applied to the marketing of his weeping Rachels and portrait busts in London.'

Nollekens' house was a corner one, standing at the intersection of the north side of Mortimer Street and the west side of Great Titchfield Street. His stonemason's yard at the back of the house had its entrance on Great Titchfield Street. Here he would sometimes stand on a fine summer's evening, enjoying the weather and ready for gossip with passing acquaintances. The extraordinary little man, ignorant to a degree, homely and familiar in speech and utterly devoid of pretentiousness, seems to have been able with a certain forthright joviality to get on with persons of all ranks from George III downwards. Certainly someone who could measure the royal nose with a pair of callipers, pricking it in the process, and then imitate the roaring of a lion a couple of inches from the king's ear, and get away with these clodhopping lapses unscathed, had a way with him – though 'Farmer George', it is said, enjoyed such deviations from the courtly norm. But Nollekens' lack of dignity, and his boorish, familiar ways, coming on top of his brazen parsimony, sometimes led to much less satisfactory encounters. One of these, described in *Nollekens and his Times*, J. T. Smith's classic, concerns the 'lady in the green calash' – a sort of mini-carriage. This elderly madam, who seems to have combined brothel-keeping in the sinister slum of St Giles's with the provision of nude models for the artists of the Berners Street area, swept into Nollekens' house in a towering rage, bawling: 'I am determined to expose you! I am, you little grub!'

'Kit!' cried Nollekens, 'call the yard-bitch'; adding with a clenched and extended fist, that 'if she kicked up any *bobbery* there, he would send Lloyd for Lefuse, the constable'. 'Ay, ay, honey', exclaimed the dame, 'that won't do. It's all mighty fine talking in your own shop. I'll tell his worship Collins, in another place, what a scurvy way you behaved to young Bet Belmanno yesterday! Why the girl is hardly able to move a limb today. To think of keeping a young creature eight hours in that room, without a thread upon her, or a morsel of any thing to eat or a drop to drink, and then to give her only two shillings to bring home! Neither Mr Fuseli nor Mr Tresham would have served me so. How do you think I can live and pay the income-tax? Never let me catch you or your dog beating our rounds again; if you do, I'll have you both skinned and hung up in Rats' Castle.'

Nollekens, cowed by this threat from someone in the criminal underworld quite capable of having him beaten up – not to mention cutting off his supply of models – paid up. Rats' Castle, it appears, was a ruined house used by rat-catchers and dog-snatchers. Stolen dogs unransomed by their owners were killed there and their skins cleaned, and presumably sold.

Among fellow artists who sometimes entertained Nollekens in their houses was a man who was almost at the extreme opposite pole in appearance and manner. Sir William Chambers, the architect, was a tall, distinguished-looking person who designed in the grand manner, and had not a little of the grand manner himself. He had a house in Berners Street, designed by himself, and a villa in Twickenham. After his retirement – still sticking to Marylebone – he lived in a small house in Norton, now Bolsover, Street. But at the outset of Nollekens' career and the height of his own in the 1770s, the rising young sculptor and the *doyen* of the architectural profession lived within a few minutes' walk of one another. An encounter between these two – the elegant-minded grandee, with his Swedish upbringing and his Gallic tastes and refinement, and the shambling, illiterate, blush-making 'Nolly' – must have been curious in the extreme. Sir William, a dominating character, was Treasurer of the Royal Academy, and commanded it even more thoroughly than that other larger-than-life figure, its President Sir Joshua Reynolds.

No doubt, many of the contacts between Chambers and Nollekens were really professional ones. The painters, sculptors, plasterers and other craftsmen who worked for, and with, the leading architects lived mostly in Marylebone, and could generally get in touch with them simply by walking down the street or round the corner. Chambers employed Nollekens to make keystones for Somerset House, and another sculptor neighbour at the top of his profession, John Bacon, to design the monument on its river front to George III and Neptune. Bacon lived in Newman Street, and Chambers encouraged him from the outset, buying his first and prize-winning relief in gesso, *Aeneas Fleeing from Troy*, and installing it over the mantelpiece at his Berners Street house. No. 53 Berners Street later became the headquarters of the Royal Society of Medicine, who have taken Bacon's plaque with them to their premises in Wimpole Street.

One of Chambers' closest friends, Joseph Wilton, the sculptor and a founder-member of the Royal Academy, had his workshops in Queen Anne Street – the part which is now Langham Street – and his house near by in Great Portland Street. He was the son of a plasterer who had made a considerable fortune out of a papier mâché factory in Edwards Street – now Langham Place. Here, with a staff of several hundreds of people, including a number of children, Wilton senior manufactured ornaments for chimneypieces and frames for looking-glasses. Wilton junior held the post of State-Coach Carver and Sculptor to George III. Like so many other leading English artists of the day, he had received his training in Italy, whence he had returned with Chambers and their mutual friend, Giovanni Cipriani, the designer and decorative artist – another founder-member of the Academy – in 1755. Wilton, like Chambers and Reynolds, had the inevitable villa to which to retire – in his case at Snaresbrook in Essex. He had also, thanks to his father's highly successful factory, an extremely ample supply of money. This he supplemented very considerably by supplying ornamental mantelpieces for most of the mansions designed by his friend Chambers, and by cornering the market in Carrara marble.

He lived on all this in a style of suitable splendour, entertained his intimates very liberally, and showed particular kindness and generosity to two other artists living in the neighbourhood – Richard Wilson and Joseph Baretti. Wilson's fame as a landscape painter of the first rank is of course now far greater than it was in his lifetime. Baretti, unknown nowadays, was an Italian critic and man of letters who had the friendship of Dr Johnson and other celebrities of his day. J. T. Smith, in *Nollekens and his Times*, describes Baretti as a sponger and a flatterer; Fanny Burney thought him 'savagely vindictive'. He must have had some virtues since Burke and Garrick, as well as Johnson, testified in his favour at his trial for murder – for stabbing a Haymarket bully. It was done in self-defence, and he was acquitted.

At the time he lived in Marylebone – first in Charlotte and then in Norton Street – both Wilson's circumstances and his appearance were very much at odds with the urbane atmosphere of those enchanting landscapes one now associates with his name. He was extremely poor – at times on his beam ends – and he was facially disfigured by an enlarged and very red nose. Whether his nasal affliction was due to his frequent visits to the Green Man, in the Euston Road – so conveniently near to his Norton (Bolsover) Street house – is probably now indeterminable. He was fond of playing skittles there, where he probably came across John Wilkes, then M.P. for Middlesex, and a strenuous vote-hunter among the well-to-do freeholders who patronised the place. J. T. Smith, writing of his own personal memories of Wilson, says that as a schoolboy he used sometimes to encounter him in the streets, and that 'his nose had then grown to such an enormous size that he held up his pocket-handkerchief to hide it.' The savage 'Peter Pindar' satirised him as 'Red-nosed Dick'. Illness and infirmity added themselves to his other afflictions in the latter part of his life. Of this time, Smith reports: 'I recollect that one morning when going to school, as I was about to cross Queen Anne Street, Mr Wilson was so unfirm that he called to me: "Little boy, let me lean upon your shoulder to cross the way." '

Fuseli, the little Swiss painter whose oddities became such a

source of anecdotes for his friends and fellow Academicians, was
also a Marylebone man. At the time of his appointment as Professor
of Painting he was living in Queen Anne Street East – in the
Foley Street part – not far from Broadcasting House. His home
for many years was at No. 37, and there he is commemorated
by a plaque. Fuseli's name remains well enough known in the
world of today. There was even a London exhibition of his works
in 1950. The strange, macabre quality of his output, the curious
distortion of his figure-drawing – particularly, his large, fleshy
women, with their elongated necks and tiny heads – have marked
him out as a subject for the Freudian investigator. The picture
which won him celebrity, and made an impact far beyond the
London art world, *The Nightmare*, exhibited in 1782 after he had
settled in England, is an odd compound of the satanic and the
erotic. The hideous horse's head with its glaring, blind eyeballs and
the flesh stripped to the musculature, the squatting horned Puck
or fawn, and the voluptuously collapsed young woman to whom
these incubi have appeared contain enough symbolism, one suspects,
to furnish students of the sub-conscious with treatise-fodder worthy
of a juicy Ph.D. thesis for some university.

Fuseli lives on today through his strange pictures. Not only are
they those of a Romantic before his time, but of a man who dared to
put his deeper fantasies on to canvas with a frankness we like to
think characterises our own age rather than his. But to his contemporaries he was also a very human figure, respected and admired for
his abilities, laughed at for the oddities of his Germanic accent,
feared for his sharp wit and frequent sarcasms. Haydon, one of his
pupils, has left a vivid picture of his first meeting with him as a
youth of eighteen in 1804:

> The maid came . . . I followed her into a gallery or showroom,
> enough to frighten anybody at twilight. Galvanised devils – mali-
> cious witches brewing their incantations (sic) – Satan bridging
> Chaos, and springing upwards like a pyramid of fire – Lady Mac-
> beth – Paolo and Francesca – Falstaff and Mrs Quickly – humour,
> pathos, terror, blood, and murder, met one at every look! I
> expected the floor to give way – I fancied Fuseli himself to be a
> giant. I heard his footsteps and saw a little bony hand slide round
> the edge of the door, followed by a little, white-headed, lion-
> faced man in an old flannel dressing gown, tied round his waist

with a piece of rope, and upon his head the bottom of Mrs Fuseli's work-basket . . . All apprehension vanished on his saying in the mildest and kindest way, 'Well, Mr Haydon, I have heard a great deal of you from Mr Hoare. Where are your drawings?'

Haydon has recorded that he 'adored Fuseli's inventive imagination'. As a man, he saw him as 'the most grotesque mixture of literature, art, scepticism, indelicacy, profanity, and kindness'. The charge of indelicacy, a failing more apparent to the nineteenth century than the eighteenth, marked the difference between their backgrounds and their age-groups. The shadow of the coming era of Victorian respectability was already upon Haydon. Fuseli liked to call a spade a spade, and was ready with hard-hitting repartee at any moment. A stranger pushing his way into his office at the Royal Academy – he was both Professor of Painting and Keeper – before the door-man could announce him, 'announced himself, hoping he did not intrude. "You do intrude," observed Fuseli – "Then, Sir, I will come to-morrow, if you please" – "No, Sir ," replied Fuseli, "I don't wish you to come tomorrow, for then you will intrude a second time; let me know your business now." '

Haydon too settled in Marylebone in 1817. His choice of Lisson Grove rather than the Berners Street area was probably due to the fact that, with the rapid growth of the district, artists were having to move farther out to get the light, fresh air, and quiet they were seeking. Certainly, he was overjoyed to get away from the noise and distractions of central London. At 22 Lisson Grove North – now 116 Lisson Grove – where he lodged with the sculptor, Charles Rossi, he had the advantage of facing open countryside and yet of being within easy reach of the amenities of urban Marylebone. One of these was the private art gallery, in Duchess Street, Portland Place, of Thomas Hope. Hope had bought his first picture, written appreciatively of his work – albeit anonymously – and presented him with £200 at a moment of great difficulty in his affairs. This wealthy pillar of the Greek Revival movement was not only an art collector, furniture designer and amateur architect, but through his writings an active moulder of public opinion on the arts. He had bought his Adam mansion in 1799 and gradually enlarged and remodelled it to suit his exquisite and costly tastes, furnishing the reception rooms in a variety of Neo-classic styles and adding a gallery to house his collection of Dutch and Flemish pictures. In furtherance of his role as an arbiter of public taste, he had opened his house as a museum, to which access was obtainable by ticket of admission.

Haydon, a visitor to the gallery, was one of the earliest enthusiasts for the Elgin Marbles. He played a considerable part in getting them acquired for the nation, and was by way of being something of a connoisseur himself. The need to refresh his mind after the crushing labours of his big historical paintings must have often sharpened his desire to surround himself with beautiful and luxurious *objets d'art*. Head over ears in debt, often half-starved, half-mad at times, yet with an innate grandeur of ambition buoying him up and staving off the predestined suicide, his gusto for gracious living had its moments. Staying with the third Lord Egremont, Turner's patron, amid the splendours of Petworth in 1826, he could write:

> Sketched and studied all day . . . I really never saw such a character as Lord Egremont. He has placed me in one of the most magnificent bedrooms I ever saw . . . The bed curtains are different coloured velvets let in on white satin. The walls, sofas, easy-chairs, carpets, green damask, and a beautiful view of the park out of the high windows . . . As I lay in my magnificent bed, and saw the old portraits trembling in a sort of twilight, I almost fancied I heard them breathe, and almost expected they would move out and shake my curtains. What a destiny is mine! One year in the Bench, the companion of gamblers and scoundrels – sleeping in wretchedness and dirt, on a flock bed, low and filthy, with black worms crawling over my hands – another reposing in down and velvet, in a splendid apartment, in a splendid house, the guest of rank and fashion and beauty! As I laid my head down on the pillow the first night, I was deeply affected, and could hardly sleep.

Haydon lived in Lisson Grove for five years, from 1817 to 1822. He was thirty-one when he went there, and there he spent some of the happiest days of his feverish, frustrated existence. There, one evening in the year of his arrival, he entertained Charles Lamb, Wordsworth, and Keats to dinner. Lamb, very drunk and highly whimsical, caused much merriment by unmercifully pulling the leg of an unfortunate 'Controller of Stamps', who had got himself invited to the party in order to meet Wordsworth. The next year another party of literary men and artists is recorded: 'Sir Walter

Scott, Lamb, Wilkie and Procter have been with me all the morning, and the most delightful morning we have had. Scott operated on us like champagne and whisky mixed . . . Scott is always cool and very amusing; Wordsworth often egotistical and overwhelming.'

Scott used to stay with the Lockharts, in Sussex Terrace, Regent's Park, when in London. Wilkie lived in Marylebone – probably in Bolsover Street at this time – and Procter (Barry Cornwall) later lived in Harley Street. In reading memoirs of the late Georgian, Regency and early Victorian eras one is constantly being reminded that London was no more than a large village, where most of the notabilities knew one another, and that almost all concerned with the arts and letters were sooner or later to gravitate to that highly desirable quarter 'New London' or Marylebone.

Haydon, hell-bent on pursuing what he called 'High Art', was ultimately destined to commit suicide. This obsession about the nature of art and his natural pugnacity, 'half-artist and half-romantic man of action' that he was, led him later in life into headlong collision with the embattled Academicians. He denounced the Academy as 'this nest of portrait painters' whose 'calumnies and perpetual attacks unseated Reynolds, impoverished West, destroyed Barry, crippled Fuseli, and for a time involved me'. Sir Martin Archer Shee, President of the Royal Academy, he dismissed with elaborate sarcasm as 'the most important painter in the solar system'. Shee, a Dubliner, had moved into Romney's house in Cavendish Square a few years before Haydon's arrival in London. Romney had sat to him before he moved out, and in Haydon's eye he was tarred with the brush of much fashionable and official image-making – an Establishment painter of the type whose guts he hated.

Before the final collapse came in 1846 – it was precipitated by the rejection of the cartoons he had prepared for the decoration of the new Houses of Parliament – he had been able to make the acquaintance of many of the leading men of the time. Such was the power of his personality that all who came into close personal contact with him were forced to believe in him. Keats lent him money, Wordsworth addressed a couple of sonnets to him, Lamb, Hazlitt and Leigh Hunt were among his friends and admirers. Sir Walter Scott admired and liked him and gave him money. The Duke of Wellington sat to him for his portrait, inviting him to stay with him at Walmer Castle for the purpose. Yet his sense of self-consequence

was colossal, and in the end he could not stomach a life which failed
to take him to the heights of his over-sized ambition. Of the brilliant
little verbal vignettes he left behind him of celebrated people he
met, two concern Mrs Siddons, whose fine house at Clarence Gate,
Regent's Park, was within walking distance of his Lisson Grove
hide-out. Haydon, having borrowed all the money he could raise,
had in 1820 hired the Great Room in the Egyptian Hall, Piccadilly –
characteristically, for a whole year. There he exhibited one of his
great canvases entitled *Christ's Entry into Jerusalem*:

> The Christ's head startled people. It was not the traditional
> head; not the type, not orthodox. Everybody seemed afraid, when
> in walked with all the dignity of her majestic presence, Mrs Sid-
> dons . . . The whole room remained silent, and allowed her to
> think. After a few minutes, Sir George Beaumont, who was
> extremely anxious [He had advanced Haydon £30!] said in a
> very delicate manner, 'How do you like the Christ?' Everybody
> listened for her reply. After a moment, in a deep, loud, tragic
> tone she said, 'It is completely successful.'

Mrs Siddons, having retired from the stage ten years or so earlier,
had taken up a commanding position in society. At her house by
Regent's Park, she entertained on a considerable scale. Most of the
fashionable notabilities were to be seen there, and as she had
queened it over the stage, so with her formidable presence and resounding tones, she queened it over London society for a couple of
decades. Her pronouncement on Haydon's Christ was decisive –
instant success followed. 'The Jerusalem', says Haydon, with
typical hyperbole, 'was considered . . . a national triumph.' So pal-
pable was the success, he adds, so decided that even the Academicians had to go and see it for themselves. Haydon was overcome
with gratitude, wrote ecstatically to Mrs Siddons, had a gracious
reply inviting him to her house, went, was 'most gloriously
received', and thereafter became a friend.

The second of his Siddons stories is about the evening in March
1821 when he went to her house to hear her give a reading from
*Macbeth*:

> It is extraordinary the awe this wonderful woman inspires.
> After her first reading the men retired to tea. While we were all
> eating toast and tinkling cups and saucers, she began again. It was
> like the effect of a mass bell at Madrid. All noise ceased; we slunk

to our seats like boors, two or three of the most distinguished men of the day, with the very toast in their mouths afraid to bite. It was curious to see Lawrence [Sir Thomas Lawrence, the portrait painter and President at the time of the Royal Academy] in this predicament, to hear him bite by degrees, and then stop for fear of making too much crackle, his eyes full of water from the constraint; and at the same time to hear Mrs Siddons' 'eye of newt and toe of frog!' and then to see Lawrence give a sly bite, and then look awed and pretend to be listening . . . I went away highly gratified, and as I stood on the landing-place to get cool, I overheard my own servant in the hall say, 'What! is that the old lady making such a noise?' 'Yes', was the answer, 'she tunes her pipes as well as ever she did.'

Mrs Siddons may have been 'this wonderful woman' to the grateful Haydon, but others, able to view her more dispassionately, judged her to be wonderful only in her acting, and distinctly off-putting as someone to meet in ordinary life. Fanny Burney, who first met her when she was a rising young actress of twenty-seven, thought her 'by no means engaging', and a few years later, at a longer meeting, found her stiff, formal and dry, with a 'deep and dragging' voice. Leigh Hunt, who was her neighbour for a year or two when he moved into the Baker Street district about the same time as she, i.e. in 1817, claims no personal knowledge of her in his *Autobiography*, but evidently saw her on the stage in her later days. 'She must always have been', he says, 'a somewhat masculine beauty; and she had no love in her, apart from other passions. She was a mistress, however, of queenly and of appalling tragic effect.' Her regular visitors at Clarence Gate included the irrepressible Sydney Smith, wittiest man in an age of wits; Samuel Rogers, the poet and sharp-tongued society gossip; Dr Johnson's Mrs Thrale, by this time Piozzi's widow; Hannah More, blue-stocking and philanthropist; Sir George Beaumont, art patron and landscape painter; and Lord Sidmouth, the Tory politician and one-time Prime Minister. The fact that Sydney Smith was among her 'regulars' suggests that the great Sarah cannot have been quite as unbending a stick as her critics made her out. Some of her contemporaries, men as well as women, thought him coarse; to her credit, Sarah, at her first meeting with him 'developed convulsions, and had to be helped from the table'.

The painter John Martin, who settled in the New Road (the Marylebone Road) in 1818, at Allsop's Buildings, near the Baker Street cross-roads took steps to make Mrs Siddons' acquaintance, and she was among the visitors to his studio in 1821. It was nearly forty years since she had sat to Reynolds and Gainsborough, but Martin in later life told his son that 'in spite of a very evident moustache, she still retained traces of her queen-like beauty'. Martin himself was a man of note. He has been described as 'the most spectacularly melodramatic history painter of the early nineteenth century'. He was known as 'Mad Martin', and in fact a brother of his did become mentally deranged, and in a fit of religious mania set fire to York Minster. But Martin's 'madness' probably consisted in his being one of those artists who, like Fuseli, were quick to feel the first stirrings of that wind of change that ushered in the era of Romanticism. After a preliminary period as an heraldic and enamel painter, he blossomed forth in 1812 with the first of his sixteen 'sublime' works, *Sadak in search of the waters of oblivion*. This was exhibited at the Royal Academy that year, and was followed by the others, all intended to display 'immeasurable spaces, innumerable multitudes, and gorgeous prodigies of architecture and landscape'. This they certainly did, and their titles, such as *Joshua commanding the Sun to stand still*, *Belshazzar's Feast*, *The Deluge*, *The Destruction of Herculaneum*, *The Great Day of His Wrath*, and so on, indicate their spectacular nature. The year after he settled in Marylebone, Martin produced yet another of these extraordinary canvases, *The Fall of Babylon*, in which tiny figures are set against a background of fantastic architecture, beneath immense skyscapes, wild, lurid and lowering.

Martin's house in the Marylebone Road was a substantial affair, with a large back garden, in which he built his first painting room. From this garden he had easy access to the then open country between Marylebone and Hampstead. All the houses in this first London bypass road were required by law to be set fifty feet back from the carriageway, and so had long front gardens as well. Regent's Park was in its first stages, still a medley of fields in process of being tamed and planted, and no buildings were yet evident anywhere in the park, except for a couple of villas and a section of Park Crescent. Baker Street and his own part of the Marylebone Road had been completed some twenty years before his arrival. The buildings were comparatively new, and so were the terrace houses on the site of what is now the west front of Baker Street Underground Station. Behind these houses was an area described on the maps of the period as 'Cow Yard' – presumably part of Allsop's Farm, on whose fields Upper Baker Street, as it was then called, was built. South of the Marylebone Road crossing was York Place, the section of Baker Street running south to Crawford Street – then called Durweston Street. Little more than a decade earlier, William Pitt the younger had lived for a while in York Place, his niece, Lady Hester Stanhope, looking after him there for the last three years of his life. At this time, the district had seemed to J. P. Malcolm, a contemporary historian, to be 'distinguished beyond all London for regularity, the breadth of the streets, and the respectability of the inhabitants, the majority of whom are titled persons, and those of the most antient families'.

The fact of Martin's complete sanity is further borne out, if further evidence is needed, by what a Royal Academy catalogue of 1951 has called his 'far-sighted plans for the development of London'. A spectacular example of these was his proposed triumphal arch to span the Marylebone Road. He sent drawings of these to the Academy in 1821. Their intention was to commemorate the victory of Waterloo, and the arch was to have been sited at the 'north end of Portland Place', i.e. on the axis of Park Crescent and Park Square. A biographer has called this project 'the first-fruits of Martin's passion to embellish London'. One may well wonder whether it was not the all-powerful Nash, at the height then of his own transformation of London, who put paid to Martin's scheme. A triumphal arch would have meant changing his plans for Park Crescent and Park Square.

Towards the end of 1838, Martin and his son, Leopold, paid a visit to Turner at his house in Queen Anne Street, near Cavendish Square. At this time, Ruskin's *Modern Painters* had not yet appeared to trumpet Turner's greatness to an undiscerning world. He was in his early sixties, and rather out of favour with a public which increasingly tended to demand pictures which 'told a story', and preferably a romantically sentimental one. Indeed, Martin's own spectacular canvases were reaching the period when critics would quite soberly compare them with the works of Turner. The visit to 23 Queen Anne Street – the site is now occupied by the Howard de Walden Estate Office, successors to the historic Portland estate – was recorded by Leopold Martin, who has told how Turner invited them to walk over to Chelsea with him and inspect his riverside hide-out in Cheyne Walk. With his passion for secrecy, he went there by the name of 'Mr Booth', and so eluded all inquisitive persons in search of a celebrity.

The Martins accepted Turner's invitation, and walked with him, via Hyde Park and Brompton, and by footpaths across market gardens, to the riverside at Chelsea. But Turner had been settled in Marylebone, at one address or another for nearly forty years, and had lived in Queen Anne Street for twenty-seven of these. No. 23 was to remain his official residence until the year before his death in 1851. Walter Thornbury, his first biographer, probably exaggerated the rather squalid impression given by these premises, both external and internal. But there seems no doubt that Turner, a bachelor, cared little about the surroundings he lived in, and that dust and dilapidation meant nothing to him. He had built himself his own picture gallery as early as 1804, when he was living at 64 Harley Street. This house was sited at the corner of Harley Street and Queen Anne Street, and when he moved in 1811 to 23 Queen Anne Street it was merely a matter of going to the first house round the corner. Here he built himself another gallery in the years 1819-21. It was top-lighted and of fine proportions – a noble room, one of his visitors called it. Since his earlier gallery had been seventy feet long by twenty wide, it is not unreasonable to assume that this was even larger. He had made a lot of money in the fifteen years since the building of the first, and become a leading R.A. and one of the outstanding figures of the world of art. He was well able to allow himself the one luxury which meant anything to him – a worthy setting for the display of his masterpieces.

Constable, like Turner and so many other artists of the period, had settled in the Marylebone district very soon after he came to London – first in Rathbone Place, and then after a brief interval at 63 and afterwards at 35 Charlotte Street, Fitzroy Square, just outside the borough. A letter of 1801 reports: 'I have got three rooms in a very comfortable house, No. 50 Rathbone Place. My large room has three windows in front. I shall make that my shop, having the light from the upper part of the middle window, and by that means I shall get my easel in a good situation.' Unlike Turner, Constable was not an artist to whom success came quickly or easily. He found great difficulty in earning a living, and not until 1814, when he was thirty-eight, did he sell a picture to any but his own personal friends. Turner was able to hit the taste of his time because in the earlier part of his career his pictures harked back to the tradition of Claude and Richard Wilson. There was too a certain dramatic element in his art which struck the popular imagination. He had started as a water-colourist in the eighteenth-century tradition of that art, and his name was already made as a skilled topographical artist before he started on his more ambitious easel pictures.

During Constable's first period in Charlotte Street, he lived almost opposite the house of Joseph Farington, perhaps the most influential Royal Academician of the day. Farington, a topographical artist with a very wide circle of acquaintances in the worlds of art and fashion, became Constable's friend and mentor. To him, he went not only for advice about his professional career, but for the kind of general wisdom to be got from a very experienced man of the world thirty years his senior. Farington's *Diaries*, covering a period from the early 1790s to his death in 1821, and not found until 1921, have proved a mine of information about the late Georgian and Regency eras. After Farington's death, the Constables, who had been living for five years in Keppel Street, Holborn, moved into his house, No. 35 Charlotte Street.

In 1824, C. R. Leslie, Constable's biographer and one of his closest friends, had been living in lodgings in Charlotte Street, with his sister Ann to keep house for him. Nearly twenty years younger than Constable, he was beginning at thirty to make a name for himself, and had just been asked to paint Sir Walter Scott's portrait. At the time of the following extract from Constable's journal, he had moved out to the premises in Lisson Grove vacated by Haydon:

> Dressed to go to Leslie's for dinner. He has got things quite comfortable, and it is a very fit house for an artist but sadly out of the way – but it is quite in the country. We had a nice dinner. Willes & Newton [fellow artists] were there. We had salmon – & roast beef – peach pie and pudding. After dinner we took a walk in the feilds [sic], and went to the new church at St John's Wood . . .

The following year, as we have seen (see Chapter 7), Leslie was to settle in St John's Wood, where Landseer had already preceded him.

The year 1821, when Constable's mentor Farington died, was also the year of Richard Cosway's death. A friend of the Prince Regent and leading miniaturist of his time, he was a fop and a fashionable

party-giver at his splendidly furnished house in Stratford Place, in
Marylebone's patrician quarter. He was a tiny little man, practising
a minuscule art, and dealing in pictures as a profitable sideline, a
teller of tall stories who firmly believed that Charles I had appeared
to him and held more than one conversation with him. Like so
many other personalities of the time, 'Tiny Cosmetic' as they
dubbed him was the target of 'Peter Pindar's' flailing sledgeham-
mer. Cosway's house in Stratford Place adjoined one of the lion-
surmounted gate piers at the entrance to the cul-de-sac. One day a
piece of paper appeared pinned to the front-door, with these lines on
it:

> When a man to a fair for a show brings a Lion,
> 'Tis usual a monkey the sign-post to tie on:
> But here the old custom reversed is seen,
> For the Lion's without – and the Monkey's within!

The tale that this piece of rudery made Cosway move himself off to
another house, some way away from the lion, is hard to believe. At
all events, the affront to his vanity seems in no way to have affected
his longevity, for he survived to be eighty-one and died in a friend's
coach bowling along the Edgware Road.

'Peter Pindar' – otherwise Dr John Wolcot – came to London in
1780 from medical practice in Truro, bringing with him young
Opie, the painter known as the 'Cornish Wonder', and launching
him on his brilliant career in London. Wolcot's house was in Chapel
Street, Portland Place, within striking distance – the phrase is
peculiarly appropriate in his case – of the community of artists,
many of whom were to become the objects of his satire on the Royal
Academicians. Only known today through chunks of his rather in-
different satirical verse, Wolcot was really a man of considerable
mark. A passionate admirer of Richard Wilson, he had sufficient
artistic knowledge to be able to give Opie his early grounding, and
as a publicist and impresario he had the drive and charm, and the
wide circle of friends, needed to launch the young man on his
immensely successful course. Far more important than this, it is
likely that through Opie's lectures, he helped to influence Constable himself. He was the pioneer in England of the view that the
artist should go to nature and eschew the prevalent practice of copy-
ing old masters. His passionately urged instruction to Opie was:
'Look to originals, stare folks in the face, canvas 'em from top to toe!'

Opie, who made his home in Berners Street, died in 1807 at forty-six. His old mentor lived on till 1819, surviving like Cosway until he was eighty-one. Mrs Opie, a novelist and a woman of distinction, enjoyed the friendship of Sydney Smith, who had taken a house in Orchard Street, Portman Square, in 1806. Here the genial wit and most unparsonic parson, who was beginning to earn considerable sums from his extremely popular lectures on moral philosophy at the Royal Institution, indulged in the hospitality he loved. Dinners for two dozen were a regular weekly event. People of all sorts were invited, but the keynote of the affairs was simplicity – his maxim 'Avoid shame, but do not seek glory – nothing so expensive as glory.' Nearly twenty years later, he was to return briefly to Marylebone, taking a house in Stratford Place for a short period in order to enable his elder daughter to be married from there. Later, as Lady Holland, she told how a pompous little man visited him there one morning, saying he was compiling a history of distinguished Somer-setshire families, and had called to ascertain what the Smith arms were. This produced the typical rejoinder: 'I regret not to be able to contribute to so valuable a work; but the Smiths never had any arms, and invariably sealed their letters with their thumbs.'

If Haydon's career was a series of frustrations, there was born in his heyday, in 1817, a painter still little known today whose tragic life had its repercussions on those of Dickens and of W. P. Frith. Richard Dadd came to London, and, as an art student, shared 'digs' with Frith and Augustus Egg, a painter friend of Dickens', in Charlotte Street. Frith remembered him in after days as an extremely gentle and engaging personality. But when he was about twenty-three he went on a trip to the East, got sunstroke in Egypt and thereafter seems to have become quietly unhinged. Nobody sus-pected anything, so quiet was his manner, and on his return his father took him down to the country for a holiday. They arrived in the afternoon at an inn in Cobham, had supper together, and then went out for a walk. Neither of them returned, and the next mor-ning the father's body was found with stab wounds in it in Cobham Wood. A hue and cry was set up, and a few days later Richard Dadd was caught and arrested in France, near Fontainebleau. He was tried, found insane, and spent the rest of his life, first in Bedlam and then in Broadmoor.

This tragic affair put behind bars a man of consummate artistic ability. Though his gifts were only imperfectly exercised in the long

dreariness and squalor of asylum life – he lived for over forty years
in captivity, dying in 1887 – enough of his pictures and drawings
have survived to show his remarkable imaginative power and great
technical capacity. His best, and perhaps best-known, oil painting is
*The Fairy-Teller's Master Stroke*, a fantastic microcosm of strange
little human figures seen amongst the blades of corn in a field – of
unknown significance, but absorbingly indicative of the problems of
the disturbed mind. His drawings are said by good judges to be
exquisite in their perfection. But great as his gifts were, and
fascinating his pictures, almost equally interesting is the form his
madness took, and the effect it had upon the imagination of a much
more extraordinary man – Charles Dickens. There were macabre
elements in Dadd's mental derangement which probably seized upon
the weird and darkly brooding side of Dickens' own imagination –
the side which made him so frequently pace nightlong the more
dreadful streets of Victorian London and gaze with fascination
upon the black, stinking waters of the Thames. The journalist and
novelist, Edmund Yates, a protégé of Dickens's, tells on the
authority of Frith how Dadd came to be arrested in France:

> He had been travelling in a coach, and his homicidal tendencies
> had been aroused by regarding the large neck disclosed by a very
> low collar, of a fellow-passenger, who waking from a sleep, found
> Dadd's fingers playing round his throat.

Yates continues, switching to the situation after Dadd had been
brought back to England:

> On searching Dadd's studio, after his arrest, they found painted
> on the wall behind a screen portraits of Egg, Stone and Frith,
> Dadd's intimate associates, *all with their throats cut* – a pleasant
> suggestion of their friend's intentions.

It is clear that the obsessive idea of a killing 'far from any good
town', as the old ballad has it, seized upon Dickens's imagination
with compulsive power, and that he was haunted by the idea of
Richard Dadd, and his savage murder of his father in the lonely
recesses of Cobham Wood. But Cobham Wood was not far from
Dickens's home at Gadshill, and, with his intense desire to drama-
tise everything that lived long and vividly in his imagination, he
would take friends to the scene of the crime and re-enact it with
every variety of circumstantial detail. Dadd committed his murder

when Dickens was only thirty-two, and in the year when he had begun to write *Martin Chuzzlewit*. Significantly, Jonas Chuzzlewit first murders his father, and then kills his accomplice, the swindler Montague Tigg, in a lonely wood. Murder most foul in some darksome spot, preferably after a long and feverish chase, was part of the melodramatic furniture of Dickens's most complicated mind.

In 1839, when Dickens and his family moved into No. 1 Devonshire Terrace, Marylebone, which was to be his home for the next eleven years, he was only twenty-seven. Yet he was already celebrated, with *Pickwick*, *Oliver Twist*, and *Nicholas Nickleby* to his credit. Even so, the move to so large a house in so smart a neighbourhood must have made him wonder whether he would be able to sustain his role of well-to-do householder. A letter preceding the move says: 'A house of great promise (and great premium), "undeniable" situation and excessive splendour, is in view. Mitton is in treaty, and I am in ecstatic restlessness.' Forster, his friend and first biographer, described 1 Devonshire Terrace as 'a handsome house with a garden of considerable size, shut out from the New Road [Marylebone Road] by a high brick wall facing the York-gate into Regent's Park.' A sketch of the house done by his friend Maclise shows a large stuccoed building, a first floor with tall windows and attics immediately above, and two large bow fronts at the side. One of the bows is topped by a balcony covered with an iron safety grill, suggesting that the nursery of the numerous children born to him there must have opened on to it. The still largely rural nature of the Marylebone Road in those days is emphasised by the long brick wall with creepers hanging over it, and by the garden trees.

In this ample residence, young Dickens ruled over a household consisting of his wife, Kate, sister-in-law, Georgina, an ever-growing brood of children, and a man-servant and four maids. There was also a groom called Topping, a dog called Timber, and the raven Grip – the model for Barnaby Rudge's bird. In the regulation of this little world, Dickens the Victorian paterfamilias, orderly, shrewd, intensely business-like, alternated with Dickens the boyish, high-spirited practical joker; Dickens the social climber with Dickens the ardent social reformer, searching out misery in its lowest kennels; Dickens the dedicated novelist and journalist with Dickens the orator and amateur actor. His household lived with a man who comprised within himself an astounding variety of persons – never knowing which one was going to come uppermost. It was Carlyle, who knew him well, who wrote after his death to Forster of his 'sparkling, clear and sunny utterances', and contrasted them with something in him he called 'dark, fateful, silent elements, tragical to look upon'. Perhaps he had in mind Dickens's obsession with crime and with violent death, and with that dark strain in him which fed so insatiably upon the gloom and terrors of the Victorian underworld.

In the early years of his residence in Marylebone, it was the social side of him which was very much to the fore. His home was a model of elegance and order. The pictures on the walls, the furnishings, the current knick-knacks, were all the very last thing in contemporary taste. Over all these symbols of his material success he watched with the eye of a martinet. His daily tours of inspection saw to it that nothing was awry anywhere in his well-ordered machine-for-living. Tradesmen's bills were paid on the dot (memories of his father in a debtors' prison had to be exorcised). To show off this spick-and-span interior, and to make himself known to his fashionable readers, as well as to impress his friends in the literary and artistic worlds, he entertained frequently. It was of a dinner he gave at 1 Devonshire Terrace in 1849 that Mrs Gaskell, the novelist, wrote:

We dressed and went to dine at Mr Dickens' . . . We were shown into Mr Dickens' study . . . It is the study where he writes all his works; and has a bow-window, about the size of Uncle Holland's drawing room. There are books all round, up to the ceiling, and down to the ground; a standing desk at which he writes; and all manner of comfortable easy chairs. There were numbers of people in the room. Mr Rogers (the old poet, who is 86, and looked very unfit to be in such a large party,) Douglas Jerrold, Mr and Mrs Carlyle, Hablot Browne, who illustrated Dickens' works, Mr Forster, Mr and Mrs Tagart, a Mr Kenyon. We waited dinner a long time for Lady Dufferin (*the* Hon. Mrs Blackwood who wrote the *Irish Emigrant's Lament*,) but she did not come till after dinner. Anne sat between Carlyle and Rogers – and I between Dickens and Douglas Jerrold. Anne heard the most sense, and I the most wit; I never heard anyone so witty as Douglas Jerrold, who is a very little almost deformed man with grey flowing hair, and very fine eyes . . . In the evening quantities of other people came in. We were by this time up in the drawing-room, which is not nearly so pretty or so home-like as the study. Frank Stone the artist, Leech and his wife, Benedict the great piano-forte player, Sims Reeves the singer, Thackeray, Lord Dudley Stuart, Lord Headfort, Lady Yonge, Lady Lovelace . . . We heard some beautiful music . . . There were some nice little Dickens' children in the room – who were so polite, and well-trained.

The remark about the well-trained children is indicative of the extreme efficiency with which Dickens ran his life during the time his career was on its upward curve. He could not, however, achieve that all-important gentlemanly touch which the Victorians so valued. Thackeray had it in excess, with all the quiet arrogance it implied (Mrs Gaskell could not bring herself to like *him*). Mrs Carlyle at least had not been impressed by Dickens' display of lavish hospitality:

Such getting up of the steam is unbecoming to a literary man. The dinner was served up in the new fashion – not placed on the table at all – but handed round – only the dessert on the table, and quantities of *artificial* flowers – but then an overloaded dessert! pyramids of figs, raisins, oranges – ach!

Fortunately for Dickens, his efforts to be a trendy party-giver were only one among many activities by which he made his impact upon his fellow human beings. His readings of his own works - at this stage only privately and to small parties of friends – went with immense success. Sometimes these would be preceded by long tramps over the open countryside to Hampstead, accompanied by intimates such as Maclise and Forster. Then the reading might take place at Jack Straw's Castle. This was the period of his life *par excellence* when the fantastic vigour of the man, and the dynamism that radiated from him most impressed all who met him. Leigh Hunt said of his face at this time that it had 'the life and soul in it of fifty human beings'. Sometimes this vigour would take a whimsical turn – even a mischievous one – as when he conceived a passion for acquiring the ability to hypnotise people, took lessons from Dr John Elliotson, one of the founders of University College Hospital, and set to work to hypnotise his wife and sister-in-law, with the result that they became 'violently hysterical'. Most of the vigour, however, left over from his writing, acting and entertaining, went into social reform and generally setting the world to rights. In *The Uncommercial Traveller* he was later to describe some of his first experiences in Marylebone of the dreadful misery of the poor and downtrodden – how he attended an inquest in the parish workhouse on the dead baby of a wretched servant girl. She had fallen on her knees in front of the coroner's jury and thanked them for not convicting her of its murder, but merely of the lesser crime of concealing its body. He had paid for her defence at her trial and helped her in prison. He tells, too, of his inspection of the workhouse on another occasion, and his inability to get the apathetic inmates to answer his questions. He gives a description of the local vestrymen – the sole municipal authority in those days – at their deliberations, often, as he shows, foolish and quarrelsome.

Dickens was so peripatetic, both by day and by night, that he was bound to see much that passed other people by. His intense interest in every aspect of life and his falcon's eye assured him of missing very little. Regent's Park, so close to his home, provided him with two incidents of low life – how stinging he could be about such terms! – one tragic, the other tragi-comic, which he duly recorded. The first occurred in 1861, during his second residence – temporary – in Marylebone, when he lived in the Park at 3 Hanover Terrace.

Towards that hour of a winter's afternoon when the lamplighters are beginning to light the lamps before they are wanted, because the darkness thickens fast and soon, I was walking in from the country on the northern side of the Regent's Park – hard frozen and deserted – when I saw an empty Hansom cab drive up to the lodge at Gloucester-gate, and the driver with great agitation call to the man there: who quickly reached a long pole from a tree, and, deftly collared by the driver, jumped to the step of his little seat, and so the Hansom rattled out at the gate, galloping over the iron-bound road. I followed running though not so fast but that when I came to the right-hand Canal Bridge, near the cross-path to Chalk Farm, the Hansom was stationary, the horse was smoking hot, the long pole was idle on the ground, and the driver and the park-keeper were looking over the bridge parapet. Looking over too, I saw, lying on the towing-path with her face turned up towards us, a woman, dead a day or two, and under thirty, as I guessed, poorly dressed in black. The feet were lightly crossed at the ankles, and the dark hair, all pushed back from the face, as though that had been the last action of her desperate hands, streamed over the ground. Dabbled all about her, was the water, and the broken ice that had dropped from her dress, and had splashed as she was got out.

Having set the scene in this masterly way, Dickens – and remember that he was a middle-aged man within a few months of his fiftieth birthday, and that he had sprinted to the spot – shows that not a single detail of the sad little drama had escaped him.

The policeman who had just got her out, and the passing costermonger who had helped him, were standing near the body; the latter with that stare at it which I have likened to being at a wax-work exhibition without a catalogue; the former, looking over his stock, with professional stiffness and coolness, in the direction in which the bearers he had sent for were expected . . . A barge came up, breaking the floating ice and the silence, and a woman steered it. The man with the horse that towed it, cared so little for the body, that the stumbling hoofs had been among the hair, and the tow-rope had caught and turned the head, before our cry of horror took him to the bridle. At which sound the steering woman looked up at us on the bridge with contempt unutterable, and then looking down at the body with a similar expression – as if it were made in another likeness than herself, had been informed with other passions, had been lost by other chances, had had another nature dragged down to perdition – steered a spurning streak of mud at it, and passed on.

Was it compassion, or an insatiable desire for the dramatic which made him write like this about such matters? Did he race to the scene in order to help, or because of his journalist's itch to get good 'copy'? His general life-style suggests that these threads in him were closely intermingled. He was a deeply sensitive, socially conscious man, who would do all he could to get a rattling good story for *Household Words* or *All the Year Round*. His second story shows him in the role of outraged paterfamilias and stern upholder of the law. His children when they were small used to be taken by their nurses to Regent's Park for air and exercise. The park had been opened to the public a few years before, and among the frequenters were hooligan elements from the then extensive slums of central

London. Dickens had been writing about the grab-and-run thieves who specialised in snatching articles of clothing from women, with derisive shouts of 'I'll have this!' He blamed the police for adopting what he called 'a contemplative attitude' towards this practice. But what seems really to have enraged him was 'the blaring use of the very worst language possible, in our public thoroughfares – especially in those set apart for recreation.' Regent's Park, it seems, was a hotbed of this particular form of molestation of the perambulating nursemaid, and Dickens feared for his children. 'I found this evil to be so abhorrent and horrible there, that I called public attention to it . . . Looking afterwards into the newest Police Act, and finding that the offence was punishable under it, I resolved, when striking occasion should arrive, to try my hand as prosecutor.'

The occasion arose soon enough – and the offender turned out to be a girl:

> The utterer of the base coin in question was a girl of seventeen or eighteen, who, with a suitable attendance of blackguards, youths, and boys, was flaunting along the streets returning from an Irish funeral, in a Progress interspersed with singing and dancing. She had turned round to me and expressed herself in the most audible manner, to the great delight of that select circle. I attended the party, on the opposite side of the way, for a mile further, and then encountered a Police-constable. The party had made themselves merry at my expense until now, but seeing me speak to the constable, its male members instantly took to their heels, leaving the girl alone. I asked the constable did he know my name? Yes, he did. 'Take that girl into custody, on my charge, for using bad language in the streets.' He had never heard of such a charge. I had. Would he take my word that he should get into no trouble? Yes, sir, he would do that. So he took the girl and I went home for my Police Act.

Dickens had great difficulty in persuading first the local police inspector and then the magistrate that such a charge could be entertained. But, armed with the Police Act, he drove his charge home with unyielding pertinacity – 'during conference I was evidently regarded as a much more objectionable person than the prisoner – with the result that the girl was given the option of a ten-shilling fine or a few days' imprisonment. *Pay-off:* Police officer remarking to Dickens: 'Why, Lord bless you, sir, if she goes to prison, that will be nothing new to *her*. She comes from Charles Street, Drury Lane!' Charles Street was one of those thieves' rookeries with which Victorian London was ringed. The moral of both these anecdotes would appear to be the same – that a brutalised and exploited lower class is hardened to both death and imprisonment, and that over-many suicides and much public indulgence in obscene insults generally reflect upon the community at large.

The game of tracing the originals of the houses inhabited by famous Dickens characters – once a favourite occupation of his fans – must have been largely put paid to by the demolition preceding the huge redevelopment schemes of the past decade. Before these transformations the Dickens topographers had pinpointed various places to their own satisfaction. Marylebone was naturally a happy hunting-ground, since Dickens spent eleven years there and wrote a dozen of his famous novels, including *The Old Curiosity Shop, Barnaby Rudge, Martin Chuzzlewit, Dombey and Son*, and *David Copperfield*. Whether Mr Dombey's house was at the corner of Mansfield Street and Queen Anne Street – 'a house of dismal state, with a circular back to it'; or Madame Mantalini's fashionable dressmaking establishment, in *Nicholas Nickleby*, could have been at 11 Wigmore Street; or Mr and Mrs Boffin, of *Our Mutual Friend*, had their residence at 43 Wimpole Street; or Mr Turveydrop's dancing academy, in *Bleak House*, was 26 Newman Street, are questions for the *cognoscenti*. What is certain is that Lord George Gordon, of Gordon Riots notoriety, lived at 64 Welbeck Street, which at the time was the second house on the left from Wigmore Street, and which has now been replaced by a late Victorian building.

It is only two years since we commemorated the centenary of Dickens's death. Time, it would seem, has done little but confirm his unique power. We may find fault with him, but we cannot replace him, for he is sunk many fathoms deep in the national consciousness. As he paced the streets in life, so he has walked the minds of succeeding generations. During his lifetime it was this moving on quality, this insatiable covering of the miles alone, this ceaseless taking in of the human scene in all the countries he visited, but above all in the streets of London, which marked him down as a kind of Flying Dutchman of the urban scene. George Augustus Sala, the journalist, who worked for him on *Household Words*, and was himself a roamer of the London streets, enumerating the many places he had encountered him in, wrote:

A hansom whirled you by the 'Bell and Horns' at Brompton, and there he was striding, as with seven-league boots, seemingly in the direction of Northend, Fulham. The Metropolitan Railway sent you forth at Lisson-grove and you met him plodding speedily towards the 'Yorkshire Stingo'. He was to be met rapidly skirting the grim brick wall of the prison in Coldbath-Fields, or trudging along the Seven Sisters-road at Holloway, or bearing under a steady press of sail, underneath Highgate Archway, or pursuing the even tenor of his way up the Vauxhall-bridge-road.

As he himself said in a letter to Forster: 'Put me down on Waterloo-bridge at eight o'clock in the evening, with leave to roam about as long as I like, and I would come home, as you know, panting to go on.'

Dickens's house in Devonshire Terrace was literally within the shadow of the parish church, St Marylebone. In the sixth year of his residence – 1846 – Robert Browning and Elizabeth Barrett were clandestinely married in the church, and shortly afterwards departed for Italy. This romantic elopement has been more than adequately publicised, and the pair turned into the classic lovers of the English world of letters. From Robert's opening shot across her bows in January 1845 – the letter beginning: 'I love your verse with all my heart, dear Miss Barrett . . . ', through the two volumes of correspondence which ensued, the first meeting in May, the proposal in Regent's Park, and the plans to defeat the inevitable parental opposition – we have had it all, not only in a plethora of books, but in *The Barretts of Wimpole Street*, and more recently in a post-war musical. What has all the fuss been about? Well, clearly it was the Barretts – Elizabeth, her father, and his large family, and not Mr Robert Browning, that big bow-wow – who first attracted the lime-light. In 1931, when *The Barretts of Wimpole Street* was put on, the sport of debunking our Victorian grandparents was in its heyday. Mr Barrett, who had always been written off as the heaviest of heavy fathers – there seems some doubt of it now – was obviously an excellent target. The runaway marriage of two poets – one of them, the lady, an invalid who kept the Greek text of Plato by her bedside bound up as a novel to deceive her doctor – was also splendid audience-fodder. And then there was 'Flush', Elizabeth's pet spaniel – stolen in Wimpole Street by the professional dog-thieves of the day, and returned on payment of ransom to the opulent-looking, cigar-smoking head of the gang, passing himself off of course as a

specialist in tracking down lost dogs. Virginia Woolf gave the whole
thing a further fillip in 1933 by devoting a whole book to re-telling
the tale of 'Flush' – and so the great Barrett-Browning saga was
inflated to monstrous size.

There were indeed elements of the *Forsyte Saga* in the situation,
which was essentially a family one. But Galsworthy, it must be
remembered, was preceded by Trollope. Had Trollope had the
handling of the matter a few years later, when he began to make
his name as a novelist, he would no doubt have treated the whole
tale on a regional basis, with Marylebone as the locale, Mr Barrett
of course as the tyrannical father, Robert Browning as the
mysterious Bohemian infiltrating the well-ordered family, the Rector of St Marylebone as the honest broker trying to patch up the
family quarrel, and a large supporting cast of Vestrymen and their
wives striking a variety of appropriate Victorian attitudes towards
the drama. Perhaps he would have had 'Flush' killed off by the
dog-thieves, and his head and paws despatched in a parcel (this
actually happened in those days) to his mistress. Trollope did not
make his name as a novelist until about ten years later – with the
publication of *The Warden*, the first of the Barsetshire series, in
1855 – and he did not settle in Marylebone until 1872. By this time
the big Barsetshire novels were all behind him, and he had raked in
a tidy part of that odd £70,000 which he tells us in his autobiography
he made by his works.

Trollope lived for eight years at 39 Montagu Square. These were
happy and productive years for him, and he was still, though near-
ing sixty when he settled there, keeping up his beloved riding to
hounds whenever he could get away into the country. He entertained a lot at his house, and played whist daily at the Garrick Club
between tea and dinner. He rode in the park for exercise, and went
about his business and to dinner parties in a brougham. His daily
writing was done in the morning, and was generally over by eleven
o'clock. At this period of his life, he had begun to suffer from
writer's cramp, and so had to employ a secretary. He was lucky
enough to find the ideal amanuensis in his niece, Florence Bland.
This patient female, who lived with the Trollopes as the daughter
of the house, was not allowed to speak a single word while he was
dictating nor to offer the slightest suggestion to the great man. One
day he tore up a whole chapter and threw it into the wastepaper
basket because she ventured on an emendation. A fiery-tempered

man, of whom it was said 'he came in at the door like a frantic windmill', he also had the generosity of disposition of the swift to wrath. Explosions in the study were often the subject of teasing comment by his womenfolk at lunch, and he would then join in the joking. The years at Montagu Square included a fair quota of foreign travel, both on the Continent and farther afield to Australia, South Africa, and Iceland. Among the books he wrote during his time in Montagu Square were *The Eustace Diamonds* (1873), *Phineas Redux* (1874), *The Prime Minister* (1876), *The American Senator* (1877), and *Is he Popenjoy?* (1878).

In 1854, the year before Trollope sprang into fame with the publication of *The Warden*, there died at Abbotsford that rather controversial figure, John Gibson Lockhart, Scott's son-in-law. After his early years in Scotland of polemics for *Blackwood's* – when, nicknamed 'The Scorpion', he indulged in the savage personalities of the day against the 'Cockney School' of writers, Hazlitt, Leigh Hunt and Keats – he settled in London at 24 Sussex Place, Regent's Park, and lived there for most of the rest of his life. As editor of the *Quarterly Review*, a novelist of competence, and author of the first and classic life of Scott, he was a figure in London literary circles for more than quarter of a century. But he was noted for the cold arrogance of his manner, and although his intimates seem to have testified to the traditional heart of gold beneath this glacial exterior, many people did not like him. One of these, a greater literary talent than his own, the author of *Moby Dick*, met him at a party at Murray the publisher's in 1849. Herman Melville has left this vivid and venomous vignette – a piece of poetic justice on a literary executioner who in his time hacked down Hazlitt and possibly hastened Keats' departure from this life:

> Lockhart was there also, in a prodigious white cravat (made from Walter Scott's shroud, I suppose). He stalked about like a half-galvanised ghost – gave me the tips of two skinny fingers when introduced to me – or rather I to him . . . After the ladies withdrew . . . I sat next to Lockhart, and seeing that he was a customer who was full of himself & expected great homage; and knowing him to be a thoroughgoing Tory and fish-blooded Churchman & conservative, & withal, editor of the *Quarterly* – I refrained from playing the snob to him like the rest – & the consequence was he grinned at me his ghastly smiles.

Round about the time Lockhart took up his abode in London, a literary and artistic personality of a very different type was just beginning to earn money by his drawings. Edward Lear, born in 1812, had shown precocious skill, and was already getting money for his sketches at the age of fifteen. The man so firmly linked in many minds only with the *Nonsense Rhymes* was much better known to his contemporaries for most of his life as a gifted landscape artist and illustrator. His connections with Marylebone were spasmodic – as indeed were the links of this indefatigable traveller with any one spot on the globe. He did, however, live first on the borders of the borough, and then within it at four separate stages of his life, and the Greater London Council have commemorated his residence in Seymour Street, Portman Square, with one of their blue plaques. When he was still under twenty the Zoological Society engaged him to make drawings of the parrots at the Regent's Park zoo. Ann, his eldest sister – she had taken on the task of looking after the shy, talented, epileptic youth when the family broke up on his father's imprisonment for debt – thereupon moved with him to Albany Street, at the eastern side of the park. There Lear produced a splendid folio volume on the parrot family, with forty-two coloured lithographic plates – an achievement which instantly made his name, and was the means of his being introduced to the thirteenth Earl of Derby, a keen naturalist, who became his patron. He lived at Derby's home, Knowsley Hall, for nearly four years, was launched on art-loving society, made numerous influential friends, and embarked upon that career of travel in search of landscape which was to be his life.

Lear's travels in the Mediterranean area, the Near East, and India are now well enough known to the public. We have become curious about the life of a man who, apart from his much-quoted nonsense jingles, left behind him so many limpid, haunting evocations of what today's poster paradises looked like before the travel agents got at them. In the intervals between these incessant journeyings, and the longer residences in sun-drenched lands, Lear would return to England – to stay with the Tennysons, look up Holman Hunt, or Franklin Lushington (the closest of his friends), or even give Queen Victoria drawing lessons. In 1850, after being based mainly abroad in Rome for ten years or so, with visits to Sicily, Greece, Corfu, Albania, Egypt and Malta, he took a studio at 17 Stratford Place, off Oxford Street, and remained there for two years, returning there

in 1861 for a further period of years. It was here that Lear first met
Holman Hunt. Hunt, who became his close friend and artistic mentor, wrote of this:

> About this time, 1852, Robert Martineau spoke to me of
> Edward Lear, and gave me an invitation to his chambers in Strat-
> ford Place to see his numberless drawings, which were in outline,
> with little to indicate light or shade. Lear overflowed with
> geniality, and at the same time betrayed anxiety as we turned over
> the drawings, avowing that he had not the ability to carry out the
> subjects in oil; in some parts of them he had written in phonetic
> spelling the character of the points which the outlines would not
> explain – 'Rox', 'Korn', 'Ski', indulging his love of fun with
> these vagaries.

Soon after this Lear went off to a farm near Hastings to sketch
with Holman Hunt. There they were joined by William Rossetti,
brother of Dante Gabriel, and by Millais. Martineau – painter of
the well-known *Last Day in the Old Home,* and his wife, lived close
by – so temporarily a small artistic colony came into being. Lear
enjoyed himself enormously, but on returning to Stratford Place
found that the ceiling of his front room had fallen in. Not long
after, the back room ceiling followed suit. Lear packed up and went
back to Hastings, 'where at least there are fresh air and muffins'.
During his next spell at Stratford Place in the 1860s he held an
exhibition there. For this effort, made in 1865, he sent out a thousand circulars in appropriate directions. He was rewarded by
catching one of the largest of sprats – the Prince of Wales (later
Edward VII), who came and bought ten sketches.

In a letter to Emily Tennyson, wife of the poet-laureate, about
his exhibition, Lear went on to remark: 'I should like to know how
Alfred likes a Pome or Tragedy by one Mr Swinburne – *Atalanta
in Caledon* (sic): I take to it extremely.' At this time, Swinburne too
was in Marylebone – in chambers at 22a Dorset Street, where he was
to remain for the next three years. It is not clear whether the two
men met at this period, or indeed at all in their lives. Lear was
twenty-five years Swinburne's senior, and because of his shyness and
physical disability not everyone's cup of tea. Swinburne, too, was a
very odd fish and, according to a recent biographer, Jean Overton
Fuller, in her *Swinburne: A Critical Biography,* seems to have been
indulging at this period in a sexual deviation which has nowhere

yet been pinned on Lear. Swinburne's novel *Lesbia Brandon* makes it clear that he was obsessed by the notion of flagellation. It seems that in July 1865 he met a young man called John Thomson, who 'had an interest, perhaps a share, in a house in St John's Wood where, in luxuriously furnished rooms, two fair-haired and rouged ladies whipped gentlemen who came to them for this service. A third, elder, lady, very respectable in appearance, welcomed the guests and took their money.' Thomson introduced Swinburne to this house – probably in Circus Road – and he became a regular client. It appears that by 1875 there were at least two well-known flagellation brothels in Marylebone – one of them in Portland Place.

In this early, dissipated period of his life, Swinburne mixed a good deal with William Morris and Rossetti. This was in his free-ranging period, before he 'shacked up' with Watts-Dunton at 'The Pines', Putney, and before, with an allowance of twopence in his pocket for his daily pint, he walked out shocking nursemaids by 'addressing them without introduction', while – in Robert Graves' delightful phrase – 'gazing ecstatically into their perambulators'. Rossetti too has his link with Marylebone, having been born in Hallam Street, the son of Gabriele Rossetti, an Italian poet and revolutionary who in exile became Professor of Italian at King's College in the Strand. His mother, Frances Polidori, sister of Byron's travelling companion, Dr Polidori, was part English, part Italian. In 1848-9, Rossetti as a budding painter shared a studio for a while with Holman Hunt in Cleveland Street from which he removed to one of his own in Newman Street. He did not leave Marylebone until 1852, when he was twenty-four. By this time he had already made the acquaintance of the chestnut-haired beauty, Elizabeth Siddal, the model whose love and companionship were to be his inspiration for the next decade till her early death in 1862, two years after they had finally married. It is general knowledge that he never really recovered from this cataclysmic shock. The burial of his poems in her grave (even though they were recovered later under pressure from his friends), the transformation into a recluse, and the final hopeless drug addiction – these are the well-known landmarks of his descent into his private Avernus. In his single-minded pursuit of a medieval dream-world both in writing and through the medium of paint, he remains one of the strangest figures thrown up by the Romantic movement in the nineteenth century. One of his minor oddities seems to have been a fetishistic devotion to chestnut-coloured hair in the female. Mrs Gaskell, the novelist, has something to say of her experience of this in 1859:

> I think we got to know Rossetti pretty well. I went three times to his studio, and met him at two evening parties – where I had a good deal of talk with him, always excepting the times when ladies with beautiful hair came in when he was like the cat turned into a lady, who jumped out of bed and ran after a mouse. It did not signify what we were talking about or how agreeable I was; if a particular kind of reddish brown, crêpe wavy hair came in, he was away in a moment struggling for an introduction to the owner of the said head of hair. He is not as mad as a March hare, but hair-mad.

By the late 1860s Marylebone was beginning to give place to Chelsea as a centre of artistic activity. The up-and-coming young men of the day, Rossetti himself, Holman Hunt, Whistler, William de Morgan, had settled there. Marylebone's century of unquestioned supremacy as artistic capital of London was coming to an end. It had begun with the great northward expansion of the West End in the eighteenth century – the creation of Regent's Park giving it a further impetus. It drew to its conclusion when Buckingham Palace became Queen Victoria's residence in the 1840s, when Belgravia was built to accommodate the palace's attendant aristocracy, and the ripple of fashionable development thus started spread westward to Chelsea. The building of the Chelsea Embankment in the 1870s emphatically marked the change. Stylish living migrated from north of Hyde Park to south of it, and with it went the artists – following as they needs must the tide of moneyed patronage.

An envoi to Marylebone as it was in the 1860s, when these changes were beginning to take place but had not yet made themselves felt, is provided in an article which appeared in the *Evening News* of 28 September 1936. In this, Malcolm Salaman, a man of eighty-one, poet, playwright and art connoisseur, recalls a childhood and youth spent in Baker Street, where his father had lived since 1834. Baker Street then, in the reign of King William IV, if no longer full of 'the most antient families' of the nobility, possessed not a single shop to contaminate its residential purity. One day in 1861, when young Salaman had been taken with his brothers and sisters into Regent's Park, their nurse cried out: 'Look, children, the Queen!' – and there were Victoria and Albert driving by in their

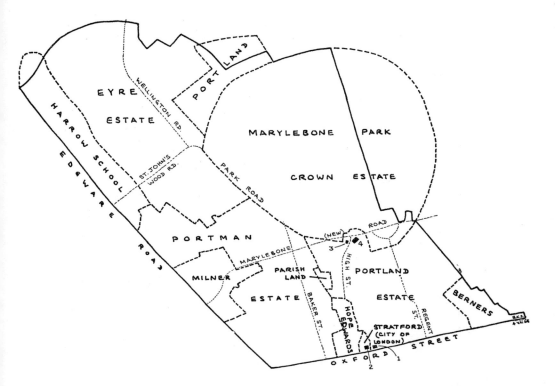

Principal estates in Marylebone
drawn by Bruce Kemp Saunders
and reproduced from Ann Saunders' *Regent's Park* (1969)

barouche. And it seems that they frequently passed along Baker
Street on their way to these drives in the park – a sign no doubt
that 'the right side of the park' (Hyde Park) was still north of it.
Mr Salaman continued:

> Traffic in Baker-street in my early schooldays was sedately
> mobile. Carriages of various styles, four-wheeled and hansom
> cabs, commercial carts, and rare omnibuses – interrupted every
> First of May by the slow-moving rustic pageant of Jack-in-the-
> Green and Maid Marian (imagine this in the crowded Baker-
> street of to-day!) – drove along in a leisurely manner. The omni-
> buses were of two kinds, the light-green Atlas, which plied as far
> as the Swiss Cottage, and the dark-green City Atlas, which ended
> its journey at the Abbey Road. Each ran once every hour, and
> beyond these stopping-places there were no omnibuses, for the
> rest was practically the country. As boys we would mount the
> Atlas, when possible climbing to seats beside the driver, clad in
> his old-fashioned cape and tall felt hat, driving behind three
> horses to far-away Swiss Cottage. There we would dismount, and
> begin our walk to Hampstead across the seven fields, in the first
> of which beside the hedge on the left, a murder had been dis-
> covered long ago; but it still thrilled me.

'Jack-in-the-Green' – for the benefit of those under 120 years of
age – was a part of the chimney-sweepers' celebration of the May-
Day festival, the Jacks – the sweeps' boys – being festooned with
green leaves from head to foot. Maid Marian, garlanded with
flowers, was the traditional May Queen.

# 9. The French Émigrés

I F Gibbon's remark is correct – that history is 'little more than the register of the crimes, follies, and misfortunes of mankind' – then Marylebone may be said to owe its French *émigrés* of past years to a couple of crimes and a folly. The crimes were the Massacre of St Bartholomew and the French Revolutionary Terror. The folly was the Revocation of the Edict of Nantes. The persecuting spirit never dies, and *émigrés* of a variety of nationalities and colours still flow into England. But they are rarely French nowadays, for the wars of religion that divided Frenchmen are over, and the great struggle which sent the 'Free French' to England a generation ago ended happily for France. The massacre in 1572 and the withdrawal in 1685 of the privileges and immunities conferred by the Edict of Nantes in 1598 were both attempts to wipe out the Huguenot community in France. Of Louis XIV's revocation of the Edict, Dr H. A. L. Fisher has written in *A History of Europe*:

> . . . he withdrew the wise toleration which his grandfather had accorded to French Protestants, prohibiting their worship, proscribing their ministers, destroying their churches, closing their schools, and so driving some of the best artificers of his kingdom into foreign lands, there to create industries in competition with his own, and to foment sentiments of enduring rancour against France.

What kind of people were these Huguenots? The fact that they were Calvinists, with all that this means in the way of stern self-discipline, is probably the central fact about them. It was the strength of their discipline which enabled them to survive so many persecutions, and it was this exercised in everyday life which helped to make them so successful as bankers, craftsmen, and teachers. The very doctrine of predestination may have contributed to their extraordinary money-making capacity. For, if a man is to be damned to eternity in the next world, do what he will in this, he may as well compensate himself to the top of his bent by using his highly-tempered faculties to gather all the money and power he can grasp. The other vital fact about the Calvinists, only slightly less significant than their total command of themselves (whether to heavenly or earthly ends) was their democratic organisation. At a time when authority and hierarchy in religion were the unquestioned order of the day, Calvin dared to found a self-ruling church, each unit of which was governed by an elected body of elders. Thus, not only were theological know-how and a sense of personal responsibility spread through the community, but the foundations were laid of that democratic spirit which was to be the mainspring of progress in the modern world. The Huguenots then were in a sense an élite – or at any rate a body from which an élite of men and ideas was to proceed, fertilising the communities into which it was injected and helping to prepare the world for fresh ways of life. France had the misfortune to chase these men and women out; Britain, some other European countries, and America had the good fortune to give them a home.

At the time of the Massacre of St Bartholomew in 1572, when elements of the first wave of persecuted Huguenots made their way to England, Marylebone was still a small village quite unconnected with London. Some of the refugees may have infiltrated as far as the village, but if so nothing now remains to establish their names and identities. It was not until Louis XIV, in his struggle against Protestant power both inside and outside France, decided that the hour was ripe to ditch the Edict of Nantes, that Huguenot *émigrés* arrived in Marylebone whose names have come down to us – though indeed little more than their names. One of the first of these was Claude Champion de Crespigny. He left France about 1687 at the ripe age of sixty-four, and brought his wife and three children with him to England. He was lucky enough to have relatives, the Pierrepoints, already settled in this country, to welcome him. He was also lucky in reaching England at a time when James II, with his fanatically Catholic outlook, was on his way out, and the Glorious Revolution of 1688 was about to put Whigs and Protestants firmly in power. He survived until 1697. His eldest son, Pierre, lived on for another forty years and became a member of the committee of the French Church in Marylebone, and one of the original directors of *La Providence*, the Huguenot benevolent fund founded in 1718. One wonders if the Crespignys' Pierrepoint relatives were kinsmen of

Lady Mary Wortley Montagu's family. Her father, the Duke of Kingston, was Evelyn Pierrepoint. Lady Mary, as we have seen, lived in Cavendish Square in the 1730s.

One of the most eloquent preachers of his day, Jacques Abbadie, spent his last years in Marylebone, then still a village. Abbadie, who was thirty-one when the Edict of Nantes was revoked, died at his lodgings in Marylebone in 1727. In the forty odd years which elapsed between these dates, he achieved a considerable degree of celebrity for himself by his preaching and his theological works. After a brief period at first as Minister of the French Church in Berlin, he attached himself to the distinguished German soldier, Marshal Schomberg, and went with him first to Holland, and then to Ireland. Schomberg was killed at the battle of the Boyne, and Abbadie went to London, where he became Minister of the French Church in the Savoy. When King William of Orange's fellow-sovereign and wife, Queen Mary, died in 1694, Abbadie devoted one of the most sonorous and splendid of his *oraisons funèbres* to her memory. William himself was of course a Calvinist, firmly believing in predestination. He made Abbadie Dean of Killaloe, in County Clare, as a reward for his propaganda on behalf of the Revolution of 1688. There he lived and worked for a period. But he retired to Marylebone in his last years, and absorbed himself in the revision of his printed works.

In 1703 a 'high-class preparatory school' was started in Marylebone by a Mr Dennis de la Place. This establishment, which took over the old manor house in Marylebone High Street (see Chapter 2) became very fashionable as the district itself became increasingly so throughout the eighteenth century. Was de la Place a Huguenot? W. H. Manchée, who in 1915–17 wrote at some length on the Huguenots of Marylebone, came to the conclusion that he was, though he admits to having found no record of him as such. The school is mentioned in 1711, in a periodical *The Post Boy*, as teaching 'Latin, French, Mathematics, etc'. The de la Places seem to have kept the ownership of the school until about 1770, when a Dr Fountaine, de la Place's son-in-law, and a Huguenot, took over. During his headmastership, George Colman the younger, the dramatist and theatre manager, was a pupil. In his autobiography, *Random Records of My Life*, he makes it clear that though the place was a prep school specialising in getting boys into Westminster School, it still gave the teaching of French pride of place in its curriculum. There were, he says, two resident French masters, one of whom helped to teach Latin. Four non-resident masters – teaching respectively writing, arithmetic, dancing and fencing – came in on days fixed for these subjects.

A Huguenot family which arrived in London via Geneva – and took a century over it – were the Chalons. Originally French, they emigrated to Switzerland when Louis XIV did away with the Edict of Nantes. In 1789 they struck camp again, and moved off to England. The immigrant Chalons had three sons, all of whom made their names as painters. The two younger sons, John James and Alfred Edward, were bachelors keeping house together in Wimpole Street. Both became Royal Academicians, and Alfred Edward was one of the most fashionable portrait painters of the first half of the nineteenth century. He was in fact the first portrait painter to paint Queen Victoria after her accession, and she appointed him her official painter in water-colours. He was only nine years old when his parents brought him to England on the outbreak of the French Revolution, and as he lived to be eighty, he had many years in which to become thoroughly anglicised. He and his brother John – painter of that Victorian favourite, *John Knox Rebuking Mary Queen of Scots* – became close friends with Constable, perhaps one of the most thoroughgoingly English of all our great painters.

Another Huguenot name of note which has connections with Marylebone is that of Thellusson. The family is of French Huguenot origin, but settled in Geneva after the Massacre of St Bartholomew. In 1737 a Thellusson was Genevan Ambassador in Paris, and that year his son Pierre was born there. Pierre emigrated to England in 1762, i.e. just about the time Britain was successfully concluding the Seven Years' War and entering upon a period of unparalleled prosperity. Pierre, anglicised as Peter, became a London merchant and shared in the great access of wealth which flowed into the capital. He entered into close business relations with other flourishing Huguenot families, such as the Eglises and the Fonblanques, and accumulated a great fortune. His son, Peter Isaac, First Baron Rendlesham, a director of the Bank of England, took a seven-year lease of the great mansion, Foley House, a couple of years after his father's death in 1797. This house, it will be remembered, was at the southern end of Portland Place – on the present Langham Hotel site – with a magnificent view northwards towards what was then Marylebone Park.

The Thellussons gave their name to an act of parliament – the Thellusson Act, the popular name of the Accumulations Act. This act was judged necessary because of the unusual provisions in the original Peter Thellusson's will. After leaving £100,000 to his wife and children, he directed that the remaining £600,000 of his fortune should accumulate during the lives of his sons, of his grandsons, and of their issue living at the time of his death. Since it was calculated that the accumulation might conceivably reach an ultimate total of £140,000,000, the Accumulations Act was passed in 1800, restraining testators from leaving funds to accumulate for more than twenty-one years. In spite of this restriction, known in legal circles as the Rule against Perpetuities, Thellusson's will was held to be valid when tested in the courts in 1805, and it led to litigation among descendants later in the nineteenth century.

One of the better known Huguenot names of the late eighteenth century was that of Sir Peter Francis Bourgeois, R.A., who was appointed landscape painter to George III. Appointments of this kind mean nothing today, but Bourgeois is still far from forgotten – not for his work as an artist – who besides the dealers and art historians has heard of that? – but as the principal benefactor of that notable collection of pictures, the Dulwich Gallery. Bourgeois lived for a time in Charlotte Street, Portland Place – now known as Hallam Street – and with him lived Noel Desenfans, who was born in Flanders in 1745 but spent the greater part of his life in England. Desenfans was one of the ablest picture dealers of his time, and his own personal collection had been unexpectedly inflated when the gallery of pictures which he had been building up for King Stanislas of Poland was no longer needed. The king was forced to abdicate in 1795, and Desenfans was left with the pictures, unpaid-for, on his hands. He tried unsuccessfully to get the British Government to buy them and found a national gallery. Many were still unsold when he died in 1807, and left his collection to his wife, and to Bourgeois. Himself a collector as well as a working painter, Bourgeois survived his friend by only four years, and left a will bequeathing the whole collection to Dulwich College. Provision was made in this that Madame Desenfans should have the pictures for her lifetime, but she generously surrendered them. The gallery, designed by Sir John Soane, was built in 1814. Since Desenfans had a strong aversion to the idea of burial, Bourgeois also provided for the building of a mausoleum to contain the coffins of the Desenfans and himself. So there they lie, the trio of Huguenots – their pictures displayed around them in Soane's enchantingly skilful and sensitive building – making a wonderfully generous return for England's hospitality.

In 1757, the year after Bourgeois' birth, there was born one of the most distinguished of all Englishmen of Huguenot descent, Sir Samuel Romilly – a great reforming name standing alongside those of Bentham, Wilberforce and Shaftesbury. The grandson of Etienne Romilly, of Montpellier, who took refuge in England in 1701 from the persecution of Louis XIV and the French Catholics, Samuel was the son of Peter Romilly, a Soho jeweller. He was born in Frith Street, one of the main French refugee areas of London, but soon after was taken by his parents – who had already lost six children in infancy – to the cleaner air and better surroundings of Marylebone. There they lived at first in lodgings, in 'Mr Mahoon's Gardens' – the French Gardens which were an extension of Marylebone Gardens themselves. These allotments had been formed by the first wave of French refugees which had come over in the time of Etienne Romilly. To the north lay open countryside bordering the newly-made Marylebone Road – the New Road which figures so largely in the history of the parish and borough. Samuel was brought up in the closely-knit Huguenot community of those days, with their own schools, and their own church, situated close to the Rose of Normandy tavern. By the time he had become a young man the family circumstances had greatly improved owing to a bequest from a wealthy relative – the Huguenots of London were a very thriving community – and the Romillys were able to move to a small house in Marylebone High Street.

The impetus which set Romilly going on his career as a barrister, and later as a law reformer, came not from his father, but from the pastor at the church attended by his parents, the French Protestant church in Threadneedle Street. John Roget, who had emigrated from Geneva, was a man with a lively mind, an eloquent tongue, and remarkable penetration, and he had the gift to see that in the young Samuel there was the stuff of a man of high distinction. He deflected him from his intention of becoming a solicitor, and persuaded his father to direct him towards the Bar. Roget, not content with this, fell in love with Samuel's sister, Catherine, married her, and thus bound the family to his gifted self, if not with hoops of steel at least with strong Genevan bands. The product of this marriage was another man of remarkable distinction, Peter Mark Roget, now only remembered because of his celebrated and still much used *Thesaurus of English Words and Phrases*, but much better known in his own time as a distinguished physician, a Fellow of the Royal Society and for many years its Secretary, and one of the founders of London University.

Roget senior, who died at a comparatively early age, did young Romilly the further service, before he himself passed from the scene, of introducing him to the works of Rousseau. The *Contrat Social* and *Émile* were then sweeping Europe; the great Genevese had died only three years earlier. Romilly, visiting Switzerland where Roget had retired in a vain effort to regain lost health, was sent by him to Geneva with introductions to his friends. There he met many of the leaders of progressive opinion in the city. On his return journey, he stayed at Passy near Paris, in the home of Madame Delessert who had known Rousseau well, and in Paris itself he was introduced to d'Alembert and Diderot, then the most influential writers in France. D'Alembert was reserved with the shy young man, but Diderot was 'all warmth and eagerness, and talked with me with as little reserve as if I had been long and intimately acquainted with him.' Rousseau, politics and religion were the principal topics of his conversation, and he inveighed with great warmth against the tyranny of the French Government. The year was 1781, and the great ideas set forth by Rousseau were working like yeast in all thinking minds, and were to produce the volcanic explosion of the French Revolution before the decade was out. Reform in its various shapes was in the air, and in that fine instrument the mind of Samuel Romilly, moulded by the same Calvinist culture which had produced Rousseau, it was already fermenting.

On the outbreak of the French Revolutionary Terror, Romilly, as may be imagined, had been deeply anxious about the fate of his friends in France. One of the first of the refugees with whom he had to concern himself was young Delessert, the son of his friend living at Passy. Delessert junior had been in command of a battalion of the National Guard. The known loyalty of many members of that body to Louis XIV immediately endangered their officers once the Revolutionary leaders had taken their decision to get rid of the King. During the summer of 1792, Delessert was denounced by the Jacobins. He got away with great difficulty, travelling without a passport. He was one of the earliest arrivals in England of that enormous army of *émigrés* which was to flood into the country over a period lasting more than twenty years. It is true that many were amnestied by Napoleon, when he became absolute master of France, and returned to their homes after an absence of ten years or less. But it remains a fact that Frenchmen brought as infants to Britain in the early 1790s were sometimes unable to return to their native country until they were grown men. Their fathers, whether Bourbon loyalists, moderate monarchists, or simply active politicians who had made enemies of the Revolutionary leaders – or, later, of Napoleon – were frequently destined to spend the best years of their manhood on the wrong side of the Channel. In addition, some 8,000 Catholic priests who had refused to take the oath to the Republic, ranging from leading members of the hierarchy to village curés, flocked to Britain during and after the Terror.

London of course took the brunt of this great migration – and Marylebone a very large share of the London émigrés. Why Marylebone? The short answer is that Marylebone, as the then most rapidly expanding and flourishing district of fashionable London, offered attractions to most classes of refugee. The future King Charles X of France – then Comte d'Artois – by living in Baker Street, with his circle of ducal associates lodged nearby, maintained a convenient distance from the Court of St James, the government offices, and the amenities of central London. He was decently, but not ostentatiously housed only a short carriage drive away from the heart of things, but paid a lesser rent than if he had been in Hanover Square or Piccadilly. He was in a quarter which though not yet the smartest was rapidly becoming so. For those émigrés to whom considerations of rank and social status were not so important, but who had to find a way of earning their living, Marylebone offered a variety of attractions. In the proximity of the exiled royalist circles there was always a chance of pickings for those willing to act as agents, publicists, or spies. Since the district was well populated with comfortably-off members of the British nobility and gentry, there were plenty of opportunities for the emigrant intelligentsia to offer themselves as tutors or governesses to the children of well-heeled families, or simply as French language masters or mistresses. A flourishing district like Marylebone needed all sorts of services – and some of these the incomers were particularly well able to supply. French pastrycooks and restaurateurs, hotel and boarding-house keepers, dress-makers and modistes, drawing and fencing masters, journalists and doctors, and masters (or otherwise) of many other avocations, sprang up as the *émigré* community grew. Marylebone, for so long a home of London's French Huguenot community, was flooded with a new tide of French life, much of it Catholic and royalist.

Like the English residents of Marylebone, the French *émigrés* who managed to get themselves lodgings in the district must have been attracted by its combination of urban amenities and rural charms. The New, or Marylebone, Road which at that time formed the northern border of the whole quarter was completely unbuilt-on on its northern side. Here, on the site of what was later to become Regent's Park, were the farms and fields of Marylebone Park. An *émigré* such as the celebrated Chateaubriand, Romantic writer and Byronic figure, who lived for a while near Marylebone High Street at the turn of the century, could reach open country on foot from his quarters in a matter of minutes. Nor, if he needed refreshment, would it be lacking. On emerging from the High Street, he had merely to cross the Five Acres field to get to the Jew's Harp tavern, 'one of the prettiest inns near London', with ample provision for dining and dancing, a skittle alley, and rustic arbours. If this well-to-do place should prove too expensive for his refugee's pocket, a walk across Salt-Petre Field, past the country house of John White, surveyor of the Portland estate, would bring him to the equally well known but more modest Queen's Head and Artichoke.

The Marylebone of the 1790s and the early 1800s was also largely unbuilt upon in the area between Baker Street and the Edgware Road. Gloucester Place was built up no farther northwards than the Dorset Street crossing, and such houses as there were on the western side had their back windows looking out across open country. The Portman estate was as yet developed only in its southern and eastern parts. Portman Square itself was completed, but Bryanston and Montagu Squares and the network of streets surrounding them had yet to be built. The barracks and stables of the 2nd Life Guards – a couple of acres of them, on the site now occupied by Marks and Spencer's head office – had a back entrance-way giving on to Gloucester Street, as the southern end of Gloucester Place was then known. It was in this undeveloped part of the parish that the emigrant French clergy succeeded in obtaining the lease of a plot of land on which they built a chapel – the Chapel of the Annunciation, known as the French Chapel Royal from having been patronised by exiled French royalty from Louis XVIII onwards.

This tiny building, which escaped demolition until as late as 1969, stood in Carton Street – then known as Little George Street – a mews street just east of Gloucester Place. The presence of French royalty, in the person of the Comte d'Artois – later King Charles X – in Baker Street, a few hundred yards away, was the reason no doubt for the siting of the chapel in this particular neighbourhood. His house, No. 46, became the nucleus of a small colony of the French nobility of the *ancien régime*, and here he held a miniature court, attended from their houses or lodgings nearby by such personages as the Duc d'Uzès, the Duc de Castries, the Duc de Choiseul, the Duc de Duras, and others of ducal rank, like de Fitz-James, De Lorges, de Maille, and de Sérent. A short distance away on the farther side of Baker Street, at No. 18 Thayer Street, lived Louise de Polastron, mistress of the Comte d'Artois. This porcelain beauty with the large pale-blue eyes and the ash-blond hair was the future king's consolation for a dynastic marriage of the most arid kind. Charles X and his brother Louis XVIII – who preceded him on the French throne at the Bourbon restoration – married sisters, daughters of Victor-Amadeus III of Sardinia. Both were ugly; Charles's was excessively stupid, and Louis's drank.

The Chapel of the Annunciation, where the little world of French Bourbon royalty in exile heard mass and celebrated its births, marriages, and deaths, was founded by the Abbé Bourret, formerly of the church of Saint-Sulpice in Paris. The site was obtained through the influence of the Bishop of St Pol de Léon, the leading *émigré* cleric in England, a big burly soldier turned divine. The bishop had arrived in Cornwall aboard a smuggling craft in 1792, and from that time onwards for a number of years had administered the affairs of the exiled clergy, who after the Terror had poured in their thousands into England. These men had refused to take the oath of loyalty to the Republic and were mostly devoted adherents of the Bourbon cause, with a loathing of the atheistic, levelling doctrines of the new France. The little chapel was consecrated in 1799. Small as it was, and unpretentious as was its exterior, it was vastly better than the cellar at the corner of Paddington Street and Dorset Mews which had been the *émigrés'* first place of worship. Indeed, the interior during the first half of the nineteenth century, when it was at its most flourishing, had a certain miniature splendour befitting its functions as the French Chapel Royal, doing duty on this side of the Channel for Notre Dame, the place of coronation, and the Abbaye St Denis, the place of burial, of French kings.

There were at this period four altars. One of these had a very fine altarpiece by Maria Cosway, wife of the famous miniaturist, showing the Annunciation. The carved canopy over the pulpit was surmounted by gilded *fleurs-de-lis*. All the rich furnishings were gifts from Catholic donors in Britain and a variety of other countries. Here the marriages of Louis XVIII, as Comte de Provence, and Charles X, as Comte d'Artois, were solemnised, and here a requiem mass was held in 1811 for the Comtesse de Provence before her interment at a ceremony in Westminster Abbey attended by d'Artois and his two sons, the Dukes of Angoulême and Berry. Edward Walford, in his *Old and New London*, a mid-Victorian work, wrote of the chapel:

> Here most, if not all, the Bourbon kings and princes who have come to England as exiles or visitors . . . have always heard Mass; to say nothing of the Emperor Louis Napoleon, Eugénie, and their son. Here have been preached the *oraisons funèbres* of the Abbé Edgeworth, of the Duc d'Enghien, and of very many royal and distinguished personages of foreign countries, such as the King of Portugal . . . Chateaubriand, Count de Montalembert and others. In this chapel the body of the duc de Montpensier lay in state previous to its interment in Westminster Abbey. Here courses of sermons have been annually preached, and 'Retreats' have been given from time to time by the most eloquent of French preachers, such as Père Ravignan, Père Gratry, and Père Lacordaire. Attached to the chapel are many religious and charitable confraternities, etc., including a branch of the Society of St Vincent de Paul, for the benefit of the French poor of the metropolis.

This remarkable little chapel, so full of history, yet tucked discreetly away in a backwater behind Portman Square (where the French Embassy was once situated) was finally closed in 1911. Its last ministering priest, Father Louis Tourzel, who died in 1910, was there thirty years and was made a Canon of Westminster Cathedral. The chapel itself, as we have seen, survived for another couple of generations – playing the strangest variety of roles as a furniture warehouse, a day nursery, a mortuary chapel, a Protestant prayer-room, a synagogue, and a sound-recording studio.

Walford mentions Chateaubriand as one whose passing was also celebrated by a funeral oration in the little French Chapel Royal. That incarnation of the Romantic spirit in literature and in life had arrived in London in 1793 more dead than alive, having packed enough dangers, hardships and illnesses into the previous couple of years to rival those undergone by almost any of the *émigrés* during that savage time. A member of the Breton *noblesse*, his first reaction to the Revolution was one of extreme pessimism. He took the view as early as 1791 that the king was lost, and that there would be no counter-revolution. His personal remedy for the situation was to pack himself off to America, which in his youthful enthusiasm he regarded as the splendid sunlit home of liberty. After five months in the New World – which turned out to be the Old World writ rather differently – he felt the urge to return and take his part in the struggle. After a rough transatlantic passage, he reached France and before long had joined the Army of the Princes, the *émigré* army preparing to invade Republican France from German and Austrian soil. Badly wounded in the early operations, he developed smallpox while still on the march, but managed to make his way to Belgium. From Ostend he got himself a berth on a ship going to Jersey, where he had relations living. He arrived there a desperately sick man, and it was only after months of nursing that he was fit enough to proceed to England.

Research suggests that Chateaubriand's first lodging was in Rathbone Place. Here he knew real want and acute hunger, for the work as a translator which he found himself hardly brought in enough to keep him alive. He shared his garret with another Breton, Hingant de la Tiemblais, who seems to have been of the same rather proud kidney. Hingant became so desperate for lack of food that he attempted suicide with a penknife. Yet as an *émigré* who had been a magistrate in France, he was entitled to an allowance from the British Government. This he had refused, just as Chateaubriand himself refused the 1s. 1d. a day which the Government allowed to all *émigrés* not in receipt of special allowances from them. Both men were deeply concerned to express their ideas through writing. Hingant was at work on a novel, and Chateaubriand in the early stages of his *Essay on Revolutions*. The impact of this book in *émigré* circles was later to win him the *entrée* to the intelligentsia in exile in England – men like Montlosier, Malouet and Mallet du Pan, and women like Madame d'Aguesseau, Mrs Lindsay, and the Princesse d'Hénin. For the same reason, the *Ultras*, the out-and-out royalists frequenting the Comte d'Artois' little court in Baker Street, viewed him as having fallen a victim to 'modern philosophy' – the polite term for those who were not prepared to work for the return of Bourbon absolutism.

Chateaubriand's first years in England were by his own account – and it must be remembered that the father of French Romanticism was inclined to see his past life through a haze of colourful impressions – very wretched ones. His pride, his poverty, his utter lack of knowledge of the English and their ways, and his damaged health, combined to isolate him. Hingant's friends had removed him to hospital after his suicide attempt. He probably went to the Middlesex, where twenty-four beds were at the disposal of the *émigrés*, and there were French nuns to nurse the sick. Deprived of his sole congenial society, and of Hingant's contribution towards the rent, Chateaubriand moved his quarters. Of this change he wrote:

> On a lower level than the needy emigrants who had been my first protectors in London were others even more poverty-stricken. There are degrees among the poor as among the rich; one can go from the man who keeps himself warm in winter by sleeping with his dog to the man who shivers in his tattered rags. My friends found me a room better suited to my diminishing fortune (one is not always at the height of prosperity); they installed me in the vicinity of Marylebone Street, in a garret whose dormer-window overlooked a cemetery: every night the watchman's rattle told me that body-snatchers had been at work.

It seems probable that Chateaubriand, writing long after the event, confused Marylebone Street with Marylebone High Street, and that his new lodgings were in a house overlooking one of the cemeteries in Paddington Street, which links the High Street with Baker Street. At all events, he was destined soon to leave London temporarily, and though he came back to these lodgings later on, he had a short but extremely happy period in the family of a cultivated and amiable clergyman in Suffolk.

One of the forward-looking *émigrés* with whom Chateaubriand later became very friendly in London was the Comte de Montlosier, a powerful personality whose hawklike glances had disconcerted him at first. They had taken a liking to one another after Montlosier had given the *Essay on Revolutions* a very frank review in the *émigré* newspaper he ran, sparing neither blame nor praise. Each week on a Wednesday, Montlosier entertained Chateaubriand to lunch, together with two other intimates, Christien de Lamoignon, who lived in Oxford Street, and the Chevalier de Panat, a former naval officer 'famed for his wit, his grubbiness and his greed'. On Saturdays, Chateaubriand returned the compliment with interest by laying on a supper party for the same party, at which punch was drunk. This, Montlosier considered a sign of affluence. Chateaubriand was no doubt earning more now that he had found his feet in the *émigré* community, and he had finally pocketed his pride and accepted the British Government's allowance. Another sign no doubt of his comparative 'affluence' was that at this time – or perhaps a little later – he had taken to himself a beautiful Creole as his mistress. She is said to have been the model for the *Atala* of his famous love story. Henriette de Belloy, widow of the Vicomte de Belloy, had been born in Haiti. In London, Chateaubriand and Malouet – perhaps the most influential of all the progressives – had been rivals for the love of this attractive woman. First she had been Malouet's mistress, now she was Chateaubriand's. Years later – in 1809, when she was forty and he nearly seventy – she married Malouet.

The Comte de Montlosier, who played an important part in Chateaubriand's life in London, had emigrated there in 1794. This able polemicist and journalist, equipped with an exceedingly well-informed and penetrating mind, came from the volcanic Auvergne district of southern France. Montlosier found himself lodgings at the Edgware Road end of the Marylebone Road, having previously stayed for a short while with other *émigrés*. Characteristically – for, to encyclopaedic reading in a variety of sciences, he added a gentleman farmer's interest in the weather – some of the earlier comments in his memoirs are on the climate:

The first thing to note about England is the nature of the climate. It is first of all marked by a notable absence of heat or cold. Myself, I would say: an absence of heat. I lived for six years on end facing a house where a trellis-work of black grapes was affixed to a thirty-foot-high wall. I saw it not exactly ripen, but become coloured, on one single occasion . . . I don't know why, but it is a fact that fruit in general does not ripen there, or ripens badly. In recent times, when Madame de Staël was in England, she told a Frenchman leaving for France who had asked her if she had any commission for him: 'When you see the sun, give it my compliments.'

From this climatic peculiarity, Montlosier made the deduction that in England both animal and vegetable vitality must be affected, and consequently that neither Nordic vigour nor French vivacity were to be found there. English meat lacked vital juices – therefore the English were lacking in vitality. That was why the English were taciturn, doled out such words as they had without grace, and were devoid of gestures. On the other hand, having no conversation to distract them, they were notably pertinacious and patient. This was the reason for their being, not inventors, but the perfectors of other people's inventions. The Englishman had an insatiable lust to make profits, where the Frenchman sought only his amusement. The French *émigrés* had brought their own arts and manufactures with them to England – but no sooner had the English set eyes on them than they made the most incredible improvements in them. The English were justly famed for their horses, their sheep, and their gardens. But none of these was English; the English had merely indefatigably improved them until they had reached their present high level. A general lack of wit in the English, as compared with the abundance of it in the French, served them well; it prevented jealous quarrels and low intrigues. In England the serious man sat enthroned, and the very word 'gay', so favourably applied in France, had a disapproving note about it.

Montlosier, who spent seven years in England, carried his theory of the English climate even farther. The Englishman, he indicates in his memoirs, goes abroad at his peril. For there – in France, Italy, America or India – he breathes a more vital air. Swollen with the butter, beer, and tea which he still insists on consuming in those happier lands, his body incorporates infinitely more vigorous and active elements. Well and good as long as he remains there. But when nostalgia or love of his motherland take him home again to his native mists, he is a lost man. His heart, accustomed to beat so much more strongly in the pure continental air, grows tired, overcome with lassitude. Profound gloom sets in, followed by collapse. He has become the victim of a well-known malady – the spleen, a consumption of the self, which by the stages of distraction or stupor, leads on to a rage for self-destruction. Hence England, a country so generally composed and calm, is the one with the most madmen, lunatic asylums, and books on madness in all Europe. The foreigner, on the other hand, who comes to live in England, soon develops rheumatism. Next, he begins to feel a vague unease in his chest, and soon he is getting palpitations. If, for reasons either of economy or his continental habits, he continues with a spare and sober diet, he is booking himself a ticket to Bedlam, or the cemetery. Sobriety on the Continent is possible; in England it is not. The air having no substance, you have to eat a lot. Four meals are not too much, and you can easily eat five. If lack of adequate air leads to excessive eating, it likewise provides a compulsive need for heavy drinking. There is said to be less of that now; but in 1794, when he reached England, 'le hard drinking' was 'tout à fait en vigueur'.

In spite of these daunting consequences of the English climate – so engagingly set forth – the Comte de Montlosier seems to have been pretty active throughout his exile on this side of the Channel. With his powerful frame, craggy face, and beak like Cyrano de Bergerac's, plus abounding energy, he was not a man to be overlooked.

Montlosier's main occupations during his exile were journalism and political pamphleteering. He varied this from time to time by utilising his knowledge of hypnosis – or magnetism as he called it – to treat the ailments of women whose cases had been brought to his notice. There were considerable risks in this – particularly for an émigré, who, if thought undesirable, could be deported under the recently-passed Alien Act. As a man of progressive views, he had, too, to contend with the growing displeasure of the royalist quarters in Baker Street, and with the competition, and later the attacks of a rival journalist, – named Peltier, who earlier on had constituted himself the mentor and helper of the young Chateaubriand. Jean-Gabriel Peltier had found such difficulty in earning a living when he first arrived in England in 1792 that he had turned himself into a showman of a rather macabre kind. He had a mahogany guillotine constructed, smaller than its Parisian prototype, but large enough to be lethal. For this gruesome machine he hired a room in which he gave displays of the despatch and neatness with which heads could be sliced off – not, of course, human heads, but those of animals. Outside the exhibition, he put up a large notice announcing the species of animal he was going to decapitate that day. One day it would announce: A GOOSE TO BE GUILLOTINED TODAY; another: SEE A PIG GUILLOTINED TODAY – and so on. For the front seats at this slaughtering he charged five shillings, and for the rest a shilling.

In 1798, Jacques Mallet du Pan, the most celebrated publicist of the Revolution in the constitutional monarchist interest, took refuge in London. Since Marylebone was *par excellence* the centre of all *émigré* political activity, he inevitably gravitated there. His lodgings were in Woodstock Street, Cavendish Square, and he was soon running a newspaper, the *Mercure Britannique*, which appeared both in French and in an English translation. Mallet, a Swiss living and working in Paris, had lost most of his possessions in the Revolution, and had arrived in England quite early on. He transferred himself, however, to Switzerland, and stayed there indefatigably pamphleteering until 1798, when French pressure on the Swiss forced him to leave and take refuge again in England. Montlosier, who was very friendly with him, described him as having a rough exterior and a manner which was repellent – a complete contrast, he says, to the extremely engaging manners of Malouet. Mallet du Pan died prematurely in 1800. But his family stayed on in England, and his descendants have been English ever since.

The monarchist progressives in the *émigré* society of London – men who were willing to forget the cruelties of the Terror and to learn from the past misdeeds of the *ancien régime* and the Bourbon monarchy – were a minority in a community which was dominated by diehard royalists and clerics. The Comte de Provence – later Louis XVIII, who did not arrive in England until 1807 after nearly twenty years' wandering about Europe as a refugee, had settled at Hartwell in Buckinghamshire. But his brother, and his successor on the French throne, the Comte d'Artois, had, as we have seen, chosen Marylebone for his London residence. He had come to London as a refugee as far back as 1793, and had later settled in Baker Street with his courtiers around him in houses nearby. Hence, Marylebone had been the centre of all French royalist activities for some years when the future Louis XVIII belatedly turned up. During this period d'Artois had naturally set the tone of the leading *émigré* society. A tall, handsome, exquisitely-dressed man with extremely engaging manners, he was an uncompromising adherent of the Bourbon monarchy's divine right to govern. Much less politically adroit than his equally absolutist brother, his unbending reactionary policy was one with which British Governments had to reckon throughout the first decade of the emigration.

D'Artois had with him in his exile his sons, the Dukes of Angoulême and Berry. Angoulême seems to have been a nonentity, and an
uncouth one at that. He had married his cousin, the daughter of
Louis XVI – known as Madame Royale – and sarcastically described
by Napoleon as 'the only man in the family'. Berry was a man of
spirit, who had seen service with the Army of the Princes, but his
manner was extremely offensive, and he was impossibly inconsiderate
and capricious. It was his fate to be assassinated in the Paris Opéra
five years after the Bourbon restoration. The British Government
made all the royal exiles allowances sufficient to enable them to
maintain themselves with modest dignity. The future Louis XVIII
received £7,200 a year; the future Charles X, £6,000 a year, and the
Dukes of Angoulême and Berry, £3,600 a year each. D'Artois was
able to keep up a certain amount of state at his Baker Street residence.
His house, near the corner of Crawford Street – then known as
Durweston Street – had a large drawing room on the first floor,
which he used for receptions. Miss Margery Weiner, in her book,
*The French Exiles, 1789–1815* has described the routine of his life:

> ... Every day the captain of his non-existent guards bowed him
> into his carriage (it was never paid for, and Howard the coach-
> maker ultimately went bankrupt) to take him down Baker Street
> to Louise's house ... Once a week he received the gentlemen who
> had belonged to the court, the Ducs d'Uzès, de Maille, de Fitz-
> James, de Lorges, de Duras, de Choiseul, de Castries, de Sérent
> ... Three times a year he gave formal dinners – New Year's Day,
> feast day of St Louis, and his own name-day, St Charles'.

The Louise referred to was Louise de Polastron, d'Artois' mistress,
who lived a short distance away in Thayer Street. In this street, she
had for neighbours the aged Duc de Castries, a Marshal of France
who had commanded the First Corps of the Army of the Princes,
and the Comte Lévis de la Tour du Pin, of the distinguished
Dauphiné family of that name. Her next-door neighbour was the
Baron de Montalembert, colonel of a French *émigré* legion in
British service.

Both the Duc de Berry and the Duc de Bourbon had English
mistresses. Berry, who did not find himself a wife till after the restoration, when he was thirty-eight, lived at 39 George Street, a couple
of doors away from the Archbishop of Narbonne, an aged and
rather unepiscopal aristocrat noted in pre-Revolution days for his

addiction to hunting on the family estate at Hautefontaine in Picardy. Berry's *petite amie*, called Amy Brown, bore him two daughters. In 1820 as he lay dying in the Opéra after the assassin had stabbed him, he called for these girls and entrusted them to the care of his wife, the Duchess Marie-Caroline. In the wave of emotion which swept royalist circles after the assassination, Louis XVIII legitimised and then ennobled them as the Comtesse d'Issoudun and the Comtesse de Vierzon. The Duc de Bourbon's mistress, Sophie Dawes, was a much better known, and certainly a greatly more formidable character. Louis-Henri-Joseph, Duc de Bourbon, later Prince de Condé, had arrived in England in 1795, after having commanded the Third Corps of the Army of the Princes. He had taken a house in Orchard Street. A widower verging on forty, he had come into contact with the captivating Sophie and quickly fallen victim to her combination of charm and dominance. He was perhaps hardly the man to be able to put up much resistance to a determined adventuress of Sophie's ruthlessly climbing type.

Born a fisherman's daughter in the Isle of Wight, she had been a workhouse girl, a servant in a brothel, and an officer's mistress before in a moment of luck for her she hooked on to the Duke, floundering in London like a fish out of water. After the Bourbon restoration she got herself married to one of his aides-de-camp, the Baron de Feuchères, who quickly disappeared, leaving Sophie in entire charge of the mentally rather sub-normal Prince de Condé, as he had then become. In the early 1820s, having no heir himself – his son the Duc d'Enghien had achieved a place in history when years before he had been cold-bloodedly murdered on the orders of Napoleon – he had been persuaded by Sophie to make a will leaving his vast fortune to the Duc d'Aumale, son of the future King Louis-Philippe. In return for this stroke, Louis-Philippe had made her a *quid pro quo* of which the most obvious element was the presentation of the Baronne de Feuchères at Louis XVIII's court. Time passed, Charles X succeeded Louis, and then came the July Revolution. Shortly afterwards, Condé was found hanged from one of the high windows of his château at Saint-Leu Taverny. This mysterious occurrence took place just after he had announced his intention of revoking his will and following the deposed Charles X into exile. Sophie was suspected, but no action was ever taken against her, and she returned to England with a substantial fortune. King Louis-Philippe, who had received her at the Tuileries several times, had the château

of Saint-Leu Taverny razed to the ground, thus leaving the matter
a deeper mystery than ever.

The life of the Bourbon princes and *noblesse* in London, from
which Sophie had emerged to establish herself in royalist circles in
Paris, was a curious mixture of *splendeurs* and *misères*. The princes
had of course their political pocket-money from the British Government, their obliging but hardly disinterested paymaster. But inevitably they and their courtiers outran their resources, and – for
instance – the bankrupting of Howard, the unfortunate coachmaker,
was not the work of d'Artois alone. Condé and other nobles of the
Baker Street quarter had bought carriages of him for which they
had been unable to pay. They had, of course, to keep up a certain
state and dignity in mixing with the British royalty and aristocracy,
and there was a decent, if modest, hospitality to be maintained. Some
of them only mixed with their own *émigré* nobility, and kept away
entirely from British society. Others, like the Duc de Berry, were
frequently to be seen at the houses and entertainments of British
personages of appropriate rank and political sympathies. Berry of
course could rely on his British Government allowance to keep his
head above water, but it was the lesser nobility of his household who
really felt the pinch of want. One such was the Comte Auguste de la
Ferronays, who was a soldier by profession and a close personal friend
of Berry's who had served with him in the Army of the Princes. An
active, stirring man whose heart was in his army career, he hated
the life of a dangling courtier and resented having to live in exile in
England. Things were made no easier by a long separation from
his young wife and children who had to be left behind in Prussia
when the Army of the Princes was disbanded.

De la Ferronays was finally reunited with his wife and children –
and indeed with her father and mother as well. The whole family
had decided to leave Prussia when the French declared war on that
state, and had come to join him at his home at 36 Manchester Street
– only a few minutes' walk away from the Duc de Berry's house in
George Street. But in the days of the carriage society, walking was
not a method of progression thought acceptable for a family of the
social standing of the de la Ferronays – at least when they went
calling. It was all very well for the Count to go on foot to his master
the Duc de Berry's house in George Street, but when he and his wife
went into society – and particularly into English society – it was
necessary for them to drive up in a well-appointed carriage. But on

the de la Ferronays' pittance of £120 a year from the Duke, plus an allowance of £60 a year from the British Government, the maintenance of one's own carriage was an unimaginable luxury. The result was that they rarely went into society. When they did, it meant begging a lift in the Duc de Berry's carriage. Or, if that was unobtainable, making themselves beholden to some titled *émigré* temporarily able to bear the expense of an equipage of style. Even then, it was sometimes not possible to get a lift home by carriage after the party was over. In that case, they were reduced to the humiliating shift of pretending to their host that their equipage had inexplicably not turned up and marching along the rank of waiting carriages, shouting: 'James! James!' – the name of their imaginary coachman – until they were out of sight and could safely take themselves home on foot.

For many years during the emigration the most numerous single class of refugees were the priests, who at one time numbered some 8,000 out of the total of some 25,000-odd *émigrés* who made Britain their home for longer or shorter periods. This very large intake of Roman Catholic clergy occurred when Catholic emancipation, in any serious sense, remained unknown in the British Isles. The Gordon Riots, which had taken place a mere decade before the outbreak of the French Revolution, were still fresh in the memory of most Londoners. The country was solidly and traditionally Protestant, and inclined to regard the Pope of Rome and his followers as a profane and iniquitous lot, never to be allowed anywhere near Old England. Yet the British Government and the Anglican clergy, and, more surprisingly, the British people, seem to have treated the French papist clerics in their midst not only with consideration, but in general with compassion. The priests, most of them ardent royalists, responded by behaving with exemplary correctness and dignity, and many of them made themselves useful to their hosts as French language tutors. The fear that they would use their position to attempt the proselytism of their hosts was never realised. Some of the credit for the relatively painless way in which they were absorbed into the community must be given to the committee so promptly set up by Burke, the Duke of Portland and others, for their relief. A number were also helped and given hospitality by the Catholic nobility of the country.

Tom Moore, the Irish poet and song-writer, arriving in London in 1799 as a young man fresh from Dublin, settled in lodgings at 85

George Street. Here he found himself in the heart of the *émigré* community, and more particularly of the district favoured by the French clergy. Might not the emigrant bishop referred to in the following extract from his *Memoirs* have been Saint-Pol de Léon himself?

> The lodgings taken for me . . . was a front room up two pairs of stairs . . . for which I paid six shillings per week. That neighbourhood was the chief resort of the poor French emigrants, who were then swarming into London, and in the back room of my floor was an old curé, the head of whose bed was placed tête-a-tête with mine, so that (the partition being very thin) not a snore of his escaped me . . . A poor emigrant bishop occupied the floor below me.

Moore also, in a letter written in April 1799 to his mother, indicates how the *émigrés* coped with the food problem by setting up their own cheap eating-houses.

> They have my breakfast laid as snug as possible every morning, and I dine at the *traiteur's* like a prince for eightpence or ninepence. The other day I had soup, *bouilli*, rice-pudding and porter for ninepence halfpenny. If that be not cheap the deuce is in it.

Among the *émigrés* the arts were represented for some time by one of France's most celebrated portrait-painters – Elizabeth Louise Vigée-Lebrun. At the time of her arrival in London in 1802 she was getting on for fifty, and had been a noted figure in the art world for twenty years. As a favourite at the court of Louis XVI and a friend of Marie Antoinette, she had found it advisable to leave France on the outbreak of the Revolution. After her departure in 1789 she went first to Italy and then, after staying in some of the leading European cities, spent five years in Russia. She had returned to Paris in 1801, but had found life under Napoleon not at all to her taste. Hence her arrival in London the following year, where she settled in Marylebone – at No. 61 Baker Street. As her self-portrait in the much reproduced *The Artist and her Daughter* shows, she had been a very pretty woman in a kind of ingénue way. But a lot of water had flowed under the bridges, and many heads had rolled in France, since she had given the world that gently idyllic picture. Her kind of society had been slaughtered, or driven from France, and she had been an exile for years in a Europe that had been stood upon its head.

Nevertheless, could this dainty creature really have developed 'rather a plebeian and masculine exterior', with 'manners far from prepossessing' by the time Madame Tussaud – of the waxworks – met her? The Comtesse de Boigne, a leading French *émigré*, who came across her in the early 1790s, found her 'very good-natured, still pretty, and rather foolish'. In June 1803, when Opie called to cast a fellow professional's eye over her output, he seems to have noticed only her pictures, and not herself. On 7 June, Farington recorded in his diary:

Opie told me that He saw Madame Le Brun's pictures today at Her House, No. 61 Baker Street. They are painted in the present French manner, but better than any He saw in Paris. – The imitation of particular things, velvet, – silk, &c., &c., very good. – Perhaps the care and correctness might be considered by the English painters with some attention, and to their advantage. But with all their merit, they afforded him no high pleasure as works of art . . . Her price for a three-quarters is 200 guineas.

During the three years of her exile in London, Vigée-Lebrun painted portraits of the Prince Regent, Byron, and other celebrities. At 200 guineas a time for a three-quarter-length portrait – and presumably more for a full-length – plus her European reputation to bring the clients flocking in, she cannot have been lacking in comfort, and indeed in a degree of luxury.

An eminent French politician who died the year Vigée-Lebrun arrived in England, and who had spent many years – between 1787 and his death – as an exile in London was Charles-Alexandre de Calonne. Calonne's name and hers had been linked in a rather scandalous way at one time, and in her memoirs she told the tale of how the scandal arose, and refuted the allegations. Calonne had been Controller-General of Finance in France from 1783 to 1787. In that year, he was dismissed by Louis XVI for failing to solve the continuing financial crisis that was so important a factor in precipitating the Revolution. He emigrated to England, taking with him his considerable art collection, and became well known in London as a collector. At one time he was the owner of Sir Joshua Reynolds' much-fancied picture, *Mrs Siddons as the Tragic Muse*, for which according to Farington he paid eight hundred guineas. Vigée-Lebrun had painted his portrait at the height of his power in 1785. This dapper, little black-eyed man, 'a most complete courtier', whose polished manner and charm won him popularity in London society, took himself off to Coblenz in 1789 and there spent the whole of his fortune trying to organise the counter-revolution with the aid of the royal *émigré* party and the Army of the Princes. His efforts proved ill-judged, and when Coblenz collapsed as a centre of resistance and a springboard in 1795, he was forced to take refuge in England again. He had borrowed heavily and was ruined. The bulk of his collection went under the hammer that same year. He seems however to have been able to put a brave face on things. The all-seeing Farington, in his diary for 18 December 1798, noted that: 'Mrs Wyndham, who lives with Lord Egremont . . . spoke warmly in favour of Monsr. CALONNE (late Prime Minister of France), said he was an enthusiast in regard to pictures, and much of a gentleman in manners.' She added, with it appears unconscious irony, that the great changes in France seemed to have made little impression on his mind. He was almost penniless when he died four years later – back in Paris at last, by Napoleon's favour.

A lesser-known *émigré* portrait-painter than Vigée-Lebrun, who nevertheless enjoyed much popularity in England, was Henri-Pierre Danloux. Danloux, who was just on forty when he arrived in London, quickly adapted his style to suit the current taste. Just as Vigée-Lebrun has recorded for us what Calonne looked like, so Danloux has done the same for the Bishop of Saint-Pol de Léon – a formidable, tormented face. Danloux settled in Marylebone at 11 Charles – now Mortimer – Street. Among his first patrons was Richard Foster, Customs official, of Thames Bank, Bucks., to whose home he was frequently invited. One of the results of this connection is his picture, *The Masters Foster*. It shows the Foster boys, perhaps ten and eight years old, moving off down a woodland path with cricket bats and a ball. In its marriage of English informality and French technical skill, this brilliantly vivacious presentation is both portraiture and narrative painting. The focus of course is on the children, whose faces are highly individualised studies, but the background, with its precise handling of the Watteau-like woods and figures, is, one feels, equally important. The children are not merely being recorded in paint for the benefit of their parents; they are the central element in an anecdote of English middle-class life in 1792.

During the last years of his life, Pitt, the heart and soul of the British struggle against the France of the Revolution and the Empire, had a house in Baker Street, near its junction with the Marylebone

Road. He was thus close to many of the leading *émigrés*. The Comtesse de Boigne, with her numerous contacts in both British and *émigré* society, had the opportunity of seeing him in this final stage of his career. He was a tired and sick man. He had taken the house after his fall from power in 1801, and installed his niece, Lady Hester Stanhope, to look after his establishment. According to the Comtesse, who was much in high society in London, Lady Hester – who afterwards made such a name for herself by her swashbuckling in the Levant, and by the oriental state she kept up in her residence on Mount Lebanon – needed her uncle to look after her. Her sister had already fallen for 'a village apothecary' now that her mother, Pitt's sister, was dead, and there was no knowing what imprudence Hester might commit.

> She did the honours of the very modest house occupied by her uncle after he had retired with a middling fortune. During this period of leisure, the latter had taken it upon himself to act as a chaperon to his niece, remaining with the utmost good nature until four or five o'clock in the morning at dances, where he was bored to death. I have often seen him sitting in a corner and waiting with exemplary patience until it suited Lady Hester to put an end to his suffering.

What a contrast with the Pitt, Chateaubriand some years earlier had seen running up the steps of the House of Commons in his elegant black coat, taking them two or three at a time, his sword at his side and his hat under his arm!

Pitt's health did not finally collapse until 1806. After his first government had fallen in 1801, he had become Lord Warden of the Cinque Ports and turned his efforts to the drilling of the Volunteers. Bodies of these had been set up all over the country for home defence at a time when most of the regular army was serving abroad. Marylebone's first volunteer corps had been enrolled in 1797 and had not been disbanded until 1801, when the Peace of Amiens ushered in a brief couple of years' respite from the prolonged struggle with France. The St Marylebone Volunteers, or the 'Blue Bottles' as they were known, from the colour of their uniform, mustered nearly eight hundred strong, and were armed with a motley collection of fowling-pieces, firelocks, bayonets, and pikes. Their parade ground was in George Street, the western end of which, it will be remembered, abutted at that time on a large unbuilt-up stretch of the parish lying behind the barracks of the 2nd Life Guards. The citizen soldiers, on their march, passed right through the heart of the *émigré* quarter – George Street being closer packed with royalist clerics and *ancien régime noblesse* than any other part of Marylebone. If their antiquated weapons inspired little confidence in the hearts of the dispirited refugees watching from their windows, at least their stalwart bearing and dogged John Bull faces indicated that the *sacrés bouledogues* would not easily yield to an invader.

On the resumption of the war in 1803, Marylebone answered the call again with the formation of the 'Royal York St Marylebone Volunteers'. The new title was a delicate compliment to the Commander-in-Chief of the British Army, the Duke of York, who lived in Marylebone. This was at a time when his affair with the beautiful and impudent Mary Anne Clarke – then installed in Gloucester Place – was in full swing. One suspects that the new corps, which remained in being for eleven years, was a force much more to be reckoned with than its predecessor. The rank and file were mainly skilled tradesmen. It was better armed, and it was 'officered by gentlemen'. Its correspondingly greater glitter was provided by a uniform consisting of 'a scarlet jacket trimmed with gold lace, and blue pantaloons'. Commanded by Colonel the Right Hon. Viscount Duncannon, it went as far afield as Hounslow Heath to indulge in its 'numerous battles, skirmishes, and gallant achievements'. Jeffry Wyatt – afterwards Sir Jeffry Wyatville, restorer of Windsor Castle for George IV – told Farington the diarist, on 19 October 1803, that he was the only professional man among the officers in this corps, and that 'all the rest are in independent circumstances'. Farington adds that the previous day they had received their colours from the Duchess of Devonshire. Her nephew, Duncannon, had afterwards entertained all the officers in the corps – some fifty of them – to dinner at his house in Cavendish Square.

The Volunteer, the public house at the north end of Baker Street whose name commemorates Marylebone's first home guard, was founded during the great struggle against Napoleon. On 20 April 1814, the day when Louis XVIII came in state to London from his retreat at Hartwell in Buckinghamshire, on his way to Paris and the crown of France, many toasts must have been drunk at this tavern at the downfall (the 'Hundred Days' had yet to come) of the 'Corsican Ogre', who had been the bogy of the British people for the best part of twenty years. It is permissible to think that some of the *émigrés* who had waited so long for this moment stepped into The Volunteer wearing white cockades and calling for a toast to the restoration of the House of Bourbon. Farington, R.A., once again depicts the scene on that memorable day:

> After painting till past three o'clock, I walked out & proceeded through Portman-square to Oxford-street, which I found lined with people on both sides & a continued line of Carriages with Ladies & Gentlemen in them . . . Cavalry were riding forwards & backwards to keep the middle of the street clear. The windows of the Houses were also filled with persons anxiously waiting for the arrival of the French Monarch. I proceeded from Oxford-street along the Edgware Road to the Halfmile stone . . . A little before 5 o'clock a great number of persons on Horseback, those who had rode to some distance to have a first view of the Cavalcade, came riding hastily forward . . . After several carriages had passed containing French noblemen, & in one of them the Duchesse d'Angoulême, the carriage of Louis 18th followed. He sat on the right hand *forward* & I was struck with the resemblance he bore to the print of His Brother the late Louis 16th . . . The last Carriage in the Cavalcade was that in which the Prince Regent rode, he having gone to Stanmore to meet the French King. A large Body of Cavalry followed the Prince Regent's Carriage, which at the rate they drove was soon out of sight.

# 10. *Americans in Marylebone*

Dɪᴅ Dr Johnson really say: 'I am willing to love all mankind, except an American'? If so, was he perhaps thinking more particularly of the wife of one of the closest of his younger friends? John Paradise was more than thirty years younger than the doctor – an able, cultured, scholarly man, born in Greece and brought up in Italy, who had married Lucy Ludwell, a Virginian heiress, in London. That was in 1769 – seven years before the American Declaration of Independence – when he was twenty-six. The Paradises lived in Charles Street (now Mortimer Street), near Cavendish Square, and they entertained lavishly. Lucy Paradise had ambitions to be a society hostess, and for a number of years she possessed the means of living it up in late Georgian London. Even if, in the rather cool atmosphere prevailing after the War of Independence, she was cold-shouldered by English hostesses who regarded the Americans as rebellious colonials, the change of political climate had its compensations. The great Thomas Jefferson, then American Minister in Paris, visited England in 1786. He and John Adams, the first minister of independent America to the Court of St James's, went on a tour of some of the stately homes and gardens of England. The two future Presidents of the United States – Jefferson a talented architect, and both connoisseurs of fine architecture and landscape gardening – took a friendly interest in the Paradises. Adams frequently dined at their house, and Jefferson was to become a life-long friend.

Lucy Paradise appears to have been the very reverse of her quiet, studious, learned husband. As Laetitia Hawkins, a contemporary writer, rather cattishly observed 'nothing could be more elegant and refined than Mrs Paradise's whole exterior'. But, it seems, appearances were deceptive in her case. She had been known to threaten a servant who brought her a dirty plate with breaking it over her head, and at one of her evening parties had quelled the *diavolo incarnato*

Baretti, Johnson's Italian protégé, by pouring the contents of a scalding hot tea-urn over his head. It is clear that she was a very spirited lady; the trouble was that she was also incurably frivolous and headstrong, and evidently rather ignorant and silly. 'Now I'll be crucified,' she announced towards the end of one of her parties, 'if Mr Friery hasn't made his escape! Miss P, go down and see if he is in the parlour with Mr P, and bring him up again!' Her unwilling daughter went and fetched up the reluctant Mr Friery – already in his overcoat. He was at once made to 'take another dance', with 'Mrs Den, an old harridan!' Behaviour of this sort, larded with much empty prattle, was not overlooked in the circles in which her husband moved. After the Paradises had left a tea-party at Dr Burney's one of the musicologist's other guests, Mrs Thrale, turned to Dr Johnson and complained that she was 'quite worn out with that silly woman, who had talked of her family and affairs till she was sick to death of hearing her'.

'Madam', said he, 'why do you blame the woman for the only sensible thing she could do – talking of her family and her affairs? For how should a woman who is as empty as a drum talk upon any other subject? – If you speak to her of the sun, she does not know it rises in the east – if you speak to her of the moon, she does not know it changes at the full; if you speak to her of the queen, she does not know she is the king's wife. How then can you blame her for talking of her family and affairs?'

Poor Mrs Paradise! Fate had a very dusty end of the road in store for her. Financial embarrassments compelled her and her husband to move out of their fine house near Cavendish Square. Retrenchment took them successively to two smaller establishments in the neighbourhood. Mr Paradise then died at the age of fifty-two. Mrs Paradise went back to the United States, lost her reason, and ended her days in an asylum. The fact that her English doctor – also medical adviser of Dr Johnson and Boswell – was Richard Warren, physician to George III, was perhaps a little ominous. The 'mad doctor' of those days was drastic enough in his treatment of his lunatic patients, and the very sight of him may well have proved sufficient to send an unstable case over the edge. The roughness of late eighteenth century medicine was summed up in the wry comment of Carlisle, a contemporary surgeon, on Dr Warren: 'Dr Warren never killed in vain' – a reference to his willingness to try some other drastic nostrum once his current specific had killed a patient.

Living in Marylebone, in Gloucester Place, at the same time as the Paradises was an American general who is now remembered chiefly for having defected to the British at the height of the War of Independence. The American view of Benedict Arnold is naturally a jaundiced one. He left his side in the lurch at a critical moment in the struggle, and was preparing to betray his command at West Point to the enemy when the capture of the British spy, Major André, led to his exposure. It sticks in the American gullet that he not only fled to the British lines, but accepted George III's commission and commanded a force sent to attack his own home state of Connecticut. Yet Arnold was no ordinary traitor, but an able and gallant soldier, admired by Washington and promoted Major-General for bravery in battle. He had fought with distinction at Saratoga, and a year later had been promoted to the command of Philadelphia. He was a man on the up-and-up in the world of military renown. Yet at a critical moment he decided to fling everything overboard. The explanation given is that he was an ambitious man, bitterly disappointed by the promotion over his head of a number of juniors. And the inference is that his planned betrayal of the insurgent cause was an act of revenge. André, the British officer with whom he had conspired, was hanged by the Americans, as a spy. Rather surprisingly, his remains were repatriated in 1821 and deposited in Westminster Abbey. One wonders how many, if any, other secret agents have had this honour. General Arnold settled in London after the war was over, lived in Gloucester Place in complete obscurity, and died in 1801 at the age of sixty.

John Adams, the first American Minister, had set up his legation at No. 9 Grosvenor Square. 'Little America' still houses U.S. diplomats and their enormous ancillary staffs in the vast embassy building of nearly two hundred years later. But between their first arrival in the square in 1785 and their latter-day return to it, American representatives have had a number of different addresses, including several in Marylebone. Rufus King, for instance, the fourth U.S. representative accredited to the Court of St. James's, had his legation at 20 Baker Street. This street had only recently been completed when he arrived in London in 1796, and he and his staff will have been accommodated in one of the elegant Georgian mansions which made it a smart neighbourhood up till the middle of the nineteenth century. King did not leave until 1803, and by the time James Monroe, his successor as Minister, arrived in 1805, the Chancellery had been moved to Great Cumberland Place, near the present Marble Arch. Monroe himself took a house in Portland Place. He came to London from the post of Minister to France, and his Francophile tendencies did not endear him to ruling circles in London.

Later, as President of the United States to enunciate the celebrated 'Monroe Doctrine' (warning Old World colonisers to keep out of the New World), he had at this time just helped to negotiate the purchase by the U.S.A. of the vast French New World territory of Louisiana. Napoleon, armed with the eighty million francs produced by this transaction, had yet further encouragement to resume hostilities against Britain. Monroe therefore, as the author or part author of this stroke, must have been barely *persona grata* when he arrived in London to represent the late rebellious colonists of America. A policy of petty pinpricks was used against him in official circles, which from Castlereagh downwards treated him with insolent disdain. At his first State Dinner, he was allocated a remote position between the representatives of a couple of petty German principalities. Thereafter he was contemptuously ignored until the Russian Ambassador intervened and proposed his health as the latest addition to London's diplomatic circles. It is said that Castlereagh himself treated him to a display of insular arrogance at a dinner party given by the celebrated Whig hostess, Lady Holland. Monroe had used the word 'equipages' in the course of conversation, with its connotation doubtless of high-bred horses, stylish coachwork, and smartly-dressed grooms bowling along some fashionable boulevard. 'Equipages?' said Castlereagh. 'Do they really have equipages in America?'

An interesting feature of these early days of Anglo-American relations was the presence on the English scene of leading American men of science. Benjamin Franklin, Count Rumford, Samuel Morse are names which immediately spring to mind. Franklin, of course, was dead before the eighteenth century was out, and his English activities were largely political. But Count Rumford was the founder of the Royal Institution, and so one of the fathers of the spread of scientific information in Britain. Samuel Morse, the third of this trio of great names, arrived in London in 1811 aged twenty – not as a scientist at all, but as a budding painter. He settled in Marylebone, living first in Great Titchfield Street, and then at 8 Buckingham Place – now 141 Cleveland Street – where his residence is commemorated by a blue L.C.C. plaque. At one of his Great Titchfield Street addresses, he shared lodgings with C. R. Leslie, another young American, then at the outset of his career as a leading English genre and portrait painter. The future biographer of Constable was then only seventeen, and like Morse had just arrived in the country from America (see Chapters 7 and 8). Appropriately enough for the two young men, Benjamin West, their fellow-countryman, was President of the Royal Academy, and for years had been the outstanding Establishment figure of the art world in London. Samuel Morse's studies under West led to his exhibiting at the Academy in 1812, and again in 1814 and 1815. He proved to be an artist of very considerable ability, and no doubt would have made a name for himself as a painter had he, 'the American Leonardo', not been still more interested in scientific discovery than in painting. As it is, his output of portraits and Romantic landscapes, done after his return to America in 1815, brought him recognition as one of the most important of early U.S. painters.

It is a mark of the early distinction of Morse's mind that in the four years he spent in England he became friendly with Turner, Lawrence, Coleridge and Wordsworth – four of the most splendid talents of the nineteenth century. It is probably characteristic of the inventor of the Morse Code that of two stories of his recollections of life in London in his day both should be concerned with sounds. He writes to a friend soon after his arrival in Marylebone:

> The cries of London, of which you have doubtless heard, are very annoying to me, as indeed they are to all strangers. The noise of them is constantly in one's ears from morning till midnight and, with the exception of one or two, they all appear to be the cries of distress. I don't know how many times I have run to the window expecting to see some poor creature in the agonies of death, but found to my surprise, that it was only an old woman crying 'Fardin' apples', or something of the kind. Hogarth's picture of the enraged musician will give you an excellent idea of the noise I hear every day under my windows . . .

And again:

> There is a singular custom with respect to knocking at the doors of houses here which is strictly adhered to. A servant belonging to the house rings the bell only; a strange servant knocks once; a

market man or woman knocks once and rings; the penny post knocks twice; and a gentleman or lady half a dozen quick knocks, or any number over two. A nobleman generally knocks eight or ten times, very loud.

This curious piece of sociological information makes it clear that the freedom of the knocker was reserved for the higher ranks of society. The poor slavey of the house was not allowed to knock at all, and one's neighbour's servant was conceded no more than a single rap. At the other end of the scale, the nobleman could be as peremptory with the knocker as he pleased. George Cruikshank, almost the exact contemporary of Morse, painted a picture with a strong Dickens flavour called *The Runaway Knock*. This showed a portly gentleman in Regency costume standing glaring on his front doorstep amidst a bevy of barking house-dogs while a couple of mischievous boys who have clearly used his knocker with more than aristocratic freedom are seen laughing over their shoulders as they run off. The women of the house are shown at the windows peeking inquisitively out. The fact that Cruikshank did not call his picture *The Runaway Ring* is clearly full of a social significance which no longer has any relevance today.

Almost all leading Americans of the late eighteenth and early nineteenth centuries seem to have been christened Benjamin. Benjamin Franklin; Benjamin West; Benjamin Thompson, Count Rumford; Benjamin Rush (one of the signatories of the Declaration of Independence); and Benjamin Silliman – yet another scientist. Silliman, Professor of Chemistry and Natural History at Yale University, toured England in 1805 and stayed for a while in Marylebone. As befitted a man of his interests, his first observation concerned a meteorological phenomenon. His journal for 2 August records:

There has been a thunderstorm this evening, with torrents of rain, which have disengaged such quantities of hepatic gas from the subterranean receptacles of filth that the air has been for hours extremely offensive. I am told that sudden and heavy rains usually produce this effect in London and that sometimes the gas is so abundant as to blacken the silver utensils in the closets.

London was a city of cesspools in the Professor's day – even the pestilential system of obligatory sewers all draining into the Thames lay forty years ahead. If it was indeed the 'hepatic gas' which produced the deposit on silver objects, it is surprising that he had not heard of a similar deposit in American cities, which were presumably in 1805 also in a rudimentary state of drainage.

A couple of weeks later, Professor Silliman's journal records the observation of a quite different kind of phenomenon.

> As I was standing in a shop in the Strand, this morning, I had the satisfaction which I had long wished for, of seeing *Lord Nelson*. He was walking through the streets, on the opposite side, in company with his chaplain, and, as usual, followed by a crowd. This is a distinction which great men are obliged to share in common with all wonderful exhibitions ... Lord Nelson cannot appear in the streets without immediately collecting a retinue, which augments as he proceeds, and when he enters a shop the door is thronged until he comes out when the air rings with huzzas, and the dark cloud of the populace again moves on and hangs upon his skirts ... My view of him was in profile. His features are sharp – and his skin is now very much burnt from his having been long at sea; he has the balancing gait of a sailor; his person is spare and of about the middle height or rather more, and mutilated by the loss of an arm and an eye, besides many other infirmities of less magnitude.

In 1815 there arrived in London, John Quincy Adams, son of the first American Minister to the Court of St James's, and like him later President of the United States. Adams came three weeks before the Battle of Waterloo and the final defeat of Napoleon. Unlike his father, he did not choose Grosvenor Square for his residence, but moved out to what was then the rural peace of the village of Ealing. He stayed only two years. His successor, Richard Rush, son of that Benjamin Rush who was one of the signatories of the Declaration of Independence, spent eight years as Minister in London, and lived at No. 20 Baker Street – the house where Rufus King had preceded him at the turn of the century. In his book, *A Residence at the Court of London*, published in 1833, some years after his return to the U.S.A., he explains that the quietness and seclusion of this part of Marylebone, and the number of furnished houses available, had attracted many foreign embassies to the district.

> This part is quite secluded, if so I may speak of a town district of more than a hundred thousand inhabitants. You hear little

noise beyond the rumble of equipages, beginning at two o'clock, abating in the evening and returning at midnight . . . I found that the Russian, Austrian and French Ambassadors had here fixed their domiciles. Every house has its area enclosed with iron palisades. The front-door steps are all of brown stone, with iron railings topped with spikes; so that the eye traces in all directions lines of this bristling iron-work. If you add, that on the broad pavements of flag, you perhaps see nobody before noon, unless a straggling servant in morning livery, or a butcher's boy with tray in hand issuing here and there from an area, you have the main external characteristics of this region when first I beheld it.

It must be remembered that the American Minister in London in Rush's day was not the representative of the richest, and possibly the most powerful, nation on earth, but the emissary of a far from affluent struggling ex-colonial community which had possessed its independence for no more than a single generation. As we have seen, only a decade earlier, Monroe had been treated by Castlereagh with a cool hauteur which he must have found hard to bear. This may have been largely due to his having identified himself so closely with the cause of Franco-American friendship, but it was also undoubtedly owing to Castlereagh's consciousness that America was not a major Power. The rent of No. 20 Baker Street was only four hundred and fifty guineas a year at a time when some other embassies were paying a thousand guineas a year for their furnished accommodation. Indeed, in some West End squares, the rent of a furnished house was 'sixty and sometimes eighty guineas *a week*'. The furnishings of these mansions – presumably some of them the town houses of the wealthier nobility – were clearly extremely opulent. Yet even a distinctly more modest style of residence – such as was the case at 20 Baker Street – appears to have impressed the American Minister. Admitting sadly that it was the policy of his government to pay small salaries, he adds:

A great number of the houses were to let, and I went through them. From the basement to the attics, every thing had an air of comfort. The supply of furniture was full. The staircases were of white stone. The windows and beds in servants' rooms had curtains. No floor was without carpeting. In many instances libraries made part of the furniture to be rented with the houses – a beautiful part.

Joseph Farington, the influential Royal Academician whose diary is so informative on this period, noted that Richard Rush was reputed to be 'a very respectable man' and that he 'delighted in pursuing his studies' – legal presumably, as he was an able lawyer. Farington approved of him because he was not, he heard, pro-French, like some other leading American politicians. The sober, steady seriousness of the man emerges from his journal. Sometimes, however, he allows himself a lighter note in describing the antics of the official diplomatic world. One such anecdote concerns a dinner party given by the Right Honourable Joseph Planta, M.P., Private Secretary in turn to Castlereagh and Canning – at his house in Queen Anne Street. Canning was present, and also Lord Goderich (then Mr Robinson) and Lord Granville. After dinner a game of questions and answers was started of a kind which suggests that a famous B.B.C. radio quiz game is far from new. Canning and Goderich set themselves up as a 'court of questioners' and instructed Rush and Granville to think of an object without disclosing it:

> The first question asked by Canning was whether the object in question belonged to the Animal or the Vegetable world. 'The Vegetable world,' was the answer. Then followed nineteen other deliberate questions at the end of which Canning exclaimed after a pause of a few moments: 'Why it cannot surely be anything else than the Wand of the Lord High Steward!' And so it was.

After Rush had completed his unusually long term of eight years as Minister in London, several Ministers followed him in rapid succession. Two of these, Louis McLane and Martin Van Buren, kept up the tradition of living in Marylebone. McLane had his residence in Chandos Street, and Van Buren in Stratford Place, the fashionable cul-de-sac off Oxford Street built by the second Earl of Aldborough. Van Buren, who later became the eighth President of the United States, found this address a pretty expensive one. He wrote at this time: 'Money – money is the thing,' finding the maintenance of this *palazzo*, together with his carriage and a large staff of servants, a heavy burden. The post of Minister in London, he described as the most agreeable he had ever held – an indication presumably that at long last the British Government's attitude towards the United States had changed from scarcely veiled hostility to cordiality. Perhaps his own manner had something to do with the agreeableness he found in his mission, for Washington Irving, who was Chargé d'Affaires when he arrived, wrote: 'I have just seen Mr Van Buren, and do not wonder you should all be so fond of him. His manners are most amiable and ingratiating; and I have no doubt he will become a favourite at this Court.' This farmer's son who began his swiftly successful career at the age of fourteen, when he started to read law, arrived in London in 1831, only to return to America the next year to take up the post of Vice-President under Andrew Jackson. His own Presidency came in 1836.

Five years after the departure of Van Buren there arrived in England an American businessman whose body in death was to lie in state in Westminster Abbey, before a British warship bore it back to his home town of Danvers, Massachusetts. George Peabody – according to Victor Hugo a man on whose face you could see the smile of God – came to England in 1837, and lived for a while at 11 Devonshire Street, near Portland Place. Peabody was forty-two when he arrived in London from America, head of a Baltimore dry goods business, and (of course) a millionaire. He was the first of those great American philanthropists of the Rockefeller brand whose overflowing riches have also been channelled abroad. He set up in England as a merchant and a banker, made a position for himself in the country, and from 1850 onwards became celebrated for the 4th July dinners with which he celebrated American Independence Day. In later life, he became ill and had to spend much time at Bath and other spas. He wrote: 'When aches and pains came upon me, I realised I was not immortal. I became anxious to use my millions for the greatest good of humanity.'

During his lifetime he gave £350,000 for the benefit of the London poor, and he bequeathed £150,000 for the trustees of the Peabody Fund to build dwellings for the working classes of London. His first idea had been to build ragged schools and set up drinking fountains all over London. But Lord Shaftesbury persuaded him that the real need was for model tenements with which to rehouse the poor and lift them out of the appalling squalor of their black slums. Peabody jumped at the idea, and he insisted that his buildings be cheerful, with all the light and air which could possibly be achieved. Fifty years after his death in 1869, the Peabody Trust already owned more than 15,000 rooms providing accommodation for some 23,000 people. Today the Trust owns fifty estates, and has assets of a nominal value of nearly five million pounds, and a real value of considerably more. When Peabody's statue near the Royal Exchange was unveiled by the Prince of Wales – later King Edward VII – in 1869, he described such generosity by a foreigner in England as unparalleled. It remained so for another couple of generations, when the setting up of Stephen Harkness's Pilgrim Trust of two million pounds demonstrated the extraordinary bounty of another American businessman to a country other than the United States.

By the time of George Peabody's death, Marylebone had a population of over 160,000 – the biggest it has ever had – and more than twice the population of today. Besides its fine residential districts, it contained a number of foul slums. Peabody's housing first aid was direly needed. In 1877, the borough's medical officer reported that people were migrating from Marylebone it was so overcrowded. One of the contributory causes of slum overpopulation had been the eviction of the poor of the St Giles's area when Oxford Street was extended eastwards as New Oxford Street in 1846. Five thousand people moved out of St Giles's following this upheaval, and most of them went into the slums of Marylebone and St Pancras. Dickens, in an article entitled *On Duty with Inspector Field*, published in book form in *Reprinted Pieces*, has described a descent by night with police into the kennels of St Giles's at this period.

Saint Giles's church clock, striking eleven, hums through our hand from the dilapidated door of a dark outhouse as we open it, and are stricken back by the pestilent breath that issues from within. Rogers to the front with the light, and let us look! Ten, twenty, thirty – who can count them! Men, women, children, for the most part naked, heaped upon the floor like maggots in a cheese! Ho! In that dark corner yonder! Does anybody lie there? Me, sir, Irish me, a widder, with six children. And yonder? Me sir, Irish me, with me wife and eight poor babes. And to the left there? Me sir, Irish me, along with two more Irish boys as is me friends. And to the right there? Me sir and the Murphy fam'ly, numbering five blessed souls . . . Thus, we make our New Oxford Streets, and our other new streets, never heeding, never asking where the wretches whom we clear out, crowd.

Only a few years later, in 1854, there were in one part alone of the parish of Marylebone, 1,132 underground or cellar dwellings.

For a contrast to this dark side of Marylebone, one must go to a writer who had much to say about the beauties of the place. A decade earlier than the mass eviction of the poor of St Giles's, an

American writer, Slidell Mackenzie, a naval officer of sensibility, had been enchanted with the finer parts of Marylebone, and particularly with the recently-opened Regent's Park (see Chapter 6). In his book, *The American in England*, he describes the Regent Street area around Oxford Circus with evident pleasure.

The shops here assume a still more elegant and fashionable character. Among them were druggists' shops the names of whose proprietors I had seen on their preparations in almost every corner of the world; their extent, neatness and elegance of arrangement were admirable. Others were occupied by French milliners addressing themselves in their signs to those only who could read French; or Parisian and Swiss confectioners, and one or two more elegantly fitted up as cafés and restaurants. The vista before me terminated at an angle where Regent Street turns into Portland Place. This is a most favourable point for the exhibition of a noble edifice. The objects on either hand prepare the eye for no measured degree of gratification. And here in fact the artist who conceived and so nobly executed in the last reign the magnificent idea of all these improvements, which give an air of grandeur to this quarter of the metropolis, has accordingly placed an edifice, the Church of All Souls . . .

As was not surprising perhaps, Slidell Mackenzie, ready as he was to be pleased with Nash's work, was unable to give many marks to a novelty so outrageous of contemporary taste as a classical fabric topped by a spire. He dismisses it as an 'architectural mis-alliance' – a mild enough criticism when compared with the mud flung at Nash by some of his fellow-countrymen.

Like Mackenzie, Caroline Kirkland, whose book, *Holidays Abroad or Europe from the West*, appeared in 1849, was fascinated by Regent's Park. She was also pleased by a meeting with Dickens, by the privacy and quiet of English homes and the excellence of London lodgings, and by Madame Tussaud's; and she was half-admiring, half-disapproving of the opulent and revealing styles of dress worn by fashionable women in public places. From the start, she stepped off on the right foot, finding the hotel of her dreams, Johnson's, apparently in Cavendish Square – although perhaps she meant in the immediate neighbourhood of the square since it seems improbable in 1848 that the Duke of Portland, the ground landlord, would have tolerated a hotel in this well-to-do enclave where he had his own town mansion. She praises the 'elegance, abundance, and service'. But in spite of these high marks for the establishment, she and her friends wanted to find a place where they could be on their own. Once again, they fell on their feet, and found John Bull able to offer them entire satisfaction in their new existence as furnished lodgers. Quiet, absolute freedom to come and go, meals at any time of the day or night and 'punctual to the moment' seem to have been the characteristics of these ideal lodgings. What they cost is not mentioned. One can only assume that the rent of these 'service digs' was so modest as to be undeserving of mention.

Mrs Kirkland's reactions to Madame Tussaud's seem to have been fairly typical of middle-class ladies of her time – pleasure at the 'grand saloon' with its light and music, interest in the effigies of contemporary artistes such as Grisi and Jenny Lind, and fascination with the relics of Napoleon and the French Revolutionary era. Fascination turned to horror, she records, at some of the early life-like representations of mangled bodies – 'Robespierre's in particular, I think, but am not certain, for I ran away.' On the other hand, the feelings aroused in her by Regent's Park were of a sort definitely ahead of her time – though it is true that 1848 was the year of revolutions in Europe:

> Many is the tired workman I have seen meeting with his child and wife in the Park, as he returned homeward with his coat on his arm, and his tin dinner-box in his hand; and when I have seen them sitting down upon a bench to listen to the fountain-music and rest their weary eyes by looking at the grass and the trees and the playful children and the careless promenaders, I have thought that was the class for whom it is worth while to make parks.

Regent's Park at the time she was writing of had been open to the public for no more than ten years. It is noteworthy that, in spite of the lakeside area being restricted to keyholders, the park was a place of resort for all classes and a real source of recreation for tired Londoners from the early years of Queen Victoria's reign onwards. The French critic and historian, Hippolyte Taine, writing somewhat later in the century, drew attention likewise to the general availability of the park, adding: 'A singularity from our point of view is that there are no keepers. Anyone who wishes may enter; yet no damage is done.' Taine may have been mistaken in thinking that entry was absolutely unrestricted. Mrs Kirkland says – but she was writing some twenty years earlier than he – that 'there is some exclusion, though but little about London's parks; one must not pass through them with a burthen, or even a parcel.' She adds, with warm-hearted fervour: 'But I would have no such restrictions. I should love to have people with bundles – the bigger the better . . . I plead earnestly for wide, generous fields, clean walks and soft-flowing water for the use of such as own nothing but hands and hearts.'

Mrs Kirkland's comments on the well-dressed people in Regent's Park 'straying through its ample walks or thronging the pavilions where were displayed the most splendid collections of flowers of the season' are not without pungency. 'But the company was truly a sight! Such an array of ball-room dresses I never saw by daylight before . . . There were not only the richest and gayest silks, satins and velvets, but transparent dresses over pink and blue silks, and all the paraphernalia of evening costume shaded only by rainbow mantillas and parasols. All this in a mixed company and in the open air was most strange to our American eyes.' The park, she added, was full of smart carriages and liveried servants, and there was no doubt of 'the rank of a large portion of the company'. Yet, though they were clearly not vulgar, jumped-up people, this ostentatious parade of brilliant clothes could not but be considered by Americans as *mauvais ton* in the circumstances, i.e. for an afternoon airing in the park. Mrs Kirkland, though not an unsophisticated woman, had spent a number of years in the Far West of America, and to the general Puritan background of her country, she probably added a certain overlay of provincialism. Her remarks are interesting, though, as suggesting that in 1848 drab Victorian industrialism had still not been long enough in the saddle to stifle that desire for colour in clothes which had prevailed before the coming of coal, steam-engines, and evangelical dullness.

During their stay in London, Mrs Kirkland and her friends paid the inevitable visit to Charles Dickens, then living in his Devonshire Terrace house, near the York Gate entrance to Regent's Park. The young Mr Dickens – he was thirty-seven and still radiating *joie-de-vivre* –fully lived up to her expectations.

We saw him at his own house, in his own pleasant library, looking out upon a bosky green garden, and furnished with all that makes libraries comfortable and attractive. It was with no little gratification that I seated myself at the desk where so many delightful things had been written, and looked upon the appliances which helped to give us *Dombey* and the *Cricket*... All was arranged with the businesslike order and neatness which is said to characterize everything done by Mr Dickens... He received us with cordial frankness and asked, with eyes full of fun 'How are you pleased with our country?' – the question of which he complained so much during his visit to the United States. For my own part, I rewarded his hospitality by stealing one of his pens, hoping there might be something inspiring in its touch.

Mrs Kirkland's impressions of the London scene were those of a passing visitor who earned her living by her pen. She was on the look-out for 'copy', and she had a keen eye and a warm heart, but neither her gifts nor her knowledge were out of the ordinary. But within a few years of her visit there was an American recording what he saw in London who had especial opportunities for observing what was going on in what was then the world's most important capital city. At a time when Palmerston was reaching the height of his power, Benjamin Moran, a young American of literary tendencies and no particular prospects, took a post as a temporary clerk in the American Legation. His father had been born in England, and had emigrated to America early in the nineteenth century. He himself had arrived in England with practically no money, and toured England, Wales, Scotland and Ireland, travelling nearly everywhere on foot. He was a romantic with a hard streak in him, a lover of England who never missed an opportunity of dwelling on the repulsive aspects of the Englishman's character, and a hardworking diplomatist who served America well in England during the difficult days of her Civil War.

James Buchanan, who was the U.S. Minister in London when Moran started his career, quickly promoted him from temporary clerk to the post of his private secretary. Buchanan, a Federalist who became a Democrat under pressure of the slavery struggle, was yet another of those American Ministers in London destined to become President of the United States. A scholarly man, of considerable penetration and judgement, he gave Moran his first lessons in diplomatic practice. As the private secretary rose, first to be Assistant Secretary and then Secretary of Legation, and finally to frequent stints as Chargé d'Affaires, he confided more and more to his private journals. From these, which cover a period of eighteen years from the early 1850s, and which were eventually published, a large-scale picture of men and events emerges.

Before looking at some of the elements which go to make up this picture, let us take a look at James Buchanan at work in London, as seen through the eyes of a celebrated American novelist. Nathaniel Hawthorne, author of *The Scarlet Letter*, was in England during the years 1853 to 1857, trying to eke out a living as a consular agent. In 1855, he visited London, and was called upon by Buchanan. The result was this vignette, recorded in his *English Notebooks* for 13 September:

> Mr Buchanan called on me on Tuesday ... So yesterday after forenoon I set out to find his residence, 56 Harley Street. It is a street out of Cavendish Square, in a fashionable quarter, although fashion is said to be ebbing away from it. The ambassador seems to intend some little state in his arrangements; but, no doubt, the establishment compares shabbily enough with the legations of other great countries, and with the houses of the English aristocracy. A servant not in livery (or in a very unrecognizable one) opened the door for me ...

This preliminary call was followed by another, in which Hawthorne took his wife, Sophia, along with him. The tone is still faintly disapproving.

> We were shown into a stately drawing-room, the furniture of which was sufficiently splendid, but rather the worse for wear – being hired furniture no doubt ... Sophia spoke to him about an order from the Lord Chamberlain for admission to view the two Houses of Parliament; and the Ambassador drew from his pocket a coloured silk handkerchief! (which ought to have gone into this week's wash) and made a knot in it in order to remind himself to ask the Lord Chamberlain. The homeliness of this little incident has a sort of propriety and keeping with much of Mr Buchanan's manner; but I would rather not have him do it before English people.

Mr Buchanan, whose portrait makes him look the spit image of Cruikshank's Mr Micawber, was a bachelor of sixty-four. Elected the fifteenth President of the United States the following year, he is said to have been the only bachelor President ever to occupy the White House. In the mid-1850s the U.S.A. was still very far from being the colossus of wealth and power it is today, and other Americans besides Hawthorne complained of the comparative shabbiness of Uncle Sam's legation, and envied the evidences everywhere of John Bull's vast resources. Richard Rush, as we have seen, had drawn attention to the very modest rent he was able to pay for No. 20 Baker Street. In fact, he amplified this with the remark that even the salaries of the representatives of the 'Imperial and Royal governments of Europe', though much larger than American salaries, were yet 'so much below the wealth of the home circles as to be no distinction'. Slidell Mackenzie, too, in contrasting the amenities of the Regent's Park quarter with a comparable part of New York, refers to the 'vast superabundance of capital' in London.

By the time Buchanan left England in 1856 to take up the Presidency, Benjamin Moran had his feet well set upon the rungs of the diplomatic ladder. The self-confident and caustic note in his diary grows noticeably as the years pass by. In 1861 the Legation was moved to Portland Place, and some of the earlier entries touch upon things he saw on his journeys to and from his office there. Even before the move, he seems to have been often in the district. On 30 January 1857 the afternoon finds him strolling along Portland Place in the direction of Regent's Park to the accompaniment of 'crowds of carriages dashing up and down', most of them 'filled with ladies muffled in furs and finery'. He notes a number of good-looking English girls walking in the park and seemingly enjoying it. 'These English females are wonderful for exercise. They'll walk Lord knows how many miles daily, go alone for miles, take care of themselves wherever they go, and come home delighted and not the least tired.' A curious remark this, for a citizen of pioneering America whose girls, one might have assumed, were ready at the drop of a hat to take over the reins of the covered waggon, or gallop the riderless horse away to the nearest sheriff's office.

Other sights seen in the streets are recorded in the earlier years. He is driving down Regent Street one day when the sight of 'a couple of couriers in red livery' warns him, knowledgeable as he is in such matters, that the Sovereign is approaching. Her carriage passes, and he notes that she is accompanied by two ladies in black, but annoyingly he cannot see her face as one of the ladies blocks the view. A regiment (a troop?) of Horse Guards passes the Legation twice daily. 'A fine set of men, but not so the officers.' He is walking down Duke Street with his friend Dr Darling when they notice a man ahead of them with oddly deformed shoulders. Suspicious, they follow him, and he turns out to be a sneak-thief, who stuffs purloined articles of clothing between his jacket and waistcoat. He goes into a shop, and they call a policeman. Shown the shop, the bobby identifies it as a receiver's; by then though it is too late to make the arrest. When summer comes round, he and Dr Darling and another friend go walking to Hampstead and Highgate, taking in Primrose Hill on the way. By green lanes and pleasant footpaths, they reach 'the very summit of the Hampstead range of hills which like the rim of a great basin rises above London at the north'. A reminder this, that we have now entirely lost sight of this piece of natural scenery beneath a mass of housing. A few years earlier, Herman Melville on a visit to England had contrasted the northward with the southward view:

> ... and so round Regent's Park to Primrose Hill. The view was curious. Towards Hampstead the open country looked green and the air was pretty clear; but cityward it was like a view of hell from Abraham's bosom. Clouds of smoke, as though you looked down from Mt Washington in a mist.

The author of *Moby Dick* records mundanely enough that, after leaving Primrose Hill, he crossed Regent's Park to the New Road and took, not a white whale but a bus. He adds 'outside'. Buses had been running along the New Road (Marylebone Road) since George Shillibeer started the first public service in 1829. Three horses, driven abreast, carried a load of twenty-two passengers – all inside in those early days – from Paddington via the Yorkshire Stingo, near the Edgware Road, to the Bank and back. The fare was a shilling, including the use of a newspaper. There were a number of turnpike gates to pass en route including, within Marylebone itself, one at Lisson Grove and another at Great Portland Street. In 1883 an enterprising gentleman called Hancock even put a steam bus on this route for a while. Steam of course was coming in in a big way on the railways which were spreading all over England, and within fifteen years or so after Herman Melville's bus trip along the New Road, Benjamin Moran was travelling on the first Underground railway in the country. On 10 January 1863 he writes:

> This morning I went down to Portland Road [i.e. Great Portland Street] from the Bishop's Road station at Paddington on the

Metropolitan or *Underground railway*. The carriages are comfortably and lighted with gas, the road is solid and admirably constructed, and the brick-work which forms the arching is among the finest masonry I have ever seen. The road is *under* ground and consists of a tunnel of near 4 miles, with a few exceptions. It will prove a great boon to London ... The ride was very soft and was accomplished, stoppages and all, in about 13 minutes to Portland Road – which was not a bad run for the first day of opening.

Unlike Mrs Kirkland in 1848, Moran ten years later had nothing favourable to say of Dickens. He does not appear to have actually met him, but he went on 16 April 1858 to hear him give a reading of the *Christmas Carol* at St Martin's Hall, Long Acre. 'His voice was husky, altho' his enunciation was distinct. As a performance however his reading was very defective ... It was the first time I saw this celebrity, and altogether the impression was favourable. That is, I was not so much inclined to kick him after seeing him as I was before ...' Moran goes on to speak of Dickens's 'evident insincerity of character', and dismisses him as 'one of those men who never adhere long to a friend.' Dickens at forty-six was beginning to show signs of wear and tear. His affairs, domestic and professional, were in a state of crisis, and he was on the brink of a new phase in his career. Within weeks of the lecture he had separated from his wife, and was soon to break with his publishers and discontinue his magazine, *Household Words*. So it may well be that his performance as a reader was affected by a certain degree of mental stress. Apart from this, he was at the very outset of his career as a professional reader (the reading which Moran heard – whether he knew it or not – was an unpaid one, done for a children's hospital), and in fact did not give the first professional reading of his career until a fortnight later. The question of his sincerity, or lack of it, is a matter of opinion. The charge that he failed to stick to his friends is not substantiated in any way by Moran.

The note of disapproval of things English in the journal tended to grow with the years. Not long before the Dickens episode, Moran went one evening with a couple of friends to 'The Oxford', a sort of *café chantant* at the corner of Oxford Street and Tottenham Court Road. Here his reaction has something of the same Puritan distaste about it as Mrs Kirkland had shown towards the fashionable parade in Regent's Park:

This is a gaudy place, and under the glare of gas light is a place to see when filled with smoking and drinking Londoners and their families. There is something about it not compatible with respectability, however, and it is only to be visited by the curious. To see men and women sitting indiscriminately at tables eating and drinking amid clouds of smoke, while listening to operatic performances on a stage at one end of the great saloon was something new but by no means calculated to create a favourable impression.

Had Mr Moran and his friends turned into 'Frampton's Salle de Danse' in the Princess's Concert Rooms, a little farther west along Oxford Street – a place of some notoriety at the time – they might have seen goings-on still more likely to disturb their equanimity. This gay night haunt had gained resoundingly adverse publicity by refusing in 1857 to observe Queen Victoria's proclamation of a national day of mourning and prayer for the victims of the Indian Mutiny. Moran and his friends would probably have been better pleased had they gone to another celebrated establishment in the neighbourhood – the Portland Rooms, known as Mott's', in New Cavendish Street. This place was distinctly 'smart' and exclusive, and strictly decorous, 'in the sense that no matter whom you brought or what you planned to do with her, she was for the nonce a lady, and you mightn't do it there.' The splendid tone of this upper class *boîte de nuit* had however on one single regrettable occasion been badly marred – when 'the irrepressible Lord Hastings let loose a sackful of rats one night, while a confederate turned out the lights.'

Moran's increasing distaste for the Englishman of the day – no doubt the patrician Englishman with whom he had to deal in the course of his highly responsible work as U.S. Chargé d'Affaires in London – is reflected in his journal. The arrogance and egoism of the Englishman had been an American diplomatic theme since the days of Adams and Jefferson. Monroe, as we have seen, had suffered from it, and there can be little doubt that the condescension of certain noble lords and their sedulous apes in the higher echelons of the civil service had made its mark on many transatlantic diplomats. Moran had clearly suffered from it, as is evident from his confiding the following parody of the National Anthem to his journal. He says that it was attributed to Grant White, an American scholar and journalist of the day, and that it made its way into *The Spectator* in 1862.

> God save me, great John Bull!
> Long keep my pocket full!
>> God save me, great John Bull.
>
> Ever victorious,
> Haughty, vainglorious,
> Snobbish, censorious,
>> God save me, great John Bull!
>
> O Lords, our gods, arise,
> Tax all our enemies,
>> Make tariffs fall!
>
> Confound French politics,
> Frustrate all Russian tricks,
> Get Yankees in a 'fix',
>> God 'bless' them all!
>
> Heaven's choicest goods in store
> On me, me only pour
>> Me, great John Bull!
>
> Then pass oppressive laws,
> Frown down the poor man's cause
> So will I sing with heart and voice
>> I, great John Bull!

Underneath these verses, Moran wrote his own comment: '. . . a faithful picture of the selfish brute it paints'.

The year before these uncomplimentary verses appeared, the Chancery of the U.S. Legation had been transferred from Cadogan House, Piccadilly, to 5 Mansfield Street, Portland Place. The move delighted Moran, who wrote that it was 'the finest house the embassy has occupied in my time. It is the property of Mr Seymour Fitzgerald, late Under Sec. of State for Foreign Affairs & contains some splendid, valuable pictures. There are original portraits of Cromwell, Lady Jane Grey, Mary Queen of Scots, Nell Gwynne & others, all of which are highly prized.' Shortly before the move, a new Minister had arrived from America. (Moran's reference to 'the embassy' is a *façon de parler*. There was no U.S. Ambassador at the Court of St James's until 1893.) Charles Francis Adams was the son of John Quincy Adams and the grandson of John Adams, both Presidents of the United States in their time, and both, as we have seen, Ministers at the Court of St James's. Adams was the appointee of Abraham Lincoln, and he held his post in Britain throughout the Civil War. His position was difficult, as British sympathy was sharply divided between the two sides, and the decline in the supply of raw cotton from the U.S.A. caused some British mills to close for a time, throwing many Lancashire men and women out of work. Adams's greatest achievement came in 1863, when he persuaded the British Government at the last moment to hold at Liverpool the iron-clad rams built for the Confederates of the South and then on the point of being shipped to them.

If the American diplomat of the nineteenth century often found members of the English ruling classes infuriatingly arrogant and self-centred, it seems that the ordinary American visitor, and even the American resident in Britain, frequently made the surprising discovery that the country and its inhabitants had a positively beneficial effect on his mental and physical health. The writer Bret Harte, who made his name with tales of the mining communities of the Far West – *The Luck of Roaring Camp, The Outcasts of Poker Flat*, etc. – settled in England in 1885 and remained there until his death in 1902. His only reason for doing so was that he found a better market here, but his biographer, Merwin, writing in 1912, nevertheless has this to say about Americans living or staying in England:

... the English climate is the natural antidote to the American ... England has a soothing effect upon the hustling American. He eats more, worries less, and becomes a happier and pleasanter animal. A similar change has been observed in high-strung horses taken from the United States to England. And so of athletes ... The temperament and manners of the English people have the same pleasant effect as the climate upon the American visitor. More important still perhaps is the ease of living in a country which has a fixed social system. The plain line drawn in England between the gentleman and the non-gentleman class makes things very pleasant for those who belong to the favored division.

# 11. *The Shape of Today*

IN a famous and memorable line, Byron tells us that: 'The mountains look on Marathon – and Marathon looks on the sea.' So, in its classic days, Marylebone looked on 'Maribone Park', and 'Maribone Park' looked on the fields. That is to say that in the late eighteenth and early nineteenth centuries, it combined the urban in its most urbane form with the rustic at its most recognisably rural in a way that made it a highly sought-after residential area. Marylebone is, of course, sought after today, but clearly not for the same reasons. A great mass of buildings, many miles deep, now intervenes between it and those distant fields. It is no longer possible with young De Quincey to 'gaze from Oxford Street up every avenue in succession which pierces through the heart of Marylebone to the fields and woods'. It is no longer even feasible, like the young Leigh Hunt, to take a house on the south side of the Marylebone Road, step across it, and make off through the countryside to the village of Hampstead. The Park of course remains, an enormous lung aerating latterday Marylebone, a green haven to which the crowds can retreat out of the swing of the sea of traffic that thunders around its approaches. But the overriding fact is that the district has lost that link with the country-side which gave an extra zest to the pleasure of living there.

Oddly enough, it is its reverse role, of being so near the heart of London while not being of it, which today constitutes one of Marylebone's principal attractions. Most of it is nearer to central London than Kensington or Chelsea are, and it is larger, more diversely endowed with amenities, and less expensive than Mayfair. Actually, the bait of relative proximity to Westminster was held out to the noble lords invited to be the first residents of Cavendish Square – that plot which was the nucleus of urban Marylebone. John Prince's estate plan of 1719 included a comparative timetable showing that it was quicker to get to Westminster, and so to Parliament, from there than from various fashionable residential districts of the day. Though fashion has now deserted those places – Bloomsbury for instance – for others 'south of the Park' – the more recently-favoured areas are also at a disadvantage of distance compared with Marylebone. The fact is that Marylebone, which has largely retained its residential character, was developed early enough to pre-empt a commanding position in relation to that official heart of London which has stood where it does for a couple of centuries.

Behind its southern 'frontier' of Oxford Street – the barrier which separates it from the West End area of shops, offices and theatres – Marylebone remains a little aloof. Step from Oxford Street into Wigmore Street, and you are at once aware of a change of atmosphere. It too is full of shops, clogged with traffic, but somehow it contrives to retain an Edwardian residential air. The shops appear to take their tone from the stately Debenham's. None of that up-today-and-down-tomorrow cast of shop-front so noticeable among the more gimmicky establishments in Oxford Street; none of that fun-fair touch so prominent there since the last war. The Rollses and Bentleys glide unctuously along, looking comfortably at home with their environment, while the buses appear to be almost touching their caps with embarrassment as they creep past the restrainedly stylish emporia – the jewellers, the confectioners, the antique dealers, the opticians. The dignified *persona* of the place – originally due to its being the shopping preserve of the Cavendish Square grandees – is still unmistakably dominant.

Indeed, the note of dignity derived from a still remoter period, the eighteenth century, pervades the whole of that grid of streets stretching from Seymour Place on the west to Portland Place on the east. In spite of a great deal of rebuilding in the last decade, this area which contains the great medical kingdom of the consultants and the still greater communications kingdom of the broadcasters, is one whose rooflines and street-fronts still predominantly conform with the rules of taste laid down in the age of Horace Walpole and the Adam brothers. Notwithstanding such modern anomalies as Broadcasting House itself, Burmah-Castrol House – that strangely satisfying glaucous-green bandbox on the Marylebone Road – the overwhelming tower block on the south-east corner of Cavendish Square, and such subordinate intrusions as Kellogg House in Paddington Street and the Marks & Spencer head office in Baker Street, the architectural uniform of the eighteenth century still prevails. Marylebone then, in its heart-land area as opposed to its extremities – St

## MODERN MARYLEBONE
### Places of interest now demolished
*Key to approximate sites*

1. Tyburn Tree (gallows)
2. Church of St John the Evangelist
3. Lord Mayor's (City) Banqueting House
4. Banqueting House Bridge over Tyburn
5. Manor House (later School House)
6. Dorset Fields (Lord's first cricket ground)
7. The Boarded House (boxing arena)
8. Alsop's Farm
9. Yorkshire Stingo public house
10. The Eyre Arms public house
11. Marylebone Old Parish Church
12. Lisson Manor House
13. Marylebone Gardens
14. Marylebone Basin (reservoir)
15. The Portman Barracks (Foot Guards)
16. Life Guards Barracks
17. The Oxford Market

18. Workhouse and Infirmary
19. Watch House (later Court House)
20. Portman (earlier Montagu) House
21. Princess's Theatre (earlier Queen's Bazaar)
22. The Quebec Chapel
23. The Portman Market
24. The Old Marylebone Theatre
25. Mrs Siddons's house
26. Dickens's house
27. Chapel of the Annunciation (French Chapel Royal)
28. The Colosseum
29. Sussex Villa
30. Albany Cottage
31. The Diorama
32. Holford House
33. St Dunstan's Villa
34. South Villa
35. Abbey Lodge
36. Master's House, St Katharine's Hospital
37. Foley House
38. Langham House
39. Harcourt (later Portland) House
40. Rose of Normandy public house

Reproduced from the Ordnance Survey 6 inch to 1 mile
© Crown Copyright

John's Wood, Maida Vale and Lisson Grove – remains at least basically true to its Georgian origins.

'Harley Street' of course is not merely the name of a street, but the label tagged onto a whole quarter within the area. Indeed, some parts of 'Harley Street' – or at least of the great medical complex of central Marylebone – are, like the Middlesex Hospital, the best part of a mile away from the famous street of consultants. Wimpole and Welbeck Streets contain some of the immediate overflow of medicos; and the rest of the medicine men, together with a tremendous array of nurses' homes, dentists' surgeries, surgical instrument shops, medical bookshops, dispensing opticians, and chemists' and druggists', as well as the headquarters of a variety of professional medical organisations, are housed in the network of smaller streets around. New Cavendish Street seems to specialise in surgical instrument displays of the most intimidating kind, diversified by the numerous opticians' offerings of gay and glittering spectacles in multitudinous shapes tailored to the feminine demands of the passing moment. Hospitals abound: the great Middlesex in Mortimer Street; the National Heart in Westmoreland Street; King Edward VII's Hospital for Officers a couple of minutes' walk away in Beaumont Street; the Samaritan Hospital for Women and the Western Ophthalmic, close to one another in the Marylebone Road; the Florence Nightingale, just off the Marylebone Road, in Lisson Grove; the London Clinic in Devonshire Place, with a frontage on the Marylebone Road; and the Royal National Orthopaedic Hospital in Great Portland Street. Nurses in a variety of uniforms move between these institutions and their hostels, ambulances dash backwards and forwards along the ruler-straight streets, the sleekly comfortable cars of prosperous consultants nose their way in and out of the traffic.

Apart from all this front-line activity against disease and the mortality of man, there are those humming headquarters of the professional medical bodies, where standards are evolved and the careers of the lights of healing weighed in the balance: the Royal Society of Medicine and the General Dental Council in Wimpole Street; the Medical Society of London in Chandos Street; the Royal College of Physicians in St Andrew's Place and the Royal College of Obstetricians in Sussex Place; the Royal College of Nursing in Henrietta Place and the Royal College of Midwives in Mansfield Street; the General Medical Council in Hallam Street and the General Optical Council in Harley Street; the National Association for Mental

Health, the Nutrition Society, and the Royal Medico-Psychological Society in Queen Anne Street; the Institute of Psycho-Analysis in New Cavendish Street; the London Association for the Blind in Crawford Street; the Royal Institute of Public Health and Hygiene and the Royal Society of Tropical Medicine and Hygiene in Portland Place. And so on, endlessly, in a few square Marylebone miles.

The picture indeed of this district is almost overwhelmingly health-orientated. How does it come about that there is such a tremendous concentration of the medical and disease-fighting battalions in this neighbourhood? Perhaps the Middlesex Hospital, founded more than two centuries ago, started the drive. Just as shops of a particular trade tend to cluster together, so perhaps do hospitals. Over and above this there is that fact that urban Marylebone came into being at a time when medical science was developing rapidly. Building land was available there – which was not the case in the older districts of London – and the area was generally reputed a healthy one. On the other hand, the borough rapidly became overcrowded in the nineteenth century, and some very bad slums grew up. The overcrowding was greatly intensified when in 1846 New Oxford Street was created to make a direct link between Oxford Street and Holborn. The formation of the new road meant the destruction of the masses of tenements belonging to the rookery of St Giles and the eviction of the tenants. These poverty-stricken people moved in great numbers into the slum areas of eastern Marylebone. At this time the forty-four public wells supplying the borough were for the most part producing water 'offensive to taste and smell'. The very few shallow sewers were insufficient for the growing population, with the result that basements were frequently flooded and there was need of 'the daily use of pumps to remove the foul liquids'. This was at a time when, for instance, a group of ten dilapidated six-roomed houses was occupied by eighty-four families. By 1877, Marylebone's medical officer of health was reporting that one out of every three children born in Marylebone died before the age of five. No wonder that he also reported that people were migrating from the borough as fast as they could, it had become so overcrowded. In 1861 the peak figure of 161,000 inhabitants had been reached; today it is no more than some 70,000 – a population explosion reversed.

The Victorian picture was a grim one, but out of it emerged the hospitals. As we have seen in the chapter on the development of

Harley Street, the doctors did not really begin to move into the district in a big way until the population peak had been reached. They went no doubt for the fashionable practices which Marylebone offered, and they stayed on to act as consultants to the hospitals which grew up around them. The area between Baker Street and Portland Place into which they moved was smart and well-to-do. But immediately to the east of it was a poor and shabby quarter, some parts of which were real slums. This quarter lay in the main to the east of Great Portland Street and extended as far eastward as Cleveland Street. Even today anyone who follows New Cavendish Street from its intersection with Marylebone High Street in the west to its junction with Cleveland Street in the east is immediately made aware of the change of atmosphere as he proceeds eastwards. Till Portland Place is reached an air of comfortable prosperity and residential ease is maintained. It is true that the first part of New Cavendish Street, where it debouches from Marylebone High Street, is a shopping quarter – but, like Wigmore Street, a shopping quarter with a difference. The solid residential neighbourhood wears its shops with an air, like a dignified dowager sporting a trouser-suit. But the shops soon give way to the indigenous array of fan-lighted doorways and doctors' nameplates, and the district reasserts its essential nature.

Once across the broad, light-filled savannah of Portland Place, and New Cavendish Street prepares to turn commercial. Beyond Great Portland Street it enters a canyon of office buildings. You are in the sleekly slick 'rag trade' empire which, as far as Great Portland Street itself is concerned, has ousted the car-dealers who once possessed the street almost wholly. Roll on farther east still, and you are in a neighbourhood to the north of the murky outskirts of the all-pervasive Middlesex Hospital, a place lurking in the shadow of the Post Office Tower where whole streets of shoddy houses have been ripped up and flung down and the area refashioned and recon-structed in the last few years. Here are now to be found a multi-plicity of modern glass, curtain-walled offices – novel growths rising in the midst of the grimy compost heap of decaying buildings which constitutes Marylebone's east end. Dwarfing the lot is the Polytechnic College of Science and Engineering, a giant of glass and concrete seeming to survey with cold technological eyes the unlovely scene below. Away to the south-east, where Newman Street makes a short stride to its outlet in Oxford Street, the computer industry has settled in. It would be well occupied predicting the precise lifespan remaining to the life-denying architectural muck-heap which Victorian industrialism made of this district.

I.B.M.'s Data Centre is in Newman Street, whereas the West End showroom of its Office Products Division is in Wigmore Street, near the western border of Marylebone. These are only items in its great chain of London offices. Its presence in both the eastern and western parts of the district points to the important role played by Marylebone as the chosen centre of the communications industry. The B.B.C. of course is the kingpin in this. From its island site at the southern end of Portland Place – or, if you prefer it, at the apex of Upper Regent Street, it bestrides the two sections of what may be called Georgian Marylebone, lying east and west of Portland Place. Its many outlying offices spread in both directions. The general public are inclined to think of the B.B.C. as summed up by Broadcasting House, Alexandra Palace, and the T.V. Centre at Shepherd's Bush. In fact, these are merely the loftiest peaks in an extensive range. Most of the more modest heights are in the immediate neighbourhood of B.H. – in the Langham Hotel; on the opposite side of Portland Place; in Langham Street; in Hallam Street; in Duchess Street; in New Cavendish Street; in Chandos Street; in Cavendish Place; and in Cavendish Square, etc. There is, too, an outlier as far away as Marylebone High Street – B.B.C. Publications. Marylebone in fact contains more B.B.C. offices than it does post offices. The B.B.C. has even taken root on one of Marylebone's oldest historic sites – the 'Rose of Normandy' site. Here the Corporation's 'Radio Times' Hulton Picture Library, with its six million photos and prints covering anything and everything but the purely topical in the field of illustration, blossoms where the famous old pub flourished for more than two hundred years. This pillar of Marylebone life, which closed down in 1956, housed the Marylebone Music Hall for the last forty years or so of the nineteenth century. The first floor was turned into an auditorium seating two hundred people, and the place was the favourite haunt of Sickert and other noted artists.

Broadcasting House has pointed its shipshaped bows down Regent Street since 1931. With Eric Gill's beguiling *Prospero and Ariel* as the figurehead on its bowsprit, and its stepped-back upper storeys, it seems a vessel at once ancient and modern preparing to enter a presumptive Regent Street waterway leading to the centre of London. It is quite a while ago since Sir Nikolaus Pevsner damned the building as wanting in form, and accused it of 'casting a blight on the whole delightful Georgian neighbourhood'. Influences a lot more blighting have been at work round about since he wrote his condemnation, and one may perhaps be allowed to feel that even a formless building may charm. There is a certain easy serenity about Val Myers' original Broadcasting House, which certainly cannot be said for its lateral extension – or for the St George's Hotel which now occupies the site of the Queen's Hall. The old B.H. is like one of those middle-aged ladies who have no 'figure' in the accepted sense, but who are sufficiently curvaceous and good-natured-looking for one to fall instantly into the easiest of relations with them. If one accepts that a contemporary architecture implies large buildings, then one must admit that Broadcasting House (before the extension) closed the Regent Street vista in a civilised manner. It also had – and has – the merit of terminating the eastern street-front of Portland Place in such a way as to allow a view of the colonnaded circular porch of All Souls Church from the north. Hence one of the functions of the cut-away façade. Let it be also remembered that if Lord Reith, its chief begetter, was not an architectural purist, he was an engineer and a perfectionist.

The erection of the Langham Hotel, which lies just across the street from Broadcasting House, was of course the first blow struck against the Georgian harmonies of the neighbourhood. This monster piece of Victorian exuberance – the scene of so many pre-1914 junketings, where 'Ouida' took up her abode and Wilde once scooped up the tiny Swinburne under one arm as he lay dead drunk on the floor, and dropped him into a chaise-longue – was launched in 1865 with a visit by the Prince of Wales, later King Edward VII. It was fitting no doubt that here (where the notorious, money-spinning Horatio Bottomley later broached his magnums of champagne and Sir Henry Wood held court during the Queen's Hall concert season) this latterday Merry Monarch should set a-going nineteenth century London's lushest palace of pleasure. With its six hundred rooms including three hundred bedrooms, its hundred-foot-long dining room, its vast hall fifty feet high, its 'Ambassadors' Audience Room', its private post office and its own water supply from a well three hundred feet deep, it sought to bring magnificence combined with comfort to the public of the then richest country in the world. Nothing comparable could be found in all Europe at the time, and apart from Claridge's none of the great luxury hotels of London had yet come into existence. The Langham was damaged by bombs during the last war, but in 1939 it was already long past its prime as a resort, and the world of fashionable entertaining and entertainment of which it had been so intimate a part had moved steadily southwards to Mayfair and Piccadilly throughout the years following its foundation. After the war, the B.B.C. shared the premises with the Metal Box Company, and now that they have taken themselves off to Baker Street, the Corporation camps out alone in the shell of a place from which all the original magnificence has departed. The atmosphere is like that of the wings of a theatre after the brilliance and colour of the stage.

The B.B.C.'s impact upon central Marylebone has of course not been confined to the buildings it has put up or occupied. These are merely the visible effects upon the townscape of an occupation which has been both wide and subtle. A less perceptible consequence of the insertion of this massive broadcasting organisation into Marylebone's living space has been the fillip it has given to places of recreation and refreshment in the neighbourhood. The Queen's Hall and St George's Hall, situated close by in Upper Regent Street, were soon affected. Before their destruction by fire bombs in 1941, the Queen's Hall was used for the broadcasting of the larger orchestras and St George's Hall was the home of B.B.C. Variety programmes. A number of pubs have benefited largely – not only from the patronage of the B.B.C.'s staff, but from that of the numerous artists, actors, writers, musicians and many others drawn into the business of getting programmes on the air. The Stag's Head in New Cavendish Street, The George in Great Portland Street, the Dover Castle in Weymouth Mews, and such other establishments as Yarner's coffee-shop in Upper Regent Street (now removed to George Street) and Shirreff's Wine Parlour in Great Castle Street, have all at one time or another been much patronised. The Bolivar in Chandos Street was for years a place of much resort. Now its premises house the B.B.C. Club.

Both Broadcasting House and the Langham have the advantage of frontages on Portland Place which, apart from Parliament Street, is the widest street in London. The Mall, its only other rival, is not a street, but the processional approach by way of St James's Park to Buckingham Palace. A very wide street, however, can have its drawbacks from the viewpoint of the pedestrian who has to cross it, as illustrated by the following excerpt from a letter which Samuel

Butler, author of *Erewhon*, sent to his friend Miss Savage on 4 December 1880:

> By the bye apropos of O.c.s. [odious creatures], I saw Mr Gladstone last week. He came out of Lord Selborne's house in Portland Place. He was looking fearfully cross and very yellow. He seemed very undecided as to where he should cross the street, and he stared at me in a helpless sort of way, as if he expected me to offer him some advice on the matter, but as there was no possibility of putting him in the way of being run over, I refrained from giving an opinion. The crossings about Portland Place are so stupidly safe.

Gladstone, close on seventy-one, was Prime Minister when this incident occurred. As he survived for another eighteen years and a couple of further Prime Ministerships, one must assume that he was rather better at crossing the road than he appeared to Samuel Butler.

If the Langham and Broadcasting House are to be reckoned as the principal villains in the business of destroying the architectural unity of Portland Place, the flats which have been introduced during the present century have certainly continued the process. In his great work *The Buildings of England*, Pevsner has denounced the treatment meted out to Portland Place as the wilful destruction of what was 'a monument of European importance'. He might have added that London, one of the great capital cities of the world, is so lacking in those streets of grandeur which grace most of the others that it least of all can afford to treat its architectural nonpareils with philistine negligence. The Royal Institute of British Architects is the last body to be accused of this kind of shortcoming. Yet the building which it put up some forty years ago on the east side of Portland Place at its intersection with Weymouth Street cannot be said to be the ideal solution to a problem which is clearly almost impossibly difficult to solve. A place of distinction, with several extremely imaginative features – the great window, for instance, rising above the main entrance to about three-quarters of the height of the façade, or the fine staircase with its ornamented glass panelling leaping lightheartedly through space – it shouts its individuality aloud. This insistence on its own architectural personality, to the detriment of the unity of the street, is underlined by the two free-standing pillars with statues on top which flank the main entrance. They seem to emphasise the importance of the R.I.B.A. building rather than the harmonies of Portland Place.

Just as the hospitals seem to jostle one another in Marylebone, so broadcasting headquarters show a tendency towards the same process. Broadcasting House till recently had Yorkshire Television as its neighbour in Portland Place. A few minutes' walk away to the east, close to Great Portland Street, is the new, highly functional-looking building which houses Independent Television News. This part of Marylebone near the park is also becoming increasingly infiltrated by student centres and organisations devoted to teaching. For instance, there is the British Council's London Student Centre, with accommodation which includes twenty-four self-contained flats, housed in a modern building with its main frontage on the west side of Portland Place.

At the other end of Portland Place, Park Crescent has risen once again to provide a delightful prelude to Park Square and Regent's Park. In this age of severely rectangular architecture, with the element of playfulness hardly ever indulged, the gleaming curve of coupled columns with the balustrade above enchants the eye. Though the Crescent still houses some of Harley Street's far-flung outposts, the principal tenant is International Students House, which occupies much of the eastern section. This consists of a hostel and club for overseas students. It is a splendidly ambitious conception, planned initially to provide a residence for 134 men students and a club for 2,000 mixed members, together with an assembly hall for 350. The scheme, the work of the International Students' Trust, a private limited company, is designed to be self-supporting, with some of its funds coming from the rents of office accommodation on the same site and some from Government grants, but the bulk from non-official sources. Away to the west on the Outer Circle of Regents' Park, reconstructed York Terrace and Sussex Place – the latter's array of glittering white domes peeping over the roofs at intervals – likewise now provide study centres and accommodation for students. York Terrace East houses the International Students House's new extension, and Sussex Place the London Graduate School of Business Studies. In these new, elegant premises the students look across to the Inner Circle, where the Bedford College students already occupy a couple of Nash's historic buildings, as well as the extensive ranges of modern buildings on the old South Villa site. Thus student youth now constitutes the majority of those enjoying 'a room with a view' over the Park.

Reference was made in an earlier chapter to the painter John

Martin, whose scheme in 1821 for a triumphal arch over the Marylebone Road was turned down. The fact that he sited his proposed Waterloo Arch at a point on the axis of Portland Place was no doubt connected with Nash's Regent Street scheme. Regent Street was originally conceived as a triumphal way linking the Regent's palace of Carlton House with the Park, with Portland Place as the last section before the Park. The proposal to build such an arch is probably the nearest the Marylebone Road has ever come to being treated as if it were Whitehall or Parliament Street – a site fit for a national monument. Martin's sepia drawings are in fact embellished with pictures of Horse Guards prancing along the route. The Act under which the New Road was created in 1756 had indeed envisaged its secondary purpose as a strategic military route along which defence forces could be rapidly despatched in time of war. It still serves its primary purpose as a ring-road by-passing central London.

It has of course been considerably widened in the course of its two centuries' existence. The Act of 1756 allowed no building within fifty feet of either side of the road. So it has been possible to achieve the necessary widenings simply by taking in more and more of the original garden space intervening between the houses and the carriageway. In 1966 the Greater London Council began a major widening scheme of that part of the road extending for about a quarter of a mile or so on either side of the Baker Street crossing. This operation, designed as 'part of the improved Inner Circular route linking Western Avenue with the City and the London Docks', cost well over £1,000,000, and produced among other improvements, a pedestrian subway at the crossing. The farsightedness of the mid-eighteenth-century planners, i.e. the group of 'gentlemen, farmers, and tradesmen' inhabiting the northern parishes of London, who chose this route when George II was king, was demonstrated once again when it was thought worth spending this large sum on a small section of the road two centuries later.

It is difficult when walking along the highly urbanised Marylebone Road of the 1970s to visualise that original rutted track running between the post-and-rail fences which shut off the fields on either side. This track – forty feet wide – skirted the northern fringes of the metropolis, linking Paddington with Marylebone, and Marylebone with Islington. At this stage it was in fact no more than a drove road, along which great herds of sheep and cattle were driven from home counties' farms to Islington and thence to Smithfield Market. But with the development of Marylebone in the late eighteenth and early nineteenth centuries, it was paved and became a route for vehicular traffic. With this improvement came the building of country villas on either side of the road, and – because of the fifty-foot building restriction – long gardens stretching between the villas and the carriage-way. It was only in the twentieth century that intense urbanisation led to the disappearance of the gardens in favour of shops and offices, and to the widening of the street to take modern motor traffic.

Large stretches of both sides of the street have been rebuilt since the last war, and a great deal of the rebuilding has taken place in the last decade. At its western end, the Marylebone Flyover now carries the roadway over the Edgware Road and links it directly with the Harrow Road. On the western section of the road, close to where Lisson Grove joins it, British Home Stores and Woolworth's have set up office buildings almost opposite one another. As if to balance Burmah-Castrol House, on its site opposite the Town Hall, a vast concrete building with an enormous overhang at roof level has arisen on the south side of the road opposite Baker Street Underground Station. This was originally dubbed the Polytechnic College of Architecture, Advanced Building Technology and Management Studies. A mass of building with a mouthful of titles, it now more modestly proclaims itself as the Polytechnic of Central London. The façade of the college is strongly reminiscent architecturally of its sister institution at the other end of Marylebone, the Polytechnic College of Science and Engineering. Behind the Marylebone Road college, on the site occupied so long by the Marylebone workhouse and infirmary, and later by the old people's home, Luxborough Lodge, is the 21-storey block of flats known as Luxborough Tower, part of the same redevelopment scheme.

The recent reconstruction of York Gate, as part of the over-all restoration of York Terrace, has shown once again the infallibility of Nash's eye for scenic possibilities. The façades in this splendid approach from the park to St Marylebone Church have been rebuilt exactly as in his day. The reconstructed interiors are no doubt a great improvement on his rather careless use of space. Cheek-by-jowl with the eastern side of York Gate stands the Royal Academy of Music. This rather comfortable-looking building occupying a long frontage was designed in 1910 by Sir Ernest George, the P.R.I.B.A. of the

day, with the help of an assistant. The tall centre block with lower
wings, the mellow red brick with stone facings and quoins, the
pediment with gigantic reclining figures, the urns at roof level and
elsewhere, all suggest an exercise in the late seventeenth-century
manner, with Wren as the chief inspiration. Next door to this building is Harley House, a very substantial block of Edwardian mansion flats which went up the same year on the site of the old Harley
House. This was a detached house standing in its own walled garden. The Queen of Oudh and family, plus a horde of Indian retainers, descended on the place in 1856 and rented it for a year. The
retinue camped out in the garden. Oudh had been annexed by the
East India Company that year, and the Queen was in exile. Nuns,
the last tenants of old Harley House, had the place for nearly forty
years.

The new Polytechnic College has sat itself down opposite Madame
Tussaud's. Today this time-defying British institution has the green
dome of the Planetarium coyly nestling, as it were, under its right
ear. The many coach-loads of tourists, both foreign and home-
grown, who each summer are deposited on the pavement at the
main entrance are thus able to 'do' the stars of the firmament and
the stars of our human scene with the maximum of speed and the
minimum of distance to cover. The Tussaud building, all pale green
shades of wall surface, giant pilasters, and large bricked-up windows
picked out in dark slate-grey beneath an attic storey of curlicue
ornamentation, is easily identifiable. But what as? If one didn't see
it proclaim itself as Tussaud's, one might imagine that it was a
furniture store out on a spree. The finger-on-lips secrecy of that
bricked-up front! Only at tourist's-eye-level are there small display
windows where souvenirs glitter and beckon.

The Zoo, like Madame Tussaud's, caters for an international mass
public. It is now in the midst of an immensely ambitious reorganisation and reconstruction programme. For this it is dependent on
outside aid, since its annual takings of some £700,000 only just
enable it to cover the yearly outgoings. Though it has long been a
national institution, it is not as many people imagine regularly provided for out of public funds. The generosity of wealthy benefactors
is behind the progress already achieved in modernising the Zoo in
so notable a manner. And this applies not only to the housing and
display of the animals (and their extremely up-to-date hospital
accommodation now completed), but to such by-products of animal-

keeping as the Nuffield Institute of Comparative Medicine and the Wellcome Institute of Comparative Physiology. In these research establishments, operating on the spot, the study of animal health and physiology is pursued with an eye on the advancement of human medicine.

One of the most eye-catching examples of the Zoo authorities' modernisation programme is the large, very high aviary designed by Lord Snowdon. Here, against a background of the green slopes of Primrose Hill, huge canted metal yard-arms as bulky as the booms of the old ocean-going grain-runners support a spider's web of tension cables. Inside this tent of looped-up cables and wires there is space enough for the largest birds to sail about, or dive suddenly, without immediately meeting prison walls. This, quite apart from the fact that the construction is a thing of beauty in itself – an artist's stylish scrawling upon space. The Penguin Pool, done before the last war (by Tecton, in 1935 when the fathers of today's visiting children were just being born), was advanced enough for its time to hold its own with Snowdon's aviary and Casson's elephant houses, both products of the 1960s. The thin, cambered spirals of concrete, up and down which the penguins march when using their pool, are a delight to the eye. They are like the curves of a half-uncoiled flat metal spring, and the fun of watching the solemn birds on the move is immensely enhanced by the way they are presented suspended in space, with their delicious oddities as it were underlined.

Sir Hugh Casson, by contrast, has all the air of having gone to the old English oast-house for the inspiration of his elephant and rhinoceros houses. One might well assume that, casting around for an existing structure which combined heat retention with an adequate supply of fresh air, he suddenly bethought him of that familiar feature of the southern English countryside. In fact, and no doubt a great deal more sensibly, Messrs. Casson and Conder, one is led to understand, had their eyes not on the Kentish hopfields, but on the African jungle. These odd roof features are meant to give the effect inside the building of tall jungle trees with the light filtering through their branches from high above – the kind of conditions in which the animals would live in their natural state. The human animals viewing them are also thoughtfully catered for. The S-shaped path which leads through this simulated jungle has viewing bays set a little aside from the track. Here *homo sapiens* can pause awhile and gaze upon the might, majesty and power of *elephas africanus* or *rhinoceros indicus* taking their ease on a platform above spectator level in the notional, shadow-dappled tropical sunlight of the cycloramic landscape. Natural light from above and the artificial light from below are no doubt intended to complete the illusion that one has left Regent's Park far behind.

The big names in Zoo architecture in its earlier decades were those of Decimus Burton and Anthony Salvin. Both were protégés of Nash, and both lived at one time or another in Marylebone. Today the names that emerge are those of Casson, Stengelhofen (the Zoo's own architect) and Snowdon. The Zoo, under its modern regime, is being treated more and more as a place where the cage must, as far as possible, vanish, and modern technology replace it by producing the appearance of the natural habitat. Bars are being widely dropped in favour of moats and dry ditches. The 'walk-through', along which the human animal proceeds as he makes his way through the landscapes devoted to the various fauna, is being imaginatively treated. Zoo water-buses operating on the quiet waters of the Regent's Canal bring the human visitor into the heart of these new-made wilds. When all the changes planned have been brought about – including the latest lake which is to act as a moat between the park and the enclosure – London will have been endowed with a Zoo-city – an arena in which all species of animals, including the human, will be able to observe one another with mutual comfort.

On the opposite side of the park, near the lake which Nash made, there stands, remarkably quietly and unobtrusively for its size, something – if we are talking of cities – that might be dubbed a city of learning. Bedford College, whose present buildings originated in 1910–13 and have been added to over the years, has a red-brick bulk and spread which must be little short in extent of Hampton Court. It is an assemblage of very large units, in the older parts of which – more particularly the library – the spirit of late seventeenth-century English collegiate architecture has been invoked with some success. Basil Champneys, the architect of Newnham College and so many other scholastic buildings, one of those long-lived Victorians who designed in many styles, was called in to rehouse Bedford College when South Villa became inadequate for its growing needs. Of the various units, the Tate Library was designed by S.R.J. Smith – son-in-law of the benefactress, Lady Tate, widow of Sir Henry Tate of Tate Gallery fame – and the Tuke Building by Maxwell Ayrton, 1927–31. After the last war, Maxwell Ayrton carried out the reconstruction of the war-damaged parts of the monster carcase of what was the oldest major establishment for the higher education of women in England, and is one of the larger schools of London University. Since 1966 it has ceased to be exclusively a women's college and, of the 1,500 odd students of this near university in a park founded by Elizabeth Jesser Reid in Bedford Square in 1849, nearly half are now men.

Leaving the park by Baker Street when you have approached by Portland Place is to proceed from the professional to the commercial. Apart from its flats, Portland Place is now given over to the professional either in the shape of consultants' rooms or, more frequently, the offices of professional associations or technical organisations. Since these are offices and not shops, it is possible for them to be housed in the existing accommodation. Hence no fascia-boards, no shop windows, no pavement displays. Instead the whole street – although Portland Place has lost much of its residential character – still wears the aspect of an avenue of dignified mansions. Baker Street, on the other hand, though retaining a number of its Georgian houses – mostly in the section just south of the Marylebone Road – has been infiltrated by shops from as far back as the middle of the nineteenth century. Until modern times, many of these were housed in the original Georgian buildings, which were simply adapted at ground-floor level to the needs of sales space. During the inter-war period, however, modern buildings began to go up, with provision made for shop-fronts as a matter of course. Since the last war, redevelopment has gone on steadily, and at an increased speed in the last decade, and a number of steel-framed curtain-walled buildings have arisen provided with both residential accommodation in the form of flats, and with big modern offices.

One of the oddest effects of the redevelopment has been the growing popularity and exploitation of the long-established Sherlock Holmes cult. As every schoolboy knows – not to mention all the rest of the Holmes brigade from diplomats to dons – Sherlock Holmes, the detective in fiction whose fame almost exceeds that of Nelson in real life, lived at 221b, Baker Street. There is of course no such number – Conan Doyle saw to that – but it seems that clues were given in the tales which suggest that Doyle had at least a definite area of the street in mind, if not a precise house. As recently as 1963, the Town Clerk of Marylebone – no less – replying to a query from one of the pundits of the cult who had had it from his father, a personal friend of Conan Doyle's, that the actual house was 21 Baker Street on the east side, identified this as the house now numbered 48 Baker Street. The sacred premises, the Town Clerk disclosed, containing the flat in which Holmes was 'done for' by the immortal Mrs Hudson, were on this assumption situated in the sixth house north of the corner of Blandford Street. It would seem therefore that, putting the matter in modern terms, Sherlock Holmes's chambers were almost opposite Marks & Spencer's head office. Should this valuable piece of information ever percolate to management levels in M & S, one can see a 'Sherlock Holmes' deer-stalker (with the St Michael tag inside it) coming on the market with – say – all the promptitude with which Holmes could drill a pattern of bullet-holes on the wall of his study.

Sherlock Holmes, it seems, is now riding the crest of the wave of redevelopment in Baker Street. A restaurant known as 'My Dear Watson' made its appearance early in 1970 in that section of the street bordering upon holy ground, if not actually within the precincts. Here one is saluted at the entrance with a 'blow-up' of the cab-filled Baker Street of Dr Watson's day, and the menu is peppered with references to the 'Sign of Four', 'The Baker Street Irregulars', and other familiar Holmesiana. Later in the year a Sherlock Holmes Hotel, sited at 108–14 Baker Street – geographically rather wide of the mark, this – opened its doors to waiting devotees. The public rooms in this establishment have been decorated in the style of Holmes's day, and one of the curiosities guests are shown is a Holmesian menu combining 'Mrs Hudson's dish of the day' and other Sherlockiana of the table. The management are dead set on luring American Holmesians over in vast numbers. They have instigated package trips from the U.S.A. which do not stop at London. They are prepared to take the transatlantic tourist to Dartmoor (*Hound of the Baskervilles*) and even to the Reichenbach Falls in Switzerland (scene of Holmes's desperate struggle with Professor Moriarty).

American Holmesians? As with the hard drugs, they are the most fanatical of addicts. Many American cities have their own Sherlock Holmes societies. They meet at least once a year and listen to addresses on the extraordinary, but little-known sides of the Master's character. Some of them celebrate Holmes's birthday. At such reunions an enormous amount of expertise is bandied about. There is talk of the forty-one languages into which the sacred text has been translated, and of the more than 750 volumes and pamphlets which have been dedicated to the supreme subject since the memorable year 1891. Such is the theme of conversation at the meetings of bodies like the 'Baker Street Irregulars', of Broadway, New York; the 'Dancing Men of Cleveland', of Boyleston Avenue, Cleveland, Rhode Island; and the 'Speckled Band', housed in the Statler Building, Boston – to name only a few of these proliferating brotherhoods. This extraordinary cult of a man who never was, has, over the years, reached the proportions of a major lunacy, spreading far beyond the English-speaking peoples.

Apart from the fact that it has erupted on Broadway in such forms as the straight play, *Sherlock Holmes*, with Basil Rathbone in the title role, and in the musical, *Baker Street*, in which the 'Baker Street Irregulars' danced against a background of London fog, and Moriarty's agents did their villainous worst, the madness spread to Switzerland in 1968. A pilgrimage to the Reichenbach Falls by members of the Sherlock Holmes Society of London was transformed, with the aid of the Swiss National Tourist Office, into a national festival. Swiss towns all along the route turned out with brass bands, Sir Paul Gore-Booth, then Head of the Diplomatic Service, played Sherlock Holmes for part of the tour, and the famous fight at the Falls was re-enacted eight times for the 278 journalists and photographers sent by seventeen countries expressly to cover this non-event. Flights to the moon pale beside this flight from reality.

Half-a-mile away to the south of the Sherlock Holmes country, Portman Square, once a model of eighteenth-century architectural deportment, seems now to spawn new and diverse buildings almost annually. Both the north and south sides have been considerably rebuilt within recent years, and now the whole of the war-damaged west side has been eliminated in favour of the Churchill Hotel. The name chosen for this 500-room hostelry, in conjunction with the fact that a New York firm of consultant architects were brought in at the planning stage, suggests that the American owners are going all out for the American tourist market. Yet another large hotel, the Portman, has since risen alongside it on the site of the old Montagu (later Portman) House at the north-west angle of the square. Since Gloucester Place, on which the Portman Hotel has its main frontage, has become practically a street of hotels, it may be assumed that this part of Marylebone, with the not inconsiderable quota of hotels to be found in its other streets, represents one of the denser tourist concentrations in London.

Another contemporary development has been the re-siting of St Paul's Church, Portman Square. This church, originally a chapel of ease for the grandees of Portman Square, was built in 1779. The square was practically complete by that date. For those residents who were too lazy or too unwell – or perhaps too disdainfully exclusive – to make the mile or so's journey to the little parish church in Marylebone High Street, or to St Peter's, Vere Street, it was convenient to have this chapel just north of them in Baker Street. Anyhow by 1779 the parish church had long been too small to cope with the needs of a parish of the size of Marylebone, and chapels of ease were beginning to appear to accommodate the overflow of worshippers. The old St Paul's had its main front on Baker Street, and a subsidiary one on Robert Adam Street. It was one of many similar little eighteenth-century preaching-boxes, with a restrainedly classical façade in brown stock brick topped by a turret. Financial, and perhaps other reasons have dictated its re-siting near the other end of Robert Adam Street. The new church is a severely functional-looking affair, built in conjunction with a block of flats and their underground garage – whose rents are intended to maintain the church in our changed late twentieth-century conditions of small congregations and few rich patrons.

The new flats look out on Manchester Street. Immediately opposite is the west front of Hertford House – the Wallace Collection. This towering wall of red brick punctuated by blind arcading with the curving tops of the arches picked out in white has a curiously satisfying quality about it. The shade of red is so rich, and the reticence of the great wall with its single row of barred windows at ground level so reminiscent of a spacious past, that one is oddly soothed and tranquillised by the sight of it. Round the corner, in George Street, Durrant's Hotel displays its long, pilastered front, still elegantly Adamesque in feeling, a hostelry somewhat different from anything else central London can offer. A stylishly-equipped carriage with emblazoned panels, drawn by a couple of bays with gleaming harness and jingling bits might come to a halt outside its entrance, and a gentleman in a flowered silk coat and a three-cornered hat descend from it, without seeming in the least out of place.

Here, where George Street runs into Marylebone High Street you are at the heart of the criss-cross of ruler-straight streets which grew out of the Cavendish Square housing estate. The curving High Street and its tributary, winding Marylebone Lane – survivals from medieval times – point the contrast with the extensive rectangular network of routes which eighteenth-century planners linked up with them. The main grid of streets is everywhere paralleled by those subsidiary arteries the mews lanes. Less prettified in general than their counterparts in Kensington, many of these erstwhile rows of stables have been converted into most desirable dwellings, and the roadway between them made a thing of pleasure to the eye. The small scale of everything about them gives a certain cosy charm. They are like village streets inserted into the urban framework, each unit in the more highly developed specimens an individual cottage.

Of course, the degree of mews culture varies, and some remain undeveloped, while others are nothing but dingy backyards of a semi-industrial character. But in the best specimens there is a quiet, tucked-away appeal, and width enough in the roadway to allow of a good share of daylight and sunshine. In such spots, some of the houses will have been equipped with many-paned bow windows or big picture windows at ground-floor level. Walls painted in delicate pastel shades will have climbing plants trained up them. Old-style street lamps on projecting wrought-iron brackets seem to be standard fixtures. Flowers in pots on window-sills, or massed in large tubs flanking the front door, are a prominent feature. Brightly-decorated garage doors abound. Painters' or other studios are not uncommon. But through all the diversity there runs unmistakably the rural and the communal note. You are in a village within a town.

One of the pioneers surely of this anti-urban spirit, and so a forerunner of the militant mews-men and mews-women of today, was Mrs Haweis. This charming, gifted woman, in many ways much ahead of her time – and in no way more than in her frank outspokenness – lived in Welbeck Street. Her husband, the Reverend H. R. Haweis, one of the most popular preachers of his day, and a rather sensational one, was Vicar in the 1860s and 1870s of the now demolished St James's Church, Westmoreland Street – the short street running northwards from New Cavendish Street that is practically a continuation of Welbeck Street. Mrs Haweis, an interior decorator and an expert on women's clothes, was the author of a book called *Beautiful Houses*. Welbeck, Harley and Wimpole Streets, she declared to be 'featureless black ravines', and in protest painted her front door moss-green with black lines barring it. This audacious gesture in an age when extreme sobriety of hue was the order of the day must have caused a considerable stir. It so enheartened Sir Charles Lyell, the eminent geologist, that he promptly painted his own front-door in Harley Street sky-blue. The Haweises were a couple who attracted friends of distinction. Gustave Doré, who when in London exercised his romantically macabre pencil in recording the squalor of the slums, used to frequent their parties in Welbeck Street, as did their near neighbour, J. R. Green, the pioneer social historian. Emanuel Oscar Deutsch, the Semitic scholar and assistant librarian at the British Museum, another Welbeck Street neighbour, was taken into their house at a time when his health was precarious. He made it his home.

Mrs Haweis would no doubt have approved of the rural touches given our latter-day mews, as of their humanising and smartening up. But she might have been less appreciative of the way some of them have been carved up, concreted over, extended laterally by the demolition of various outbuildings, and made into large, ramp-equipped car parks, lock-up garage areas, and loading bays for the industrial backsides of impeccably well-mannered business frontages on the main streets. Ruskin, who had extended his experiments in social amelioration to Marylebone at a time when the Haweises were still living there, would no doubt have denounced the pollution of London by the motor-car in no uncertain terms. In 1874, he had chosen Paddington Street – only a few streets away from their home, but then a very poor neighbourhood – as the spot for opening a shop for the sale of tea at cheap prices. For some years he had been financing Octavia Hill, one of the leading social workers of the age, and he had learnt that the poor were often outrageously cheated in buying their 'screws of tea' – small quantities rolled up in paper. His effort to meet this situation in Paddington Street by setting up shop and installing a couple of old servants of his mother's as saleswomen, failed. He was defeated by an inadequate sales technique, and by, as he reported, 'the steady increase in the consumption of spirits in the neighbourhood'.

Today, Paddington Street has 'come up'. However, Ruskin's shop, at the Chiltern Street corner, still stands. It is now occupied by a greengrocer's. But facing it, on Chiltern Street, is a multi-storey car-park, and across the road, on the other side of Chiltern Street, is Kellogg House, a thirteen-storey modern office block, a mass of glass and curtain-walling set diagonally on its site and looking straight across at the little shop where Ruskin's 'screws of tea' pathetically failed to connect with enough of the poverty-stricken to make it a success. The handful of open ground on the farther side of Kellogg House, a burial-ground in Ruskin's day, is now a small public garden. Opposite this, where Marylebone's second burial-ground used to back on to the local workhouse, is another public garden over-looked by the white immensities of Luxborough Tower and the Polytechnic of Central London. Paddington Street is still no Park Lane, but its new-minted pub, its school, its modest shops and rest-aurants, proclaim it a little farther raised from the dust than when Ruskin walked its squalid Victorian pavements.

At the time of Ruskin's Paddington Street shop, Octavia Hill was living in Nottingham Place, a turning off that street. Here, and in a house in the Marylebone Road, she lived for more than fifty years. But it was in another part of the borough, Lisson Grove, that much of her good work was done. This district suffered from the dis-advantage of having become largely an urban slum almost as soon as it lost its rural character in the first quarter of the nineteenth century. Irish labour had flowed into the Church Street area in the heart of the district at the time of the building of the Regent's Canal. Tem-porary shacks had been put up to house them, and thereafter the erection of high-density, cheap dwellings had been allowed to go on unchecked. Octavia Hill appears to have been the first to tackle the task of rehousing some of the inhabitants of this early slum. She took over the management of a particularly bad tenement called Christ-church Buildings, acquired other neighbouring sites, and persuaded friends and backers to build cottages in the area to replace existing hovels. This policy she reinforced by pursuing the eviction of unde-sirable tenants and their replacement by respectable types.

The movement begun by Octavia Hill has never looked back, though it must often have seemed to her successors – the St Maryle-bone Housing Association and L.C.C. (later G.L.C.) and the Maryle-bone Borough Council (later the Westminster Council) – that pro-gress was exceedingly slow. Over the years, the slum clearance campaign has in fact made a great deal of headway. A walk, for instance, along Broadley Street, a former slum area, in an east to west direction, shows at least three separate stages in the rehousing chronicle. First (actually in Broadley Terrace, the eastern extension of the street), the rather massive-looking blocks of tenement flats called Portman Buildings, dating from the 1880s and pre-Borough

Council days. Dark red brick with prominent vertical bands of elaborately moulded terracotta running up from pavement to parapet, they typify the institutional sort of structures favoured in Victorian times. Solid, heavy, gloomily bare, religiously uncomfortable in aspect, they suggest that if God's in His heaven, the Devil's not far away round the corner. There is a kind of moral judgment in their very bricks.

Halfway along Broadley Street comes the inter-war period's answer to the rehousing problem. Red brick again – but this time not the sultry red of hell-fire, but the pleasant, easy King George V-type-of-town-hall red, reminiscent of hundreds of thousands of middle-class dwellings in the age when the local cinema flourished – the now far-off 1930s. Four or five large blocks round a quadrangle planted with trees. Tall, splendidly-tiled roofs on which prominent brick chimney-stacks rise proudly. Entrance to the quadrangle through a lofty archway in Lyon House, the block facing Broadley Street. Low relief sculpture here and there. Inscription on wall of arch recording opening of premises in 1935, under gracious auspices. Every inch of the buildings shouting aloud of the opening of purse-strings and the benevolent spreading of middle-class comfort in unfamiliar surroundings.

Comes the western end of the street, and one is suddenly plump in the middle of the 1960s. The bleakly moral and the comfortably 'tween-the-wars middle-class have given way to the strictly-tailored utilitarian amenities of the new society. Municipal housing financed out of the rates and government grants. But public funds are not all that elastic, and the flats that emerge from them look a bit reach-me-down contrasted with the bespoke tailoring of Lyon House and its nicely-turned-out residential units. Nevertheless, the new blocks are vastly superior to most of the older houses in Lisson Grove. Four to six storeys high, they are reasonably pleasant to look at, have many of the modern amenities, and keep to the level of the general roofline of the area. Like their inter-war predecessors along the street, they are built round central squares. These contain recreational facilities and children's play areas.

But the ancient, dreadful buildings are falling fast everywhere in Lisson Grove. The hoveldom of the early industrial era is on its last legs. Church Street, where tall tower blocks of flats already rise from near the site of the old Portman Market, is being transformed into a modern shopping centre. Lisson Grove – the street, not the district – is having its darker satanic monstrosities rubbed out. The long, unlovely stretch north of Ashmill Street lies deservedly flattened. Ashmill! The name has a sulphurous whiff about it suggestive of the age of coal which spawned this district. Perhaps the mysterious 'White Lead Manufactory', marked hereabouts on eighteenth-century maps, shot its superfluous cinders on to the green at this point and got itself undeservingly commemorated.

The greatest contemporary fact about Lisson Grove is the major redevelopment scheme, now under way. On the former site of the huge railway yards bordering the Regent's Canal, has arisen an estate intended to house well over 5,000 people. An account of the invasion in the late 1890s of this once pleasant residential area by the Great Central Railway, and the creation of Marylebone Station, has been given in the chapter on Regent's Park. Here it is only necessary to recall that it is the reorganisation and modernisation of the railway system, with the consequent elimination of lines, which have enabled this land to be reclaimed for housing. The main area lies on the opposite side of Lisson Grove from Church Street. In the days before the railway, Church Street was continued eastwards, under the name of Alpha Road, and ran into Park Road. But the new scheme is not intended to open this communication again and so Lisson Grove will remain without a direct link with the park.

In essence, the idea appears to be the creation of a new more-or-less self-contained suburb of Marylebone. If it is correct that the 28-acre site cost about £124,000 an acre, and that the revised cost of building – it was decided to drop the tall tower blocks after the Ronan Point disaster – is alone working out at considerably over £11,000,000 it would seem to be a very ambitious scheme indeed. Some 5,500 people are now to be accommodated in a number of seven-storey buildings constructed around tree-lined squares. These contain flats and maisonettes purpose-built for different sizes of family. At the time of writing, it is stated that heating will be from a central boiler system, and rubbish disposal by way of chutes, the rubbish being pneumatically delivered, first to a silo and then to incinerators. Motor access roads will lead to garage space underneath the buildings. The main pedestrian route will be a west–east one, continuing the line of Church Street, but not extending over the railway to reach Park Road. A bridge over the canal will however link the estate with the St John's Wood Road area. The amenities offered are to include shops, a pub, a health centre, a home for the aged, a site for a school, a children's home and a boys' hostel.

Will this huge hive of concrete really provide a satisfactory background to the lives of London citizens subjected to modern pressures? The density of individuals to the built-up acre will be higher than in, say Roehampton, or even the Churchill Gardens estate in Pimlico, and the surroundings devoid of Roehampton's pleasant parkland or the advantage of a Thames-side frontage. It is true that when the Regent's Canal has been de-industrialised, the canal-side amenities planned for the new estate will considerably add to its attractions. Scenically speaking, though, even after the canal banks have been terraced and brightened up, it will hardly be the equal of either Roehampton or Pimlico. No doubt, it will benefit by the experience gained by the planners over the years since these estates were built.

The architectural transformation of Lisson Grove includes another feature of note. This is the creation of the Cockpit Theatre in Gateforth Street, a small lane running northwards from Church Street. This miniature drama centre, opened in 1969, is equipped for theatre-in-the-round. It is housed in the Inner London Education Authority's new building, and provides a place where teachers and children can experiment with dramatic techniques, as well as a forum for new movements in music and the graphic arts, with a strong emphasis on audience participation. It is characteristic of the way in which this hitherto underprivileged neighbourhood is flowering that it was possible for this delightful new centre to be sited there. This is an experiment which not only promises much for local youth, but reaches out towards the contemporary awareness that life itself is an art. It is wholly right and proper that drama should re-establish itself in the Church Street area. After all, it was only in 1962 that the bomb-damaged Old Marylebone Theatre, further along Church Street, was finally destroyed by fire. It had long ceased to be a theatre. But the survival of the structure in its ruinous state served to remind residents that they and their forebears had had a theatre in their midst for more than a hundred years.

St John's Wood, like Lisson Grove, has its dramatic connections. In Victorian times the name that most readily occurs is that of Douglas Jerrold, playwright and journalist. He lived in 'The Wood', and in our own day, Bernard Miles started the Mermaid Theatre there in a hall in his back garden. Both districts also have names

indicating their rural origin. Again, they are alike in not only having
been built up in the nineteenth century, but largely rebuilt in the
twentieth. Montgomery Eyre, the principal authority on the history
of St John's Wood, whose book appeared in 1913, would be dumb-
founded were he alive again to see it today. A mere sixty years – a
couple of generations – have elapsed since he described it. In the
preface to his book we read of: '. . . a thousand and one gardens, a
thousand and one miniature groves of almond and lilac half-hidden
behind ivied walls'. Whole streetfuls of the old villas and their
spreading gardens have now been swept away. In their stead, blocks
of flats of all sizes and heights, interspersed by closely-packed rows
of neat neo-Georgian boxes, half-garage and half-dwelling space,
occupy the major part of the district. Only in places like Hamilton
Terrace, Elm Tree Road, Marlborough Place, and Carlton Hill do
some stretches of the picturesque old villas remain. Some of the old
terrace houses still survive also in St John's Wood Terrace. Here the
disused Congregational Chapel has been turned into a film studio.
Coats of white and beige paint have splendidly revived its Corinthian
portico and the delicate details of the façade. Next door but one, the
Woronzow Almshouses, dating from the early nineteenth century,
have been rebuilt in the neo-Georgian style as a number of two-
roomed homes, and continue the note of contemporary well-being.

The major transformation which has taken place since Eyre's day
is that St John's Wood has almost completely lost its semi-rural
character. With this, it has ceased to be a retreat largely reserved
for artists, writers, nondescript Bohemians, and rich men and their
mistresses. Such elements of the population still no doubt live there.
But it is no longer their preserve, and they exist there only as a small
portion of that mass of residents of all kinds, and many nations,
which has flowed in since St John's Wood, like the rest of Marylebone, became a part of inner London, and almost wholly urbanised.
Nothing more vividly illustrates the altered composition of the inhabitants than the fact that when a three-and-a-quarter-acre site
recently became available in the Loudoun Road area, it was promptly
acquired for the building of a very large American school, capable
of handling 1,500 children. The American community in St John's
Wood had a substantial addition made to it when in the mid-1960s,
an American Marine detachment moved into barracks in Allitsen
Road. It is understood that this military body is stationed there for
the defence of the U.S. Embassy in case of emergency.

Another large modern school in the St John's Wood area is the amalgamation representing the Quintin and Kynaston boys' schools, with an extensive frontage on the Finchley Road. This long, low complex of buildings, with units built at different levels, occupies a large acreage of former rough woodland, which it shares with the George Eliot Junior and Infant schools and the Marylebone Institute, an adult education centre with its frontage on Marlborough Hill. Recent changes in the St John's Wood skyline have included the appearance of several massive multi-storey blocks of flats on either side of St John's Wood Road. Two of these slabs overlook Lord's Cricket Ground, and are appropriately called 'Lord's View'. Within their purview also is the rebuilt, entirely modernised Lord's Tavern. Here there is a splendid, extremely spacious banqueting suite above the tavern. A foil to the smartly contemporary character of this new building is the massive Ionic temple façade of the Liberal Jewish Synagogue on the other side of the road.

Marylebone is rich in synagogues. The Jewish community seems to have been ready to provide a fresh one each time a sizeable section of worshippers broke away from the Orthodox persuasion – or at least from a previous breakaway body. From the time of the Central London Synagogue in Great Portland Street – a building in the Moorish style for which part of the money was put up by the Rothschild family – and the West London Synagogue, in Upper Berkeley Street (with a façade in Romanesque idiom) to the United Synagogue in Great Cumberland Place, and the St John's Wood Synagogue, in Grove End Road – the largest and most modern of the lot as it now presents itself – a century and more has elapsed, and the architectural styles have changed from oriental to occidental. The Liberal Synagogue, dating from 1925, is in effect neo-classical, and shows how far the congregation had come in its emancipation from traditional and eastern influences. The St John's Wood Synagogue, completed in 1964, is entirely contemporary in style. It has the look of a large, elegant hangar, the curving copper-sheathed roof, and walls of pale brown brick, presenting the cleanest and simplest of lines. Only the Stars of David set in the entrance façade distinguish it – at least to the gentile eye – from a secular concert hall.

St John's Wood is the northernmost part of Marylebone, and in the steady northward drive of London since the eighteenth century, the last of its districts to be developed and urbanised. Even with the greatly increased densities of today, future building will have to take place on sites where previous buildings have been demolished. This, of course, has been the case in the rest of Marylebone for a much longer period. Over the whole fifteen hundred odd acres of it, from Oxford Street to Boundary Road, the predictable pattern of the coming years is one of rising density and more and more multi-storey structures. Marylebone as it is today began to take shape in the early 1960s. After a decade of rebuilding, with multi-storey curtain-walled buildings springing up at many points, it has entered the 1970s no longer an independent borough – for the enlarged City of Westminster has absorbed it – but more alive than ever, and filled with institutions which are an integral part of modern life.

What is the future to be? As long as the City of Westminster remains the administrative centre of London, and the beating heart of the capital's life, Marylebone, because of its geographical position, must continue to be a key area. And, since like attracts like, it is to be expected that its modern function as the headquarters of medicine and communications in the metropolis, and one of the focal points of educational activities, will grow. But it seems unlikely that the needs of the late twentieth century in these fields – and in others which will probably add themselves to these as the life of the technological society becomes more complex – can continue to be met out of the present pool of older buildings.

Nor indeed is this desirable in the long run. Many houses in central Marylebone are more than 150 years old, and some nearer 200, and although numbers of them have been extensively repaired, or reconstructed, they cannot be expected to last indefinitely. They are the products of an industrial society in its infancy, and every year become more and more remote from the rapidly-changing requirements of contemporary life. Preservation orders have been placed on numbers of these old buildings on the grounds that they are part of our historic heritage and are of high artistic merit. These are good reasons for protecting them for a time from the depredations of speculative builders, or indeed from the less well-considered decisions sometimes taken by local government bodies which have just come into power. But they are unconvincing grounds for the indefinite retention of obsolete buildings at a time when new bottles are required into which to pour the wine of a challengingly new era. Marylebone as it is today is no bad example of an intelligently pursued policy of preservation – intelligent, that is, in the circumstances of a particular period. The Harley Street area and its eighteenth-century classicism survived the dislike of our nineteenth-century ancestors. They regarded it as outdated and dreary, and found it totally at odds with their Gothic Revival dream-world. But they laid no violent hands on it, and it lived on into our own disturbed and war-racked age, in which it was prized for its ordered grace and discipline, and above all perhaps for the implication inherent in it, as in all classical architecture, that a city can and must be an harmonious whole.

# Bibliography

W. H. D. Adams, *A Book about London*, 1890

Alison Adburgham, *Shops and Shopping, 1800-1914*, 1964

A. Adrian, *Georgina Hogarth and the Dickens Circle*, 1957

Robert Allbutt, *London Rambles with Charles Dickens*, 1886

H. C. W. Angelo, *Reminiscences of Henry Angelo*, 2 vols. 1828

J. W. von Archenholz, *A Picture of England*, 2 vols. 1789

E. Bright Ashford, *Lisson Green: a Domesday Village in St Marylebone*, 1960

—, *St. John's Wood: the Harrow School and Eyre Estates*, 1965

—, *Tyburn Village and Stratford Place*, 1969

Priscilla Bailey, *Sarah Siddons*, 1953

C. H. Baker and M. I. Collins, *The Life of James Brydges, Duke of Chandos*, 1949

T. Balston, *Life of John Martin*, 1948

Elizabeth D. Bancroft, *Letters from England 1846-9*, 1904

Albert W. Barnes, *A Dickens Guide*, 1929

E. M. Bell, *Octavia Hill 1838-1912*, 1942

T. Besterman, *The Druce – Portland Case*, 1935

Reginald Blunt, *Mrs Montagu . . . Her Letters and Friendships*, 2 vols. 1923

James Boaden, *Memoirs of Mrs Siddons, 1827-31*, 2 vols. 1827

A. T. Bolton, *The Architecture of Robert and James Adam, 1758-94*, 1922

James Boswell, *The Life of Samuel Johnson*, 2 vols, 1791

Martin S. Briggs, *Everyman's Concise Encyclopaedia of Architecture*, 1959

John Britton and A. C. Pugin, *Public Buildings of London*, 2 vols. 1825-8

P. R. Broemel, *The History and Romance of Cavendish Square and Its Vicinity*, 1925

C. P. Bryan, *Roundabout Harley Street*, 1932

Arthur Bryant, *The Years of Endurance, 1793-1802*, 1942

Thomas Burke, *The Streets of London*, 1941

Frances Burney, *Letters and Diaries*, 1846

John Busse, *Mrs Montagu . . .*, 1928

Thomas Campbell, *Life of Mrs Siddons*, 2 vols. 1834

E. Beresford Chancellor, *The History of the Squares of London*, 1907

—, *The Private Palaces of London*, 1908

—, *Wanderings in Marylebone*, 1926

William D. Chapple, *George Peabody*, 1933

François René de Chateaubriand, *Mémoires d'outre-tombe*, 6 vols. 1902

P. Christophorov, *Sur les Pas de Chateaubriand en Exil*, 1960

Basil F. L. Clarke, *Parish Churches of London*, 1966

Emily J. Climenson, *Elizabeth Montagu . . .*, 2 vols. 1906

George Clinch, *Marylebone and St Pancras*, 1890

Howard Colvin, *Biographical Dictionary of English Architects, 1660–1840,*
    1954

Ann Cox-Johnson, *John Bacon, R.A., 1740–99*, 1961. *See also* Ann Saunders

*The Creevey Papers*, ed. Sir H. Maxwell, 2 vols. 1903

J. Mordaunt Crook, articles in *Country Life*, 4 and 11 July 1968

G. H. Cunningham, *London . . .*, 1927

P. Cunningham, *Handbook of London*, 1850

Anthony Dale, *James Wyatt*, 1956

Dorothy Davis, *A History of Shopping*, 1966

Baroness Deichmann, *Impressions and Memories*, 1926

Mary Granville Delany, *The Autobiography of Mrs Delany*, 3 vols. 1861

Charles Dickens, *The Letters of Charles Dickens to the Baroness Burdett-
    Coutts*, ed. C. Osborne, 1931

—, *Little Dorrit*, 1857

—, *Reprinted Pieces*, 1899

—, *The Uncommercial Traveller*, 1861

*The Letters of George Eliot*, ed. G. S. Haight, 7 vols. 1954–6

James Elmes, *Metropolitan Improvements*, 1831

A. Montgomery Eyre, *Saint John's Wood: its histories, its houses, its haunts,
    and its celebrities*, 1913

*The Farington Diary*, ed. James Greig, 8 vols. 1922–8

John William Ferry, *A History of the Department Store*, 1960

A. J. Finberg, *Life of J. M. W. Turner*, 1961

*Letters of Mrs Fitzherbert*, ed. Sir Shane Leslie, 1928

John Fleming, Hugh Honour and Nikolaus Pevsner, *The Penguin Dictionary
    of Architecture*, 1966

P. Flemming, *Harley Street*, 1939

A. S. Foord, *Springs, Streams and Spas of London*, 1910

John Forster, *The Life of Charles Dickens*, 1873

Willi Frischauer, *The Clinic*, 1967

William Powell Frith, *My Autobiography and Reminiscences*, 3 vols. 1887

Jean Overton Fuller, *Swinburne: a Critical Biography*, 1968

*The Letters of Mrs Gaskell*, ed. J. A. V. Chapple and Arthur Pollard, 1966

Mrs M. D. George, *London Life in the Eighteenth Century*, 1930

John Gore, *Creevey's Life and Times*, 1934

Lord Ronald Gower, *Life of Romney*, 1882

Frank Green, *London Homes of Dickens*, 1951

*Reminiscences and Recollections of Captain Gronow*, ed. John Raymond, 1964

P. J. Grosley, *A Tour to London*, 2 vols. 1772

*Guide to the City of Westminster*

John Gwynn, *London and Westminster Improved*, 1766

F. H. Hallam, *Random Sketches of . . . Marylebone*, 1885

Robert Halsband, *The Life of Lady Mary Wortley Montagu*, 1961

Wilmot Harrison, *Memorable London Houses*, 1889
Sir Paul Harvey, *The Oxford Companion to English Literature*, 3rd ed., 1946
*The Autobiography of Benjamin Robert Haydon*, ed. Alexander P. O. Penrose, 1927
Rayner Heppenstall, *Portrait of the Artist as a Professional Man*, 1969
R. W. Hidy, *House of Baring in American Trade and Finance . . .*, 1949
W. H. Holden, *Houses with a History in St Marylebone*, 1950
J. E. Holroyd, *Baker Street By-ways*, 1959
Bea Howe, *Arbiter of Elegance*, 1968
David Hughson, *London . . . and Its Neighbourhood 30 Miles Around*, 1805
Robert Huish, *Memoirs of . . . Caroline, Queen of Great Britain*, 2 vols. 1821
—, *Memoirs of George the Fourth*, 2 vols. 1830
*The Autobiography of Leigh Hunt*, ed. J. E. Morpurgo, 1949
Alan A. Jackson, *London's Termini*, 1968
Leonard Jacobs, *The Streets of St Marylebone*, 1955
H. Jephson, *The Sanitary Evolution of London*, 1907
Caroline S. M. Kirkland, *Holidays Abroad, or Europe from the West*, 1849
Margaret Lane, *Edgar Wallace*, 1938
Anne Leslie, *Mrs Fitzherbert*, 1960
C. R. Leslie, *Autobiographical Recollections*, 2 vols. 1860
W. S. Lewis, *Three Tours through London in 1748, 1776, 1797*, 1941
Bryan Little, *The Life and Work of James Gibbs*, 1955
C. Lloyd, *Lord Cochrane, Earl of Dundonald*, 1947
W. J. Loftie, *History of London*, 2 vols. 1883
*London*, ed. C. Knight, 1841–4
Daniel Lysons, *The Environs of London*, 1792–6
A. Slidell Mackenzie, *American in London*, 1848
*The Diaries of William Charles Macready*, ed. William Toynbee, 2 vols. 1911–1912
J. P. Malcolm, *Londinium Redivivum*, 4 vols. 1807
T. A. Malton, *A Picturesque Tour through the Cities of London and Westminster*, 2 vols, 1792
W. H. Manchee, 'Marylebone and Its Huguenot Associations', in *Proceedings of the Huguenot Society of London*, vol. 11, no. 1, 1915
R. Mander and J. Mitchenson, *The Lost Theatres of London*, 1968
Alfred Marks, *Tyburn Tree. Its History . . .*, 1908
H. S. Marks, *Pen and Pencil Sketches*, 2 vols, 1894
André Maurois, *Miss Howard and the Emperor*, 1957
H. and P. Massingham, *The London Anthology*, 1950
*Mayhew's London*, ed. Peter Quennell, 1951
*The London Journal of Gansevoort Melville*, ed. H. Parkes, 1948
H. C. Merwin, *Life of Bret Harte*, 1911
G. E. Mitton, *Hampstead and Marylebone*, 1902
Comte de Montlosier, *Souvenirs d'un Émigré, 1791–98*, 1951
*The Journal of Benjamin Moran, 1857–65*, ed. S. A. Wallace and F. E. Gillespie, 2 vols. 1948–9
R. B. Mowat, *Americans in England*, 1935

Peter and Linda Murray, *A Dictionary of Art and Artists*, 1960

Ian Nairn, *Modern Buildings in London*, 1964

—, *Nairn's London*, 1966

Sutton Nicholls, *London Described*, 1731

John Northouck, *History of London*, 1773

E. G. Oakes, *Sir Samuel Romilly*, 1935

John Oliver and Peter Bradshaw, *Saint John's Wood Church, 1814–1964*, 1955

Sir William Orpen, *The Outline of Art*, 1950

Louis Osman, *Report of Lecture at the Royal Society of Arts, 20 May 1957, on Duke of Chandos's Cavendish Square Scheme, by Louis Osman*

J. B. Papworth, *Select Views of London*, 1816

Franklin Parker, *George Peabody Founder . . .*, 1956

Étienne-Davis, Duc de Pasquier, *The Memoirs of Chancellor Pasquier, 1767–1815*, 1967

Anthony Paul, *A History of Manchester Square*, 1971

Hesketh Pearson, *The Smith of Smiths*, 1934

Thomas Pennant, *Some Account of London*, third edition, 1793

*Diary of Samuel Pepys*, Everyman Library, 3 vols, 1906

Sir Nikolaus Pevsner, *Buildings of England: London, except for the Cities of London and Westminster*, 1952

Hugh Phillips, *Mid-Georgian London . . .*, 1964

Baron Roger de Portalis, *Henri-Pierre Danloux et son Journal durant l'Émigration*, 1910

Reginald Pound, *Harley Street*, 1967

F. Praeger, *Wagner as I Knew Him*, 1892

S. I. Prime, *Life of Samuel F. B. Morse*, 1875

Ida Procter, *Masters of British Nineteenth Century Art*, 1961

Peter Quennell, *Hogarth's Progress*, 1955

Ernest Raymond, *To the Wood No More*, 1959

Cyrus Redding, *Fifty Years' Recollections*, 3 vols, 1858

Elizabeth Rigby (afterwards Lady Eastlake), *Journals . . . of Lady Eastlake*, 2 vols, 1875

John Rothenstein, *Turner, 1775—1851*, 1949

Royal Academy Exhibition Catalogues: *The First Hundred Years of the Royal Academy 1769–1868*, 1951–2; *European Masters of the Eighteenth Century*, 1954–5; *British Portraits*, 1956–7

Richard Rush, *A Residence at the Court of London*, 1833

Frank Rutter, *Modern Masterpieces*, 1935

Michael Sadleir, *Forlorn Sunset*, 1947

Enid Cecil Samuel, *The Villas in Regent's Park and Their Residents*, 1959

Ann Saunders, *Handlist of Painters, Sculptors and Architects Associated with St Marylebone 1760–1960*, 1963

—, *Regent's Park: a Study of the Development of the Area to the Present Day*, 1969

H. St George Saunders, *History of the Middlesex Hospital*, 1947

William Sharp, *Life of Robert Browning*, 1890

F. H. W. Sheppard, *Local Government in St Marylebone 1688–1835*, 1953

Walter Sydney Sichel, *Emma, Lady Hamilton*, 1907

Friedrich Sieburg, *Chateaubriand*, 1961

Benjamin Silliman, *Journal of Travels in England*, 1810

Louis Simond, *Journal of a Tour and Residence in Great Britain 1810–11*, 1815

Sir Sacheverell Sitwell, *Narrative Pictures*, 1937

John Slater, *History of the Berners Estate*, 1918

Alastair Smart, *Life of Allan Ramsay*, 1952

John Thomas Smith, *Nollekens and His Times . . .*, 2 vols, 1828

—, *A Book for a Rainy Day*, 3rd ed., 1861

Naomi G. R. Smith, *The Private Life of Mrs Siddons*, 1933

Thomas Smith, *A Topographical and Historical Account of the Parish of St Mary-le-bone*, 1833

J. L. Smith-Dampier, *Who's Who in Boswell?*, 1935

Herbert Spencer, *London's Canal*, 1961

A. J. D. Stonebridge, *St Marylebone: a Sketch of Its Historical Development*, 1952

J. Stuart, *Critical Observations of the Buildings and Improvements in London*, 1771

Dr S. Sutherland, *Old London's Spas, Baths, and Wells*, 1915

*Survey of London: North of the Thames*, ed. Sir Walter Besant, 1911

Hippolyte Taine, *Notes on England*, 1871

Walter Thornbury, *Life of J. M. W. Turner*, 1877

Captain Edward Topham, *Life of John Elwes*, 1797

Madame Tussaud, *Souvenirs*, 1837

E. and J. Underwood, *America in England*, 1949

E. R. Vincent, *An Italian in Regency England*, 1953

*Wallace Collection Catalogue*, 1938

Will M. Wallace, *A Traitorous Hero*, 1954

David Watkin, *Thomas Hope and the Neo-Classical Idea*, 1968

Margery Weiner, *The French Exiles, 1789–1815*, 1960

Clare Williams, *Sophie in London in 1786*, 1933

Virginia Woolf, *Flush: a Biography*, 1933

Warwick W. Wroth, *The London Pleasure Gardens of the 18th Century*, 1896

E. Yates, *Recollections and Experiences*, 2 vols, 1884

John Yeowell, *The French Chapel Royal in London*, 1958

G. M. Young, *Gibbon*, 1939

Various editions of the following: *Encyclopaedia Britannica, Chambers Encyclopaedia, Larousse, Dictionary of National Biography, Chambers Biographical Dictionary*, and *The Complete Peerage*. Also articles in *The Gentleman's Magazine*, 1803; *Contract Journal*, 29 May 1968; and *Building*, 17 October 1969.

## OTHER SOURCES OF INFORMATION

Howard de Walden Estates Ltd; Portman Family Settled Estates; Greater London Council's Historic Buildings Division, their Middlesex and London Records, and their Prints and Drawings Collection; the Royal Institute of British Architects; the Royal College of Physicians; the Royal Society of Medicine; the Royal Medico-Psychological Association; the Middlesex Hospital; the United States Embassy in London; the Dickens Fellowship; the International Students House; Bedford College; and the Peabody Trust.

# Index

A View of S.t Mary le Bone. from the Bafon